Fostoria Tableware

1924 – 1943

THE CRYSTAL FOR AMERICA

IDENTIFICATION & VALUE GUIDE

Milbra Long and Emily Seate

COLLECTOR BOOKS
A Division of Schroeder Publishing Co., Inc.

The current values in this book should be used only as a guide. They are not intended to set prices, which vary from one section of the country to another. Auction prices as well as dealer prices vary greatly and are affected by condition as well as demand. Neither the authors nor the publisher assumes responsibility for any losses that might be incurred as a result of consulting this guide.

Searching For A Publisher?

We are always looking for knowledgeable people considered to be experts within their fields. If you feel that there is a real need for a book on your collectible subject and have a large comprehensive collection, contact Collector Books.

Front cover: Plate Etching 279, June, in Topaz
Back cover: From a Fostoria Bicentennial Brochure

Cover design by Michelle Dowling
Book design by Terri Stalions
Color photography by Charles R. Lynch

COLLECTOR BOOKS
P.O. Box 3009
Paducah, Kentucky 42002-3009

Milbra Long and Emily Seate
P.O. Box 784
Cleburne, TX 76033-0784

Copyright © 1999 by Milbra Long and Emily Seate

CONTENTS

NO METHOD OF REPRODUCTION, HOWEVER WELL DONE, CAN TRUTHFULLY REFLECT THE CLARITY, BRILLIANCE AND COLOR OF THE FINEST MODERN AMERICAN GLASSWARE— FOSTORIA. THE PHOTOGRAPHS IN THIS CATALOG, THERE- FORE, CANNOT PORTRAY THE PERFECTION OF THE GLASS ITSELF, OR MIRROR THE RADIANT LOVELINESS OF ITS COLOR.

It was Fostoria who originated the complete dinner service of glass, which has been accepted by authorities on table decoration everywhere. It is styled to sell, because it conforms to the new trend of the times for beauty in merchandise.

But Fostoria does not exist merely to be beautiful. It is as durable as china and is absolutely practicable for serving hot and cold foods. No amount of hard wear or usage can dim its original lustre.

The fact that the score of different materials used in the making of Fostoria glass must all measure up to the same high standard of purity . . . that they must pass rigorous tests in the thoroughly equipped Fostoria chemical laboratory . . . that the clarity, brilliance and tint of the glass must conform to the specifications set by the designers — is responsible for the vision of the artist becoming a reality.

Thus the name, "Fostoria," has become a symbol in the public mind for the finest modern American glass. This has been accomplished first by the beauty and high quality of every piece of glass that bears the Fostoria label . . . by sound styling and the knowledge that merchandise in good taste sells best.

It is our earnest desire to do everything we can to help you increase your sales of Fostoria glassware, and to that end you will always find ready assistance and advice by writing to the Fostoria Glass Company, Mounds- ville, West Virginia.

From the 1933 Fostoria catalog

ACKNOWLEDGMENTS

We are grateful to the Lancaster Colony Corporation, Inc. of Columbus, Ohio, for permission to use the materials and logo of the Fostoria Glass Company, Inc.

Many thanks to J. R. Johnston for the use of priceless pieces from his extensive Baroque collection.

Our appreciation and respect for Collector Books grows with each book we author. We especially thank Billy Schroeder and Lisa Stroup for doing their best to bring to the reader this history of the patterns made by the Fostoria Glass Company as authentically and beautifully as is possible with today's technology.

DEDICATION

This book and all the other books of the "Crystal for America" series are dedicated to the employees of the Fostoria Glass Company, Inc. whose skilled hands created fine Fostoria crystal.

Every man's work . . .

Handmade Fostoria crystal is a source of pride for those who make it, as well as for those who own it. The work is challenging, not everyone can do it. It represents achievement and personal satisfaction for many skilled workers.

And for those who do own Fostoria ware, it is a link with the past—a time when virtually every household article was lovingly fashioned by hand. It brings with it a personal history lacking in the machine-made and mass-produced.

Fostoria has been around a long time—since 1887. And things aren't done a whole lot differently now than they were back then. Some of the products have changed, but the skills and processes are much the same. And there's still a lot of family involvement in the business—a kind of craftsmanship applied to management.

If you're ever in Moundsville, we invite you to tour the Fostoria plant. It's quite a spectacle to see hands making so many beautiful things from glass. It's an old-fashioned way of doing things. And the result is old-fashioned quality.

From Fostoria
Bicentennial Brochure

"Every man's work is always a portrait of himself."
– Samuel Butler

INTRODUCTION

When we began this labor of love, we thought it would be best to divide the material into two books: 1924 – 1943 and 1944 – 1986. It was not to be. In the twenty years between 1924 and 1944, the Fostoria Glass Company offered more diverse products than at any other time. Many of those products were simply numbered bowls, comports, shakers, vases, and the like. No resource would be complete without giving full attention to the miscellaneous numbered pieces as well as the patterns. Thus, after much thought, we decided to continue our presentation of the Fostoria Glass Company between 1924 and 1986 with three volumes, all of which will complement and extend the information originally presented in *Fostoria Stemware*. Following this volume will be *Fostoria Tableware: 1944 – 1986* and *Fostoria: Useful and Ornamental,* which will be devoted to the multitude of miscellaneous pieces.

The Fostoria Glass Company was thorough in its presentation of products. Until 1933, the company relied on catalogs of varying sizes and price lists to present wares and ordering information. In the 1920s, Fostoria used large general catalogs published annually or every few years. Price lists generally were offered at the beginning of each new year, with supplementary price lists of new goods dated July and less often, September. In 1933, dealers were provided with a leather binder containing individual pages which could be removed or replaced over the years as products were discontinued or added. Each catalog page was dated with month, day, and year. (We have elected to omit dates for reasons of space.) Within the binders were card stock dividers labeled Pressed Patterns, Etchings, Cuttings, Carvings, Decorations, Tableware, Vases, Barware, and Miscellaneous. New catalog pages were sent along with the January price lists, although July or September supplementary price lists might include catalog pages relating to any new offerings within the price lists. Some new products were announced with New Goods sheets which contained not only listings, but pictures or line drawings of the new offerings. The leather-bound catalog pages continued until the early 1960s when the company began including line drawings and some photographs in the price lists, thus combining the two.

Our research took us through each of these catalogs and price lists, and required tedious tracing of each piece in each pattern. By looking so closely at the material, we made discoveries that would not have been possible otherwise. We found pieces dropping out of a pattern and reappearing, sometimes years later, and we noticed a few mistakes, usually transposed numbers, or numbers with one digit in error.

The decorations section of this book contains everything we know, even our speculations. Nearly all the decorations ever listed by the Fostoria Glass Company are shown. Some decorations have been found for which there seems to be no name or number, and we have included them as "unknown" decorations.

We have tried to show designs for every etching, cutting, and decoration, but if there is any doubt and the pattern had stemware, the design will be shown in *Fostoria Stemware*.

The Fostoria Glass Company was well organized throughout its history. One essential element to tracking pieces through the years was the numbering system. Fostoria numbered nearly everything. Oftentimes one can guess at a date of production or kind of piece from the number alone. Pressed patterns had four numbers, and the rest had two or three. More often than not, patterns are sequential. In addition, it would be well to remember that the names of pressed patterns (sometimes called blanks) are like maiden names. If a cutting, etching, or decoration was put on a pattern, the name of the cutting, etching, or decoration was used. For example, Golden Glow is a decoration that was placed on the Sunray pattern. Once the Sunray pattern was decorated, it was married to its decoration and called by its married name, Golden Glow. Another example is the Navarre etching which was put on a multitude of different pressed patterns such as Baroque, Fairfax, Lafayette, Sonata, Contour, but when any of the pieces was etched with Navarre, it was always called Navarre.

Several of the patterns introduced by Fostoria before World War II continued to be made after the war. American is one of those patterns. Thus, we have divided the American pattern between this book and *Fostoria Tableware: 1944 – 1986.* Pieces introduced after 1943 or which continued to be offered after 1943 will be found in the next book instead of this one. The same is true for Navarre. In addition, Colony, Raleigh, and Coronet will be found in the 1944 – 1986 book, again, for reasons of space. Some patterns which were introduced before 1943 and continued to be made had introductory pieces dropping out after just a few years of production. The Romance etching falls into this category. We found it more logical to include those patterns, and the patterns that used Raleigh and Coronet as the dinnerware blank, in *Fostoria Tableware: 1944 – 1986.*

We invite your questions and comments, but please enclose a self-addressed, stamped envelope if you wish a reply. Whether you are new to Fostoria glassware, or are a longtime collector, we hope this book, and the ones to follow, will help you value the Fostoria Glass Company as we do.

Shown here on a celluloid display piece, the brown paper sticker placed on Fostoria products from 1924 to 1957.

THE FOSTORIA GLASS COMPANY

After natural gas was discovered in Findlay, Ohio, in 1886, leaders from this central Ohio community promised "free gas" to attract industry to the area. Nearby Fostoria, Ohio, was the location chosen by a new company that had been recently organized in Wheeling, West Virginia. Lucian B. Martin, the president, had the reputation of being the most experienced and best glass salesman in that region, working for Hobbs, Brockunier and Company. Teamed up with William S. Brady as secretary, J.B. Russell as manager, and Charles E. Beam and Harry Humphreville as mould makers, that formidable group started what became the longest lived, largest, and best known glass house in the United States: the Fostoria Glass Company. The factory was constructed, skilled workers recruited from other established glass factories, and the first glass made before the end of 1887.

In the earliest days, Fostoria made oil lamps, hand-painted vases, pressed glass for home and hotel, and tall candelabra for banquet tables. The Victoria pattern, reportedly made only in the Fostoria, Ohio, plant before 1891, is much sought after by today's collectors and would rival fine French crystal in clarity and finish.

Though the natural gas supply was short lived, the forethought and experience of the new company's leaders made relocation of the factory to Moundsville, West Virginia, a quick reality. To the management and to many of the workers, it was like coming home, and by the end of 1891, the plant in Moundsville was in operation. Management was, and continued to be, the key to the success of this great company.

In Moundsville, it was necessary to switch from natural gas to coal as the source of energy. Since natural gas is much cleaner, a producer plant was designed to convert coal to natural gas. In 1948, when a pipeline brought natural gas from Louisiana and Texas to the area, Fostoria abandoned the producer plant in favor of the pipeline.

Fostoria may have made the smartest move of its entire history when in 1915 it introduced a pressed pattern reminiscent of ice cubes and named it American. As heavy as cut lead crystal but much more durable, American soon rivaled the give-away depression glass for its popularity with the American housewife. Speculation has been made that Fostoria exported its wares. We are in possession of a Spanish-language 1922 price list that would seem to support that speculation.

By 1918, Fostoria was producing elaborate lines for the American table, some including as many as 25 different stems with delicate etchings such as Oriental. As many as three or four different pitchers, finger bowls, grapefruit servers, and 6", 7", and 8" plates completed the line. In fact, it could be said that Fostoria served the rich with these patterns, and the middle class with the American pattern. (Some collectors would argue that the middle class got the best of that situation.)

Big changes came in the decade of 1920 – 1930. Five furnaces were in operation, and management was keenly aware that if the factory continued to operate at capacity, customer demand had to be cultivated and maintained at that same high level. For that reason, Fostoria invested in a new sales system.

It had been customary for a sales representative to be employed by several glass companies at the same time. The Fostoria Company began to hire and train salesmen to represent Fostoria exclusively. Management had a plan which encompassed a comprehensive marketing strategy, one that would stimulate consumer demand and confidence. Department stores, jewelry stores, and gift shops were carefully chosen to carry Fostoria glassware.

In 1924, the same year color was introduced, Fostoria waged a national advertising campaign. Unheard of in the glass industry, the campaign was probably the boldest yet most successful step in the company's history. Advertising showing the beautiful colors and designs appeared in women's magazines, such as *Good Housekeeping, Ladies' Home Journal, Vogue, Ladies Home Companion*, and others. By the time the Great Depression began in 1929, Fostoria had become a household word.

In 1926, Fostoria introduced the first complete dinner service, appropriately called Pioneer, with a dinner plate, cup and saucer, bowls, shakers, and a host of other pieces. Originally offered in crystal and three colors, amber, green, and blue, Fostoria had made pieces in a total of 12 different colors besides crystal before Pioneer in color was discontinued in 1943. Not content with one dinner service, Fostoria created Fairfax, Lafayette, Mayfair, and the extraordinary Baroque line, all available in color as well as in crystal. American and Colony were best sellers in crystal, as were Century, Contour, and Sonata later.

The Fostoria Glass Company, arguably the best run glass company in America, was always ahead of its time. Management recognized the value of advertising and through print media persuaded the American public to use the new crystal dinnerware instead of china, making sure to include that a dinner service in glass could be used with both hot and cold food. Advertisements of the time speak of a new scientific method for making glass that was durable yet beautiful and highly suited for the most discriminating table. One advertisement speaks of Fostoria glassware as a dinner service which would do credit to the hostess's cook, one indication of the target group for crystal dinnerware.

Company directors invested company funds in the raw materials needed to make glassware, and they employed designers, both on staff and free-lance, to create new temptations for the American market, which they made it their business to know well. New York City was the center for design in the United States at that time, and those who ran the Fostoria Company kept in close touch with what was new and desirable. In addition, those who lived then report that a constant chatter was heard among the heads of the great glass houses of the time: Heisey, Cambridge, U.S. Glass, Imperial, Tiffin, Duncan and Miller, Morgantown, and Fostoria. If one looks closely at the designs of each of these companies, similarities may be found, even in color. One of the best examples of this is a color which Fostoria introduced as Wisteria, A.H. Heisey as Alexandrite, Tiffin Glass Company as Twilight, and the Cambridge Glass Company as Heatherbloom.

The Fostoria Company was one of the first to use the Bedeaux system, a French method for establishing how long a skilled worker should take to be able to do his job efficiently. The workers themselves determined the standard. One glass cutter has told about being timed doing a cutting over and over, and how the average of his times was used to determine the standard for that cutting. Pay was accorded to cutters by that standard.

In 1928, Fostoria introduced two new colors, a pale blue called Azure, and an equally delicate orangy pink first called Dawn, and later Rose. The richest, truest, and most beautiful yellow color made by any of the glass companies was introduced in 1929 as Topaz. The word "rich" also applied to the cost, as pieces in this color were listed separately and at slightly higher prices. Topaz was expensive to make, and Fostoria, being managed by good business people, passed that extra cost on to the customer. In the 1930s, every company made glassware in rich dark greens, deep blues, purples, and reds. Fostoria was no exception, and created Empire Green, Regal Blue, Burgundy, and Ruby. The Wisteria color mentioned earlier also came into being at this time.

The extraordinary abundance of color, etching, and decoration prevalent from the early twenties through 1943 represent a never-to-be-repeated time in the history of glass making in America. The glass made by Fostoria during this period rivals any in the world for quality of craftsmanship, color, and design. A very special kind of worker was needed to produce this glass: one who could endure working conditions few would tolerate today. Besides the intense heat, workers routinely were exposed to hydrofluoric acid, sulphuric acid, and other harsh and dangerous chemicals. Hard, physical labor, skill, experience, and timing were essential to producing this glassware. At the end of the production line sat the inspectors, whose keen eyes sought out the unacceptable flaws, passing only on those pieces which met the highest standards. We are honored to be able to dedicate our books to these workers.

During World War II, Fostoria made glass sights for bombers and other glass pieces needed for the war effort. Reportedly, scarcity of materials caused Fostoria to retool old moulds and break up others so that the materials could be reused. Certainly, the time between the stock market crash of 1929 and the middle of World War II was a confusing one for Fostoria, and perhaps for other businesses as well. Price lists reflect this confusion with introductions that appear in only one supplement and never appear again, and with pieces that drop out and reappear, sometimes renamed. Many, many cuttings were introduced during this period, some lasting one or two years.

"Master Etchings" are from this period as well, and must be considered an advertising ploy. The first time the adjective "master" is added to etchings is in the 1936 catalog. At that time Fostoria was gearing up for a fiftieth anniversary celebration, as well as trying to sell its products during a depressed time. The idea of owning a "master" etching as opposed to an "ordinary" etching was no doubt thought to be appealing to the consumer. In our opinion, all the etchings from the Fostoria Glass Company must be considered to have been created by master designers.

W.A.B. Dalzell had become president in 1902, and provided unequaled leadership and resourcefulness until 1928. His son, William F. Dalzell, became the innovative imagination behind many of the progressive changes in the 1920s. W.F. Dalzell established a chemical research laboratory which enabled the company to maintain high quality standards. In 1925, he created a special design department and brought in top artists to create new lines. He was the main force behind colored tableware and the national advertising campaign that ensured Fostoria's place in history.

Calvin B. Roe, who was a close associate of W.A.B. Dalzell, became president upon Dalzell's death in 1928, and guided the company through the difficult years of the Depression and World War II. He retired from the presidency in 1945 to become chairman of the board, and William F. Dalzell became president. During his tenure as president, the Fostoria Glass Company reached its peak in size and production in 1950. Robert F. Hannum, who had been with the company since 1928, served as president from 1958 – 1968. At his death in 1968, David Beaty Dalzell, son of William F. Dalzell and grandson of W.A.B. Dalzell, became president. David Dalzell managed the company through times that were even more difficult than the Depression years since he had to find ways to keep demand high for hand made glass in the face of a virtual avalanche of foreign imports. As early as the 1920s, Fostoria had realized the need for higher tariffs to prevent foreign imports from taking too big a bite from the market. By the 1970s and 1980s it was too late for intervention.

By 1944, Fostoria had stopped making color altogether in favor of crystal. Color was not reintroduced until the 1950s, again in tints dictated by the design group in New York City. Fostoria had its Pink and Turquoise and from time to time created sensational pieces in Ebony and Crystal combinations. The 1960s and 1970s saw Rust, Plum, Lilac, Flaming Orange, Sun Gold, and many other colors. Some of the more unusual later designs included Regal stemware, which was a stainless steel overlay on glass; Lyric, a fat, short goblet with a Pink base; and Silver Triumph and Gold Triumph, a glass bowl glued to a metal tripod-like base. Through it all, there was Navarre.

Introduced in 1936, Navarre was one of the Master Etchings. Baroque, Lafayette, Fairfax, Sonata, Contour, Twenty-Four Seventy, and a few odd pieces were combined to make the dinner service, at one time numbering more than 60 pieces, not including the stemware. One of the more interesting facts about Navarre is that Fostoria was still introducing pieces to this line as late as January 1, 1982, just months before the company stopped making blown ware.

In 1973, Fostoria created new stems in this line — in color! The highly collectible Pink and Blue Navarre stemware was first offered to the customer 37 years after Navarre was first introduced. When the Navarre pattern was sold to the Lenox Company in 1982, it represented nearly 9% of Fostoria's entire bridal stemware business.

In the early 1950s, the presidents of the Fostoria Glass Company, Imperial Glass Company, and the A.H. Heisey Glass Company were contacted by the National Park Service with a proposal that they work together to design and build a glass house in the soon to be built Jamestown Colony National Park. Each of these presidents along with others from other glass houses worked together to make a glass house that would be as close as possible to the original. Thatching of roofs was studied, as well as the glass blowing techniques of that early period. When the project was complete, everything was as close to the original as possible except that the new furnace was gas powered instead of wood-fired as the original one had been. When the park was opened in 1957, 350 years after the founding of the colony, a complete glass blowing crew was on hand from the Fostoria Glass Company. In 1958, Fostoria introduced another best-seller, the Jamestown pattern, on the 350th anniversary of the first glass made at the Jamestown Colony.

Kenneth B. Dalzell was the last president, coming into office in 1982 upon the retirement of his father. On December 28, 1983, Lancaster Colony Corporation purchased the Fostoria Glass Company, and permanently closed the factory in March of 1986.

When the Fostoria factory in Moundsville, West Virginia, was closed, the Fostoria Glass Company had been in business for 99 years. Through a great depression, two wars and several conflicts, the coming of unions, and the onslaught of imports, Fostoria had survived for nearly a century. In the final analysis, cheaper imports, the high cost of labor, the heightened awareness of and lack of tolerance for pollutants from manufacturing concerns, and the move of the American public toward the convenience of fast food and throw-away dishes closed the doors on this great glass house.

Fostoria gave the American public glassware to set the most formal and elaborate table. It gave us tempered glassware that would hold up with minimum care but looked and felt like fine crystal, because it was. Finally, Fostoria gave us a look at America, and what, through the designers in New York City, we were told we wanted: tall, graceful stems and champagne flutes; short, practical stems; platters and shakers; and always, American.

PRICING

Normally, one bases prices on supply and demand, and the going rate in the market place. Since this book is primarily concerned with tableware, the authors have developed a set of criteria which, in addition to the above considerations, is based on the relationship of pieces within a pattern.

Each dinnerware pattern had typical pieces; some had more, some fewer. Just as the tiny cordial is more difficult to find and thus, more expensive in stemware patterns, some pieces are considered more valuable in tableware than others. Often times, value is determined by the fact that some pieces were used more than others, and some had harsher use. Dinner plates became scratched and chipped, vases were stained when water sat in them, and ice tubs were scratched by the tongs used to pick up the ice pieces. Therefore, one criteria is that prices differ within a pattern. Typically, the jug will be expensive, especially the 5000 jug, as will the dinner plate, vases, candelabra (with bobeches), and those pieces that were made for only a few years.

This book covers the golden era of a great glass company. It contains rare and not so rare patterns, with few of the patterns listed made beyond 1944, and after 1943, none offered in color with the exception of a very few reintroductions. Therefore, the age of this glassware and the length of time it was offered also are pricing factors.

Quality is another factor. The Oakwood decoration is the most expensive pattern in this book, and quite frankly, was difficult for the authors to value. It is a labor intensive pattern with a brocade etching, iridescence, and gold leaf, all hand-applied and hand-finished. Oakwood is rare, with

pieces in Azure made for two years, and pieces in Orchid made for just one. None of the pattern has been made since 1929, yet it can be found in the marketplace.

Supply and demand also figure into our pricing criteria. We have seen a surge in demand for needle etchings on color that would not have been anticipated a few years ago. Another change is with the amber color. Once seldom considered, Fostoria's Amber is making a decided comeback. Some patterns may never be popular. The multitude of cuttings offered for a few years by Fostoria and then dropped, only to be replaced by other cuttings for a few years, are good examples. However, we have noticed that all things tend to run in cycles, so cuttings could become popular in the future. After all, some collectors prefer the purity of cut crystal with the sparkle of refracted light it adds to a table setting.

The current marketplace was used as a factor in determining values. It did not weigh more heavily than quality, rarity, or supply and demand. When one considers that all the patterns in this book were hand made and hand finished by deftly skilled laborers who blew it into molds, pressed it, turned and twisted it with exquisite timing, the glassware becomes priceless. It represents a time in the history of America that will never be repeated: a time when glassware was mass produced by hand.

The authors include single values rather than ranges; values are 1999 retail market prices. A good rule of thumb in pricing is to realize values may vary up to 20% either up or down.

PRESSED PATTERNS

2056 American
2183 Colonial Prism
2222 Colonial Tea Room Service
Twenty-Three Fifteen
2321 Priscilla
2350 Pioneer
2375 Fairfax
2412 Queen Anne
2419 Mayfair
2424 Kent
Twenty-Four Twenty-Nine
2430 Diadem/ 504 Crown Decoration
Twenty-Four Thirty-Three
2440 Lafayette
2449 Hermitage
Twenty-Four Seventy
2496 Baroque
2501 Rosette
2510 Sunray/Glacier/Golden Glow
2513 Grape Leaf
2545 Flame
2550 Spool
2592 Myriad
2620 Wistar

2056 AMERICAN

Made in Crystal, Amber, Blue and Canary Only

No. 2056. 6 in. Bon Bon.

No. 2056. Hair Receiver.

No. 2056 Small Cigarette and Cover.

No. 2183. Puff and Cover.

No. 2056½ Cologne.

No. 2056 Square Puff and Cover.

No. 2056. Confection and Cover.

No. 2056. 5 in. Pin Tray.

No. 2056. Large Cigarette and Cover.

No. 2056½ 10 in. Comb and Brush Tray.

Intended by Fostoria to harken back to the days of colonial America when it was introduced in 1915, the American pattern is first and foremost practical and reminiscent of the sturdiness of the folk who founded this country. However, when a freshly washed piece is held in sunlight, the brilliant elegance of fine, fire-polished glass is abundantly evident, displaying why this pattern has become the most sought after, and sometimes fought over, glass in our history.

In order to present this pattern to best advantage, the authors divided the American pattern so that all pieces originally offered from 1915 through 1943 are included in this book. Pieces introduced after 1943, as well as milk glass pieces, will be covered in a following volume.

Because the American pattern was made for so long (1915 – 1986 in Moundsville), research is difficult. In addition, table settings have changed over the years, and the American pattern changed with them. This long-lived and adaptable line often dropped pieces, only to have them reappear under a different name a few years later, and the company continued to introduce new pieces into the 1980s.

The authors have found many items of interest to the collector of the American pattern. For example, a Tea Set is listed in 1918 which was composed of the Sugar and Cover, Cream, Butter and Cover, and Spoon. The crystal five-piece Boudoir Set used the Match Box from 1918 – 1924, but then switched to the Oval Ash Tray with match stand. The only time that tiny little box was called a Match Box was when it was offered with the Boudoir Set, otherwise, it was the Hair Pin Box. When used in the colored Boudoir Set in 1925 – 1926, the Glove Box became the Large Cigarette; the Jewel Box became the Small Cigarette; and the Handkerchief Box was the Confection and Cover.

The 10½" Oblong Tray has a checkered history. It was used in the Ice Cream Set, the Condiment Set, the Decanter Set, and the Boudoir Set in crystal. Sometimes it was listed as a 10" Oblong Tray, and it became the 2056½ Comb and Brush Tray when it was offered in color. The Hair Receiver shown with the pieces in color above was never listed as part of the Boudoir Set in price lists, although it naturally would seem to belong. The Puff and Cover shown on the same catalog page is from the 2183 Colonial Prism line and is not part of the American pattern. The 2056½ Ice Jug (half-gallon) did not have an ice lip until 1937. The 13½" Oval Ice Cream is not pictured but is the same shape as the 12" Platter.

Other examples of a piece known by several names are the High Foot for the 14" Punch Bowl as the 7" Vase; the Candy Jar as the handleless Sugar and Cover; the 9½" and 11" Centerpieces as the low foot for the 14" and 18" Punch Bowls.

Research on the Cologne Bottles revealed that in most price lists they were simply Small and Large, with sporadic inclusions of 6 ounces for the Small Cologne and 8 ounces for the Large. In 1928 only, they were listed as having 4½ ounces and 8 ounces. Probably, this listing is a misprint. In 1925, the Boudoir Set in color lists simply a 2056½ Small Cologne.

The 2056½ Bagged Vase is similar to the 10" Cupped Vase of the same period and could have been made from the same mold. The Bagged Vase has deeper shoulders, and the clear band that turns in on the Cupped Vase flares on the Bagged Vase.

In 1925, a Table Salt is listed along with the Individual Salt. In other pressed patterns, a Table Salt was a Master Salt, but since no picture was shown, this cannot be positively confirmed for the American pattern. From 1944 to July of 1947, no shakers were made, only the Individual Salt. During the few years before World War II, Fostoria Glass Tops and Silver Tops were used on shakers until 1943. When these shakers reappeared in late 1947, Fostoria Glass Tops, Silver Tops, and Chrome Tops were used, with Silver dropping out in 1948 and Glass in 1949.

Until 1925 there was a 5½" Ice Cream Tray. The 1925 price list includes a 5¼" Ice Cream Saucer instead of the Tray. The rim of the later version turns up more which accounts for the difference in diameter. In 1933, the Ice Cream Saucer became the 5½" Ice Cream. A 10" Square Plate was listed in 1924 – 1925. Most likely this is the same as the 10" Square Tray listed from 1926 – 1943.

Cups in this pattern have been somewhat confusing. Until 1938 there were two styles of punch cups which were called custards: the regular custard and the flared custard. The custards were renamed punch cups in 1938 and continued with that title until Fostoria started numbering individual pieces within a line in 1957. The regular cup was given the number 615 and the flared cup 616. In 1971, the 396 footed coffee cup also was used as the 614 footed punch cup. There are variations in the height, width of the band around the top, and placement of handles on the earlier cups. Information on the pointed handles has not surfaced, but we see these quite frequently.

Collectors will find the Catsup Bottle and Stopper in this volume. Made from 1939 – 1943, it dropped out of the line only to return briefly in 1957 – 1958 as the Condiment Bottle and Stopper. The Marmalade was never listed as having a glass spoon. A chrome spoon was listed in 1937 – 1941 and a silver plated spoon from 1942 – 1943. Despite the popularity of the American pattern from its inception, it did not become a complete dinner service until 1932 when a cup and saucer, and a 9½" dinner plate were added to the line.

So many things can and have been said about this incredible pattern. Rare is the citizen who has not seen or heard of American. It has graced formal dinner and luncheon tables, and wedding and graduation receptions for more than 80 years. No other glassware pattern in the history of glassmaking in America has so captured the heart of its people. The American pattern still is so popular that some folks do not know the Fostoria Glass Company made anything else.

During the Great Depression, Fostoria introduced Master Etchings, innovative designs, and a multitude of cuttings, carvings, and decorations. But what the company sold, according to former president David Dalzell, what kept them going on a daily basis, was the American pattern. It is doubtful that there will ever come a time when one can say he or she knows everything about this long-lived pattern.

Almond, 3¾" Oval, 1916-1927; 1935-1944; $22.00

Appetizer, Individual Square (Also listed as Square Ice Cream), 1934-1943;1957-1958; $34.00

Appetizer Set, 7-piece, 1934-1943;1957-1958; $365.00. Included 10½" Oblong Tray and 6 Individual Square Appetizers

Appetizer Set, 7-piece, 1935-1936; $400.00. Included 2528 11¾" Tray and 6 Individual Square Appetizers

Ash Tray, 2⅞" Square, 1936-1973; $12.00

Ash Tray, Oval with Match Stand, 1915-1958; $34.00. Ebony, 1925-1926; $67.00

Banana Split, 1915-1927; market

Basket, Reed Handle, 1940-1958; $95.00

Water Cress Set

Boat, 8½" Small, 1916-1985; $22.00
    Green, 1925-1926; $84.00
Boat, Large, 1916-1985; $28.00
    Green, 1925-1926; $110.00
Boat, Sauce and Plate, 1938-1958; $68.00
Bon Bon, 3-toed, 1925-1982; $32.00
    Amber, Blue, Canary, 1925-1926; $135.00
Bottle, Bitters and Tube, 1934-1943; $135.00
Bottle, Catsup and Stopper, 1939-1943; $145.00
Bottle, Cordial and Stopper, 1934-1943; $130.00
Bottle, Water, 1916-1927; $700.00/market
Boudoir Set, 5-piece, 1915-1927; $1,245.00. Included 10½" Oblong Tray, Quart Jug, 7¼" Candle, Match Box, 8 oz. Tumbler (Match Box replaced in 1925 by Oval Ash Tray with Match Stand; $450.00)
Boudoir Set, 8-piece. Included 10" Comb and Brush Tray, Bon Bon, Large Cigarette and Cover, Small Cigarette and Cover, Confection and Cover, Small Cologne, Square Puff Box, 5" Oval Pin Tray. Amber, 1925-1926; market. Blue, 1925-1926; market. Canary, 1925-1926; market
Bowl, 7" Cupped, 1939-1973; $58.00
Bowl, Finger and Plate, 1915-1943; $84.00
Bowl, 12" Footed Fruit (Same as Tom and Jerry), 1915-1970; $225.00
Bowl, 16" Footed Fruit, 1915-1965; $165.00
Bowl, 8" Footed, Handled, 1924-1945; $95.00
Bowl, 8½" Handled, 1934-1972; $62.00
Bowl, 11¾" Oval, 1938-1982; $65.00
Bowl, Oval Vegetable, 1938-1982; $35.00
Bowl, 2-part Vegetable, 1940-1974; $38.00
Bowl, 14" Punch, High Foot, 1915-1941; $400.00
Bowl, 14" Punch, Low Foot, 1915-1982; $295.00
Bowl, 18" Punch, Low Foot, 1915-1980; $450.00
Bowl, 11½" Rolled Edge, 1939-1974; $50.00
Bowl, 3½" Rose, 1918-1958; $24.00
Bowl, 5" Rose, 1935-1958; $37.00
Bowl, 13" Shallow Fruit, 1939-1974; $125.00
Bowl, 10½" 3-toed, 1937-1985; $39.00
Bowl, 7¼" Watercress and 8" Plate, 1921-1927; $85.00

American Large Green Boat, Mother-of-pearl iridescent Cover for Round Puff Box, 5½" Ice Cream.

Box, Pomade and Cover, 1916-1927; $550.00
Box, Round Puff and Cover, 1915-1928; $500.00
Box, 3" Square Puff and Cover, 1915-1943; $375.00
    Amber, Blue, Canary, 1925-1926; $800.00
Box, Hair Receiver and Cover, Crystal, 1916-1927; $800.00. Amber, 1925-1926; $1,100.00. Blue, 1925-1926; $1,200.00. Canary, 1925-1926; $1,200.00
Box, 3½" Hair Pin and Cover, 1915-1927; $825.00
Box, Match (Same as Hair Pin), 1915-1927; $825.00
Box, 4¾"x 3½" Cigarette and Cover, 1936-1958; $65.00
Box, 5½" Jewel and Cover, 1915-1928; $400.00
Box, 6" Handkerchief and Cover, 1915-1942; $350.00
Box, 9½" Glove and Cover, 1915-1928; $575.00
Box, Cigarette, Small (Called Jewel Box in Crystal), Amber, 1925-1926; $900.00. Blue, 1925-1926; $1,000.00. Canary, 1925-1926; $1,000.00
Box, Cigarette, Large (Called Glove Box in Crystal), Amber, 1925-1926; $1,400.00. Blue, 1925-1926; $1,500.00. Canary, 1925-1926; $1,500.00
Box, Confection and Cover (Called Handkerchief Box in Crystal), Amber, 1925-1926; $900.00. Blue, 1925-1926; $1,000.00. Canary, 1925-1926; $1,000.00
Box, Candy, 3-part and Cover, 1937-1972; $78.00
Box, Flower (same as Oblong Butter Cover), 1940-1948; $22.00
Butter, Oblong and Cover, 1940-1985; $35.00
Butter, Round and Cover, 1915-1974; $95.00
Candelabra, Duo with U.D.P., 1936-1942 (pair); $395.00
Candlestick, Duo, 1936-1958 (pair); $300.00
Candlestick, 3", 1937-1982 (pair); $32.00
Candlestick, 6", 1933-1982 (pair); $87.00
2056½ Candlestick, 7", (pair) 1924-1944; $245.00
Candlestick, 7¼", (pair) 1915-1927; $295.00
Candlestick, Twin, (pair) 1937-1982; $140.00
Candy Jar and Cover, 1937-1974; $40.00
Candy Tray, 5"x 7", 1916-1927; $150.00
Celery, 6" tall, 1915-1929; $56.00
Celery, 10" Tray, 1916-1985; $27.00
Centerpiece, 11" 3-cornered, 1940-1982; $48.00
Centerpiece, 9½", 1935-1982; $65.00
Centerpiece, 11", 1935-1980; $75.00
Centerpiece, 15", 1935-1944; $195.00
Cheese and Cracker, 1939-1970; $64.00
Chiffonier, 2¼"x4½"x 3¼", 1918-1927; $3,000.00 to market
Coaster, All-over design, 3¾", 1937-1978; $11.00
2056½ Cologne, 6 oz. Small, DS, Crystal, 1925-1943; $135.00. Amber, 1925-1926; $350.00. Blue, 1925-1926; $465.00. Canary, 1925-1926; $465.00
Cologne, 8 oz. Large, DS, 1915-1943; $145.00
Comport, 5" High Foot, 1924-1982; $38.00
Comport and Cover, 5" High Foot, 1924-1982; $54.00
Comport, 8½", 1915-1926; $65.00
Comport, 9½", 1915-1926; $65.00
Condiment Set, 5-piece, 1918-1928; $195.00. Included 10" Oval Tray, two 5 oz. Oil Bottles, DS (7 oz. in 1928), two No. 1 Shakers, "W" Tops (HN Tops in 1928)

American Boudoir Set: 10½" Tray, 8 oz. Tumbler, Quart Jug, Oval Ash Tray with Match Stand, 7¼" Candlestick.

Condiment Set, 6-piece, 1938-1943, 1952-1958; $500.00. Included 9" Cloverleaf Tray, two 5 oz. Oil Bottles (DS), two No. 2 Shakers (FGT), Mustard, Cover and Spoon

Cream, 4¾ oz. Individual, 1916-1982; $12.00

Cream, 9½ oz. Large, 1915-1982; $16.00

Cream, 3 oz. Tea, 1939-1974; $14.00

Crushed Fruit and Cover, 1915-1927; $1,500.00 to market

Crushed Fruit Spoon, 1915-1927; $375.00 to market

Cup, Custard Flared (Punch), 1915-1937; $12.00

Cup, Custard Regular (Punch), 1915-1937; $12.00

Cup, Footed (Coffee) , 1932-1985; $12.00

Decanter and Stopper, 24 oz., 1934-1965; $125.00

Decanter Set, 7-piece, 1934-1943; $240.00. Included 24 oz. Decanter and Stopper and six 2 oz. Whiskeys.

Decanter Set, 8-piece, 1934-1943;1957-1960; $350.00. Included 10½" Oblong Tray, 24 oz. Decanter and Stopper, and six 2 oz. Whiskeys.

Floating Garden, 10" (Same as Oval, 10"), 1934-1973; $78.00

Floating Garden, 11½" (Same as Oval, 11½"), 1934-1958; $85.00

2956½ Flower Pot and perforated Cover, 1915-1923; $1,200.00 to market

Hotel Cracked Ice, 1917-1927; $3,000.00 to market

Ice Bucket with Metal Handle, 1940-1970; $65.00

Ice Cream, 5½" Tray, 1916-1924;1933-1944; $67.00

Ice Cream, 5¼" Saucer, 1925-1932; $67.00

Ice Cream, 3½" Square Handled (Same as Appetizer), 1918-1927; $36.00

Ice Cream Tray, 10⅝", 1918-1927; $150.00

Ice Cream Oval Tray, 13½", 1916-1927; $195.00 (Listed as 14", 1916-1920)

Ice Cream Set, 7-piece, 1918-1927; $365.00. Included 10½" Oblong Tray and six Handled Ice Creams (Same as Appetizer Set)

Ice Dish, 1940-1958 (Priced with liner); $68.00. Liners: Tomato Juice, Crab Meat, Fruit Cocktail

Ice Tub, Small, and 8" Plate, 1925-1958; $88.00

Ice Tub, Large, and 9" Plate, 1916-1958; $115.00

Jam Jar and Cover (Same as Pickle Jar), 1935-1943; $475.00

Jar, Cracker, and Cover (Same as Cookie and Pretzel), 1915-1928; $265.00

Jar, Pickle, and Cover (Same as Jam), 1916-1925; $475.00

Jar, Pretzel, and Cover (Same as Cookie and Cracker), 1933-1944; $265.00

Jar, Straw, and Cover, 1915-1928; $275.00

Jelly, Footed Flared, 1916-1928; $110.00

Jelly, Footed Regular, 1916-1982; $35.00

Jelly, Footed Regular, and Cover, 1916-1982; $48.00

Jelly, Deep Flared, 1925; $65.00

Jelly, Deep Regular, 1925; $65.00

Jug, 7¼" Quart, 1918-1974; $90.00

Jug, 6½" 3-pint Ice, 1938-1982; $85.00

Jug, 8", 3-pint, 1918-1974; $125.00

Jug, 8", ½ Gallon, 1918-1973; $125.00

2056½ Jug, 8¼", ½ Gallon Ice, 1915-1936, $165.00. Green, 1925-1926; $800 to market

2056½ Jug, ½ Gallon (69 oz.) Ice Lip, 1937-1982; $125.00

Lamp, Candle (3" Candle, Peg Candle Insert, Wax Pot, Shade), 1939-1943; 1954-1970 (pair); $250.00

Lamp, 12" Hurricane (Base and Chimney), 1939-1943; 1953-1958 (pair); $500.00

Lemon Dish, 1915-1944; $30.00

Lemon Dish and Cover, 1915-1944; 1947-1970; $54.00

Lily Pond, 12", 1940-1974; $95.00

Marmalade, Cover and Spoon, 1937-1943; $125.00. Chrome Spoon, 1937-1941. Silver Plated Spoon, 1942-1943 (Never a glass spoon listed)

Mayonnaise, 2-part, 2 Ladles, 1939-1974; $64.00

Mayonnaise, Plate, Ladle, 1935-1973; $64.00

Molasses Can, 11 oz. Large, ENT (Ewer Nickel Top), Glass handle,1916-1927; market

Molasses Can, 6 oz., Metal Handle (Same as 6 oz. Syrup), 1916-1918; Market

Mug, 12 oz. Beer, 1933-1943; $85.00

Mug, Tom and Jerry, 1935-1944; $45.00

Mustard, Cover, and Spoon, 1935-1965; $64.00

Nappy, 4¼" Regular, 1915-1928; $35.00

Nappy, 4½" Regular, 1915-1982; $18.00. Green, 1925-1926; $75.00

Nappy, 4¾" Fruit, 1915-1982; $18.00

Nappy, 5" Regular, 1915-1985; $15.00

Nappy, 5" Regular, and Cover, 1924-1982; $25.00

Nappy, 6" Regular, 1915-1982; $18.00

Nappy, 7" Regular, 1915-1982; $20.00

Nappy, 8" Regular, 1915-1985; $20.00. Green, 1925-1926; $95.00

Nappy, 8" Deep, 1915-1959; $55.00
Nappy, 10" Deep, 1916-1985; $55.00
Nappy, 4¾" Flared, 1915-1928; $37.00
Nappy, 6" Flared, 1915-1928; $40.00
Nappy, 7" Flared, 1915-1928; $45.00
Nappy, 8" Flared, 1915-1928; $50.00
Nappy, 9" Flared, 1915-1928; $60.00
Nappy, 10" Flared, 1915-1928; $70.00
Nappy, 4½" Handled Regular, 1915-1982; $15.00
Nappy, 4½" Handled Square, 1915-1982; $15.00
Nappy, 5" Handled, 3-cornered, 1915-1982; $15.00
Nappy, 5½" Handled Flared, 1915-1944; $24.00
Nappy, 7" Shallow, 1915-1928; $40.00
Nappy, 8" Shallow, 1915-1928; $50.00
Nappy, 10" Shallow, 1915-1928; $65.00
Oil, 5 oz., D.S., G. S., 1915-1982; $54.00
Oil, 7 oz., D.S., G.S., 1915-1972; $60.00
Olive, 6", 1916-1982; $18.00
Old Fashioned Set, 9-piece, 1934-1938; $550.00. Included 12" Round Tray, 24 oz. Decanter and Stopper, one Bitters Bottle and Tube, and six 6 oz. Old Fashioned Cocktails
Oval, 4½" (Commonly called an Almond), 1918-1958; $24.00
Oval, 9", 1918-1927; $75.00
Oval, 10" (Same as Floating Garden), 1918-1927; $78.00
Oval, 11½" (Same as Floating Garden), 1918-1927; $85.00
Pickle, 8", 1916-1982; $22.00
Pitcher, Pint Cereal, 1937-1973; $37.00

American Old Fashioned Set: 12" Round Tray, Decanter, Bitters Bottle, six Old Fashioned Cocktails.

Plate, 6" Bread and Butter, 1932-1982; $10.00
Plate, Cream Soup, 1939-1958; $15.00
Plate, Crescent Salad, 1937-1944; $75.00
Plate, 6" Ice Tea, 1915-1928; $10.00
Plate, 6" Syrup, 1939-1944; $10.00
Plate, 6½" Finger Bowl, 1915-1943; $18.00
Plate, 7" Salad, 1934-1982; $15.00
Plate, 8" Salad, 1928-1933; $25.00
Plate, 8" Crushed Ice Tub, 1915-1958; $25.00
Plate, 8" Watercress, 1921-1927; $25.00
Plate, 8½" Salad, 1935-1982; $33.00
Plate, 9" Sandwich, 1915-1974; $33.00
Plate, 9" Ice Tub, 1916-1928; $24.00
Plate 9½" Dinner, 1932-1982; $24.00
Plate, 10" Square (May be same as 10" Square Tray), 1924-1925; $195.00
Plate, 10½" Sandwich, 1915-1982; $35.00
Plate, 11½" Sandwich, 1915-1974; $38.00
Plate, 12" Footed Cake, 1938-1983; $48.00
Plate, 13½" Oval Torte, 1939-1973; $95.00
Plate, 14" Torte, 1934-1985; $45.00
Plate, 18" Torte, 1935-1980; $175.00
Plate, 20" Torte, 1932-1943; $195.00
Plate, 24" Torte, 1928-1931; market
Platter, 10½" Oval, 1933-1970; $55.00
Platter, 12" Oval, 1933-1973; $65.00
Preserve, Handled and Cover, 1915-1944; $80.00
Relish, 2-part, 1935-1985; $30.00
Relish, 3-part, 1935-1944; $65.00
2056½ Relish, Combination 3-part, 1939-1982; $68.00
Relish, 4-part Square, 1935-1943; $195.00
2056½ Relish, 4-division, 1939-1971; $70.00
Salad Set, 3-piece, 1935-1982; $125.00. Included 14" Torte Plate, 10" Deep Nappy (Salad Bowl), Salad Fork and Spoon (wood)
Salt, Individual, 1924-1982; $8.00
Salt, Table, 1925; market
Salver, 10" Round, 1916-1982; $165.00
Salver, 10" Square, 1924-1982; $185.00
Saucer, 6", Plain Center, 1932-1982; $6.00
Shaker, No. 1, 3", 1916-1945 (Priced as a pair), Tops: HNT (Heavy Nickel Top), $50.00; HST (Heavy Silver Top), $55.00; FGT (Fostoria Glass Top), $75.00; SPT (Silver Plated Top), $65.00; W (Glass disc with heavy nickel band), $75.00; available at different times
2056½ Shaker, No. 2, 3¼" (Priced as a pair) HNT (Heavy Nickel Top), $50:00; HST (Heavy Silver Top), $55.00; PT (Pearl Disc with non-corrosive band), 1918, $75.00; FGT (Fostoria Glass Top), 1934-1940, $75.00; "S" (Silver) Top, 1941-1943; 1947-1948, $65.00. Chrome "A", 1949-1985; $32.00
Shaker, 2" Individual (Priced as a pair), FGT (Fostoria Glass Top), 1938-1949, $48.00; Chrome Top "C", 1939-1983; $38.00

Shaker Set, 3-piece, 1938-1949. Included Individual Shaker Tray and 2 Individual Shakers FGT, 1938-1949, $68.00; Silver/Chrome Tops, 1941-1974, $58.00

Shaker, Sugar, Heavy Nickel Top, 1916-1927, 1978-1982; $125.00

Smoker Set, 5-piece, 1935-1958; $100.00. Included Cigarette Box and Cover and four 2⅞" Square Ash Trays

Soup, Handled Cream, 1938-1958; $54.00

Spoon, 1915-1933; $45.00

Sugar and Cover, 6¼", 1915-1982; $40.00

Sugar, 5¼" Handled and Cover, 1924-1982; $45.00

Sugar, 2½" Individual, 1916-1982; $12.00

Sugar and Cream Set, Individual, 3-piece, 1939-1974; $38.00. Included Sugar and Cream Tray, Individual Sugar and Cream

Sugar and Cream Set, Tea, 3-piece, 1939-1974; $45.00. Included Sugar and Cream Tray, Tea, Sugar and Cream

Sugar, 2¼" Tea, 1939-1974; $14.00

2056½ Syrup, 6 oz. Screw Top, NP (Same as Small Molasses), 1916-1918; $300.00 to market

Syrup, 6½ oz. Sani-Cut Server, 1939-1943; $195.00

Syrup, 6½ oz. Dripcut, 1957-1982; $75.00

Syrup, 10 oz., Cover, and Plate, 1939-1944; $300.00

Tid Bit, 3-toed, 1938-1982; $28.00

Tid Bit Set with Metal Handle, 1933-1943; $60.00

Tom and Jerry Set, 9-piece, 1935-1944; $550.00. Included 12" Footed Fruit Bowl and 8 Tom and Jerry Mugs

Toothpick, 2⅜", 1916-1981; $20.00

Topper, Ash Tray, 1939-1958; $28.00

Topper, 2½" for matches, 1939-1958; $30.00

Topper, 3" Cigarette Holder, 1939-1958; $35.00

Topper, 4", 1940-1958; $45.00

Tray, Individual Shaker, 1938-1974, $20.00

Tray, 5" Oval Pin, 1918-1923; 1932-1939; $300.00/market

Tray, 5½" Oval, 1924-1927; $300.00/market

2056½ Tray, 5" Oblong, 1917-1943; $140.00; colors 1925-1926, $300.00/market

Tray, 5"x 7" Candy, 1916-1927; $300.00

Tray, 6" Oval Pin, 1918-1943; $65.00

Tray, 9" Cloverleaf Condiment, 1938-1943; 1952-1958; $225.00

Tray, 10" to 10½" Oblong, Crystal, 1918-1928; $150.00. Amber, 1925-1926; $300.00. Blue, 1925-1926; $350.00. Canary, 1925-1926; $350.00

Tray, 10½" Oblong, 1932-1958; $150.00

Tray, 10" Oval (Same as Condiment), 1915-1925; $115.00

2056½ Tray, 10" Condiment Tray, 1924-1928; $115.00

Tray, 10" Square (May be same as 10" Square Plate), 1924-1943; $195.00

Tray, 10½" Oval, 1920-1943; $115.00

Tray, 10½" Oval Comb and Brush or Condiment, 1916-1923; $115.00

Tray, 10⅝" Ice Cream, 1924-1927; $150.00

Tray, 11½" Oval, 1918; Market

Tray, 12" Oval (Same as 12" Oval Platter), 1920-1927; $65.00

Tray, 12" Round, 1924-1943; $195.00

2056½ Tray, 13½" Oval Ice Cream (14" in 1918), 1916-1920; market

Tray, Cake with Metal Handle, 1935-1943; $75.00

Tray, Handled Lunch, 1939-1973; $85.00

Tray, Handled Utility, 1942-1982; $50.00

Tray, Sugar and Cream, 1939-1974; $15.00

Tricorne, 6½," 3-toed, 1941-1943; $120.00

Urn, 6" Square, 1940-1970; $75.00

Urn, 7½" Square, 1939-1970; $85.00

2056½ Vase, Bagged, 1924-1927; $1,200.00 to market

Vase, 6" Footed Cupped Bud, 1940-1982; $30.00

Vase, 6" Footed Flared Bud, 1940-1982; $30.00

Vase, 6" Flared, 1935-1970; $35.00

Vase, 7" Flared (High Foot for Punch Bowl), 1918-1959; $125.00

Vase, 8" Flared, 1935-1970; $50.00

Vase, 9½" Flared, 1937-1939; $195.00

Vase, 10" Cupped, 1925-1943; $135.00

Vase 10" Flared, 1939-1970; $90.00

Vase, Small Porch, 1915-1927; market

Vase, Large Porch, 1915-1927; market

Vase, 9" Square Footed, 1933-1974; $85.00

Vase, 12" Square Footed, 1924; market

Vase, 6" Straight, 1933-1970; $56.00

Vase, 8" Straight, 1915-1970; $55.00

Vase, 10" Straight, 1915-1958; $95.00

Vase, 12" Straight, 1915-1944; $145.00

Vase, Sweetpea, 1935-1958; $65.00

Vase, Swung, 9" to 12", 1937-1944; $165.00

Vase, Swung, 14" to 16", 1915-1927; $225.00

Vase, Swung, 18" to 20", 1915-1927; $350.00

Vase, Swung, 23" to 26", 1915-1927; $500.00

Watercress Set, 2-piece, 1921-1927; $85.00. Included 8" Plate and 7¼" 3-toed Water Cress Bowl

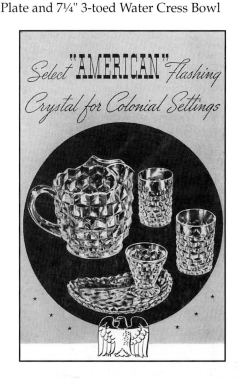

Select "AMERICAN" *Flashing Crystal for Colonial Settings*

No. 2056 Sundae
Capacity 6 oz.

No. 2056 Banana Split
Length 9 inches
Width 3½ inches

Crushed Fruit Spoon
Length 9 inches

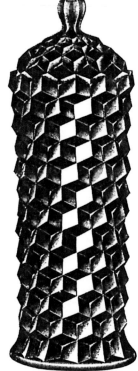

No. 2056 Straw Jar and Cover
Height 12 inches
Diameter at Top 4 inches

No. 2056 Crush Fruit and Cover
Height 10 inches
Diameter at Top 5¾ inches
Cover made to accommodate Crush Fruit
Spoon

No. 2056 Cracker Jar and Cover
Height 8¾ inches
Diameter at Top 5¾ inches

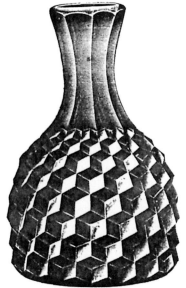

No. 2056 Water Bottle
Height 9¼ inches. Capacity 44 oz.

No. 2056½ ½ Gallon Ice Jug
Actual Capacity 69 oz.

No. 2056 Molasses Can
Height 6¾ inches
Capacity 11 oz.

No. 2056 Syrup
N. P. Screw Top
Height 5¼ inches
Capacity 6 oz.

No. 2056 Sugar Shaker
Height 4¾ inches
Also furnished with pepper top.

No. 2056 Chiffonier
Height 2¼ inches
Length 4¼ inches
Width 3¼ inches

No. 2056—Boudoir Set
Tray 10⅝x7½ inches
Quart Jug
7¼-inch Candle
Match Box 3½x1¾x1½ inches high
Tumbler 8-ounce capacity

No. 2056 Spoon
Height 3¾ inches

2056 Shaker
W. Top
Height 3¼ in.

No. 2056 Condiment Set
Length of Tray 10 inches

AMERICAN PATTERN
No. 2056 LINE

No. 2056 Flower Pot and perforated
Cover
Height 5½ inches
Diameter 9½ inches

No. 2056 Large Porch Vase.
Height 8 to 10 inches
Top Diameter 7 to 8 inches.

No. 2056 15 in. Swung Vase
Height from 14 to 16 inches.
20 in. Vase Height 18 to 20 inches
25 in. Vase Height 23 to 26 inches

No. 2056 Small Porch Vase
Height 8 to 10 inches
Top Diameter 5 to 6 inches

No. 2056 7 in. Shallow Nappy
Height 1¾ inches

No. 2056 9½ inch Comport
Height 5½ inches
No. 2056 8½ inch Comport
Height 4 inches

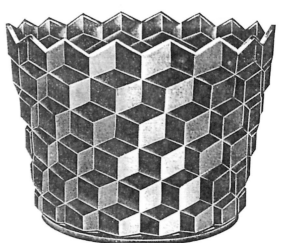

No. 2056 Hotel Cracked Ice
Capacity 10½ pints Height 7 inches Top diameter 10 inches

AMERICAN PATTERN
No. 2056 LINE

2056—6 in. B. & B. Plate
2056—7 in. Salad Plate

2056—Footed Cup
2056—Saucer

2056—8½ in. Salad Plate
2056—9½ in. Dinner Plate

2056½—Shaker, F.G.T.
Height 3¼ in.

2056—10½ in. Oval Platter
2056—12 in. Oval Platter

2056—No. 1 Shaker, H.N.T.
Height 3 inches

2056—Individual Sugar
Height 2½ in.

2056—Individual Cream
Height 2¾ in.
Capacity 4¾ oz.

2056—Sugar and Cover
Height 6¼ in.

2056—Cream
Height 4¼ in.
Capacity 9½ oz.

2056½
Handled Sugar and Cover
Height 5¼ in.

2056— 6 in. Olive
2056— 8 in. Pickle
2056—10 in. Celery

2056—Individual Salt
Height 1 in.

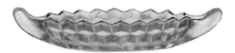

2056—8½ in. Small Boat
2056—12 in. Large Boat

2056—Quart Jug—Height 7¼ in.
2056—3 Pint Jug—Height 8 in.
2056—½ Gallon Jug—Height 8 in.

2056—Finger Bowl
Top Diameter 4½ in.
2056—Finger Bowl Plate, 6½ in.

AMERICAN PATTERN

No. 2056 LINE

2056—4¾ in. Nappy (Fruit)

2056—4½, 5, 6, 7 in. Nappy

2056—5½ in. Ice Cream

2056—Mayonnaise and Plate
and Ladle
Height 3 in.

2056—5 oz. Oil, D/S
Height 6¼ in.
2056—7 oz. Oil, D/S
Height 6¾ in.

2056— 9 in. Sandwich Plate
2056—10½ in. Sandwich Plate
2056—11½ in. Sandwich Plate

2056—8 in. Nappy, Reg.
2056—8 in. Nappy, Deep
2056—10 in. Nappy, Deep

2056—10½ in. Handled Cake Tray
Metal Handle

2056—14 in. Torte Plate
2056—18 in. Torte Plate
2056—20 in. Torte Plate

2056—Mustard and
Cover and Spoon
Height 3¾ in.

2056—Tid Bit Set
Metal Handle
Height 10½ in.

2056—3 Piece Salad Set—Height 5 in.
Consisting of
1/12 Doz. 2056—10 in. Deep Nappy
1/12 Doz. 2056—14 in. Torte Plate
1/12 Doz. 2056—Salad Fork and Spoon, Wood

AMERICAN PATTERN
No. 2056 LINE

2056—3¾ in. Almond

2056—4½ in. Oval

2056—4½ in. Hld. Nappy,
Square

2056—4½ in. Hld. Nappy,
Reg.

2056—5½ in. Hld. Nappy,
Fld.

2056—5 in. Hld. Nappy,
3 Cor.

2056—10 in. Round Salver
Height 7¼ in.

2056—10 in. Square Salver
Height 7¼ in.

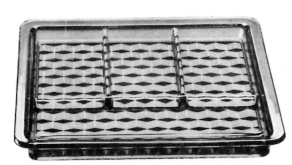

2056—4 Part Square Relish
10 in. Square

2056—3 Part Relish
Length 9½ in. Width 6 in.

2056—2 Part Relish
Length 9 in. Width 5½ in.
12 in. Overall

2056—Appetizer Set, 7 Piece
Consisting of
1/12 Doz. 2056—10½ in. Oblong Tray
1/2 Doz. 2056—Individual Appetizers
Height 1¾ in., Length 10½ in., Width 8¾ in.

AMERICAN PATTERN
No. 2056 LINE

2056—Jelly and Cover
Height 6¾ in., Diameter 4½ in.

2056—3 Toed Bon Bon
Diameter 7 in.

2056—Jam Jar
and Cover
Capacity 12 oz.
Height 6 in.

2056—5 in. Comport
Height 6¼ in.
With Cover, Height 9 in.

2056—Handled Preserve and Cover
Height 4¼ in., Diameter 5¾ in.

2056—Lemon and Cover
Height 3½ in., Diameter 5½ in.

2056½—5 in. Oblong Tray
Width 2½ in.

2056—6 in. Oval Tray

2056—Small Ice Tub and Plate
Top Diameter 5⅝ in., Height 3¾ in.
2056—Large Ice Tub and Plate
Top Diameter 6½ in., Height 4½ in.

2056—Oval Ash Tray
Length 5½ in.

2056—Square Puff Box and Cover
3⅛ in. square, Height 2¾ in.

2056—Cigarette Box
and Cover
Length 4¾ in.
Width 3½ in.

2056—6 oz. Small Cologne
Height 5¾ in.
2056—8 oz. Large Cologne
Height 7¼ in.

2056—Handkerchief Box and Cover
Length 5⅝ inches—Width 4⅝ inches

AMERICAN PATTERN
No. 2056 LINE

2056—2-oz. Whiskey
Height 2½ in.

2056—12 in. Round Tray

2056—2½ oz. Wine
Hexagon Foot
Height 4⅜ in.

2056—6-oz.
Old Fashioned Cocktail
Height 3⅜ in.

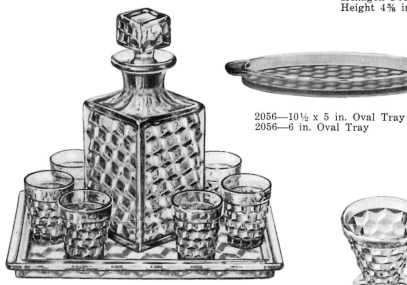

2056—10½ x 5 in. Oval Tray
2056—6 in. Oval Tray

2056—8 Piece Decanter Set
Consisting of
1/12 Doz. 2056—Decanter and Stopper
1/2 Doz. 2056—2 oz. Whiskey
1/12 Doz. 2056—10½ in. Oblong Tray

2056
3-oz. Footed Cocktail
Height 2⅞ in.

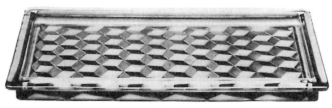

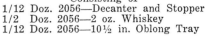

2056—10½ in. Oblong Tray
Width 7½ in.

2056
Bitters Bottle with Tube
Cap. 4½ oz.   Height 5¾ in.

2056—Decanter and Stopper
Cap. 24-oz., Height 9¼ in.
2056—Cordial Bottle and Stopper
Cap. 9-oz., Height 7¼ in.

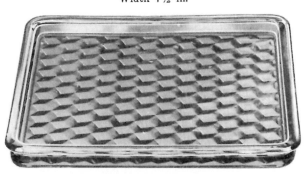

2056—10 in. Square Tray

23

AMERICAN PATTERN
No. 2056 LINE

2056—Pretzel Jar and Cover
Height 8⅞ in.

2056—12 in Footed Fruit Bowl
Small Punch Bowl or Tom and Jerry Bowl
Capacity 1¾ gal. Height 7¼ in.

2056—12 oz. Beer Mug
Height 4½ in.

2056
Tom and Jerry Mug
Capacity 5½ oz.
Height 3¼ in.

2056—Custard, Fld.

2056—14 in. Punch Bowl and High Foot (Illustrated)
Capacity 2 Gallons
2056—18 in. Punch Bowl
Capacity 3¾ Gallons
Low Foot is used with 18 in. Punch Bowl
Low Foot can also be furnished for 14 in. Punch Bowl

2056—Custard, Reg.

AMERICAN PATTERN
No. 2056 LINE

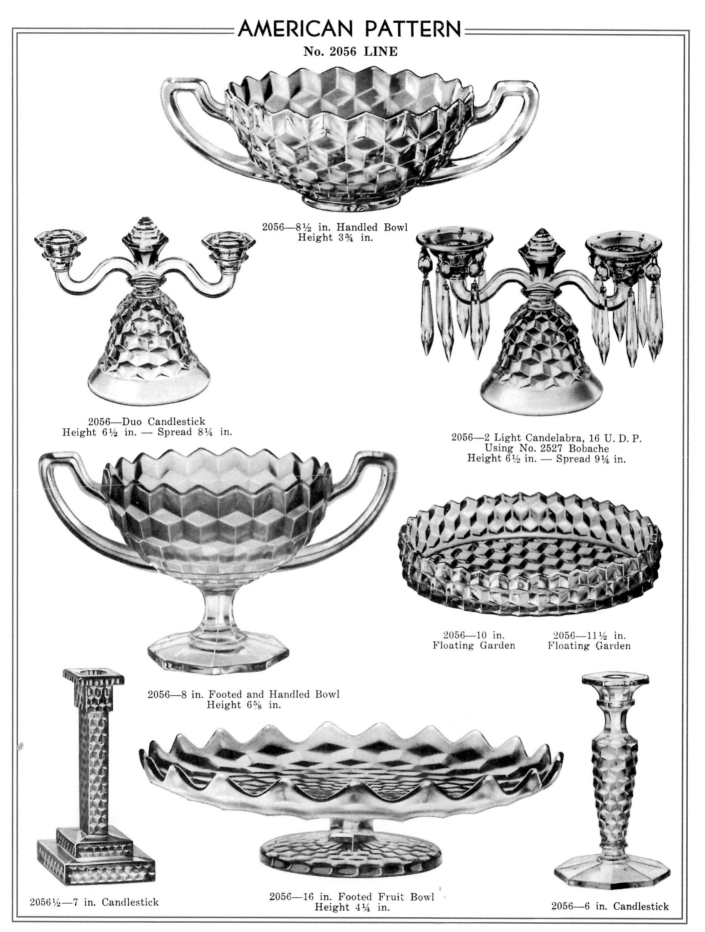

2056—8½ in. Handled Bowl
Height 3¾ in.

2056—Duo Candlestick
Height 6½ in. — Spread 8¼ in.

2056—2 Light Candelabra, 16 U. D. P.
Using No. 2527 Bobache
Height 6½ in. — Spread 9¼ in.

2056—10 in.
Floating Garden

2056—11½ in.
Floating Garden

2056—8 in. Footed and Handled Bowl
Height 6⅝ in.

2056½—7 in. Candlestick

2056—16 in. Footed Fruit Bowl
Height 4¼ in.

2056—6 in. Candlestick

AMERICAN PATTERN
No. 2056 LINE

2056—Sweetpea Vase
Height 4½ in.

2056—3½ in. Rose Bowl
2056—5 in. Rose Bowl

2056— 6 in. Vase
2056— 8 in. Vase
2056—10 in. Vase
2056—12 in. Vase

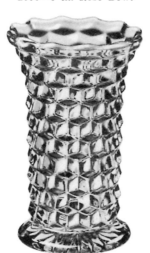

2056½
8 in. Vase, Flared

2056½
6 in. Vase, Flared

2056—9 in. Square
Footed Vase

2056—9½ in. Centerpiece—Height 3⅝ in.
2056—11 in. Centerpiece—Height 4⅜ in.

2056—10 in. Cupped Vase

2056
15 in. Centerpiece
Height 4¼ in.

AMERICAN PATTERN
No. 2056 LINE

2056
Toothpick

2056—Butter and Cover

2056½—6 Piece Condiment Set
Consisting of:
1/6   Doz. 2056 —5 oz. Oil, D/S
1/6   Doz. 2056½—Shaker, F.G.T.
1/12 Doz. 2056 —Mustard and Cover and Spoon.
1/12 Doz. 2056 —9 in. Condiment Tray

2056
3 in. Candlestick

2056—7 in. Vase

2056
3 in. Candlestick

AMERICAN PATTERN
No. 2056 LINE

2056—Vase
Swung 9 in. to 12 in.

2056—Square Ash Tray
2⅞ in. Square

2056—Coaster
Diameter—3¾ in.

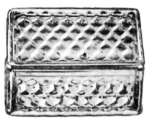

2056—5 Piece Smoker Set
Consisting of:
1/12 Doz. 2056 Cigarette Box and Cover
1/3 Doz. 2056 Square Ash Trays

2056—Pint Cereal Pitcher
Height 5⅜ in.

2056½—Ice Jug
Capacity ½ Gallon, Height 8¼ in.

AMERICAN PATTERN
No. 2056 LINE

2056—10½ in. Bowl, 3 Toes
Height 3½ in.

2056½—Twin Candlestick
Height 4⅜ in.   Spread 8½ in.

2056—Crescent Salad Plate
Length 7½ in.   Width 4⅜ in.

2056—Marmalade and Cover and Spoon
Height 5½ in.
Using Chromium Spoon

2056—3 Part Candy Box and Cover
Height 4 in. Width 6⅛ in.

2056—9½ in. Vase, Flared

AMERICAN PATTERN
No. 2056 LINE

2056
Ind. Shaker, Square
Height 2 in.

2056—3-Piece Ind. Shaker Set
Length 4 in. Height 2¼ in.
Consisting of:
1/12 doz. 2056—Ind. Shaker Tray
1/6 doz. 2056—Ind. Shaker, F.G.T.

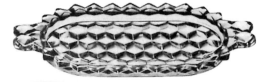

2056—6 oz. Sundae
Height 3⅛ in.

2056—6¾ in. Sugar and Cream Tray
Width 4 in.

2056—3-Piece Ind. Sugar and Cream Set
Height 3¼ in.
Consisting of:
1/12 doz. 2056—6¾ in. S. & C. Tray
1/12 doz. 2056—Ind. Sugar
1/12 doz. 2056—Ind. Cream

2056—9 in. Oval Vegetable Dish
Width 6¾ in.

2056—Cream Soup
2056—Cream Soup Plate

2056
9 oz. Footed Tumbler
Height 4⅜ in.

2056—Sauce Boat
Length 6¾ in. Width 5 in.
2056—Sauce Boat Plate
Length 8 in. Width 6½ in.

2056—12 in. Footed Cake Plate

2056—3 Pint Ice Jug
Height 6½ in.

AMERICAN PATTERN
No. 2056 LINE

2056—11¾ in. Oval Bowl
Height 2⅞ in.

2056—3 Toed Tid Bit
Diameter 8 in.
Height 1½ in.

2056—Syrup and Cover and Plate
Syrup Height 3¾ in.—Capacity 10 oz.
Plate Diameter 6 in.

2056½—Combination Relish, 3 Part
Length 11 in—Width 7½ in.

2056½—10 in. Vase, Flared

2056—Cheese and Cracker
Height 4 in.
Diameter Plate 11½ in.
Diameter Cheese 5¾ in.

AMERICAN PATTERN

No. 2056 LINE

2056—Topper Ash Tray
Top Diameter 2⅛ in.

2056½—Sani-Cut Server
Height 5¼ in.
Capacity 6½ oz.

2056½—Tea Sugar
Height 2¼ in.

2056½—Tea Cream
Height 2⅜ in.
Capacity 3 oz.

2056—Hurricane Lamp Complete
Height 12 in.
Consisting of
Hurricane Lamp Base
Hurricane Lamp Chimney

Candle Not Included

2056½—4 Division Relish
Length 9 in. Width 6½ in.

2056—3 in. Candle Lamp Complete
Height 8½ in.
Consisting of—
1/12 Doz. 26/1—3 Piece Candle Lamp
1/12 Doz. 2056—3 in. Candlestick
1/12 Doz. Wax Light

2056— 6 in. Square Urn
2056—7½ in. Square Urn

2056—12 in. Handled Lunch Tray

AMERICAN PATTERN

No. 2056 LINE

2056—Ice Dish
Tomato Juice Liner Illustrated
Patent No. 1858728

2451—4 oz. Crab
Meat Liner
Blown

2451—5 oz. Tomato
Juice Liner
Blown

2451—5 oz. Fruit
Cocktail Liner
Blown

2056½—Flower Box (Butter Cover)
Length 5¾ in. Height 1½ in. Width 2¼ in.

2056—6 in. Footed Bud Vase,
Flared

2056—6 in. Footed Bud Vase, Cupped

2056½—Oblong Butter and Cover
Length 7½ in. Height 2⅛ in. Width 3¼ in.

2056—2 Part Vegetable Dish
Length 10 in. Height 2⅛ in. Width 7 in.

2056—4 in. Topper
Top Diameter 6 in.

AMERICAN PATTERN
No. 2056 LINE

2056—11½ in. Rolled Edge Bowl
Height 2¾ in.

2056—3 Toed Tricorne
Length 6½ in.
Height 3 in

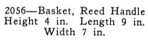

2056—Basket, Reed Handle
Height 4 in.   Length 9 in.
Width 7 in.

2056—12 in. Lily Pond
Height 2¼ in.

2056—11 in. 3-Cornered Centerpiece
Height 3¾ in.

2056—Ice Bucket
Height 4½ in.   Top Diameter 6 in.
Metal Handle and Tongs
Tongs Priced Separately

AMERICAN PATTERN
No. 2056 LINE

2056—13½ in. Oval Torte Plate

2056—5 in. Comport and Cover
Height 9 in.

2056—Catsup Bottle and Stopper
Height 6¾ in   Capacity 8½ oz.

2056—5 in. Nappy and Cover
Height 5 in.

2056—2 Part Mayonnaise
Diameter 6¼ in.
Height 3¾ in.

2056—2½ in. Topper
Top Diameter 3¾ in.

2056—3 in. Topper
Top Diameter 4½ in.

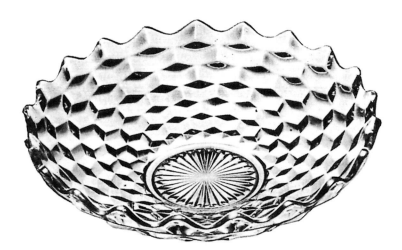

2056—13 in. Shallow Fruit Bowl
Height 3 in.

2183 COLONIAL PRISM

1918 – 1927

The puff and cover shown with the American pattern on page 10 are often mistaken for American. Stemware is featured in *Fostoria Stemware,* page 44.

Boat, 8½" Small; $12.00
Boat, 11" Large; $16.00
Bowl, 6½" Footed, Crimped; $15.00
Bowl, 6½" Footed, Flared; $18.00
Bowl, 8½" Combination Nut; $18.00
Bowl, 8½" Orange; $15.00
    Amber, 1925-1927; $28.00
    Blue, 1925-1927; $37.00
    Green, 1925-1927; $30.00
    Canary, 1925-1926; $37.00
Bowl, 12" Cabarette; $20.00
    Amber, 1925-1935; $25.00
    Blue, 1925-1927; $45.00
    Green, 1925-1939; $25.00
    Canary, 1925-1926; $45.00
    Orchid, 1927; $30.00
    Azure, 1928-1939; $30.00
    Rose, 1928-1935; $30.00
Bowl, 12" Fruit; $20.00
Bowl, 14¾" Fruit; $25.00
Bowl, Punch and Foot; $150.00
2183½ Butter and Cover, 2-handled; $85.00
Celery, tall, 6"; $22.00
Celery, 10" Tray; $18.00
2183½ Celery, 12" Tray; $20.00
Comport, 5½"; $24.00
Comport and Cover, 5½"; $32.00
Condiment Set (2-6 oz. Oil; 2 shakers, condiment tray);
    $95.00
Condiment Tray; $12.00
Cream; $10.00
Cream, Hotel; $8.00
2183½ Cream; $12.00
Custard; $6.00
Custard, Flared; $6.00
Finger Bowl and Plate; $11.00
Fruit Salad; $6.00
Grapefruit Plate; $5.00
Ice Tub, 4½"; $15.00
Ice Tub, 6½"; $18.00
Ice Tub Plate; $12.00
Ice, Hotel Crushed, 9¾"; $45.00
Jar and Cover, Footed; $50.00
Jelly and Cover, 4" Footed; $30.00
Jelly, 5" Footed; $22.00
Jug, Quart; $50.00
Jug,½ Gallon; $65.00
Jug,½ Gallon Ice; $65.00
Jug, 3-Quart Ice; $65.00
Lemon Dish; $15.00

Lemon Dish and Cover; $20.00
Lemon Dish, 6" Flared; $10.00
Milk Pitcher, 10 oz.; $18.00
Nappy, 3¼" Regular; $6.00
Nappy, 4½" Regular; $6.00
Nappy, 4½" 3-cornered, Handled; $7.00
Nappy, 4½" Handled, Flared; $7.00
Nappy, 4½" Handled Square; $7.00
Nappy, 5" Regular; $7.00
Nappy, 6" Regular; $7.00
Nappy, 7" Regular; $8.00
Nappy, 8" Regular; $8.00
Nappy, 4¾" Flared; $9.00
Nappy, 6" Flared; $7.00
Nappy, 7" Flared; $8.00
Nappy, 8" Flared; $8.00
Nappy, 9" Flared; $12.00
Nappy, 7" Shallow; $7.00
Nappy, 8" Shallow; $8.00
Nappy, 8" Regular, Deep; $10.00
Nappy, 10" Flared, Deep; $15.00
Olive, 5¾"; $8.00
Oil, 5½ oz. (DS or GS); $28.00
Oil, 6½ oz. (DS or GS); $28.00
Oval, 6"; $8.00
Oval, 7½"; $10.00
Oval, 9"; $12.00
Oval, 10½"; $15.00
Pickle, 8" Dish; $10.00
2183½ Pickle, 10" Tray; $12.00
Pickle Jar and Cover; $48.00
Plate, 9¼"; $10.00
Plate, 4½" Ice Tea; $4.00
Preserve and Cover, 5½" Handled; $25.00
Puff and Cover
    Amber, 1925-1926; $38.00
    Blue, 1925-1926; $50.00
    Canary, 1925-1926; $50.00
Shakers (HNT, SPT, Pearl Top, Glass Top); $25.00
Squat Sugar and Cover; $18.00
Sugar and Cover; $18.00
Sugar and Cover, Hotel; $15.00
2183½ Sugar and Cover, 2-handled; $15.00
Tankard, Footed; $50.00
Toothpick; $22.00
Vase, 8"; $28.00
Vase, 10"; $32.00
Vase, 12"; $40.00
Vase, 12" Swung; $45.00
2183½ Vase, 13" Swung; $55.00

2222 4½-oz. Low Sherbet
2222 4½-oz. High Sherbet
Gr-Am
Priced on page 37

2222½ 14-oz. Ice Tea
2222½ 8-oz. Table Tumbler
2222½ 5-oz. Tumbler
Gr-Am
Priced on page 37

713½ Shaker, G. T.
Gr-Am-Crys
Priced on page 40

2222 Individual
Cream
Gr-Am
Priced on page 37

2222 4-oz. Oil G. S.
2222 6-oz. Oil G. S.
Gr-Am
Priced on page 37

2222 Goblet
Gr-Am
Priced on page 37

COLONIAL TEA ROOM SERVICE

Amber and Green, 1929 – 1932

In 1973, the Olive and Pickle were remade in lead crystal as part of the Centennial II line. Stemware is featured in *Fostoria Stemware*, page 45. Prices will be the same for either color.

2222 Bowl, Finger, and Plate; $15.00
2222½ Sugar and Cover; $15.00
2222 Cream, Individual, no handle; $11.00
2222 Oil, 4 oz. (GS); $18.00
2222 Oil, 6 oz. (GS); $20.00
1372 Oyster Cocktail and Liner; $12.00
713½ Shaker, Glass Top (pair); $22.00
2222½ Water Bottle; $22.00

Colonial Prism Amber Cabarette Bowl

TWENTY-THREE FIFTEEN

Pieces in this line were introduced in crystal and in color simultaneously with the first dinnerware service, 2350 Pioneer. Etched and cut patterns using the Pioneer pattern often added pieces from the 2315 line. Colors offered were Amber, Green, Blue, Canary, and Orchid, with Rose and Azure added in 1928.

This was an extremely difficult pattern to research as pieces were added and dropped in different years, and not all pieces were made in all the colors. Note that Bowls A, C, and D were made in Spiral Optic in colors of Amber, Blue, Green, and Orchid in 1927 only. Bowls A and B were made in plain Orchid that same year. There were two Creams, but only one Sugar. The 2315½ Cream added in 1927 seems to go with the Sugar better than the original 2315 Cream, which was not made in the Orchid color. An example of the 2315 cream with the Coronado decoration is shown on page 322.

The Grapefruit and Mayonnaise look very much alike but used different plates. The Mayonnaise was also used with the Lettuce Plate to make a set. The Salver and the Sugar and Cream in Amber and Green were the only pieces made after 1930. Only a few pieces were made in Rose and Azure, and none in Topaz.

273 Royal Etching: Footed Mayonnaise/Grapefruit, Bowl A, Cream with unknown cutting, Bowl D.

Bowl A, 10½" Footed Console
    Crystal, 1925-1927; $20.00
    Amber, 1926-1927; $22.00
    Amber Spiral Optic, 1927; $22.00
    Green, 1926-1927; $22.00
    Green Spiral Optic, 1927; $22.00
    Blue, 1925-1927; $24.00
    Blue Spiral Optic, 1927; $24.00
    Canary, 1926; $25.00
    Orchid, 1927; $24.00
    Orchid Spiral Optic, 1927; $24.00
Bowl B, 11½" Footed Console
    Crystal, 1925-1927; $20.00
    Amber, 1926-1927; $20.00
    Blue, 1926-1927; $24.00
    Green, 1926-1927; $20.00
    Orchid, 1927; $24.00
    Canary, 1926; $26.00
Bowl C, 10½" Footed Console,
    Crystal, 1925-1927; $20.00
    Amber, 1926-1927; $20.00
    Amber Spiral Optic, 1927; $22.00

Blue, 1926-1927; $25.00
Blue Spiral Optic, 1927; $25.00
Green, 1926-1927; $22.00
Green Spiral Optic, 1927; $22.00
Canary, 1926; $26.00
Orchid, 1927; $24.00

No. 2315. Mayonnaise.

No. 2315. Grape Fruit.

Bowl D, 8¾"
    Crystal, 1925-1927; $20.00
    Amber, 1926-1927; $22.00
    Amber Spiral Optic, 1927; $22.00
    Blue, 1926-1927; $28.00
    Blue Spiral Optic, 1927; $28.00
    Green, 1926-1927; $22.00
    Green Spiral Optic, 1927; $22.00
    Canary, 1926; $30.00
    Orchid, 1927; $26.00
Cream, Footed
    Crystal, 1925-1927; $15.00
    Amber, 1926-1927; $18.00
    Green, 1926-1927; $18.00
    Blue, 1925-1927; $22.00
    Canary, 1926; $25.00
2315½ Cream, Footed
    Crystal, 1929; $15.00
    Amber, 1927-1929; $18.00
    Green, 1927-1929; $18.00
    Blue, 1927; $25.00
    Orchid, 1927; $25.00
Sugar, Footed
    Crystal, 1925-1929; $15.00
    Amber, 1926-1929; $15.00
    Green, 1926-1929; $15.00
    Blue, 1925-1927; $20.00
    Canary, 1926; $25.00
    Orchid, 1927; $22.00
Grapefruit, Footed and 2283 Plate, 7"
    Crystal, 1925; $15.00
    Amber, 1926-1927; $15.00
    Green, 1926-1927; $15.00
    Blue, 1925-1927; $20.00
    Canary, 1926; $22.00
    Orchid, 1927; $20.00
Mayonnaise, Footed and 2332 Plate, 7" (also
    used as a Grapefruit)
    Crystal, 1925-1930; $15.00
    Amber, 1926-1930; $15.00
    Green, 1926-1930; $15.00
    Blue, 1925-1927; $20.00
    Canary, 1926; $22.00
    Orchid, 1927; $20.00
    Rose, 1928-1930; $18.00
    Azure, 1928-1930; $18.00
Mayonnaise with 13" Lettuce Plate
    Crystal, 1928-1930; $30.00
    Amber, 1928-1930; $30.00
    Green, 1928-1930; $30.00
    Orchid, 1928; $35.00
    Rose, 1928-1930; $35.00
    Azure, 1928-1930; $35.00
Plate, 13" Lettuce
    Crystal, 1928-1930; $15.00

2315—Cream.

2315½—Cream.
Also made in orchid.

2315—Sugar.
Also made in orchid.

    Amber, 1928-1930; $15.00
    Green, 1928-1930; $15.00
    Orchid, 1928; $20.00
    Rose, 1928-1930; $18.00
    Azure, 1928; $18.00
Salver
    Crystal, 1928-1930; $30.00
    Amber, 1928-1930; 1933-1934; $32.00
    Green, 1928-1930; 1933-1934; $34.00
    Orchid, 1928; $45.00
    Rose, 1928-1930; 1933-1934; $40.00
    Azure, 1928-1934; $40.00
Sugar and Cream
    Crystal, 1925; $30.00
    Amber, 1925-1933; $30.00
    Blue, 1925-1927; $42.00
    Green, 1925-1933; $33.00
    Canary, 1925-1926; $50.00

2315—10½ in. Bowl "A" Flared.
Made Plain or in Spiral Optic.
Crystal not made in Spiral Optic.

2315—8½ in. Bowl "D" Regular.
Made Plain or in Spiral Optic.

2315—11½ in. Bowl "B" Cupped.
Made Plain Only.

2315—10½ in. Bowl "C" Rolled Edge.
Made Plain or in Spiral Optic.

2321 PRISCILLA

Stemware is featured in *Fostoria Stemware,* page 45.

Bouillon
  Crystal, 1925-1929; $6.00
  Amber, 1925-1930; $7.00
  Green, 1925-1930; $7.00
  Blue, 1925-1927; $11.00
  Rose, 1929-1930; $11.00
  Azure, 1929-1930; $11.00
*Bridge Set (Mah Jongg Plate, Sherbet or Handled Custard)
  Amber, 1925; $18.00
  Green, 1925; $18.00
  Blue, 1925; $22.00
  Canary, 1925; $22.00
Cream
  Crystal, 1925-1929; $6.00
  Amber, 1925-1930; $7.00
  Green, 1925-1930; $7.00
  Blue, 1925-1927; $11.00
  Rose, 1929-1930; $11.00
  Azure, 1929-1930; $11.00
Cream and Bouillon on 2000 Condiment Tray
  Amber, 1929-1931; $37.00
  Green, 1929-1931; $37.00
  Rose, 1929-1931; $45.00
  Azure, 1929-1931; $45.00
Cream Soup (also used as Mayonnaise)
  Crystal, 1925-1929; $15.00
  Amber, 1925-1929; $16.00
  Green, 1925-1929; $16.00
  Blue, 1925-1927; $18.00
  Canary, 1925-1926; $20.00

Cup and Saucer
  Crystal, 1926-1929; $11.00
  Amber, 1926-1929; $12.00
  Green, 1926-1929; $12.00
  Blue, 1926-1927; $14.00
*Mah Jongg with Sherbet
  Crystal, 1925-1927; $16.00
  Amber, 1925-1927; $18.00
  Green, 1925-1927; $18.00
  Blue, 1925-1927; $22.00
  Ebony, 1925-1926; $20.00
  Canary, 1925-1926; $22.00
Jug, 3-pint
  Crystal, 1925-1929; $95.00
  Amber, 1925-1929; $100.00
  Green, 1925-1929; $100.00
  Blue, 1925-1927; $125.00
Plate, 8"
  Crystal, 1925-1927; $6.00
  Amber, 1925-1927; $7.00
  Green, 1925-1927; $8.00
  Blue, 1925-1927; $15.00
  Ebony, 1925-1926; $10.00
  Canary, 1925-1926; $18.00

*The design of the Mah Jongg Set doesn't seem to match the other Priscilla pieces. The 8" Luncheon Plate was used with an insert added for the sherbet to fit. The Handled Custard was also used in the Bridge Set. The Mah Jongg Set may be found decorated as shown in the section on Decorations.

Canary 2321 Mah Jongg Set, Azure Condiment Set: Tray, Cream, and Bouillon.

No. 2321. Sugar.

Shakers made in all Colors

No. 2111
Shakers, F. G. T.

No. 2128
Shakers, F. G. T.

No. 2127
Shakers, F. G. T.

No. 2321. Cream.

No. 2321. Mayonnaise.

No. 2321. Bouillon.

No. 2321
Footed Custard, Handled.

No. 2321
Footed Tumbler, Handled.

No. 2321 3 Pint Pitcher.

2350 PIONEER

Much as those brave souls who carved new homesteads and ranches from the lands in the American West, the Fostoria Glass Company became a pioneer in glass manufacturing when it boldly offered the first complete dinner service in crystal. Beginning in 1926, Fostoria launched an extensive advertising campaign to convince the housewife that Fostoria crystal was as durable as china, and absolutely practical for serving either hot or cold foods. With 30 pieces in the original offering, Pioneer could be used to set the most elegant table entirely with crystal, except for silverware. Full-page advertisements appeared in magazines of the period to illustrate tables set with glassware in the many colors in which Pioneer was offered.

Many etched, cut, and decorated patterns used pieces from the Pioneer pattern, and the 2350½ Cup was used over and over, even with a 2419 Mayfair saucer. As is so often true of Fostoria, the ½ added to the number indicated that the piece was different from the first offering; in this case, the cup is footed.

The Pioneer pattern is plain, with no optic and few frills. To be sure of identification, one should know the colors in which the pieces were made. An additional clue comes from handles which are grooved on either side with a small half-drop of glass evident where the top of the handle connects with the bowl of the cup. The sugar and cream, and the cup were offered both footed and flat. A major difference between the Pioneer pattern and the Fairfax pattern is that Fairfax was made with the regular optic. We do not know of any pieces in the Pioneer pattern which had an optic, and we know of only one piece in the Fairfax pattern that did not have an optic, the Fairfax ash tray.

In 1927 several sets were offered in Crystal, Amber, Green, and Blue. This was no doubt a marketing strategy as no new pieces were added. Although the Canary color was used extensively for candlesticks, bowls, and other complementary pieces in 1926, we did not find any items listed in Canary in the Pioneer pattern.

Ash Tray, Small, 3¾"
    Crystal, 1927-1939; $16.00
    Amber, 1927-1939; $16.00
    Green, 1927-1939; $16.00
    Ebony, 1928-1937; $18.00
    Rose, 1928-1939; $20.00
    Azure, 1928-1934; $24.00
    Topaz/Gold Tint, 1929-1939; $20.00
    Orchid, 1927-1928; $24.00
Ash Tray, Large
    Crystal,1928-1940; $18.00
    Amber, 1928-1940; $18.00
    Green,1928-1934; $18.00
    Ebony, 1928-1936; $22.00
    Rose, 1928-1934 ; $25.00
    Azure, 1928-1934; $25.00
    Topaz, 1929-1934; $25.00
Bouillon and Saucer
    Crystal, 1926-1934; $11.00
    Amber, 1926-1934; $12.00
    Green, 1926-1934; $12.00
    Blue, 1926-1927; $14.00
2350½ Bouillon, Footed
    Crystal, 1927-1934; $8.00
    Amber, 1927-1934; $9.00
    Green, 1927-1934; $9.00
Bowl, 5" Fruit
    Crystal, 1926-1943; $7.00
    Amber, 1926-1940; $7.00
    Green, 1926-1939; $7.00
    Blue, 1926-1927; $14.00
Bowl, 6" Cereal
    Crystal, 1926-1943; $8.00
    Amber, 1926-1940; $9.00
    Green, 1926-1934; $9.00
    Blue, 1926-1927; $18.00
Bowl, 7" Soup
    Crystal, 1926-1943; $11.00
    Amber, 1926-1934; $14.00
    Green, 1926-1934; $14.00
    Blue, 1926-1927; $24.00
Bowl, 9" Oval Baker
    Crystal, 1926-1943; $20.00
    Amber, 1926-1940; $20.00
    Green, 1926-1937; $23.00
    Blue, 1926-1927; $35.00
Bowl, 10" Salad
    Crystal, 1926-1927; $24.00
    Amber, 1926-1927; $24.00
    Green, 1926-1927; $6.00
    Blue, 1926-1927; $38.00
Bowl, 10½" Oval Baker
    Crystal, 1926-1934; $20.00
    Amber, 1926-1932; $22.00
    Green, 1926-1934; $24.00

After Dinner Cups and Saucers in Ruby, Green Beverly, Amber Vesper and Ebony. Burgundy Footed Cup and Saucer.

    Blue, 1926-1927; $37.00
Butter and Cover
    Crystal, 1926-1932; $65.00
    Amber, 1926-1934; $70.00
    Green, 1926-1934; $70.00
    Blue, 1926-1927; $115.00
Celery, 11"
    Crystal, 1926-1934, 1943; $18.00
    Amber, 1926-1934; $18.00
    Green, 1926-1934; $18.00
    Blue, 1926-1927; $22.00
Comport, 8"
    Crystal, 1926-1930; $25.00
    Amber, 1926-1930; $27.00
    Green, 1926-1930; $27.00
    Blue, 1926-1927; $32.00
    Rose, 1928-1929; $30.00
    Azure, 1928-1929; $32.00
    Orchid, 1927-1928; $30.00
Cream Soup
    Crystal, 1926-1934, 1943; $14.00
    Amber, 1926-1934; $16.00
    Green, 1926-1934; $18.00
    Blue, 1926-1927; $28.00
2350½ Cream Soup, Footed
    Crystal, 1927-1934, 1943; $15.00
    Amber, 1927-1934; $18.00
    Green, 1927-1932; $22.00
Cream Soup Plate
    Crystal, 1926-1934, 1943; $5.00
    Amber, 1926-1934; $6.00
    Green, 1926-1934; $6.00
    Blue, 1926-1927; $7.00
    Ebony, 1926-1934; $6.00
Cup and Saucer
    Crystal, 1926-1940; $11.00
    Amber, 1926-1939; $12.00
    Green, 1926-1939; $12.00

Blue, 1926-1927; $14.00
2350½ Cup, Footed and Saucer
    Crystal, 1926-1950; $10.00
    Amber, 1926-1940; $12.00
    Green, 1926-1940; $12.00
    Blue, 1926-1927; $14.00
    Ebony, 1926-1940; $12.00
    Regal Blue, 1934-1940; $28.00
    Burgundy, 1934-1942; $26.00
    Empire Green, 1934-1942; $26.00
    Ruby, 1934-1942; $26.00
Cup and Saucer, After Dinner
    Crystal, 1927-1932; $12.00
    Amber, 1926-1940; $14.00
    Green, 1926-1935; $16.00
    Blue, 1926-1927; $20.00
    Ebony, 1926-1938; $18.00
    Regal Blue, 1934-1937; $48.00
    Burgundy, 1934-1940; $40.00
    Empire Green, 1934-1939; $38.00
    Ruby, 1934-1936; $48.00
Egg Cup
    Crystal, 1927-1932; $22.00
    Amber, 1927-1932; $25.00
    Green, 1927-1932; $25.00
    Rose, 1928-1932; $30.00
    Azure, 1928-1932; $30.00
Grapefruit and Crystal Liner
    Crystal, 1926-1927; $23.00
    Amber, 1926-1927; $25.00
    Green, 1926-1927; $25.00
    Blue, 1926-1927; $30.00
Nappy, 8"
    Crystal, 1926-1927; $15.00
    Amber, 1926-1927; $18.00
    Green, 1926-1927; $18.00
    Blue, 1926-1927; $22.00
Nappy, 9"
    Crystal, 1926-1927; $16.00
    Amber, 1926-1927; $16.00
    Green, 1926-1927; $17.00
    Blue, 1926-1927; $25.00
Pickle
    Crystal, 1926-1934, 1942-1943; $10.00
    Amber, 1926-1934; $12.00
    Green, 1926-1934; $14.00
    Blue, 1926-1927; $18.00
Plate, 6"
    Crystal, 1927-1959; $5.00
    Amber, 1926-1940; $6.00
    Green, 1926-1940; $6.00
    Blue, 1926-1927; $8.00
    Ebony, 1926-1940; $6.00
Plate, 7"
    Crystal, 1927-1959; $5.00

Amber, 1926-1940; $6.00
    Green, 1926-1940; $7.00
    Blue, 1926-1927; $10.00
    Ebony, 1926-1940; $6.00
Plate, 8"
    Crystal, 1927-1959; $6.00
    Amber, 1926-1940; $7.00
    Green, 1926-1940; $8.00
    Blue, 1926-1927; $15.00
    Ebony, 1926-1940; $8.00
Plate, 9"
    Crystal, 1926-1959; $11.00
    Amber, 1926-1940; $12.00
    Green, 1926-1940; $14.00
    Blue, 1926-1927; $25.00
    Ebony, 1926-1940; $12.00
Plate, 10"
    Crystal, 1926-1959; $15.00
    Amber, 1926-1940; $18.00
    Green, 1926-1940; $20.00
    Blue, 1926-1927; $34.00
    Ebony, 1926-1940; $18.00
Plate, 12" Chop
    Crystal, 1927-1927; $18.0
    Amber, 1926-1927; $18.00
    Green, 1926-1927; $20.00
    Blue, 1926-1927; $34.00
Plate, 13" Chop
    Crystal, 1927-1934; $18.00
    Amber, 1926-1934; $20.00
    Green, 1926-1934; $20.00
    Blue, 1926-1927; $27.00
Plate, 15" Round
    Crystal, 1926-1930; $20.00
    Amber, 1926-1934; $22.00
    Green, 1926-1934; $22.00
    Blue, 1926-1927; $35.00
Platter, 10½"
    Crystal, 1926-1934; $22.00
    Amber, 1926-1934; $22.00
    Green, 1926-1934; $24.00
    Blue, 1926-1927; $32.00
Platter, 12"
    Crystal, 1926-1943; $22.00
    Amber, 1926-1940; $22.00
    Green, 1926-1940; $24.00
    Blue, 1926-1927; $35.00
Platter, 15"
    Crystal, 1926-1931; $24.00
    Amber, 1926-1934; $24.00
    Green, 1926-1934; $24.00
    Blue, 1926-1927; $35.00
Relish, 3-part
    Crystal, 1928-1934; $12.00
    Amber, 1928-1934; $14.00

Green, 1928-1934; $14.00
Rose, 1928-1932 ; $16.00
Azure, 1928-1934; $16.00
Topaz, 1929-1934; $15.00
Sauce Boat and Plate
    Crystal, 1926-1934; $30.00
    Amber, 1926-1934; $32.00
    Green, 1926-1934; $35.00
    Blue, 1926-1927; $48.00
Sugar and Cream
    Crystal, 1926-1932; $16.00
    Amber, 1926-1932; $18.00
    Green, 1926-1932; $20.00
    Blue, 1926-1927; $30.00
Sugar Cover
    Crystal, 1926-1930; $18.00
    Amber, 1926-1930; $18.00
    Green, 1926-1930; $20.00
    Blue, 1926-1927; $32.00
2350½ Sugar and Cream, Footed
    Crystal, 1926-1957; $16.00
    Amber, 1926-1940; $18.00
    Green, 1926-1940; $20.00
    Blue, 1926-1927; $30.00
    Ebony, 1928-1940; $20.00
    Rose, 1928-1935; $22.00
    Ruby, 1935-1940; $35.00
2350½ Sugar and Cover

Crystal, 1927-1932; $20.00
Amber, 1927-1932; $22.00
Green, 1927-1932; $22.00
Blue, 1927; $35.00
Salad Set: Six 7" Plates and 12" Plate
    Crystal, 1927-1928; $48.00
    Amber, 1927-1928; $56.00
    Green, 1927-1928; $60.00
    Blue, 1927; $75.00
Cold Meat Set: Six 8" Plates, Six Footed Cups
    and Saucers, 12" Oval Platter
    Crystal, 1927-1928; $118.00
    Amber, 1927-1928; $135.00
    Green, 1927-1928; $135.00
    Blue, 1927; $200.00
Bridge Set: Six 8" Plates, Six Footed Cups and Saucers,
    Footed Sugar and Cream, 13" Plate
    Crystal, 1927; $130.00
    Amber, 1927; $132.00
    Green, 1927; $135.00
    Blue, 1927; $225.00
Breakfast Set: Six 8" Plates, Six Footed Cups and
    Saucers, Six 6" Cereal, 10½" Platter, 9" Plate, Foot-
    ed Sugar and Cream
    Crystal, 1927-1930; $185.00
    Amber, 1927-1930; $200.00
    Green, 1927-1930; $225.00
    Blue, 1927; $350.00

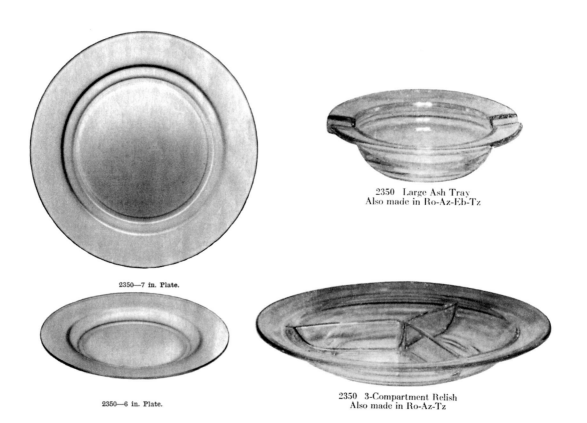

2350—7 in. Plate.

2350 Large Ash Tray
Also made in Ro-Az-Eb-Tz

2350—6 in. Plate.

2350 3-Compartment Relish
Also made in Ro-Az-Tz

No. 2350 DINNERWARE, "PIONEER" DESIGN.
MADE IN AMBER, BLUE, GREEN AND CRYSTAL.
PRICED PAGE 4 — No. 2 SUPPLEMENT PRICE LIST.
Patent Applied For.

2350—Butter and Cover.

2350—Cream Soup.
2332—7 in. Cream Soup Plate.

2350—Bouillon.
2350—Saucer.

2350½—Ftd. Tea Cup.
2350—Saucer.

2350—After Dinner Cup.
2350—A. D. Saucer.

2350—Cup.
2350—Saucer.

2350—Sugar and Cover.

2350—Cream.

2350½—Sugar.

2350½—Cream.

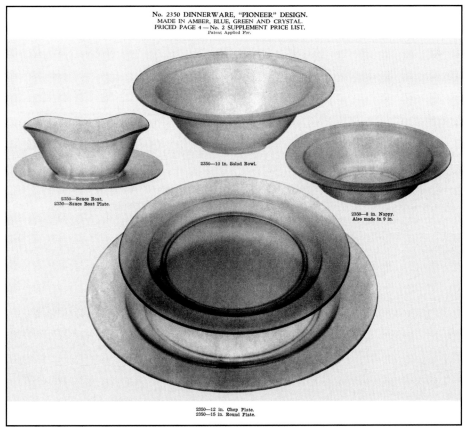

No. 2350 DINNERWARE, "PIONEER" DESIGN.
MADE IN AMBER, BLUE, GREEN AND CRYSTAL.
PRICED PAGE 4 — No. 2 SUPPLEMENT PRICE LIST.
Patent Applied For.

2350—Sauce Boat.
2350—Sauce Boat Plate.

2350—10 in. Salad Bowl.

2350—8 in. Nappy.
Also made in 9 in.

2350—12 in. Chop Plate.
2350—15 in. Round Plate.

2350½—Ftd. Cream Soup.
2350—Cream Soup Plate.
Cream Soup not made in blue.

2350—Ash Tray.
Not made in Blue.
Also made in Orchid.

2350½—Ftd. Bouillon.
2350—Saucer.
Bouillon not made in Blue.

2350—8 in. Pickle.

2350—Egg Cup.
Not made in Blue.

2350—8 in. Comport.
Also made in Orchid.

2350—11 in. Celery.

2350—10 in. Baker.
Also made in 9 in.

2350—Grape Fruit.
2350—G. F. Liner.
Liner made in crystal only.

2375 FAIRFAX

Once the Fostoria Glass Company had created and marketed the first dinner service in the Pioneer pattern, it set about creating the definitive table service, one that was both elegant and durable, practical and acceptable for the most formal of table settings. Fairfax became the largest and most complete of the dinnerware lines and was used for the huge patterns of June, Versailles, Trojan, and Kashmir.

The Fairfax line is distinctive for several reasons. Each of the pieces has a regular optic, and cup handles, although reminiscent of Pioneer, do not have the extra dollop of glass at the top of the handle. The Lemon Dish, Sweetmeat, Bon Bon, and Whipped Cream may be found with squared-off one-part handles, as well as the bow-like two-part ones. Panels between the ribs of the optic are flattened, creating a not quite scalloped look to the piece. The sugar bowl with its flattened panels could cause one to doubt that the lid fits properly. If the reader will look at the picture of the covered sugar in the catalog pages, it is evident that the lid was intended to sit on top of the flattened panels and is not the tight fit one might expect. The lid to the sugar bowl has an optic, as do all lids in the Fairfax line. The Pioneer covered sugar has a lid that fits more snugly and does not have an optic although it is the same size as the Fairfax lid, and except for the optic could be mistaken for it. The Fairfax ice bucket may be distinguished from the 2378 ice bucket since it has the regular optic and the 2378 line does not, but sometimes the optic is so faint you have to use your fingers to feel it on the inside of the piece.

Many other lines were used with Fairfax but were not listed as Fairfax. The 2378 Whipped Cream Pail and Sugar Pail often were included with Fairfax. The 5000 Jug with its regular optic looks like it should be Fairfax, but was not listed with Fairfax. Several different stemware lines were shown in advertising with Fairfax dinner services, notably 5098 and 5099. Both Vernon (877 stemware) and Verona (890 stemware) used Fairfax to complete the pattern, and Club Design B used pieces from Fairfax as well as Mayfair and Pioneer.

As with most patterns, when one-half was added to the number (2375½) the piece was different in some way, most often adding a foot. For example, the 2375 cup had no foot, the 2375½ cup did. As with other patterns, sometimes pieces were renamed. For example, the 12" Oval Bread which is listed only in 1927, most likely became the 12" Oval Platter.

Fairfax was made in many colors and with the Mother of Pearl finish. The reader is reminded that Fostoria changed the name of its Topaz color to Gold Tint in 1937. Most of those colors are still available, but as in all things, some colors are currently more desirable than others. Rose and Azure seem to be most collectible along with Green and Topaz. Orchid, although short lived and therefore rare, has not caught on with collectors at present. Most likely this is because, unless the color is decorated as in the Oakwood pattern, or cut, as is shown in the Arvida pattern, orchid does not seem to have the same brilliance as other colors. The Mayonnaise Ladle was offered in colors at first. It would be reasonable to assume that once the colored ladle was dropped from the line, a crystal ladle was used instead. Since there was no sugar and cream tray in the Fairfax line, the 2429 Service Tray with Lemon Insert was used. The Service Tray with the Sugar and Cream is shown on page 68. The Fairfax ash tray is quite small and has two indentations for cigarettes instead of one.

here is modern glassware in colors..shapes..patterns..pieces.. to delight every hostess

F O S T O R I A

is made in an entire dinner service, absolutely practicable for the serving of hot foods...with matching or harmonizing fostoria stemware, each table-setting becomes a lovely picture

Christmas gifts of glowing glass...table service inspired by antique grace and modern elegance

F O S T O R I A

A vase of Azure...A flower bowl of Dawn...A cigarette box of Amber, Green or etched white Crystal...Or a whole dinner service in the incomparable golden glass called Topaz: All these indicate a wide range of tasteful possibilities for Christmas giving

Ash Tray
    Crystal, 1928-1935; $12.00
    Rose, 1928-1934; $20.00
    Azure, 1928-1935; $20.00
    Green, 1928-1935; $18.00
    Amber, 1928-1935; $15.00
    Orchid, 1928; $22.00
Bon Bon, 2 Handles
    Crystal, 1928-1943; $18.00
    Rose, 1928-1936; $22.00
    Azure, 1928-1936; $22.00
    Green, 1928-1940; $20.00
    Amber, 1928-1939; $18.00
    Orchid, 1928; $25.00
    Topaz/Gold Tint, 1929-1939; $20.00
    Ebony, 1929-1938; $20.00
    Mother of Pearl, 1928-1934; $18.00

Bottle, Salad Dressing
  Crystal, 1932-1943; $120.00
  Rose, 1932-1934 ; $175.00
  Azure, 1932-1934; $175.00
  Green, 1932-1934; $165.00
  Amber, 1932-1938; $148.00
  Topaz/Gold Tint, 1932-1938; $165.00
Bouillon, Footed
  Crystal, 1927-1943; $12.00
  Rose, 1928-1939; $18.00
  Azure, 1928-1939; $18.00
  Green, 1927-1940; $15.00
  Amber, 1927-1940; $15.00
  Orchid, 1927-1928; $18.00
  Topaz/Gold Tint, 1929-1943; $15.00
Bowl, 5" Fruit
  Crystal, 1927-1942; $16.00
  Rose, 1928-1940; $20.00
  Azure, 1928-1942; $20.00
  Green, 1927-1940; $18.00
  Amber, 1927-1940; $18.00
  Orchid, 1927-1928; $25.00
  Topaz, 1929-1943; $18.00
  Mother of Pearl, 1928-1942; $16.00
Bowl, 6" Cereal
  Crystal, 1927-1943; $20.00
  Rose, 1928-1939; $24.00
  Azure, 1928-1943; $24.00
  Green, 1927-1939; $24.00
  Amber, 1927-1940; $22.00
  Orchid, 1927-1928; $26.00
  Topaz/Gold Tint, 1929-1941; $22.00
  Mother of Pearl, 1928-1938; $20.00
Bowl, 7" Soup
  Crystal, 1927-1943; $28.00
  Rose, 1928-1938; $45.00
  Azure, 1928-1935; $50.00
  Green, 1927-1940; $37.00
  Amber, 1927-1940; $35.00
  Orchid, 1927-1928; $54.00
  Topaz/Gold Tint, 1929-1937; $37.00
Bowl, 9" Oval Baker
  Crystal, 1927-1943; $42.00
  Rose, 1928-1940 ; $65.00
  Azure, 1928-1943; $65.00
  Green, 1927-1940; $60.00
  Amber, 1927-1935; $60.00
  Orchid, 1927-1928; $75.00
  Topaz/Gold Tint, 1929-1938; $60.00
Bowl, 10½" Oval Baker
  Crystal, 1927-1940; $47.00
  Rose, 1928-1937; $70.00
  Azure, 1928-1935; $75.00
  Green, 1927-1936; $70.00

  Amber, 1927-1939; $60.00
  Orchid, 1927-1928; $78.00
  Topaz, 1929-1935; $70.00
Bowl, 12"
  Crystal, 1928-1943; $35.00
  Rose, 1928-1939; $48.00
  Azure, 1928-1938; $50.00
  Green, 1928-1940; $45.00
  Amber, 1928-1939; $42.00
  Orchid, 1928; $50.00
  Topaz/Gold Tint, 1929-1940; $45.00
  Mother of Pearl, 1928-1943; $35.00
Bowl, Large Dessert
  Crystal, 1929-1940; $35.00
  Rose, 1929-1936; $54.00
  Azure, 1929-1933; $60.00
  Green, 1929-1935; $54.00
  Amber, 1929-1939; $38.00
  Topaz, 1929-1940; $48.00
Butter and Cover
  Crystal, 1927-1943; $85.00
  Rose, 1928-1940; $135.00
  Azure, 1928-1939; $165.00
  Green, 1927-1940; $125.00
  Amber, 1927-1940; $115.00
  Orchid, 1927-1928; $165.00
  Topaz/Gold Tint, 1929-1943; $115.00
Cake, 10" Handled
  Crystal, 1929-1945; $40.00
  Rose, 1929-1938; $60.00
  Azure, 1929-1943; $64.00
  Green, 1929-1940; $60.00
  Amber, 1929-1940; $55.00
  Topaz/Gold Tint, 1929-1938; $60.00
  Ebony, 1930-1935; $60.00

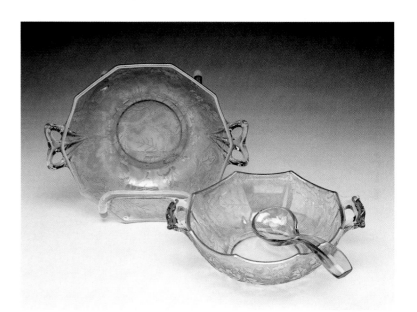

Orchid Oakwood Sweetmeat, Bow Handles; Orchid Oakwood Whipped Cream, Square Handles, Orchid Ladle

Candlestick, 3" (pair)
   Crystal, 1928-1943; $25.00
   Rose, 1928-1940; $35.00
   Azure, 1928-1940; $35.00
   Green, 1928-1940; $35.00
   Amber, 1928-1938; $30.00
   Orchid, 1928; $35.00
   Topaz/Gold Tint, 1929-1939; $35.00
   Mother of Pearl, 1928-1943; $25.00
Candlestick, 2375½ (pair)
   Crystal, 1928-1935; $40.00
   Rose, 1928-1935; $50.00
   Azure, 1928-1935; $55.00
   Green, 1928-1935; $50.00
   Amber, 1928-1935; $45.00
   Orchid, 1928; $65.00
   Topaz, 1929-1935; $50.00
   Mother of Pearl, 1928-1934; $40.00
Celery, 11½"
   Crystal, 1927-1943; $20.00
   Rose, 1928-1940; $28.00
   Azure, 1928-1941; $28.00
   Green, 1927-1940; $28.00
   Amber, 1927-1939; $25.00
   Orchid, 1927-1928; $28.00
   Topaz/Gold Tint, 1929-1938; $28.00
   Mother of Pearl, 1928-1942; $20.00
Centerpiece, 12" Round
   Crystal, 1928-1941; $45.00
   Rose, 1928-1935; $60.00
   Azure, 1928-1935; $60.00
   Green, 1928-1932; $60.00
   Amber, 1928-1935; $40.00
   Orchid, 1928; $60.00
   Topaz, 1929-1933; $60.00
   Mother of Pearl, 1928-1934; $45.00
Centerpiece, 15" Round
   Rose, 1928-1932; $75.00
   Azure, 1928-1932; $75.00
   Green, 1928-1932; $70.00
   Amber, 1928-1932; $65.00
   Orchid, 1928; $85.00
2375½ Centerpiece, Oval, 13" and Flower Holder
   Crystal, 1928-1932; $75.00
   Rose, 1928-1932 ; $125.00
   Azure, 1928-1932; $145.00
   Green, 1928-1932; $125.00
   Amber, 1928-1932; $100.00
   Orchid, 1928; $150.00
2371 Flower Holder (top piece in color;
   plain glass bottom)
   Crystal, 1928-1930; $35.00
   Rose, 1928-1930; $45.00
   Azure, 1928-1930; $50.00
   Green, 1928-1930; $45.00
   Amber, 1928-1930; $40.00

Orchid, 1928; $45.00
Cheese and Cracker
   Crystal, 1930-1938; $50.00
   Rose, 1930-1937; $65.00
   Azure, 1930-1938; $65.00
   Green, 1930-1934; $60.00
   Amber, 1930-1934; $60.00
   Topaz/Gold Tint, 1930-1938; $60.00
Comport, 7"
   Rose, 1928-1934; $54.00
   Azure, 1928-1938; $54.00
   Green, 1928-1938; $50.00
   Amber, 1928-1936; $45.00
   Orchid, 1928; $55.00
Cream Soup and Plate
   Crystal, 1927-1943; $34.00
   Rose, 1928-1940; $45.00
   Azure, 1928-1941; $45.00
   Green, 1927-1940; $40.00
   Amber, 1927-1940; $34.00
   Orchid, 1927-1928; $45.00
   Topaz/Gold Tint, 1929-1941; $35.00
   Mother of Pearl, 1928-1934; $34.00
Cup and Saucer
   Crystal, 1927-1939; $14.00
   Rose, 1928-1940; $18.00
   Azure, 1928-1941; $18.00
   Green, 1927-1940; $15.00
   Amber, 1927-1940; $12.00
   Orchid, 1927-1928; $20.00
Cup, Footed and Saucer

Amber Butter and Cover, Salad Dressing Bottle

Crystal, 1927-1959; $12.00
Rose, 1928-1940; $18.00
Azure, 1928-1943; $18.00
Green, 1927-1940; $15.00
Amber, 1927-1940; $12.00
Orchid, 1927-1928; $20.00
Topaz/Gold Tint, 1929-1943; $16.00
Mother of Pearl, 1928-1943; $12.00
Cup and Saucer, After Dinner
Crystal, 1927-1943; $15.00
Rose, 1928-1940; $25.00
Azure, 1928-1941; $25.00
Green, 1927-1940; $20.00
Amber, 1927-1940; $15.00
Orchid, 1927-1928; $25.00
Topaz/Gold Tint, 1929-1938; $20.00
Ice Bucket, N.P. Handle
Crystal, 1929-1941; $50.00
Rose, 1929-1940; $65.00
Azure, 1929-1941; $68.00
Green, 1929-1940; $65.00
Amber, 1929-1935; $60.00
Topaz/Gold Tint, 1929-1941; $65.00
Lemon Dish, 2 Handles
Crystal, 1928-1943; $18.00
Rose, 1928-1940; $22.00
Azure, 1928-1936; $24.00
Green, 1928-1938; $22.00
Amber, 1928-1939; $18.00
Orchid, 1928; $24.00
Topaz/Gold Tint, 1929-1943; $18.00
Ebony, 1929; $18.00
Mayonnaise, Plate
Crystal, 1928-1945; $38.00
Rose, 1928-1932; $60.00
Azure, 1928-1941; $50.00
Green, 1928-1936; $50.00
Amber, 1928-1936; $45.00
Orchid, 1928; $50.00
Topaz/Gold Tint, 1929-1937; $50.00
Mother of Pearl, 1928-1934; $38.00
Mayonnaise Ladle
Crystal, 1928-1965; $16.00
Amber, 1928-1935; $24.00
Green, 1928-1938; $27.00
Rose, 1928-1935; $32.00
Azure, 1928-1934; $40.00
Topaz/Gold Tint, 1929-1938; $38.00
Orchid, 1928; $45.00
Nappy , 7" Round
Crystal, 1933-1943; $32.00
Rose, 1933-1938; $40.00
Azure, 1933-1935; $45.00
Green, 1933-1938; $40.00
Amber, 1933-1938; $30.00
Topaz/Gold Tint, 1933-1937; $40.00

Nappy, 8" Round
Crystal, 1927-1932; $38.00
Rose, 1928-1935; $45.00
Azure, 1928-1938; $45.00
Green, 1927-1938; $40.00
Amber, 1927-1937; $30.00
Orchid, 1927-1928; $45.00
Topaz, 1929-1934; $45.00
Oil, Footed
Crystal, 1929-1943; $125.00
Rose, 1929-1938; $175.00
Azure, 1929-1934; $200.00
Green, 1929-1938; $175.00
Amber, 1929-1938; $150.00
Topaz/Gold Tint, 1929-1938; $175.00
Pickle, 8½"
Crystal, 1927-1943; $27.00
Rose, 1928-1940; $32.00
Azure, 1928-1941; $34.00
Green, 1927-1940; $32.00
Amber, 1927-1940; $28.00
Orchid, 1927-1928; $32.00
Topaz/Gold Tint, 1929-1938; $30.00
Plate, 6"
Crystal, 1927-1950; $6.00
Rose, 1928-1940; $12.00
Azure, 1928-1943; $12.00
Green, 1927-1940; $10.00
Amber, 1927-1940; $8.00
Orchid, 1927-1928; $12.00
Topaz/Gold Tint, 1929-1943; $10.00
Mother of Pearl, 1928-1943; $6.00
Plate, 7"
Crystal, 1927-1959; $7.00

Sugar and Cream, Tea Sugar and Cream, Sauce Dish and Plate, Comport

Rose, 1928-1940; $14.00
Azure, 1928-1943; $14.00
Green, 1927-1940; $14.00
Amber, 1927-1940; $9.00
Orchid, 1927-1928; $14.00
Topaz/Gold Tint, 1929-1943; $12.00
Mother of Pearl, 1928-1942; $7.00
Plate, 8"
    Crystal, 1927-1943; $10.00
    Rose, 1928-1940; $16.00
    Azure, 1928-1943; $16.00
    Green, 1927-1940; $16.00
    Amber, 1927-1940; $12.00
    Orchid, 1927-1928; $16.00
    Topaz/Gold Tint, 1929-1943; $15.00
Plate, 9"
    Crystal, 1927-1944; $15.00
    Rose, 1928-1940; $26.00
    Azure, 1928-1943; $26.00
    Green, 1927-1940; $26.00
    Amber, 1927-1940; $18.00
    Orchid, 1927-1928; $28.00
    Topaz/Gold Tint, 1929-1943; $24.00
    Mother of Pearl, 1929-1942; $15.00
Plate, 10"
    Crystal, 1927-1944; $30.00
    Rose, 1928-1940; $54.00
    Azure, 1928-1943; $58.00
    Green, 1927-1940; $50.00
    Amber, 1927-1940; $40.00
    Orchid, 1927-1928; $55.00
    Topaz/Gold Tint, 1929-1943; $50.00
    Mother of Pearl, 1928-1943; $30.00
Plate, Canape
    Crystal, 1929-1932; $18.00
    Rose, 1929-1932; $30.00
    Azure, 1929-1932; $30.00
    Green, 1929-1932; $30.00
    Amber, 1929-1932; $22.00
    Topaz, 1929-1932; $25.00
    Ebony, 1929-1932; $22.00
Plate, 10" Grill
    Crystal, 1930-1937; $35.00
    Rose, 1930-1937; $55.00
    Azure, 1930-1934; $60.00
    Green, 1930-1937; $55.00
    Amber, 1930-1937; $40.00
    Topaz/Gold Tint, 1930-1937; $55.00
Plate, 12" Oval Bread
    Crystal, 1927; $47.00
    Green, 1927; $65.00
    Amber, 1927; $45.00
    Orchid, 1927; $65.00
Plate, 13" Chop
    Crystal, 1927-1937; $47.00
    Rose, 1928-1937; $65.00

Azure, 1928-1934; $68.00
Green, 1927-1937; $60.00
Amber, 1927-1937; $50.00
Orchid, 1927-1928; $65.00
Topaz/Gold Tint, 1929-1937; $60.00
Mother of Pearl, 1928-1937; $47.00
Platter, 10½" Oval
    Crystal, 1927-1943; $47.00
    Rose, 1928-1938; $65.00
    Azure, 1928-1932; $75.00
    Green, 1928-1940; $65.00
    Amber, 1928-1938; $50.00
    Orchid, 1928; $85.00
    Topaz/Gold Tint, 1929-1941; $65.00
Platter, 12" Oval
    Crystal, 1927-1943; $47.00
    Rose, 1928-1940; $65.00
    Azure, 1928-1941; $75.00
    Green, 1927-1938; $65.00
    Amber, 1927-1940; $45.00
    Orchid, 1927-1928; $65.00
    Topaz/Gold Tint, 1929-1943; $65.00
    Mother of Pearl, 1928-1938; $47.00
Platter, 15" Oval
    Crystal, 1927-1940; $65.00
    Rose, 1928-1939 ; $77.00
    Azure, 1928-1934; $95.00
    Green, 1927-1940; $75.00
    Amber, 1927-1940; $65.00
    Orchid, 1927; $110.00
    Topaz, 1929-1934; $95.00
Relish, 8½"
    Crystal, 1927-1943; $27.00
    Rose, 1928-1940; $34.00
    Azure, 1928-1938; $38.00
    Green, 1927-1940; $34.00
    Amber, 1927-1940; $27.00
    Orchid, 1927-1928; $38.00
    Topaz/Gold Tint, 1929-1943; $34.00
    Mother of Pearl, 1928-1942; $27.00
Relish, 11½"
    Crystal, 1927-1941; $32.00
    Rose, 1928-1935; $38.00
    Azure, 1928-1935; $42.00
    Green, 1927-1935; $38.00
    Amber, 1927-1940; $32.00
    Orchid, 1927-1928; $42.00
    Topaz/Gold Tint, 1929-1941; $38.00
Sauce Boat and Plate
    Crystal, 1927-1940; $95.00
    Rose, 1928-1937; $115.00
    Azure, 1928-194; $115.00
    Green, 1927-1940; $100.00
    Amber, 1927-1940; $85.00
    Orchid, 1927-1928; $125.00
    Topaz/Gold Tint, 1929-1937; $115.00

Shaker, Footed, FGT (Pair)
    Crystal, 1928-1943; $65.00
    Rose, 1928-1939; $95.00
    Azure, 1928-1940; $95.00
    Green, 1928-1940; $90.00
    Amber, 1928-1940; $75.00
    Orchid, 1928; $125.00
    Topaz/Gold Tint, 1929-1940; $90.00
    Ebony, 1931-1940; $85.00
Sugar and Cream
    Crystal, 1927-1932; $40.00
    Green, 1927-1932; $50.00
    Amber, 1927-1932; $45.00
    Orchid, 1927-1928; $65.00
Sugar and Cream, Footed
    Crystal, 1928-1944; $35.00
    Rose, 1928-1940; $48.00
    Azure, 1928-1943; $48.00
    Green, 1927-1940; $42.00
    Amber, 1927-1940; $40.00
    Orchid, 1927-1928; $65.00
    Topaz/Gold Tint, 1929-1943; $45.00
    Mother of Pearl, 1928-1943; $35.00
Sugar and Cover, Footed
    Crystal, 1928-1938; $35.00
    Rose, 1928-1938; $48.00
    Azure, 1928-1938; $48.00
    Green, 1928-1938; $42.00
    Amber, 1928-1934; $40.00
    Orchid, 1928; $65.00
    Topaz/Gold Tint, 1929-1938; $45.00
Sugar and Cream Set (includes 2429 Service
    Tray with Insert)
    Crystal, 1930-1932; $175.00
    Rose, 1930-1932; $225.00
    Azure, 1930-1932; $235.00
    Green, 1930-1932; $225.00
    Amber, 1930-1932; $200.00
    Topaz, 1930-1932; $220.00
Sugar and Cream, Tea
    Crystal, 1930-1943; $34.00
    Rose, 1930-1940; $50.00
    Azure, 1930-1943; $50.00
    Green, 1930-1940; $45.00
    Amber, 1930-1940; $38.00
    Topaz/Gold Tint, 1930-1940; $45.00
    Ebony, 1930-1941; $40.00
    Ruby, 1934-1942; $65.00
Sweetmeat, 2 Handles
    Crystal, 1928-1959; $16.00
    Rose, 1928-1940; $20.00
    Azure, 1928-1943; $20.00
    Green, 1928-1938; $20.00
    Amber, 1928-1940; $18.00
    Orchid, 1928; $27.00

    Topaz/Gold Tint, 1929-1943; $20.00
    Mother of Pearl, 1928-1934; $16.00
Tray, Handled Lunch
    Crystal, 1928-1959; $37.00
    Rose, 1928-1940; $45.00
    Azure, 1928-1943; $45.00
    Green, 1928-1938; $45.00
    Amber, 1928-1940; $40.00
    Orchid, 1928; $55.00
    Topaz/Gold Tint, 1929-1943; $45.00
    Mother of Pearl, 1928-1934; $37.00
Whipped Cream
    Crystal, 1928-1943; $18.00
    Rose, 1928-1940; $22.00
    Azure, 1928-1940; $22.00
    Green, 1928-1934; $24.00
    Amber, 1928-1940; $20.00
    Orchid, 1928; $30.00
    Topaz/Gold Tint, 1929-1943; $22.00
    Mother of Pearl, 1928-1934; $18.00

FAIRFAX PATTERN

No. 2375 DINNERWARE

See price list for colors

2375—6, 7, 8, 9, 10, 13-in. Plate

2375—10 in. Grill Plate

2375—Cup
2375—Saucer

2375½—Footed Cup
2375 —Saucer

2375—After Dinner Cup
2375—After Dinner Saucer

2375—Footed Bouillon
2375—Saucer

2375—5 in. Fruit
2375—6 in. Cereal
2375—7 in. Soup
2375—7 in. Round Nappy
2375—8 in. Round Nappy

2375—Cream Soup
2375—Cream Soup Plate

2375— 9 in. Oval Baker
2375—10½ in. Oval Baker

2375—10½ in. Oval Platter
2375—12 in. Oval Platter
2375—15 in. Oval Platter

2375—8½ in. Pickle
2375—8½ in. Relish—Same as Pickle,
but with 1 partition

2375—11½ in. Relish
2375—11½ in. Celery—Same as Relish,
but without partitions

53

FAIRFAX PATTERN

No. 2375 DINNERWARE

See price list for colors

2375—Sauce Boat
2375—Sauce Boat Plate

2375—Butter and Cover

2375—Shaker, F. G. T.
Height 3⅛ in.

2375½—Footed Sugar
Height 3⅛ in.

2375½—Footed Cream
Height 3¾ in.
Capacity 6¾ oz.

2375½—Tea Sugar
Height 2½ in.

2375½—Tea Cream
Height 3 in.
Capacity 3¼ oz.

2375—Mayonnaise
Top Diameter 5⅝ in.—Height 2¾ in.
2375—Mayonnaise Plate
2375—Ladle

2375—11 in. Handled
Lunch Tray

2375—Sweetmeat, 2 Handles
Length 6 in.

2375—Footed Cheese
2375—Cracker Plate
Length 10 in.

2375—Whipped Cream,
2 Handles
Length 5½ in.

FAIRFAX PATTERN
No. 2375 DINNERWARE
See price list for colors

2375—Bon Bon, 2 Handles
Length 7 in.

2375—Lemon Dish, 2 Hdles.
Length 6¾ in.

2375—Cake Plate, 2 Hdles.
Length 10 in.

2375—Large Dessert,
2 Handles
Length 8½ in.

2375—Ice Bucket with Tongs
Height 6 in.
Top Diameter 5⅛ in.

2375—Footed Oil
Height 9¼ in.
Capacity 5 oz.

2375—Salad Dressing Bottle
Height 7 in.
Capacity 4¾ oz.

2375—3 in. Candlestick

2375—12 in. Bowl

2375—3 in. Candlestick

FAIRFAX PATTERN
No. 2375 DINNERWARE
See price list for colors

2375½—Ftd. Sugar & Cover.

2375½—Ftd. Cream.

Canape Set.
Ro-Az-Gr-Am-Tz.
4101—2½ oz. Ftd. Tumbler.
2375—Canape Plate.
Plate also made in Ebony.
Priced Page 15.

2375—Sugar.

2375—Cream.

2375—7 in. Comport.

2375 Ash Tray
Not made in Topaz

2375½—Candle

2375½—13 in. Oval Centerpiece.
2371—Flower Holder.

2412 QUEEN ANNE

(also see Colony, Blank 2412)
1926 – 1927 except as noted.
Crystal, Amber, Blue, and Green

The twisted stem was a favorite theme throughout the life of the Fostoria Glass Company. The earliest representation of this was called Cascade which was made before the turn of the century. The Colony pattern was an extensive dinnerware service rivaled only by the American pattern. Prices for crystal would be 25% less than for color.

Bowl, 9" Shallow, Low Foot, Solid Color; $195.00
Bowl, 9" Shallow, High Foot, Solid Color; $225.00
Bowl, 9" Shallow, High Foot, Colored Base; $200.00
Candelabra, 2-light, Colored Pedestal (pair); $600.00/
     market
Candlestick, 9", Solid Color (pair); $300.00
Centerpiece, 11", Solid Color; $225.00
Lustre, 14½", Colored Pedestal (pair); $400.00
Vase, 12", Solid Color; $250.00
Vase, 14", Solid Color, 1926; market

Green High Foot Bowl,
14½" Lustres

2412—11 in. Centerpiece.
Not made in crystal.

2412—9 in. Shallow Low Foot Bowl.
Also made with high foot.

2412—9 in. Candle.

2412—12 in. Vase.
Patent No. 69,662.

2412—14½ in. Lustre & U. D. Prisms.
Candleholder, Bobache and Prisms are
made in Crystal only.
Pedestal made in Crystal or Colors.

2412—9 in. High Foot Bowl.
Made in solid colors.
Also made crystal with colored Foot.
Also made low foot—Solid colors only.

2412—14½ in. Lustre & U. D. Prisms.
Candleholder, Bobache and Prisms are
made in Crystal only.
Pedestal made in Crystal or Colors.

2419 MAYFAIR

Named for the smartest residential section of London in the early part of the twentieth century, Mayfair was the fashionable new dinnerware line for 1930. With square-shaped plates and cup handles, it seemed a natural to go with the 4020 stemware line with its square base and round wafers as part of the stem. By 1931, another stemware line had been added, this time with squares built right into the stem. The square shapes were definitely in vogue in this Art Deco period. Advertising illustrates the Mayfair pattern and 4020 stemware combining colors and arranging tables in ways not used before. The drama of Ebony and Crystal was softened with the addition of pieces in Rose and Azure. The ever popular Amber was combined with pieces in Green to achieve interest and variety, or used alone for a more dramatic effect. In the advertisement below, the 2375 Fairfax shaker is shown with the 4095 open salt in place of the Mayfair shakers. The use of multiple single candlesticks in the 2430 Diadem pattern emphasizes the need for ingenuity on the part of the savvy hostess.

It would be well to note that the Handled Cream Soup did not use a plate and the Mayonnaise and the Jelly are difficult to distinguish between since they are nearly the same size. In a home where the hostess had used Mayfair for years, we discovered that the Jelly was sometimes used for a flat soup. The Mayfair line did not have its own jug, but used the 4020 Jug. Oftentimes, the 2350½ Pioneer footed cup was used with the Mayfair saucer in patterns.

Both 4020 stemware and 6003 stemware are shown in their entirety in *Fostoria Stemware*.

Feb. 1931 Good Housekeeping

Ash Tray
> Crystal, 1931-1943; $12.00
> Rose, 1931-1940; $16.00
> Green, 1931-1940; $16.00
> Amber, 1931-1940; $14.00
> Topaz/Gold Tint, 1931-1938; $16.00
> Wisteria, 1931-1936; $26.00
> Regal Blue, 1933-1937; $24.00
> Burgundy, 1933-1938; $22.00
> Empire Green, 1933-1937; $24.00
> Ruby, 1934-1937; $24.00

> Ebony, 1931-1938; $22.00
> Silver Mist, 1935-1938; $12.00

Bon Bon, Handled
> Crystal, 1931-1939; $18.00
> Rose, 1931-1938; $23.00
> Green, 1931-1938; $23.00
> Amber, 1931-1934; $23.00
> Topaz, 1931-1936; $23.00
> Wisteria, 1931-1934; $35.00

Bowl, 5" Fruit
> Crystal, 1931-1943; $16.00

Rose, 1931-1940; $22.00
Green, 1931-1940; $22.00
Amber, 1931-1940; $20.00
Topaz/Gold Tint, 1931-1943; $20.00
Bowl, 6" Cereal
    Crystal, 1931-1943; $17.00
    Rose, 1931-1938 ; $24.00
    Green, 1931-1938; $24.00
    Amber, 1931-1938; $22.00
    Topaz/Gold Tint, 1931-1938; $24.00
Bowl, 7" Soup
    Crystal, 1931-1936; $20.00
    Rose, 1931-1938; $24.00
    Green, 1931-1938; $24.00
    Amber, 1931-1938; $22.00
    Topaz/Gold Tint, 1931-1938; $24.00
Bowl, 10" Baker
    Crystal, 1931-1940; $28.00
    Rose, 1931-1940; $46.00
    Green, 1931-1940; $42.00
    Amber, 1931-1940; $35.00
    Topaz/Gold Tint, 1931-1943; $40.00
Cake, Handled
    Crystal, 1931-1943; $32.00
    Rose, 1931-1939; $55.00
    Green, 1931-1934; $55.00
    Amber, 1931-1936; $48.00
    Topaz/Gold Tint, 1931-1943; $52.00
    Wisteria, 1931-1936; $78.00
    Ebony, 1931-1938; $55.00
Celery, 11"
    Crystal, 1931-1939; $32.00
    Rose, 1931-1939; $48.00
    Green, 1931-1939; $48.00
    Amber, 1931-1934; $40.00
    Topaz/Gold Tint, 1931-1939; $44.00
Comport
    Crystal, 1931-1937; $34.00
    Rose, 1931-1933; $56.00
    Green, 1931-1938; $48.00
    Amber, 1931-1938; $42.00
    Topaz, 1931-1935; $48.00
    Ebony, 1931-1938; $48.00
Cream Soup
    Crystal, 1931-1940; $32.00
    Rose, 1931-1940; $36.00
    Green, 1931-1940; $36.00
    Amber, 1931-1940; $32.00
    Topaz/Gold Tint, 1931-1937; $34.00
Cup, Footed and Saucer
    Crystal, 1930-1943; $20.00
    Rose, 1930-1940; $26.00
    Green, 1930-1940; $26.00
    Amber, 1930-1940; $18.00
    Topaz/Gold Tint, 1930-1943; $22.00
    Ebony (Saucer only), 1930-1940; $9.00

Syrup, Cover and Saucer, Sugar and Cream on Condiment Tray, Oil Bottle, Sauce Bowl and Stand

Cup, After Dinner , and Saucer
    Crystal, 1930-1939; $22.00
    Rose, 1930-1938; $27.00
    Green, 1930-1938; $24.00
    Amber, 1930-1937; $18.00
    Topaz/Gold Tint, 1931-1939; $24.00
    Ebony (Saucer only), 1930-1937; $9.00
Jelly, Handled
    Crystal, 1931-1939; $14.00
    Rose, 1931-1939; $18.00
    Green, 1931-1939; $18.00
    Amber, 1931-1934; $14.00
    Topaz/Gold Tint, 1931-1939; $17.00
    Ebony, 1931-1934; $18.00
Lemon, Handled
    Crystal, 1931-1938; $14.00
    Rose, 1931-1938; $18.00
    Green, 1931-1938; $18.00
    Amber, 1931-1938; $14.00
    Topaz, 1931-1934; $16.00
    Wisteria, 1931-1936; $32.00
Mayonnaise, 5¾", Handled
    Crystal, 1931-1942; $14.00
    Rose, 1931-1935 ; $18.00
    Green, 1931-1935; $18.00
    Amber, 1931-1938; $14.00
    Topaz/Gold Tint, 1931-1942; $16.00

Four-part Relish, Cup and Saucer

Oil, 6 oz.
    Crystal, 1931-1937; $39.00
    Rose, 1931-1934; $75.00
    Green, 1931-1938; $65.00
    Amber, 1931-1937; $48.00
    Topaz/Gold Tint, 1931-1938; $57.00
Pickle, 8½"
    Crystal, 1931-1942; $20.00
    Rose, 1931-1939; $28.00
    Green, 1931-1934; $32.00
    Amber, 1931-1939; $20.00
    Topaz/Gold Tint, 1931-1942; $22.00
Plate, 6"
    Crystal, 1930-1943; $8.00
    Rose, 1930-1938; $12.00
    Green, 1930-1940; $10.00
    Amber, 1930-1939; $8.00
    Topaz/Gold Tint, 1930-1942; $10.00
    Wisteria, 1932-1936; $18.00
    Azure, 1930-1934; $16.00
    Ebony, 1930-1940; $10.00
Plate, 7"
    Crystal, 1930-1942; $8.00
    Rose, 1930-1940; $12.00
    Green, 1930-1940; $12.00
    Amber, 1930-1940; $8,00
    Topaz/Gold Tint, 1930-1943; $10.00
    Wisteria, 1932-1936; $20.00
    Azure, 1930-1933; $18.00
    Ebony, 1930-1940; $10.00
Plate 8"
    Crystal, 1930-1943; $10.00
    Rose, 1930-1940; $13.00

    Green, 1930-1940; $12.00
    Amber, 1930-1940; $10.00
    Topaz/Gold Tint, 1930-1942; $10.00
    Wisteria, 1932-1934; $20.00
    Ebony, 1930-1940; $11.00
Plate, 9"
    Crystal, 1931-1943; $18.00
    Rose, 1931-1938; $28.00
    Green, 1931-1940; $24.00
    Amber, 1931-1940; $18.00
    Topaz/Gold Tint, 1931-1942; $20.00
    Wisteria, 1931-1936; $55.00
    Ebony, 1931-1938; $24.00
Platter, 12"
    Crystal, 1931-1940; $27.00
    Rose, 1931-1940; $48.00
    Green, 1931-1940; $48.00
    Amber, 1931-1940; $27.00
    Topaz/Gold Tint, 1931-1943; $34.00
Platter, 15"
    Crystal, 1931-1934; $45.00
    Rose, 1931-1938; $56.00
    Green, 1931-1937; $56.00
    Amber, 1931-1938; $45.00
    Topaz/Gold Tint, 1931-1938; $48.00
Relish, 8½", 2-part
    Crystal, 1931-1943; $14.00
    Rose, 1931-1940; $18.00
    Green, 1931-1935; $18.00
    Amber, 1931-1940; $14.00
    Topaz/Gold Tint, 1931-1938; $16.00
Relish, 4-part
    Crystal, 1931-1943; $16.00
    Rose, 1931-1940; $20.00
    Green, 1931-1940; $20.00
    Amber, 1931-1938; $16.00
    Topaz/Gold Tint, 1931-1943;
    $18.00
    Ruby, 1934-1936; $34.00
    Ebony, 1931-1938; $25.00
    Silver Mist, 1935-1938; $16.00
Relish, 5-part
    Crystal, 1931-1943; $30.00
    Rose, 1931-1940; $43.00
    Green, 1931-1940; $40.00
    Amber, 1931-1938; $32.00
    Topaz/Gold Tint, 1931-1943; $36.00
    Silver Mist, 1935-1938; $30.00
Sauce Bowl and Stand
    Crystal, 1931-1934; $42.00
    Rose, 1931-1938; $54.00
    Green, 1931-1938; $48.00
    Amber, 1931-1932; $42.00
    Topaz, 1931-1935; $48.00
Shaker (Priced each)
    Crystal, 1931-1943; $27.00

Rose, 1931-1940; $32.00
Green, 1931-1940; $32.00
Amber, 1931-1938; $30.00
Topaz/Gold Tint, 1931-1938; $32.00
Ebony, 1931-1934; $34.00

Sugar and Cream
Crystal, 1931-1938; $40.00
Rose, 1931-1938; $48.00
Green, 1931-1938; $45.00
Amber, 1931-1938; $40.00
Topaz/Gold Tint, 1931-1937; $44.00

Sugar and Cream, Footed
Crystal, 1931-1943; $40.00
Rose, 1931-1940; $48.00
Green, 1931-1940; $45.00
Amber, 1931-1940; $40.00
Topaz/Gold Tint, 1931-1943; $42.00

Sugar and Cream, Tea
Crystal, 1931-1943; $38.00
Rose, 1931-1939; $45.00
Green, 1931-1940; $44.00
Amber, 1931-1940; $38.00
Topaz/Gold Tint, 1931-1940; $42.00
Wisteria, 1931-1936; $72.00

Regal Blue, 1933-1942; $68.00
Burgundy, 1933-1942; $68.00
Empire Green, 1933-1939; $69.00
Ebony, 1931-1940; $52.00

Syrup, Cover and Saucer
Crystal, 1931-1940; $65.00
Rose, 1931-1940; $85.00
Green, 1931-1937; $85.00
Amber, 1931-1940; $75.00
Topaz/Gold Tint, 1931-1940; $78.00

Tray, Condiment
Crystal, 1931-1937; $30.00
Rose, 1931-1934 ; $37.00
Green, 1931-1934; $35.00
Amber, 1931-1937; $30.00
Topaz, 1931-1934; $35.00

Tray, Handled Lunch
Crystal, 1931-1938; $52.00
Rose, 1931-1934; $65.00
Green, 1931-1938; $58.00
Amber, 1931-1938; $52.00
Topaz, 1931-1934; $65.00
Ebony, 1931-1934; $52.00

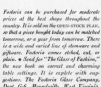

MAYFAIR PATTERN
No. 2419 DINNERWARE
Made in Rose, Green, Amber, Crystal and Topaz
(Except as noted below the item)

2419—6, 7, 8, 9 in. Plate
6, 7, 8 in. sizes also made
in Az-Eb-Wis
9 in. size also made in
Eb-Wis

2419—8½ in. Relish

2419—10 in. Baker

2419—Sauce Bowl and Stand
Not made in Amber

2419—Sugar

2419—Cream

2419—Cream Soup

2419— 8½ in. Pickle
2419—11 in. Celery

2419—After Dinner Cup
2419—After Dinner Saucer
Saucer also made in Ebony

2419—Footed Cup
2419—Saucer
Saucer also made in Ebony

2419—5 in. Fruit
2419—6 in. Cereal
2419—7 in. Soup

2419—12 in. Platter
2419—15 in. Platter

MAYFAIR PATTERN
No. 2419 DINNERWARE
Made in Rose, Green, Amber, Crystal and Topaz
(Except as noted below the item)

2419½—Footed Sugar

2419½—Footed Cream

2419—Syrup and Cover
2419—Syrup Saucer

2419—Ash Tray
Diameter 4 in.
Also made in Eb-Wis

2419—Tea Sugar
Also made in Eb-Wis

2419—Tea Cream
Also made in Eb-Wis

2419—Shaker
Height 2⅞ in.
Also made in Ebony

2419—4 Part Relish
Length 8½ in.
Also made in Ebony

2419—6 oz. Oil G/S

2419—5 Part Relish
Length 13¼ in.

MAYFAIR PATTERN
No. 2419 DINNERWARE
Made in Rose, Green, Amber, Crystal and Topaz
(Except as noted below the item)

2419—6 in. Comport
Also made in Ebony

2419—11 in. Handled
Lunch Tray
Also made in Ebony

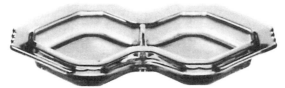

2419—Condiment Tray
Length 8¾ in.

2419—Bon Bon, 2 Hdles.
Length 6½ in.
Also made in Wisteria

2419—Jelly, 2 Hdles.
Length 6 in.
Also made in Ebony

2419—Cake Plate
Length 9½ in.
Also made in Eb-Wis

2419—Mayonnaise, 2 Hdles.
Length 5¾ in.

2419—Lemon Dish, 2 Hdles.
Length 6¼ in.
Also made in Wisteria

2424 KENT

This short-lived pattern was not a complete dinner service but was used for many of the carved patterns produced before and during World War II. It is heavy, brilliant crystal, practical and elegant.

Almond, Individual, 1940-1943; $18.00
Ashtray, 3", 1939-1943; $18.00
Bowl, 8" Regular, 1939-1943; $28.00
Bowl, 9½" Flared, 1939-1943; $34.00
Bowl, 11½" Fruit, 1939-1943; $36.00
Candlestick, 3½", 1939-1943; $27.00
Candlestick, Duo, 1940-1943; $35.00
Candy Jar and Cover, 1939-1943; $38.00
Cigarette Box and Cover, 1939-1943; $39.00
Comport, 5½" Low, and Cover, 1940-1943; $42.00
Mayonnaise, Plate, Ladle, 1939-1943; $46.00
Plate, 12", 1939-1943; $36.00
Salt, Individual, 1940-1943; $16.00
Sweetmeat, 1939-1943; $15.00
Urn, 5" Flared, Footed, 1940-1943; $42.00
Urn, 5½" Regular, Footed, 1940-1943; $42.00
Urn, 6½" Flared, Footed, 1939-1943; $45.00
Urn, 7½" Regular, Footed, 1939-1943; $48.00

2424—Almond
Height 1 in.
Diameter 1⅝ in.

2424—5½ in. Low Comport and Cover
Height 5½ in.

2424—Individual Salt
Height ¾ in.   Length 2¾ in.
Width 2 in.

2424—5 in. Footed Urn, Flared

2424—Duo Candlestick
Height 4¾ in.   Spread 6 in.

2424—5½ in. Footed Urn, Regular

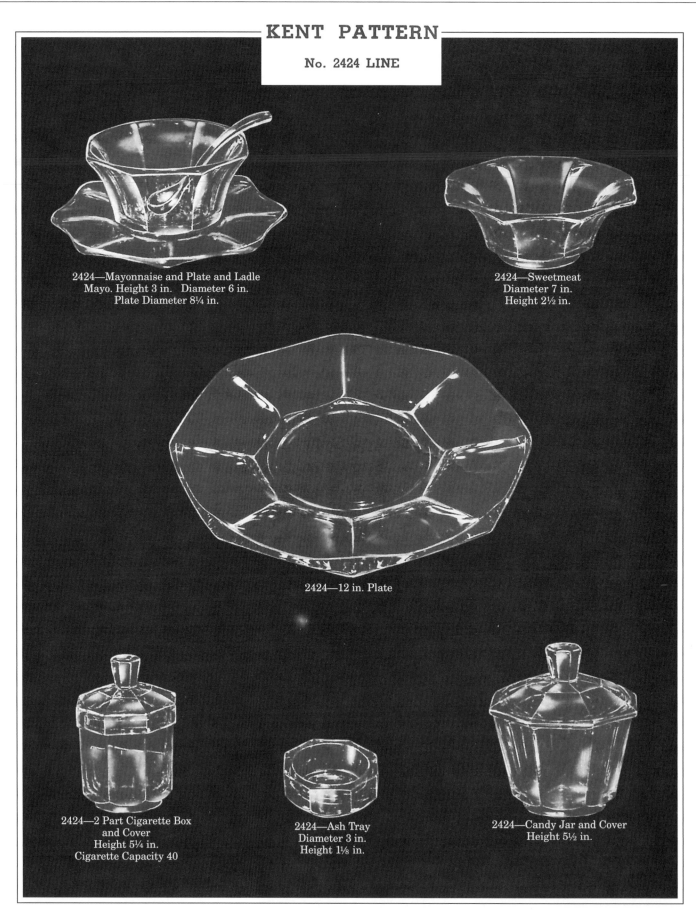

KENT PATTERN

No. 2424 LINE

2424—Mayonnaise and Plate and Ladle
Mayo. Height 3 in.   Diameter 6 in.
Plate Diameter 8¼ in.

2424—Sweetmeat
Diameter 7 in.
Height 2½ in.

2424—12 in. Plate

2424—2 Part Cigarette Box
and Cover
Height 5¼ in.
Cigarette Capacity 40

2424—Ash Tray
Diameter 3 in.
Height 1⅛ in.

2424—Candy Jar and Cover
Height 5½ in.

KENT PATTERN
No. 2424 LINE

2424—9½ in. Bowl, Flared
Height 3⅛ in.

2424—8 in. Bowl, Regular
Height 3½ in.

2424—3½ in. Candlestick

2424—11½ in. Fruit Bowl
Height 2¼ in.

2424—6½ in. Footed Urn, Flared

2424—7½ in. Footed Urn, Regular

TWENTY-FOUR TWENTY-NINE

The Service Tray and the Cordial Tray are very similar. Knowing that they were not made in the same colors should help to distinguish between them. In addition, the Lemon Dish insert does not fit in the center space of the Cordial Tray. The outside dimensions of both trays are the same, but the inside dimensions of the Cordial Tray are greater since it was made to accommodate the 2494 Cordial Bottle and eight 4024 Cordials.

Service Tray and Lemon Dish insert
    Crystal, 1929-1932; $85.00
    Amber, 1929-1932; $95.00
    Green, 1929-1932; $110.00
    Rose, 1929-1932; $125.00
    Azure, 1929-1932; $135.00
    Topaz, 1930-1932; $110.00

Cordial Tray
    Crystal, 1934-1936; $75.00
    Silver Mist, 1934-1935; $85.00
    Regal Blue, 1934-1936; $125.00
    Empire Green, 1934-1936; $125.00
    Burgundy, 1934-1936; $125.00

Service Tray, Lemon Insert, and 2375½ Sugar and Cream

Silver Mist Cordial Tray, Cordial Bottle, Cordials in Regal Blue, Burgundy, Empire Green, Silver Mist Foot

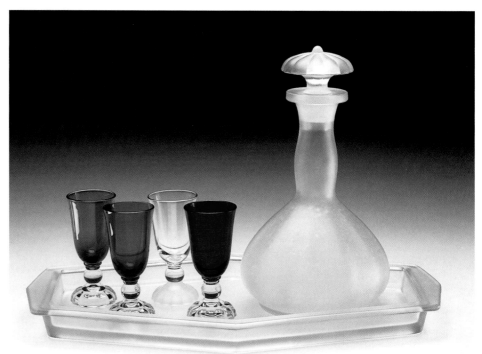

2430 DIADEM

CROWN
Decoration 504

Ebony with gold base

The only time this line was referred to as Diadem was on the introductory page in 1930; after that it was No. 2430. In addition, the Crown Decoration was put on two vases from the 2428 line, the 7½" Vase and the 10" Vase. The only piece offered in Wisteria was the Candy Jar and Cover. The 11" Bowl and either the 2" or the 9½" Candlesticks make a beautiful console set.

The Candy Jar and Cover continued to be made in colors through 1934, and in crystal for the 286 Manor etching through 1935. The bottom to the Candy Jar was most likely used as the 3¾" Vase. In 1938 several of the pieces in this short-lived line were reissued in crystal only, with those pieces dropping out by 1943. In 1954, several pieces were brought back in Ebony.

Bowl, 11"
    Crystal, 1930-1933;1938-1942; $32.00
    Rose, 1930-1933; $45.00
    Azure, 1930-1933; $45.00
    Green, 1930-1933; $42.00
    Amber, 1930-1933; $42.00
    Ebony, 1930-1933; 1954-1957; $42.00
    Topaz, 1930-1933; $42.00
    504 Crown Decoration, 1930-1932; $68.00
Candlestick, 2" (pair)
    Crystal, 1938-1942; $35.00
    Ebony, 1954-1958; $45.00
Candlestick, 9½" (pair)
    Crystal, 1930-1932; $115.00
    Rose, 1930-1932; $135.00
    Azure, 1930-1932; $135.00
    Green, 1930-1932; $125.00
    Amber, 1930-1932; $120.00
    Ebony, 1930-1932; $130.00
    Topaz, 1930-1932; $130.00
Candy Jar and Cover, ½ pound
    Crystal, 1930-1934; 1938-1943; $36.00
    Rose, 1930-1934 ; $48.00
    Azure, 1930-1934; $48.00
    Green, 1930-1934; $45.00
    Amber, 1930-1934; $45.00
    Ebony, 1930-1934, 1954-1958; $45.00
    Topaz, 1930-1934; $45.00
    Wisteria, 1931-1932; $135.00
    504 Crown Decoration, 1930-1932; $125.00
Jelly, 7"
    Crystal, 1930-1932; 1938-1940; $18.00
    Rose, 1930-1932; $21.00
    Azure, 1930-1932; $22.00
    Green, 1930-1932; $21.00
    Amber, 1930-1932; $18.00
    Ebony, 1930-1932; $20.00
    Topaz, 1930-1932; $20.00
    504 Crown Decoration, 1930-1932; $38.00
Mint, 5½"
    Crystal, 1930-1932; 1938-1942; $18.00
    Rose, 1930-1932; $21.00
    Azure, 1930-1932; $22.00

    Green, 1930-1932; $21.00
    Amber, 1930-1932; $20.00
    Ebony, 1930-1932; $20.00
    Topaz, 1930-1932: $21.00
Vase, 3¾"
    Crystal, 1938-1940, $34.00
Vase, 8"
    Crystal, 1930-1934; 1938-1943; $48.00
    Rose, 1930-1934; $67.00
    Azure, 1930-1934; $67.00
    Green, 1930-1934; $62.00
    Amber, 1930-1934; $60.00
    Ebony, 1930-1933; $65.00
    504 Crown Decoration, 1930-1932; $125.00

FOSTORIA can be purchased for moderate prices throughout the United States in complete sets or individual pieces. Replacements can be made at any time because Fostoria is sold ON THE OPEN-STOCK PLAN. The Fostoria colors are Amber, Green, Rose, Azure, Crystal, Ebony, and the golden Topaz. Fragile as this glass seems, it resists rapid changes in temperature as well as china does, and so is absolutely practicable for serving hot and cold foods. Send for "The New Little Book About Glassware." It contains invaluable suggestions on table settings and decorative pieces. The Fostoria Glass Company, Dept. G-10, Moundsville, West Virginia.

Rose is used effectively on doilies of pale green in this luncheon for eight people. Fall flowers in the centerpiece accent the color. The salad course is shown in Amber at the upper right, while at the upper left bridge accessories are suggested . . . a candy jar, a sixteen-ounce tumbler and a plate that can be used either under the tumbler, or for salad.

No. 2430 LINE

2430—7 in. Jelly
Height 1⅜ in.

2430—5½ in. Mint
Height 1⅜ in.

2430—2 in. Candlestick

2430—11 in. Bowl
Height 3 in.

2430—2 in. Candlestick

2430—3¾ in. Vase

2430—8 in. Vase

2430—½ Lb. Candy Jar and Cover
Height 5¾ in.

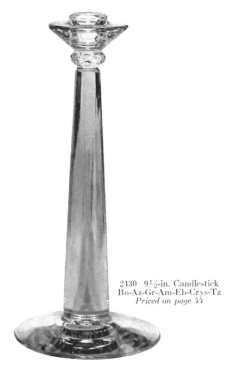

2430 9½-in. Candlestick
Ro-Az-Gr-Am-Eb-Crys-Tz
Priced on page 44

Wisteria Candy Jar and Cover; Ebony Candy Jar and Cover, Crown Decoration

TWENTY-FOUR THIRTY-THREE

1931 – 1932

It would be easy to name this pattern after the three gracefully curved columns which separate the bowl from the base of each piece. The authors fondly call this pattern "Tripod." Extremely short-lived, Twenty-Four Thirty-Three was used for some of the most elegant of etchings. Pieces were used for Manor, New Garland, Minuet, and Wildflower etchings. The Ebony based pieces are consummate Art Deco.

The 3" Candlestick was listed in January 1932 as a 4" Candlestick with Manor etching, and the September 1932 price list includes an 8" Candlestick in Minuet; one more indication that the early 1930s were a confusing time for everyone. Most likely those candlesticks never were made.

Tall Comport, Amber Base, Wisteria Bowl; Candlestick, Wisteria Bowl; Low Comport, Ebony Base, Green Base

Comport, 6" Low
Crystal, $28.00
Green Base, $32.00
Amber Base, $30.00
Ebony Base, $32.00
Rose Bowl, $32.00
Azure Bowl, $35.00
Topaz Bowl, $32.00

Comport, 6" Tall
Crystal, $42.00
Green Base, $54.00
Amber Base, $50.00
Ebony Base, $54.00
Rose Bowl, $54.00
Azure Bowl, $57.00
Topaz Bowl, $52.00
Wisteria Bowl, $85.00

Candlestick, 3"
Crystal, $28.00
Green Base, $32.00
Amber Base, $30.00
Ebony Base, $32.00

Rose Bowl, $32.00
Azure Bowl, $35.00
Topaz Bowl, $32.00
Wisteria Bowl, $48.00

Bowl "A", 12"
Crystal, $52
Green Base, $67.00
Amber Base, $65.00
Ebony Base, $67.00
Rose Bowl, $67.00
Azure Bowl, $75.00
Topaz Bowl, $65.00
Wisteria Bowl, $125.00

Bowl "D", 7½"
Crystal, $50.00
Green Base, $56.00
Amber Base. $55.00
Ebony Base, $56.00
Rose Bowl, $56.00
Azure Bowl, $58.00
Topaz Bowl, $55.00

Mock oranges make an unusual and appropriate centerpiece for breakfast, contrasting effectively with the Topaz glass used in this setting. Lower left illustrates the new Fostoria pitcher; lower right, a new vase.

Fostoria is gay at breakfast

2433   12-in. Bowl "A"
Solid Crystal
Gr-Am-Eb Base with Crys Bowl
Crys Base with Ro-Az-Tz-Wis Bowl
Priced on page 43

2433   3-in. Candlestick
Solid Crystal
Gr-Am-Eb Base with Crys Bowl
Crys Base with Ro-Az-Tz-Wis Bowl
Priced on page 43

2433   6-in. Tall Comport
Solid Crystal
Gr-Am-Eb Base with Crys Bowl
Crys Base with Ro-Az-Tz-Wis Bowl
Priced on page 43

2433   6-in. Low Comport
Solid Crystal
Gr-Am-Eb Base with Crys Bowl
Crys Base with Ro-Az-Tz Bowl
Priced on page 43

2433   7½-in. Bowl "D"
Solid Crystal
Gr-Am-Eb Base with Crys Bowl
Crys Base with Ro-Az-Tz Bowl
Priced on page 43

2440 LAFAYETTE

Quite possibly the most elegant of all the dinnerware patterns with its double optic and delicately scalloped edges, Lafayette was used as the dinner service for such etchings as Chateau, Midnight Rose, and Springtime. Often it was paired with the 2470 Line, and consistently used the 2470 Sugar and Cream Tray to exhibit its Sugar and Cream. Upon closer inspection, the curls found in the handles and bases of the 2470 Line are also seen on the cup, sugar and cream, and cream soup handles in Lafayette. The handles for the Relishes, the 2-part Mayonnaise, Oval Sauce and Tray, Handled Lemon, Handled Sweetmeat, and Oval Cake Plate are distinctive, with two curls implied in the open work. Once those handles have been seen and the double optic observed, pieces in the Lafayette pattern cannot be mistaken.

The Oval Mayonnaise is unique to this pattern. Both American and Baroque have an oval-shaped sauce and tray, but neither is as dramatically elegant as Lafayette. Every piece of this pattern was made in both Crystal and Topaz, with quite a few pieces being offered in Wisteria. Further, Fostoria used the Lafayette pattern to display the "strong" colors of the 1930s: Regal Blue, Empire Green, Burgundy, and Ruby. No fewer than 12 pieces were offered in the first three colors, with the Mayonnaise, the 13" Torte, the 2- and 3-part Relishes and the Sauce Dish and Tray being the only pieces from this line made in Ruby. Several pieces were also made with the Silver Mist decoration, and quite a few were made in Amber, Green, and Rose. Interestingly, no piece in the Lafayette pattern was made in Azure.

Almond, Individual
  Crystal, 1932-1937; $22.00
  Rose, 1932-1937; $24.00
  Green, 1932-1937; $24.00
  Amber, 1932-1937; $24.00
  Topaz/Gold Tint, 1932-1937; $24.00
  Wisteria, 1932-1936; $36.00
Bon Bon, 5" Handled
  Crystal, 1933-1942; $16.00
  Rose, 1933-1937; $22.00
  Green, 1933-1939; $20.00
  Amber, 1933-1937; $18.00
  Topaz/Gold Tint, 1933-1942; $20.00
  Wisteria, 1933-1935; $30.00
  Regal Blue,1933-1940; $30.00
  Burgundy, 1933-1940; $30.00
  Empire Green, 1933-1940; $30.00
Bowl, 5" Fruit
  Crystal 1932-1943; $20.00
  Topaz/Gold Tint, 1932-1943; $22.00
  Wisteria, 1932-1937; $32.00
Bowl, 6" Cereal
  Crystal, 1932-1943; $22.00
  Topaz/Gold Tint, 1932-1943; $24.00
  Wisteria, 1932-1935; $35.00
Bowl "D", 7"
  Crystal, 1931-1938; $33.00
  Rose, 1931-1938; $42.00
  Green, 1931-1938; $42.00
  Amber, 1931-1938; $40.00
  Topaz/Gold Tint, 1931-1938; $42.00
  Wisteria, 1931-1938; $55.00
Bowl, 8" Nappy
  Crystal, 1932-1943; $35.00
  Topaz/Gold Tint, 1932-1943; $40.00
  Wisteria, 1932-1938; $55.00
Bowl, 10" Oval Baker
  Crystal, 1932-1943; $38.00
  Topaz/Gold Tint, 1932-1938; $43.00
  Wisteria, 1932-1938; $60.00

Bowl "B", 10"
  Crystal, 1931-1940; $38.00
  Rose, 1931-1940; $42.00
  Green, 1931-1936; $42.00
  Amber, 1931-1940; $40.00
  Topaz/Gold Tint, 1931-1940; $42.00
Bowl, 12" Salad
  Crystal, 1931-1940; $38.00
  Rose, 1932-1938; $42.00
  Green, 1932-1938; $42.00
  Amber, 1932-1936; $40.00
  Topaz/Gold Tint, 1931-1940; $42.00
  Wisteria, 1931-1938; $62.00

Regal Blue 13" Torte, 3-part Relish; Ruby 2-part Relish, 2-part Mayonnaise; Sugar and Cream, Burgundy Oval Tray

Cake, 10½" Oval
Crystal, 1933-1946; $44.00
Rose, 1933-1934; $48.00
Green, 1933-1935; $48.00
Amber, 1933-1935; $45.00
Topaz/Gold Tint,1933-1942; $45.00
Regal Blue, 1933-1940; $65.00
Burgundy, 1933-1940; $65.00
Empire Green, 1933-1940; $65.00
Celery, 11½"
Crystal, 1932-1946; $32.00
Rose, 1932-1940; $38.00
Green, 1932-1940; $38.00
Amber, 1932-1940; $35.00
Topaz/Gold Tint, 1932-1943; $37.00
Wisteria, 1932-1935; $54.00
Cream Soup
Crystal, 1931-1940; $40.00
Topaz, 1932; $54.00
Wisteria, 1931-1938; $65.00
Cup and Saucer
Crystal, 1931-1961; $22.00
Topaz/Gold Tint, 1931-1940; $26.00
Wisteria, 1931-1938; $48.00
Regal Blue, 1934-1942; $48.00
Burgundy, 1934-1942; $48.00
Empire Green, 1934-1942; $48.00
Cup and Saucer, AD
Crystal, 1932-1942; $24.00
Topaz, 1932-1936; $32.00
Wisteria, 1932-1935; $125.00
Lemon, 5" Handled
Crystal, 1933-1940; $20.00
Rose, 1933-1940; $22.00
Green, 1933-1940; $22.00
Amber, 1933-1940; $20.00
Topaz, 1933-1935; $22.00
Wisteria, 1933-1935; $30.00
Regal Blue, 1933-1940; $28.00
Burgundy, 1933-1940; $28.00
Empire Green, 1933-1940; $28.00
Mayonnaise, 6½", 2-part
Crystal, 1933-1942; $25.00
Rose, 1933-1940; $33.00
Green, 1933-1940; $33.00
Amber, 1933-1940; $28.00
Topaz/Gold Tint,1933-1942; $28.00
Wisteria, 1933-1938; $52.00
Regal Blue, 1934-1940; $45.00
Burgundy, 1934-1939; $45.00
Empire Green, 1934-1940; $45.00
Ruby, 1934-1938; $48.00
Silver Mist, 1935-1938; $30.00
Olive, 6½"
Crystal, 1932-1948; $20.00

Rose, 1932-1940; $23.00
Green, 1932-1940; $23.00
Amber, 1932-1940; $22.00
Topaz/Gold Tint, 1932-1943; $24.00
Wisteria, 1932-1938; $40.00
Pickle, 8½"
Crystal, 1932-1946; $21.00
Rose, 1932-1940; $26.00
Green, 1932-1940; $26.00
Amber, 1932-1940; $24.00
Topaz/Gold Tint, 1932-1943; $24.00
Wisteria, 1932-1934; $45.00
Plate, 6"
Crystal, 1932-1961; $10.00
Topaz/Gold Tint, 1931-1943; $14.00
Wisteria, 1931-1937; $20.00
Plate, 7"
Crystal, 1931-1961; $10.00
Topaz/Gold Tint, 1931-1943; $14.00
Wisteria, 1931-1937; $22.00
Plate, 8"
Crystal, 1931-1961; $12.00
Topaz/Gold Tint, 1931-1943; $15.00
Wisteria, 1931-1937; $26.00
Plate, 9"
Crystal, 1931-1961; $26.00
Topaz/Gold Tint, 1931-1943; $32.00
Wisteria, 1931-1937; $50.00
Plate, 10"
Crystal, 1931-1942; $35.00
Topaz, 1931-1935; $45.00
Wisteria, 1931-1938; $110.00
Plate, 13" Torte
Crystal, 1932-1960; $45.00
Rose, 1932-1940; $52.00
Green, 1932-1940; $52.00
Amber, 1932-1940; $50.00
Topaz/Gold Tint, 1932-1943; $50.00
Wisteria, 1932-1938; $110.00
Regal Blue, 1934-1939; $110.00
Burgundy, 1934-1940; $95.00
Empire Green, 1934-1938; $110.00
Ruby, 1934-1939; $110.00
Silver Mist, 1934; $48.00
Platter, 12"
Crystal, 1932-1938; $45.00
Topaz/Gold Tint, 1932-1937; $50.00
Wisteria, 1932-1936; $95.00
Platter, 15"
Crystal, September 1932; $50.00
Topaz, September 1932; $58.00
Relish, 2-part, Handled
Crystal, 1933-1942; $25.00
Rose, 1933-1940; $32.00
Green, 1933-1940; $32.00

Amber, 1933-1940; $30.00
Topaz/Gold Tint, 1933-1942; $30.00
Wisteria, 1933-1938; $45.00
Regal Blue, 1933-1940; $45.00
Burgundy, 1933-1940; $45.00
Empire Green, 1933-1940; $45.00
Ruby, 1934-1942; $45.00
Silver Mist, 1935-1938; $28.00
Relish, 3-part, Handled
    Crystal, 1933-1942; $28.00
    Rose, 1933-1940; $35.00
    Green, 1933-1940; $35.00
    Amber, 1933-1939; $34.00
    Topaz/Gold Tint, 1933-1942; $34.00
    Wisteria, 1933-1938; $50.00
    Regal Blue, 1934-1940; $50.00
    Burgundy, 1934-1940; $50.00
    Empire Green, 1934-1940; $50.00
    Ruby, 1934-1942; $50.00
    Silver Mist, 1935-1938; $30.00
Sauce Dish, 6½" Oval
    Crystal, 1933-1943; $25.00
    Rose, 1933-1940; $35.00
    Green, 1933-1940; $35.00
    Amber, 1933-1940; $32.00
    Topaz/Gold Tint, 1933-1942; $32.00
    Wisteria, 1933-1938; $55.00
    Regal Blue, 1934-1937; $55.00
    Burgundy, 1934-1940; $55.00
    Empire Green, 1934-1940; $55.00
    Ruby, 1934-1937; $60.00
    Silver Mist, 1935-1938; $28.00
Sugar and Cream, Footed
    Crystal, 1931-1961; $35.00
    Rose, 1932-1940; $55.00

Green, 1932-1940; $55.00
Amber, 1932-1940; $50.00
Topaz/Gold Tint, 1931-1939; $50.00
Wisteria, 1931-1938; $95.00
Regal Blue, 1934-1939; $95.00
Burgundy, 1934-1939; $95.00
Empire Green, 1932-1940; $95.00
Sweetmeat, 4½", Handled
    Crystal, 1933-1942; $18.00
    Rose, 1933-1940; $22.00
    Green, 1933-1940; $22.00
    Amber, 1933-1940; $20.00
    Topaz/Gold Tint, 1933-1942; $20.00
    Wisteria, 1933-1937; $32.00
    Regal Blue,1933-1940; $32.00
    Burgundy, 1933-1940; $32.00
    Empire Green, 1933-1940; $32.00
Tray, 8½" Oval
    Crystal, 1933-1942; $25.00
    Rose, 1933-1940; $32.00
    Green, 1933-1940; $32.00
    Amber, 1933-1940; $30.00
    Topaz/Gold Tint, 1933-1942; $30.00
    Wisteria, 1933-1935; $55.00
    Regal Blue, 1934-1936; $55.00
    Burgundy, 1934-1940; $52.00
    Empire Green, 1934-1940; $52.00
    Ruby, 1934-1938; $55.00
    Silver Mist, 1935-1938; $28.00
Vase, 7"
    Crystal, 1931-1938; $48.00
    Rose, 1931-1938; $58.00
    Green, 1931-1935; $65.00
    Amber, 1931-1938; $54.00
    Topaz, 1931-1934; $58.00

Wisteria Almond, Sugar and Cream, Cup and Saucer, After Dinner Cup and Saucer, 7", 8", 9", 10" Plates

LAFAYETTE PATTERN

No. 2440 DINNERWARE

See price list for colors

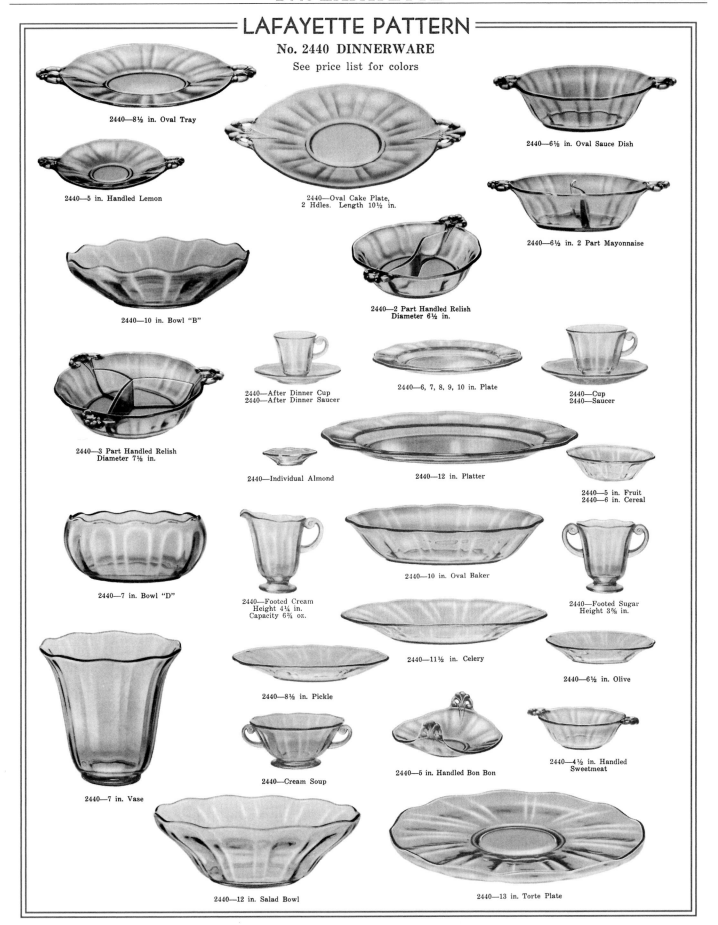

2440—8½ in. Oval Tray

2440—5 in. Handled Lemon

2440—Oval Cake Plate,
2 Hdles. Length 10½ in.

2440—6½ in. Oval Sauce Dish

2440—6½ in. 2 Part Mayonnaise

2440—10 in. Bowl "B"

2440—2 Part Handled Relish
Diameter 6½ in.

2440—3 Part Handled Relish
Diameter 7½ in.

2440—After Dinner Cup
2440—After Dinner Saucer

2440—6, 7, 8, 9, 10 in. Plate

2440—Cup
2440—Saucer

2440—Individual Almond

2440—12 in. Platter

2440—5 in. Fruit
2440—6 in. Cereal

2440—7 in. Bowl "D"

2440—Footed Cream
Height 4¼ in.
Capacity 6¾ oz.

2440—10 in. Oval Baker

2440—Footed Sugar
Height 3⅝ in.

2440—11½ in. Celery

2440—6½ in. Olive

2440—8½ in. Pickle

2440—7 in. Vase

2440—Cream Soup

2440—5 in. Handled Bon Bon

2440—4½ in. Handled
Sweetmeat

2440—12 in. Salad Bowl

2440—13 in. Torte Plate

77

2449 HERMITAGE

This wonderful pressed pattern was first listed in the September 1932 supplement. The early years of that decade seem to have been a time when the Fostoria Company was struggling not only with problems caused by the Great Depression but also with the newly organized labor unions. Some of the pieces listed were never shown in the catalogs. Since the 5" Bowl and the 7" Nappy are not pictured, the authors wonder if these were duplicates of the 5" Fruit and the 7" Soup. We have seen all the pitchers except the Hall Boy, and since it was not shown on a catalog page, we are not sure what it looked like. The Cocktail Shaker and the Bar Bottle were very similar except for the tops. The Grapefruit was slightly larger than the Ice Dish, but had the same three dividers built in to hold the liner. The Ice Dish could use either the 2451 blown liner, or the 2479 pressed one which was made in Crystal only. The Wisteria liners will be the most difficult to locate since they were made for a shorter period.

Hermitage was offered in all the pastels of the time. The idea of sets no doubt arose from the influx of bar ware after the repeal of Prohibition. Fostoria extended the idea of mixing colors with the Rainbow Assortments offered in those sets. Now that this pattern has become harder to complete in one color, the idea of mixing colors seems even more appealing.

Stemware was a highlight of the Hermitage pattern, and all pieces are shown in *Fostoria Stemware,* page 46.

Ash Tray
 Crystal, 1932-1943; $10.00
 Green, 1932-1940; $12.00
 Amber, 1932-1940; $12.00
 Azure, 1932-1940; $13.00
 Topaz/Gold Tint, 1932-1938; $12.00
 Ebony, 1932-1934; $12.00
Ash Tray Set
 Crystal, 1932-1943; $40.00
 Green, 1932-1940; $48.00
 Amber, 1932-1940; $48.00
 Azure, 1932-1940; $50.00
 Topaz/Gold Tint, 1932-1937; $48.00
Bottle, Bar, and Stopper
 Crystal, 1932-1938; $87.00
Bowl, Finger
 Crystal, 1932-1943; $15.00
 Green, 1932-1940; $20.00
 Amber, 1932-1938; $20.00
 Azure, 1932-1935; $25.00
 Topaz/Gold Tint, 1932-1942; $20.00
 Wisteria, 1932-1936; $35.00
Bowl, 5"
 Crystal, 1932-1933; $15.00
 Green, 1932-1933; $20.00
 Amber, 1932-1933; $20.00
 Topaz, 1932-1933; $20.00
2449½ Bowl, 5" Fruit
 Crystal, 1932-1943; $15.00
 Green, 1932-1938; $20.00
 Amber, 1932-1938; $20.00
 Azure, 1932-1938; $25.00
 Topaz/Gold Tint,1932-1938; $20.00
 Wisteria, 1932-1936; $35.00
2449½ Bowl, 6" Cereal
 Crystal, 1932-1943; $22.00

Green, 1932-1935; $27.00
 Amber, 1932-1938; $24.00
 Azure, 1932-1938; $28.00
 Topaz/Gold Tint, 1932-1937; $25.00
 Wisteria, 1932-1934; $38.00
2449½ Bowl, 6½" Coup Salad
 Crystal, 1932-1943; $24.00
 Green, 1932-1937; $28.00
 Amber, 1932-1938; $26.00
 Azure, 1932-1938; $32.00
 Topaz/Gold Tint, 1932-1938; $26.00
 Wisteria, 1932-1934; $42.00
2449½ Bowl, 7" Nappy

Decanter, Bar Bottle, Ice Dish and Liner, Claret, Pickle, Old Fashioned, Celery

Crystal, 1933-1938; $24.00
Amber, 1933-1938; $26.00
Azure, 1933-1934; $34.00
Topaz/Gold Tint, 1933-1937; $28.00
2449½ Bowl, 7" Soup
Crystal, 1932-1938; $24.00
Amber, 1932-1938; $26.00
Azure, 1932-1934; $34.00
Topaz/Gold Tint, 1932-1937; $28.00
2449½ Bowl, 7½" Coup Salad
Crystal, 1932-1942; $25.00
Green, 1932-1938; $28.00
Amber, 1932-1938; $26.00
Azure, 1932-1938; $35.00
Topaz/Gold Tint, 1932-1938; $27.00
Wisteria, 1932-1934; $45.00
Bowl, 8" Deep
Crystal, 1932-1940; $32.00
Green, 1932-1934; $40.00
Amber, 1932-1935; $34.00
Azure, 1932-1934; $48.00
Topaz, 1933-1935; $40.00
Wisteria, 1932-1936; $75.00
Bowl, 10" Flared
Crystal, 1932-1940; $32.00
Green, 1932-1935; $40.00
Amber, 1932-1935; $38.00
Topaz, 1932-1934; $38.00
Bowl, 10" Shallow
Crystal, 1932-1935; $32.00
Green, 1932-1935; $40.00
Amber, 1932-1934; $38.00
Azure, 1932-1934; $45.00
Topaz, 1932-1934; $40.00
Wisteria, 1932-1935; $75.00
Candlestick, 6" (pair)
Crystal, 1932-1939; $64.00
Green, 1932-1935; $70.00
Amber, 1932-1934; $70.00
Azure, 1932-1934; $85.00
Topaz, 1932-1935; $75.00
Wisteria, 1932-1935; $150.00
Celery, 11"
Crystal, 1932-1940; $24.00
Green, 1932-1935; $30.00
Amber, 1932-1935; $28.00
Azure, 1932-1934; $36.00
Topaz/Gold Tint, 1932-1938; $28.00
Wisteria, 1932-1934; $48.00
Coaster
Crystal, 1932-1943; $10.00
Green, 1932-1936; $12.00
Amber, 1932-1934; $12.00
Azure, 1932-1934; $15.00
Topaz/Gold Tint, 1932-1938; $12.00
Wisteria, 1932-1934; $22.00

Cocktail Shaker (similar to Bar Bottle)
Green, 1932-1933; $95.00
Azure, 1932-1933; $110.00
Comport, 6"
Crystal, 1932-1938; $27.00
Green, 1932-1935; $35.00
Amber, 1932-1935; $34.00
Azure, 1932-1935; $38.00
Topaz/Gold Tint, 1932-1938; $34.00
Wisteria, 1932-1936; $52.00
Cup and Saucer
Crystal, 1932-1943; $25.00
Green, 1932-1940; $32.00
Amber, 1932-1939; $30.00
Azure, 1932-1942; $34.00
Topaz/Gold Tint, 1932-1939; $32.00
Wisteria, 1932-1936; $52.00
Decanter and Stopper
Crystal, 1932-1940; $65.00
Green, 1932-1938; $95.00
Amber, 1932-1938; $85.00
Azure, 1932-1937; $110.00
Topaz/Gold Tint, 1932-1938; $85.00
Wisteria, 1932-1936; $135.00
Grapefruit
Crystal, 1932-1938; $30.00
Green, 1932-1934; $40.00
Amber, 1932-1934; $35.00
Topaz, 1932-1934; $40.00
Grapefruit Liner
Crystal, 1932-1938; $20.00
Ice Dish and Plate
Crystal, 1932-1943; $30.00
Green, 1932--1938; $42.00
Amber, 1932-1936; $42.00
Azure, 1932-1938; $45.00
Topaz/Gold Tint, 1932-1939; $42.00
Wisteria, 1932-1936; $55.00

HERMITAGE PATTERN
No. 2449 LINE
Made in Azure, Green, Amber, Crystal, Topaz and Wisteria
(Except as noted below the item)

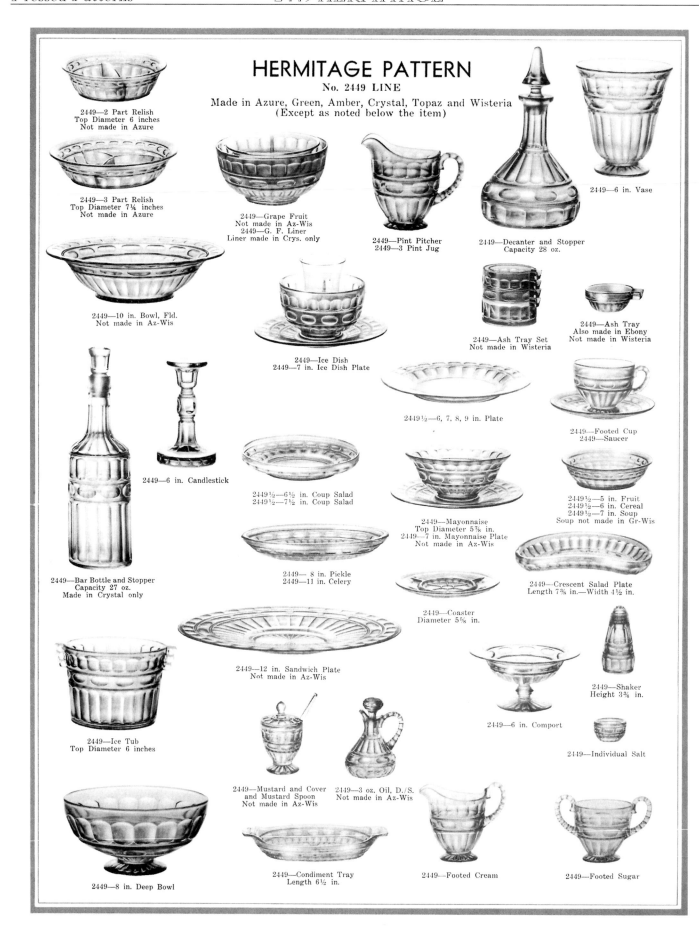

2449—2 Part Relish
Top Diameter 6 inches
Not made in Azure

2449—3 Part Relish
Top Diameter 7¼ inches
Not made in Azure

2449—Grape Fruit
Not made in Az-Wis
2449—G. F. Liner
Liner made in Crys. only

2449—Pint Pitcher
2449—3 Pint Jug

2449—Decanter and Stopper
Capacity 28 oz.

2449—6 in. Vase

2449—10 in. Bowl, Fld.
Not made in Az-Wis

2449—Ice Dish
2449—7 in. Ice Dish Plate

2449—Ash Tray Set
Not made in Wisteria

2449—Ash Tray
Also made in Ebony
Not made in Wisteria

2449½—6, 7, 8, 9 in. Plate

2449—Footed Cup
2449—Saucer

2449—6 in. Candlestick

2449½—6½ in. Coup Salad
2449½—7½ in. Coup Salad

2449½—5 in. Fruit
2449½—6 in. Cereal
2449½—7 in. Soup
Soup not made in Gr-Wis

2449—Mayonnaise
Top Diameter 5⅞ in.
2449—7 in. Mayonnaise Plate
Not made in Az-Wis

2449—Bar Bottle and Stopper
Capacity 27 oz.
Made in Crystal only

2449—8 in. Pickle
2449—11 in. Celery

2449—Crescent Salad Plate
Length 7⅜ in.—Width 4½ in.

2449—Coaster
Diameter 5⅝ in.

2449—12 in. Sandwich Plate
Not made in Az-Wis

2449—Shaker
Height 3¾ in.

2449—6 in. Comport

2449—Individual Salt

2449—Ice Tub
Top Diameter 6 inches

2449—Mustard and Cover
and Mustard Spoon
Not made in Az-Wis

2449—3 oz. Oil, D./S.
Not made in Az-Wis

2449—8 in. Deep Bowl

2449—Condiment Tray
Length 6½ in.

2449—Footed Cream

2449—Footed Sugar

2451 Liner, Blown (Tomato Juice, Crab Meat, Fruit Cocktail)
Crystal, 1932-1943; $10.00
Green, 1932-1938; $15.00
Amber, 1932-1936; $15.00
Azure, 1932-1938; $18.00
Topaz/Gold Tint, 1932-1939; $15.00
Wisteria, 1932-1935; $24.00
Crab Meat, 1932-1935; $25.00

2479 Liner, Pressed (Tomato Juice, Crab Meat, Fruit Cocktail)
Crystal, 1932-1943; $18.00

Ice Tub
Crystal, 1932-1940; $34.00
Green, 1932-1934; $40.00
Amber, 1932-1938; $38.00
Azure, 1932-1938; $45.00
Topaz, 1932-1934; $40.00
Wisteria, 1932-1936; $67.00

Mayonnaise and Plate
Crystal, 1932-1938; $32.00
Green, 1932-1938; $45.00
Amber, 1932-1934; $40.00
Topaz/Gold Tint, 1932-1938; $45.00

Ladle
Crystal, 1932-1938; $20.00

Mustard and Cover
Crystal, 1932-1940; $32.00
Green, 1932-1938; $38.00
Amber, 1932-1938; $36.00
Topaz/Gold Tint, 1932-1940; $36.00

Mustard Spoon
Crystal, 1932-1940; $20.00

Oil, 3 oz.
Crystal, 1932-1943; $45.00
Green, 1932-1940; $54.00
Amber, 1932-1940; $50.00
Topaz/Gold Tint, 1932-1943; $50.00

Pickle, 8"
Crystal, 1932-1943; $20.00
Green, 1932-1935; $24.00
Amber, 1932-1935; $22.00
Azure, 1932-1935; $26.00
Topaz, 1932-1935; $24.00
Wisteria, 1932-1934; $47.00

Pitcher, Pint Cereal
Crystal, 1932-1943; $42.00
Green, 1932-1934; $48.00
Amber, 1932-1938; $45.00
Azure, 1932-1934; $50.00
Topaz/Gold Tint, 1932-1938; $45.00
Wisteria, 1932-1936; $72.00

Pitcher, Hall Boy Jug
Crystal, 1932-1935; $65.00
Green, 1932-1934; $78.00

Amber, 1932-1934; $75.00
Topaz, 1932-1934; $75.00
Wisteria, 1932-1934; $125.00

Pitcher, Quart Ice Jug
Crystal, 1932-1938; $60.00
Green, 1932-1934; $75.00
Amber, 1932-1934; $70.00
Topaz, 1932-1936; $75.00
Wisteria, 1932-1934; $125.00

Pitcher, 3-Pint Jug
Crystal, 1932-1939; $65.00
Green, 1932-1934; $85.00
Amber, 1932-1938; $70.00
Azure, 1932-1936; $95.00
Topaz, 1932-1935; $75.00
Wisteria, 1932-1936; $155.00

2449½ Plate, 6"
Crystal, 1932-1944; $7.00
Green, 1932-1936; $10.00
Amber, 1932-1938; $10.00
Azure, 1932-1940; $10.00
Topaz/Gold Tint, 1932-1940; $10.00
Wisteria, 1932-1936; $20.00

2449½ Plate, 7"
Crystal, 1932-1944; $10.00
Green, 1932-1938; $14.00
Amber, 1932-1938; $12.00
Azure, 1932-1938; $12.00
Topaz/Gold Tint, 1932-1943; $12.00
Wisteria, 1932-1936; $24.00

2449½ Plate, 8"
Crystal, 1932-1943; $10.00
Green, 1932-1934; $14.00
Amber, 1932-1934; $12.00
Azure, 1932-1942; $12.00
Topaz/Gold Tint, 1932-1942; $12.00
Wisteria, 1932-1934; $24.00

Plate, 8" (Ground Bottom)
Crystal, 1931-1939; $11.00
Green, 1931-1935; $15.00
Amber, 1931-1938; $12.00
Azure, 1931-1935; $14.00
Topaz, 1931-1935; $14.00
Wisteria, 1931-1936; $28.00

2449½ Plate, 9"
Crystal, 1932-1944; $20.00
Green, 1932-1938; $25.00
Amber, 1932-1940; $22.00
Azure, 1932-1940; $25.00
Topaz/Gold Tint, 1932-1940; $22.00
Wisteria, 1932-1936; $45.00

Plate, Crescent Salad, Star Bottom
Crystal, 1932-1944; $26.00
Green, 1932-1934; $32.00
Amber, 1932-1940; $30.00

THE GLASS OF FASHION

8 A. M. JUNE MORNING

Nothing so befits a fresh spring morning as a breakfast service of sparkling Fostoria. This quaint pattern, the "Hermitage", is *particularly* in vogue just at the minute for luncheon as well as breakfast. In 6 lovely colors. You'll be pleasantly surprised to learn how modestly "Hermitage" is priced.

Azure, 1932-1934; $34.00
Topaz, 1932-1934; $32.00
Wisteria, 1932-1934; $54.00
2449½ Plate, Crescent Salad, Plain Bottom
Crystal, 1933-1944; $22.00
Plate, 12" Sandwich
Crystal, 1932-1943; $28.00
Green, 1932-1938; $34.00
Amber, 1932-1938; $30.00
Topaz, 1932-1934; $34.00
Relish, 2-part
Crystal, 1933-1942; $24.00
Green, 1933-1935; $30.00
Amber, 1933-1938; $28.00
Topaz/Gold Tint, 1933-1938; $30.00
Wisteria, 1933-1934; $48.00
Relish, 3-part
Crystal, 1933-1943; $26.00
Green, 1933-1935; $32.00
Amber, 1933-1938; $30.00
Topaz, 1933-1935; $32.00
Wisteria, 1933-1934; $53.00
Salt, Individual
Crystal, 1932-1943; $12.00
Green, 1932-1938; $18.00
Amber, 1932-1938; $16.00
Topaz, 1932-1935; $18.00
Salver, 11"
Crystal, 1932-1938; $32.00
Green, 1932-1937; $40.00
Amber, 1932-1936; $38.00
Azure, 1932-1934; $42.00
Topaz, 1932-1934; $40.00
Wisteria, 1932-1934; $65.00
Shaker (Priced individually)
Crystal, 1932-1943; $18.00
Green, 1932-1936; $22.00
Amber, 1932-1937; $20.00
Azure, 1932-1936; $26.00
Topaz/Gold Tint, 1932-1942; $21.00
Wisteria, 1932-1936; $32.50
Sugar and Cream
Crystal, 1932-1943; $27.00
Green, 1932-1938; $35.00
Amber, 1932-1938; $32.00
Azure, 1932-1935; $40.00
Topaz/Gold Tint, 1932-1943; $32.00
Wisteria, 1932-1936; $65.00

Tray, Condiment
Crystal, 1932-1943; $18.00
Green, 1932-1938; $23.00
Amber, 1932-1934; $23.00
Topaz/Gold Tint, 1932-1938; $23.00
Vase, 6"
Crystal, 1932-1939; $38.00
Green, 1932-1936; $47.00
Amber, 1932-1938; $45.00
Topaz/Gold Tint, 1932-1938; $45.00
*Set B – 18-piece Refreshment Set: 6 Tumblers, 13 oz.;
6 Tumblers, 2 oz. ; 6 Old Fashioneds, 6 oz. All colors, 1933
*Set C – Cocktail Set: Cocktail Shaker; 6 Cocktails, 4 oz.
All colors, 1933
*Set D – Bar Set: 1 Bar Bottle and Stopper; 6 Tumblers,
2 oz. Crystal, 1933
*Set E – Old Fashioned Set: 6 Old Fashioned Cocktails,
6 oz. All colors, 1933
*Set F – Tall Drink Set: 6 Tumblers, 13 oz. All colors,
1933
*Set G – Decanter Set: Decanter and Stopper; 6 Tumblers, 2 oz. All colors, 1933
*Set H – Demitasse Set: 6 After Dinner Cups and
Saucers. All colors, 1933 except Wisteria
*Set I – Inspiration Set: 6 Cocktails, 4 oz. All colors,
1933
*Set J – Sugar and Cream Set. All colors, 1933

*Also offered as "Rainbow Assortment."

TWENTY-FOUR SEVENTY

The accessory pieces offered in this line were used with a number of patterns, notably the 286 Manor etching. With its classic lines and curls, this line is reminiscent of the 2440 Lafayette pattern and often was used with patterns having Lafayette as a dinner service. In fact, the 2470 sugar and cream tray was used to hold the Lafayette sugar and cream. The handles in this pattern are easily identified with their four ridges bordered on either side by a classic curl. Especially elegant are the 2470 Candlesticks and 12" Bowl because they were featured in color combined with crystal. It would be well to remember that the Wisteria color was never etched or cut, therefore, the bowl and candlesticks would only be found with a Wisteria bowl if they were plain. An etched piece might have a Wisteria base. In 1952, the 10" Vase was offered in two additional colors: Cinnamon and Spruce; only the bowl was colored. Cinnamon lasted through 1957 and Spruce through 1958.

Not many etched or cut patterns used Twenty-Four Seventy, so it is often found in beautiful, unadorned crystal or color. Never plentiful, any pieces of this line are prized.

Bon Bon
    Crystal, 1933-1939; $18.00
    Rose, 1933-1938; $24.00
    Green, 1933-1938; $24.00
    Amber, 1933-1934; $22.00
    Topaz, 1933-1934; $24.00
Bowl, 7"
    Crystal, 1934-1943; $20.00
    Rose, 1934-1940; $28.00
    Green, 1934; $30.00
    Amber, 1934-1936; $26.00
    Topaz, 1934-1936; $28.00
    Wisteria, 1933-1936; $45.00
Bowl, 9" Service Dish
    Crystal, 1933-1934; $38.00
    Rose, 1933-1934; $65.00
    Green, 1933-1934; $65.00
    Amber, 1933-1934; $60.00
2470½, Bowl, 10½"
    Crystal, 1933-1962; $55.00
    Rose, 1933-1938; $75.00
    Green, 1933-1940; $70.00
    Amber, 1933-1940; $65.00
    Topaz/Gold Tint, 1933-1942; $65.00
    Wisteria, 1933-1938; $125.00
    Ruby, 1934; $115.00
Bowl, 12"
    Crystal, 1933-1940; $65.00
    Rose Bowl, 1933-1934; $95.00
    Green Base, 1933-1934; $95.00
    Amber Base, 1933-1938; $75.00
    Topaz/Gold Tint Bowl, 1933-1938; $85.00
Candlestick, 5½" (pair)
    Crystal, 1933-1938; $68.00
    Rose Bowl, 1933-1934; $95.00
    Green Base, 1933-1934; $95.00
    Amber Base, 1933-1934; $90.00
    Topaz Bowl, 1933-1935; $90.00
    Wisteria Base, 1933-1934; $150.00
2470½ Candlestick, 5½" (pair)
    Crystal, 1933-1945; $60.00
    Rose, 1933-1940; $85.00

    Green, 1933-1940; $85.00
    Amber, 1933-1940; $80.00
    Topaz/Gold Tint, 1933-1938; $80.00
    Wisteria, 1933-1938; $135.00
    Regal Blue, 1935; $200.00
    Burgundy, 1935; $200.00
    Empire Green, 1935; $200.00
    Ruby, 1934-1942; $150.00
Comport, 6" Low
    Crystal, 1933-1943; $28.00
    Rose Bowl, 1934; $37.00
    Green Base, 1934-1938; $35.00
    Amber Base, 1934-1938; $32.00
    Topaz/Gold Tint Bowl, 1934-1938; $35.00
    Wisteria Base, 1933-1938; $48.00
Comport, 6" Tall
    Crystal, 1933-1934; $48.00
    Rose Bowl, 1933-1934; $75.00
    Green Base, 1933-1934; $75.00
    Amber Base, 1933-1934; $65.00
    Topaz Bowl, 1933-1934; $68.00
    Wisteria Base, 1933-1934; $97.00

Ruby 2470½ Bowl, 10½", 7" Amber Bowl, Sugar and Cream Tray

Topaz 2470½ Candlesticks

Lemon, 2-Handled
Crystal, 1933-1939; $20.00
Rose, 1933-1938; $24.00
Green, 1933-1938; $24.00
Amber, 1933-1935; $22.00
Topaz, 1933-1934; $24.00
Plate, 10" Cake
Crystal, 1933-1938; $38.00
Rose, 1933-1938; $65.00
Green, 1933-1938; $65.00
Amber, 1933-1938; $60.00
Topaz/Gold Tint, 1933-1938; $62.00
Relish, 3-part Round
Crystal, 1933-1938; $35.00
Rose, 1933-1938; $62.00
Green, 1933-1938; $62.00
Amber, 1933-1938; $55.00
Topaz/Gold Tint, 1933-1938; $58.00
Relish, 4-part Oval
Crystal, 1933-1938; $43.00
Rose, 1933-1934; $68.00
Green, 1933-1934; $68.00
Amber, 1933-1934; $58.00
Topaz, 1933-1934; $58.00
Sweetmeat, 2-Handled
Crystal, 1933-1939; $20.00
Rose, 1933-1934; $24.00

Green, 1933-1938; $24.00
Amber, 1933-1934; $22.00
Topaz/Gold Tint, 1933-1938; $22.00
Tray, Sugar and Cream
Crystal, 1933-1942; $22.00
Rose, 1933-1940; $28.00
Green, 1933-1940; $28.00
Amber, 1933-1937; $25.00
Topaz/Gold Tint, 1933-1937; $25.00
Tray, 9¾" Round
Rose, 1933-1934; $65.00
Green, 1933-1934; $65.00
Amber, 1933-1934; $60.00
Topaz, 1933-1934; $65.00
Ebony, 1933-1934; $60.00
Vase, 8"
Crystal, 1935-1943; $54.00
Regal Blue Bowl, 1935-1938; $75.00
Burgundy Bowl, 1935-1939; $70.00
Empire Green Bowl, 1935-1938; $75.00
Ruby Bowl, 1935-1940; $75.00
Vase, 10"
Crystal, 1933-1943, 1952-1958; $60.00
Green Bowl, 1933-1937; $95.00
Topaz/Gold Tint Bowl, 1933-1938; $75.00
Wisteria Bowl, 1933-1938; $125.00
Regal Blue Bowl, 1934-1942; $115.00
Burgundy Bowl, 1934-1942; $95.00
Empire Green Bowl, 1934-1942; $95.00
Ruby Bowl, 1934-1942; $115.00
Azure Bowl, 1936; $150.00
Vase, 11½"
Crystal, 1934-1943; $65.00
Regal Blue Bowl, 1934-1939; $125.00
Burgundy Bowl, 1934-1939; $115.00
Empire Green Bowl, 1934-1939; $115.00

Wisteria 5½" Candlestick, 4-part Relish, Low Comport

No. 2470 LINE

See price list for colors

2470—Sugar and Cream Tray
Length 8¾ in.

2470—3 Part Round Relish
Diameter 9¼ in.

2470—Cake Plate, 2 Hdles.
Length 10¼ in.
2470—Lemon Dish, 2 Hdles.
Length 7 in.

2470—Bon Bon, 2 Hdles.
Length 7 in.

2470—Sweetmeat, 2 Hdles.
Length 6 in.

2470—6 in. Low Comport

2470—5½ in. Candlestick

2470—12 in. Bowl

2470—5½ in. Candlestick

2470½
5½ in. Candlestick

2470½—10½ in. Bowl
2470½—7 in. Bowl

2470½
5½ in. Candlestick

2470—8 in. Vase
2470—10 in. Vase
2470—11½ in. Vase

2496 BAROQUE

The name evokes the richly ornamented music of J. S. Bach. A child of the fertile mind of designer George Sakier, Baroque features a fleur-de-lis motif and handles reminiscent of bent bamboo with tastefully ornamented joints. The coffee cup has no fleur-de-lis, making the handle important to identification. A pre-Baroque line (2484) is included with Baroque and featured handles which looked more like outstretched wings. The 2484 10" Handled Bowl, the 2484 7" Vase, the 2484 Duo Candlestick, the 2496 Duo Candlestick, and the 2496 Trindle Candlestick first appeared in 1935 listed with candlesticks, bowls, and vases and not called Baroque.

The Baroque line had its beginning in the summer of 1936 and the complete line was not offered until 1937, the year which marked Fostoria's golden anniversary (1887 – 1937). To honor its fiftieth year, Fostoria chose to rename its rich yellow Topaz; from that year on, it was called Gold Tint.

Baroque in color lasted from 1937 – 1943 with a few pieces dropping out before that date. Baroque pieces in Silver Mist were few and are listed here. A quick scan of the production dates reveals that much of the line was no longer being made in 1944, and only the 2- and 3-light candelabra in the 2484 Line were still available after 1965. Some pieces, such as the flared and 3-cornered nappies, were included for much longer in, for example, the Navarre pattern, but not the beautiful, unetched Baroque crystal.

One controversy about this line concerns the greenish-blue color sometimes called Azure Tint. The authors did find one reference to Azure Tint in a brochure from 1937 indicating that Fostoria may have considered calling the color Azure Tint to match the renamed Topaz. Nowhere else is the term "Azure Tint" used. Fostoria did have difficulty maintaining consistency in the Azure color. The careful collector will notice that some pieces may be found in slightly differing shades of blue. Oftentimes the shadings are more evident between a blown piece and a pressed piece. These differences may be found in Azure Meadow Rose, Azure Lido, Azure June, and so forth.

The condiment set was never shown in any catalogs, although it was clearly indicated in price lists. The preserve is also elusive, but was simply a larger version of the jelly and cover. The 2484 vase and the 2496 vase appear similar until one places them side by side so that both shape and size differences become apparent. The similarity between the 3- and 4- part relishes and the floating garden is noteworthy since they differ only in the dividers. The trindle candle is a most interesting piece because it was made in six colors not normally associated with Baroque and in Silver Mist. It has been seen in Ebony but was not listed that way.

Stemware was included in this line, and the reader is invited to refer to *Fostoria Stemware*, page 47, for sizes and production dates.

Trindle Candlesticks: Crystal, Amber, Azure, Burgundy, Empire Green, Regal Blue, Ruby, Gold Tint, Silver Mist. (The Azure, Burgundy, Regal Blue, and Silver Mist are from the Collection of J. R. Johnston.)

Ash Tray, Oblong
    Crystal, 1936-1943; $12.00
    Azure, 1936-1943; $16.00
    Gold Tint, 1937-1943; $16.00
Bon Bon, 3-toed
    Crystal, 1937-1965; $26.00
    Azure, 1937-1943, $35.00
    Gold Tint, 1937-1940; $38.00
Bowl, 3-toed Nut
    Crystal, 1937-1943; $25.00
    Azure, 1937-1943; $38.00
    Gold Tint, 1937-1943; $38.00
Bowl, Rose 3½"
    Crystal, 1937-1943; $35.00
    Azure, 1937-1939; $52.00
    Gold Tint, 1937-1943; $48.00
Bowl, 5" Fruit
    Crystal, 1937-1944; $18.00
    Azure, 1937-1943; $22.00
    Gold Tint, 1937-1943; $22.00
Bowl, 7" Cupped
    Crystal, 1936-1943; $45.00
    Azure, 1936-1938; $75.00
    Gold Tint, 1937-1943; $67.00
2484 Bowl, 10" Handled
    Crystal, 1935-1948; $67.00
    Amber, 1935-1938; $125.00
    Azure, 1936-1940; $125.00
    Topaz/Gold Tint, 1935-1939; $125.00
    Green, 1935-1938; $125.00
    Silver Mist, 1935-1940; $110.00
Bowl, 10½" Salad
    Crystal, 1936-1965; $49.00
    Azure, 1936-1942; $65.00
    Gold Tint, 1937-1943; $65.00
Bowl, 10½" Handled
    Crystal, 1936-1958; $58.00
    Azure, 1936-1943, $115.00
    Gold Tint, 1937-1940; $115.00
Bowl, 11" Rolled Edge
    Crystal, 1936-1965; $48.00
    Azure, 1936-1940; $74.00
    Gold Tint, 1937-1939; $78.00
Bowl, 12" Flared
    Crystal, 1936-1965; $45.00
    Azure, 1936-1941; $65.00
    Gold Tint, 1937-1943; $58.00
Bowl, Footed Punch, 1½ gallon
    Crystal, 1936-1943; $395.00
    Azure, 1936-1938; $1200.00
Cake, 10" Handled
    Crystal, 1936-1965; $38.00
    Azure, 1936-1943; $67.00
    Gold Tint, 1937-1942; $70.00
Candlestick, 4" (pair)
    Crystal, 1936-1965; $38.00

Azure 7" Vase (Courtesy of J.R. Johnston); Gold Tint 8" Vase

    Azure, 1936-1943; $65.00
    Gold Tint, 1937-1942; $65.00
Candlestick, 5½" (pair)
    Crystal, 1936-1958; $60.00
    Azure, 1936-1943; $85.00
    Gold Tint, 1937-1943; $80.00
Candlestick, Duo (priced each)
    Crystal, 1935-1965; $28.00
    Azure, 1936-1943; $52.00
    Gold Tint, 1937-1943; $50.00
    Silver Mist, 1935-1938; $28.00
Candlestick, Trindle (priced each)
    Crystal, 1936-1958; $35.00
    Amber, 1936-1938; $82.00
    Azure, 1936-1940; $85.00
    Burgundy, 1935-1938; $110.00
    Empire Green, 1935-1938; $110.00
    Green, 1936-1938; $85.00
    Regal Blue, 1935-1937; $125.00
    Ruby, 1936-1937; $125.00
    Topaz/Gold Tint, 1936-1940; $75.00
    Silver Mist, 1935-1938; $35.00
2484 Candlestick, 7¾", UDP Lustre
    Crystal, 1936-1978; $55.00
    Azure, 1936-1940; $120.00
    Gold Tint, 1937-1942; $110.00
2484 Candlestick, 2-light, Candle Drips
    Silver Mist, 1935-1938; $55.00
2484 Candelabra, 2-light, UDP
    Crystal, 1935-1978; $65.00
    Azure, 1936-1943; $150.00
    Topaz/Gold Tint, 1935-1943; $135.00

2484 Candelabra, 3-light, UDP
  Crystal, 1936-1982; $85.00
  Azure, 1936-1943; $175.00
Candy, 3 part and Cover
  Crystal, 1937-1962; $65.00
  Azure, 1937-1942; $95.00
  Gold Tint, 1937-1943; $90.00
Celery, 11"
  Crystal, 1936-1958; $27.50
  Azure, 1936-1942; $48.00
  Gold Tint, 1937-1939; $48.00
Cigarette Box and Cover
  Crystal, 1936-1943; $85.00
  Azure, 1936-1943; $145.00
  Gold Tint, 1937-1939; $145.00
Cheese and Cracker
  Crystal, 1937-1958; $52.00
  Azure, 1937-1940; $75.00
  Gold Tint, 1937-1939; $75.00
Comport, 5½"
  Crystal, 1936-1958; $30.00
  Azure, 1936-1943; $57.00
  Gold Tint, 1937-1943; $55.00
Comport, 6½" Tall
  Crystal, 1937-1943; $60.00
  Azure, 1937-1938; $80.00
  Gold Tint, 1937-1938; $75.00
Condiment Set, 4-piece: Regular Shakers, Mustard, Tray
  Crystal, 1937-1943; $195.00
  Azure, 1937-1943; $350.00
  Gold Tint, 1937-1943; $325.00
Cream Soup and Plate
  Crystal, 1937-1943; $64.00
  Azure, 1937-1939; $125.00
  Gold Tint, 1937-1942; $95.00
Cup and Saucer
  Crystal, 1936-1965; $22.00
  Azure, 1936-1943; $34.00
  Gold Tint, 1937-1943; $32.00
Cup, Punch
  Crystal, 1936-1943; $20.00
  Azure, 1936-1938; $32.00
Floating Garden, 10"
  Crystal, 1936-1943, $75.00
  Azure, 1936-1942; $95.00
Ice Bucket and Tongs, Chrome Handle
  Crystal, 1936-1958; $62.00
  Azure, 1936-1938; $125.00
  Gold Tint, 1937-1943; $97.00
Jelly
  Crystal, 1936-1943; $35.00
  Azure, 1936-1943; $75.00
  Gold Tint, 1937-1939; $85.00
Jelly and Cover
  Crystal, 1936-1958; $75.00
  Azure, 1936-1943; $125.00

Gold Tint Preserve and Cover (Courtesy of J. R. Johnston), Azure Sweetmeat, Azure Jelly and Cover

  Gold Tint, 1937-1939; $150.00
Jug, 3-Pint
  Crystal, 1936-1943; $195.00
  Azure, 1937; $1,200.00
  Gold Tint, 1937; $900.00
Jug, 3-Pint Ice
  Crystal, 1937-1943; $225.00
  Azure, 1937-1942; $695.00
  Gold Tint, 1937-1938; $800.00
Mayonnaise, 6½", 2-part
  Crystal, 1936-1943; $42.00
  Azure, 1936-1943; $55.00
  Gold Tint, 1937-1942; $55.00
2496½ Mayonnaise, Plate, Crystal Ladle
  Crystal, 1937-1958; $65.00
  Azure, 1937-1940; $135.00
  Gold Tint, 1937-1943; $125.00
Mint, Handled
  Crystal, 1936-1943; $17.00
  Azure, 1936-1939; $28.00
  Gold Tint, 1937-1938; $30.00
Mustard, Cover, Spoon
  Crystal, 1937-1944; $68.00
  Azure, 1937-1938, $95.00
  Gold Tint, 1937-1943; $85.00
Oil, 3½ ounces
  Crystal, 1937-1958; $95.00
  Azure, 1938-1938; $575.00
  Gold Tint, 1937-1943; $350.00
Nappy, Handled Regular
  Crystal, 1937-1944; $16.00
  Azure, 1937-1943; $24.00
  Gold Tint, 1937-1941; $24.00
Nappy, Handled Flared
  Crystal, 1937-1965; $15.00

Azure, 1937-1943; $24.00
Gold Tint, 1937-1941; $24.00
Nappy, Handled 3-Cornered
   Crystal, 1937-1965; $15.00
   Azure, 1937-1943; $24.00
   Gold Tint, 1937-1941; $24.00
Nappy, Handled Square
   Crystal, 1937-1944; $16.00
   Azure, 1937-1943; $24.00
   Gold Tint, 1937-1941; $24.00
Pickle, 8"
   Crystal, 1936-1958; $22.00
   Azure, 1936-1943; $38.00
   Gold Tint, 1937-1942; $38.00
Plate, 6"
   Crystal, 1936-1965; $12.00
   Azure, 1936-1943; $20.00
   Gold Tint, 1937-1943; $20.00
Plate, 7"
   Crystal, 1936-1965; $12.00
   Azure, 1936-1943; $22.00
   Gold Tint, 1937-1943; $22.00
Plate 8"
   Crystal, 1936-1965; $14.00
   Azure, 1936-1943; $25.00
   Gold Tint, 1937-1943; $25.00
Plate, 9"
   Crystal, 1936-1965; $34.00
   Azure, 1936-1943; $60.00
   Gold Tint, 1937-1943; $60.00
Plate, 14" Torte
   Crystal, 1936-1965; $50.00
   Azure, 1936-1943; $85.00
   Gold Tint, 1937-1943; $85.00
Platter, 12" Oval
   Crystal, 1937-1944; $60.00
   Azure, 1937-1942; $125.00
   Gold Tint, 1937-1938; $125.00
Preserve and Cover
   Crystal, 1937-1940; $195.00
   Azure, 1937-1942; $225.00
   Gold Tint, 1937-1942; $225.00
Relish, 2-part
   Crystal, 1936-1965; $24.00
   Azure, 1936-1943; $38.00
   Gold Tint, 1937-1942; $38.00
Relish, 3-part
   Crystal, 1936-1965; $35.00
   Azure, 1936-1943; $65.00
   Gold Tint, 1937-1943; $55.00
Relish, 4-part
   Crystal, 1936-1943; $65.00
   Azure, 1936-1940; $125.00
Salad Set: 10½" Bowl, 14" Torte, Wooden Fork and Spoon
   Crystal, 1936-1945; $110.00
   Azure, 1936-1942; $165.00

Gold Tint, 1937-1943; $165.00
Sauce, 6½" Oblong
   Crystal, 1936-1943; $32.00
   Azure, 1936-1940; $80.00
   Gold Tint, 1937-1942; $75.00
Serving Dish, 8½"
   Crystal, 1936-1963; $25.00
   Azure, 1936-1943; $50.00
   Gold Tint, 1937-1942; $50.00
Shaker, FGT (priced as set)
   Crystal, 1937-1943; $95.00
   Azure, 1937-1942; $200.00
   Gold Tint, 1937-1942; $200.00
Shaker, Individual, FGT
   Crystal, 1937-1942; $90.00
   Azure, 1937-1938; $200.00
   Gold Tint, 1937-1938; $200.00
Smoker Set, Cigarette Box, 4 Ash Trays
   Crystal, 1936-1943; $135.00
   Azure, 1936-1943; $225.00
   Gold Tint, 1937-1939; $225.00
Sugar and Cream, Footed
   Crystal, 1936-1965; $35.00
   Azure, 1936-1943; $85.00
   Gold Tint, 1937-1943; $80.00
Sugar and Cream, Individual
   Crystal, 1936-1965; $35.00
   Azure, 1936-1943; $85.00
   Gold Tint, 1937-1943; $80.00
Sugar, Cream and Tray
   Crystal, 1937-1965; $52.00
   Azure, 1937-1943; $125.00
   Gold Tint, 1937-1940; $135.00
Sweetmeat
   Crystal, 1936-1943; $22.00
   Azure, 1936-1940; $38.00
   Gold Tint, 1937-1938; $40.00
Tid Bit, 3-toed
   Crystal, 1937-1965; $23.00
   Azure, 1937-1943; $38.00
   Gold Tint, 1937-1940; $40.00
Tray, 6½" Sugar and Cream
   Crystal, 1937-1965; $25.00
   Azure, 1937-1943; $40.00
   Gold Tint, 1937-1940; $50.00
Tray, 8" Oblong
   Crystal, 1936-1943; $30.00
   Azure, 1936-1939; $65.00
   Gold Tint, 1937-1943; $60.00
Tray, 11" Oval
   Crystal, 1937-1938; $65.00
   Azure, 1937-1938; $95.00
   Gold Tint, 1937-1938; $95.00
2484 Vase, 7"
   Crystal, 1935-1948; $87.00
   Azure, 1936-1940; $145.00

Gold Tint, 1937-1942; $125.00
Vase, 8"
    Crystal, 1937-1942; $95.00
    Azure, 1937-1939; $165.00
    Gold Tint, 1937-1942; $140.00
Vegetable Dish, 9½"
    Crystal, 1937-1944; $54.00
    Azure, 1937-1940; $95.00
    Gold Tint, 1937-1938; $95.00

Condiment Sets in Azure, Crystal, Gold Tint

2496—6, 7, 8, 9 in. Plate

2496—Footed Cup
2496—Saucer

2496—Footed Sugar
Height 3½ in.

2496—Footed Cream
Height 3¾ in.
Capacity 7½ oz.

2496—Individual Sugar
Height 2⅞ in.

2496—Individual Cream
Height 3⅛ in.
Capacity 4 oz.

2496—8 in. Pickle

2496—11 in. Celery

BAROQUE PATTERN

No. 2496 LINE

See Price List for Colors

2496—Cream Soup
2496—Cream Soup Plate

2496—5 in. Fruit

2496—12 in. Oval Platter

2496—11 in. Oval Tray

2496—9½ in. Vegetable Dish

2496—Ice Jug
Capacity 3 Pint, Height 7 in.

2496—3 Pint Jug
Height 6½ in.

BAROQUE PATTERN

No. 2496 LINE

See Price List for Colors

2496—Ice Bucket
Height 4⅜ in. Top Diameter 6½ in.
Chromium Handle and Tongs
Tongs priced separately

2496—5 Piece Smoker Set
Consisting of:
1/12 Doz. 2496—Cigarette Box and Cover
Length 5½ in. Width 3½ in.
1/3 Doz. 2496—Oblong Ash Tray
Length 3¾ in. Width 2¼ in.

2496—Handled Nappy, Reg.
Diameter 4⅜ in.

2496—Handled Nappy, Fld.
Diameter 5 in.

2496—10 in. Cake Plate, 2 Handles

2496—5½ in. Comport
Height 4¾ in.

2496—Handled Nappy, 3 Cor.
Length 4⅝ in.

2496
8½ in. Serving Dish, 2 Handles

2496—Handled Nappy, Square
4 in. Square

2496—3 Toed Tid Bit, Flat
Diameter 8¼ in.

2496½—
Individual Shaker, F.G.T.
Height 2 in.

2496—Shaker, F.G.T.
Height 2¾ in.

2496—3 Toed Bon Bon
Diameter 7⅜ in.

2496—Jelly and Cover
Height 7½ in. including cover

2496—3 Toed Nut Bowl, Cupped
Diameter 6¼ in.

2496—3½ in. Rose Bowl

2496—8 in. Vase

2496—3 Part Candy Box and Cover
Height 2½ in.—Width 6¼ in.

BAROQUE PATTERN

No. 2496 LINE

See Price List for Colors

2496—6½ in. Oblong Sauce Dish
Width 5¼ in.

2496—8 in. Oblong Tray
Width 7 in.

2496—6½ in. 2 Part Mayonnaise
Width 5¼ in.

2496—Handled Mint
4 in. Square

2496—4 Part Relish
Length 10 in.   Width 7½ in.

2496—3 Part Relish
Length 10 in.   Width 7½ in.

2496—2 Part Relish
6 in. Square

2496—7 in. Bowl, Cupped
Height 4¾ in.

2496—Sweetmeat
6 in. Square

2496—14 in. Torte Plate

2496—3 Piece Salad Set
Consisting of
1/12 Doz. 2496—10½ in. Salad Bowl—Ht. 3¾ in.
1/12 Doz. 2496—14 in. Torte Plate
1/12 Doz. Salad Fork and Spoon—Wood

BAROQUE PATTERN

No. 2496 LINE

See Price List for Colors

2496 Trindle Candlestick
Height 6 in. Spread 8¼ in.

2496—5½ in. Candlestick

2496—Duo Candlestick
Height 4½ in. Spread 8 in

2484—Lustre, 8 U. D. P.
Height 7¾ in.
DESIGN PATENT NO. 94442

2484—3 Light Candelabra, 24 U. D. P.
Using 2482 Bobache
Height 9½ in. Spread 12⅜ in.
DESIGN PATENT NO. 91688

2484—7 in. Vase

2484—2 Light Candelabra, 16 U. D. P.
Using 2484 Bobache
Height 8¼ in. Spread 10 in.
DESIGN PATENT NO. 91686

2496—12 in. Bowl, Flared — Height 3½ in.

2496—11 in. Bowl, Rolled Edge — Height 3⅜ in.

2496—10½ in. Handled Bowl — Height 3⅜ in.

BAROQUE PATTERN

No. 2496 LINE

See Price List for Colors

2496
4 in. Candlestick

2496—10 in. Floating Garden
Width 7½ in.

2496
4 in. Candlestick

2496—3 Piece Sugar and Cream Set
Consisting of:
1/12 Doz. 2496—Individual Sugar
1/12 Doz. 2496—Individual Cream
1/12 Doz. 2496—6½ in. Sugar and Cream Tray

2484—10 in. Handled Bowl
Gr-Am-Crys-Tz

2496—6½ in.
Sugar and Cream Tray
Width 3¾ in.

2496
Cheese and Cracker
Height 3¼ in.
Diameter Plate 11 in.
Diameter Cheese 5¼ in.

2496—5½ in. Comport
Height 4¾ in.
2496—6½ in. Tall Comport
Height 5¾ in.

2496—3½ oz.
Oil and Stopper
Height 5½ in.

2496—Mustard and
Cover and Spoon
Height 3¾ in.

2496—Footed Punch Bowl
Capacity 1½ Gallon
Height 8¼ in.   Top Diameter 13¼ in.
2496—6 oz. Punch Cups

2496½—Mayonnaise
and Plate and Ladle
Height 3½ in.

Celebrate with Fostoria!

here's a Jubilee Surprise FOR YOU!

14-INCH SERVING PLATE IN GOLD-TINT
$1 39*   Reg. Price $2.00

RELISH DISH IN GOLD-TINT
$1 29*   Reg. Price $1.75

FOR ONE MONTH ONLY · · APRIL 15th TO MAY 15th

Fostoria is celebrating its Golden Jubilee! Such an event deserves something very special! So Fostoria offers two of its treasured pieces at radically lower prices: The Baroque Pattern 14-inch Serving Plate and the 3-compartment Relish Dish, as illustrated above.

This extraordinary opportunity is also Fostoria's method of introducing its lovely new color —Gold-Tint.

GOLD-TINT . . . THE COLOR FOR THE GOLDEN JUBILEE

Gold-Tint reflects the exciting sparkle of champagne. It is a subtle color with the mysterious radiance of liquid gold and the brilliancy of a gem. A color so exquisite decorators decree that settings combining *Gold-Tinted* pieces with clearest crystal will be the smartest of table fashions for 1937.

For one month only this greatest value in Fostoria history is on sale at the better stores. There, too, you will see complete Golden Jubilee Displays of America's Finest Glassware.

FREE—JUBILEE GIFT FOR YOU

As a Jubilee gift for you, Fostoria offers "Modern Decorative Tables for All Occasions." Write for Booklet 37-H. Fostoria Glass Company, Moundsville, West Virginia.

FOR 50 YEARS THE GLASS OF FASHION

*Prices slightly higher in the West.

Golden   *Fostoria*   Jubilee
MADE IN U.S.A.
1887   1937

COMPANION PIECES IN THE BAROQUE PATTERN

An entire table service is available in this charmingly traditional pattern. All moderately priced.

You will adore the graceful lines, the golden brilliancy, of this Compote, for yourself or as a much appreciated but inexpensive gift.

Sparkling cubes will high light the golden tint of this quaintly French Ice Bucket. You must see these popular pieces to really appreciate them. Your dealer has a wide selection.

2501 ROSETTE

Crystal Intaglio

The Rosette design when first shown was described as Crystal Intaglio and was listed with etchings, strikingly simple, yet elegant. The design was incised on the bottom or underside of all pieces except the Cigarette Box where it is on the underside of the lid only. Even though the pattern was assigned number 2501 in the January 1936 catalog, in the July 1, 1936 catalog, it was called Rosette design with each piece using the number from the pressed pattern from which it was drawn. Rosette did not have any pieces that belonged exclusively to the line, but borrowed from other lines. The advertising shows a Crescent Relish borrowed from the Hermitage Line, where the same piece was called a Crescent Salad. The Rosette design came back for a time in the 1970s.

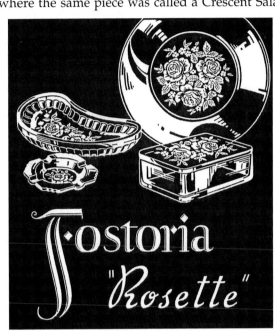

2496 Ash Tray, Oblong, 1936-1943; $16.00
2496 Plate, 7", 1936-1938; $15.00
2496 Plate, 14" Torte, 1936-1943; $65.00
2501 Ash Tray, Individual, 1934-1943; $15.00
2501 Ash Tray, 5" Large, 1934-1939; $20.00
2501 Bowl, 9" Flared, 1934; $35.00
2501 Cigarette Box and Cover, 1934-1943; $68.00
2501 Crescent Relish, 1934; $38.00
2501 Plate, 7", 1934-1943; $15.00
2501 Plate, 8", 1934-1941; $16.00
2501 Plate, Oval Cake, 1934-1943; $52.00
2501 Plate, 13" Torte, 1934-1943; $65.00
2501 Tray, Oval, 1934; $45.00
2510 Ash Tray, Individual, 1936-1939; $15.00
2510 Ash Tray, Square, 1936-1940; $12.00
2510 Tray, Sugar and Cream, 1936-1942; $35.00

2496—7 in. Plate
Etch. Rosette

2510—6½ in. Sugar and Cream Tray
Etch. Rosette
Width 3¾ in.

2496—14 in. Torte Plate
Etch. Rosette

ROSETTE DESIGN
No. 2501 LINE
Made in Crystal Intaglio

2501—Large Ash Tray
Diameter 5 in.

2501—Ind. Ash Tray
Diameter 4 in.

2496—Oblong Ash Tray
Etch. Rosette
Length 3¾ in.   Width 2¼ in.

2501—Oval Cake Plate
Length 10½ in.

2510½—Individual Ash Tray
Etch. Rosette
Diameter 2½ in.

2510—Square Ash Tray
Etch. Rosette
3 in. Square

2501—7, 8 in. Plate

2501
Cigarette Box and Cover
Length 4¾ in., Width 3½ in.

2501—13 in. Torte Plate

2510 SUNRAY/GLACIER

GOLDEN GLOW

Decoration 513

For a formal table with a tailored look, the savvy hostess chose the Sunray pattern with its ribbed and ridged edges and handles. Often shown with 6017 Sceptre stemware and the Quadrangle candles, Sunray was a very large and complete dinner service in its own right, complete with stemware and candelabra. Most of the pieces in the Sunray pattern were offered as Glacier, which had Silver Mist ribs. A few pieces were offered with Amber stained ribs and were called Golden Glow. Stemware is featured in *Fostoria Stemware*, page 47.

Almond, Individual, Footed
    Sunray, 1935-1943; $24.00
Ash Tray, Individual
    Sunray, 1936-1942; $20.00
    Glacier, 1936-1942; $22.00
Ash Tray, Square
    Sunray, 1936-1943; $16.00
    Glacier, 1936-1943; $18.00
    Golden Glow, 1935-1937; $22.00
Bon Bon, Handled
    Sunray, 1935-1943; $20.00
    Ruby, 1936-1940; $45.00
Bon Bon, 3-toed
    Sunray, 1935-1943; $28.00
    Ruby, 1935-1936; $54.00
Bowl, Frozen Dessert
    Sunray, 1935-1940; $18.00
    Glacier, 1935-1938; $20.00
    Azure, 1936-1938; $28.00
    Green, 1936-1938; $28.00
    Amber, 1936-1938; $28.00
    Topaz/Gold Tint, 1936-1938; $28.00
Bowl, 5" Fruit
    Sunray, 1935-1943; $20.00
    Glacier, 1935-1943; $22.00
Bowl, Handled Nappy, Regular
    Sunray, 1935-1943; $16.00
    Ruby, 1935-1940; $45.00
    Glacier, 1935-1943; $22.00
    Golden Glow, 1935-1937; $28.00
Bowl, Handled Nappy, Flared
    Sunray, 1935-1943; $16.00
    Ruby, 1935-1940; $45.00
    Glacier, 1935-1943; $22.00
    Golden Glow, 1935-1937; $28.00
Bowl, Handled Nappy, Square
    Sunray, 1935-1943; $16.00
    Ruby, 1935-1939; $45.00
    Glacier, 1935-1943; $22.00
    Golden Glow, 1935-1937; $28.00
Bowl, Handled Nappy, 3 Corner
    Sunray, 1935-1943; $16.00
    Ruby, 1935-1939; $45.00
    Glacier, 1935-1943; $22.00
    Golden Glow, 1935-1937; $28.00
Bowl, 9½" Nappy, Flared
    Sunray, 1935-1943; $27.00

Bowl, 10" Handled
    Sunray, 1935-1943; $38.00
    Glacier, 1935-1938; $42.00
Bowl, 13" Rolled Edge
    Sunray, 1935-1938; $45.00
    Glacier, 1935-1941; $45.00
Bowl, 12" Salad
    Sunray, 1935-1938; $45.00
Candlestick, 3" (priced each)
    Sunray, 1936-1943; $24.00
    Glacier, 1937-1943; $28.00
Candlestick, 5½" (priced each)
    Sunray, 1936-1943; $32.00
    Glacier, 1936-1943; $38.00
Candlestick, Duo (priced each)
    Sunray, 1935-1943; $67.00
    Glacier, 1935-1943; $70.00
Candelabra, 2-light, UDP (priced each)
    Sunray, 1935-1942; $95.00
    Glacier, 1935-1938; $110.00
Candy and Cover
    Sunray, 1935-1940; $65.00
    Glacier, 1935-1938; $75.00
    Golden Glow, 1935-1937; $85.00
Celery, 10" Handled
    Sunray, 1935-1943; $38.00
    Glacier, 1935-1943; $42.00
    Golden Glow, 1935-1937; $48.00

Golden Glow Jelly and Cover, Rose Bowl, 2-part Relish; Ruby Sunray Oval Tray, Pickle, Divided Sweetmeat

Cigarette and Cover
    Sunray, 1935-1943; $68.00
    Glacier, 1935-1943; $75.00
    Golden Glow, 1935-1937; $85.00
Cigarette Box, Oblong
    Sunray, 1936-1942; $75.00
    Glacier, 1937-1943; $82.00
Cheese and Cover, or Butter and Cover
    Sunray, 1936-1938; $48.00
    Glacier, 1937-1938; $50.00
Coaster, 4"
    Sunray, 1935-1943; $10.00
Comport
    Sunray, 1935-1940; $36.00
    Glacier, 1935-1938; $40.00
    Golden Glow, 1935-1937; $45.00
Condiment Tray, 8½"
    Sunray, 1936-1943; $65.00
    Glacier, 1935-1938; $70.00
Condiment Set, 5-piece
    Sunray, 1936-1942; $245.00
    Glacier, 1936-1938; $265.00
Cream Soup and Plate
    Sunray, 1935-1943; $58.00
    Glacier, 1935-1943; $62.00
Cup and Saucer
    Sunray, 1935-1943; $16.00
    Glacier, 1935-1943; $18.00
Decanter, Oblong
    Sunray, 1936-1943; $125.00
    Glacier, 1937-1938; $135.00
Decanter, Oval, 18 oz.
    Sunray, 1935-1937; $150.00
Decanter Set, 8-piece
    Sunray, 1936-1943; $265.00
Decanter Set, Oval Decanter, six 2-oz. Whiskeys, Oblong Tray
    Sunray, 1935-1937; $300.00
Ice Bucket, Chrome Handle and Tongs
    Sunray, 1935-1939; $65.00

Cigarette and Cover   Divided Sweetmeat. Hld.   Ice Bucket   Tumbler

Ruby, 1935-1936; $150.00
    Glacier, 1935-1939; $68.00
Ice Bucket, Silver Plate Handle and Tongs
    Sunray, 1940-1943; $75.00
    Glacier, 1940-1943; $80.00
Jelly and Cover
    Sunray, 1935-1939; $58.00
    Glacier, 1935-1938; $64.00
Jug, 2-Quart
    Sunray, 1935-1942; $85.00
    Glacier, 1935-1942; $90.00
Jug, Ice, 1935-1943
    Sunray, 1935-1942; $85.00
Mayonnaise, Plate and Ladle
    Sunray, 1935-1943; $58.00
    Glacier, 1935-1938; $65.00
    Golden Glow, 1935-1937; $75.00
Mustard, Cover and Spoon
    Sunray, 1936-1943; $42.00
    Glacier, 1936-1938; $48.00
Oil and Stopper, 3 oz.
    Sunray, 1935-1943; $56.00
    Glacier, 1935-1943; $60.00
Onion Soup and Cover
    Sunray, 1935-1943; $58.00
    Glacier, 1935-1938; $62.00
Pitcher, Pint, Cereal
    Sunray, 1936-1939; $36.00
Plate, 6"
    Sunray, 1935-1943; $8.00
    Glacier, 1936-1943; $10.00
Plate, 7"
    Sunray, 1935-1943; $10.00
    Glacier, 1936-1943; $12.00
Plate, 8"
    Sunray, 1935-1943; $10.00
    Glacier, 1936-1943; $12.00
Plate, 9"
    Sunray, 1935-1943; $18.00
    Glacier, 1936-1943; $22.00
Plate, 11" Torte
    Sunray, 1935-1940; $38.00
    Ruby, 1935-1940; $95.00
    Glacier, 1935-1938; $42.00
    Golden Glow, 1935-1937; $45.00
Plate, 12" Sandwich
    Sunray, 1935-1943; $34.00
    Ruby, 1935-1940; $95.00
    Glacier, 1935-1943; $38.00
    Golden Glow, 1935-1937; $44.00
Plate, 15" Torte
    Sunray, 1935-1943; $44.00
    Ruby, 1935-1939; $115.00
    Glacier, 1935-1943; $50.00
    Golden Glow, 1935-1937; $55.00

Plate, 16" Flat
  Sunray, 1935-1943; $45.00
  Ruby, 1935-1940; $115.00
  Glacier, 1935-1943; $50.00
  Golden Glow, 1935-1937; $55.00
Relish, 2-part
  Sunray, 1935-1943; $28.00
  Ruby, 1935-1936; $55.00
  Glacier, 1935-1943; $30.00
  Golden Glow, 1935-1937; $35.00
Relish, 3-part
  Sunray, 1935-1943; $30.00
  Ruby, 1935-1940; $65.00
  Glacier, 1935-1943; $32.00
  Golden Glow, 1935-1937; $45.00
Relish, 4-part
  Sunray, 1935-1943; $38.00
  Ruby, 1935-1936; $75.00
  Glacier, 1935-1943; $40.00
  Golden Glow, 1935-1937; $55.00
Salad Set, 3-piece
  Sunray, 1935-1938; $85.00
  Glacier, 1935-1938; $95.00
Salt Dip
  Sunray, 1936-1943; $22.00
  Glacier, 1936-1943; $24.00
Shaker, FGT (priced each)
  Sunray, 1935-1943; $26.00
  Glacier, 1935-1943; $30.00
Shaker, Individual, FGT (priced each)
  Sunray, 1935-1943; $22.00
  Glacier, 1936-1938; $25.00
Smoker Set, 5-piece, Cigarette and Cover, 4 Individual
  Ash Trays
  Sunray, 1936-1943; $150.00
  Glacier, 1936-1938; $165.00
Smoker Set, 5-piece, Cigarette and Cover, 4 Square Ash
  Trays
  Sunray, 1936-1943; $135.00
  Glacier, 1936-1938; $150.00

Smoker Set, No. 3: 2 Individual Ash Trays, Cigarette
  and Cover on Sugar and Cream Tray
  Sunray, 1936-1943; $125.00
  Glacier, 1936-1938; $135.00
Sugar and Cream, Footed
  Sunray, 1935-1943; $34.00
  Glacier, 1935-1943; $37.00
Sugar and Cream, Individual
  Sunray, 1935-1943; $34.00
  Glacier, 1935-1943; $37.00
Sugar and Cream Tray
  Sunray, 1936-1943; $22.00
  Glacier, 1936-1943; $25.00
Sugar and Cream Set
  Sunray, 1936-1943; $57.00
  Glacier, 1936-1943; $60.00
Sweetmeat, Divided
  Sunray, 1935-1943; $28.00
  Glacier, 1935-1938; $30.00
  Golden Glow, 1935-1937; $34.00
Tray, 7" Oval Handled
  Sunray, 1935-1943; $26.00
  Glacier, 1935-1938; $28.00
  Golden Glow, 1935-1937; $32.00
Tray, 8½" Condiment
  Sunray, 1936-1942; $65.00
  Glacier, 1936-1938; $70.00
Tray, 10" Square
  Sunray, 1936-1943; $60.00
  Glacier, 1936-1938; $64.00
Tray, 10½" Oblong
  Sunray, 1936-1943; $55.00
  Glacier, 1936-1938; $60.00
Vase, 3½" Rose Bowl
  Sunray, 1935-1942; $35.00
  Glacier, 1935-1940; $40.00
  Golden Glow, 1935-1937; $55.00
Vase, 5" Rose Bowl
  Sunray, 1936-1942; $40.00
  Glacier, 1936-1938; $45.00
Vase, 6" Crimped
  Sunray, 1936-1943;
  $58.00
  Glacier, 1936-1938;
  $65.00

2510—Ice Jug
Capacity 2 Quarts   Height 7½ in.

2510½
2-oz. Whiskey
Height 2¼ in.

2510—Coaster
Diameter 4 in.

2510—2 Quart Jug
Height 8½ in.

101

SUNRAY PATTERN

No. 2510 LINE
See price list for colors

2510
Shaker F. G. T.
Height 4 in.

2510½
Ind. Shaker F. G. T.
Height 2¼ in.

2510
Salt Dip

2510—5-in. Fruit

2510—Frozen Dessert
Height 2¼ in.

2510—Cup   2510—Saucer

2510—Onion Soup and Cover
Height 4 in.
Suitable for Candy Jar and Cover

2510—6, 7, 8 and 9 in. Plate

2510—Cream Soup
2510—Cream Soup Plate

2510—Individual Cream
Height 3⅜ in.
Capacity 4½ oz.

2510—3 Piece Sugar and Cream Set
Consisting of
1/12 Doz. 2510—Individual Sugar
1/12 Doz. 2510—Individual Cream
1/12 Doz. 2510—6½ in. Sugar and Cream Tray

2510—Footed Cream
Height 4 in.
Capacity 8 oz.

2510—Individual Sugar
Height 2¾ in.

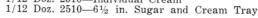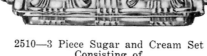

2510—6 in. Pickle   Width 4¼ in.

2510—Footed Sugar
Height 3¾ in.

2510—6½ in. Sugar and Cream Tray
Width 3¾ in.

2510—10 in. Celery

SUNRAY PATTERN
No. 2510 LINE — See price list for colors

2510—Pint Cereal Pitcher
Height 5 in.

2510—Mustard and
Cover and Spoon
Height 3¾ in.

2510
3 oz. Oil and Stopper
Height 4¾ in.

2510—11 in. Torte Plate
2510—15 in. Torte Plate

2510—Mayonnaise
2510—Mayonnaise Plate
2510—Ladle
Height 3 in.

2510—12 in. Sandwich Plate
2510—16 in. Flat Plate

2510—9½ in. Nappy, Fld.
Height 2⅞ in.

2510—2 Part Relish
Length 10 in.

2510—4 Part Relish
Diameter 8 in.

2510—3 Part Relish
Diameter 6½ in.

SUNRAY PATTERN

No. 2510 LINE

See price list for colors

2510—Handled Nappy, Reg.
Diameter 5 in.

2510—Handled Nappy, Fld.
Diameter 6 in.

2510—Handled Nappy, Square
5 in. Square

2510—Handled Nappy, 3 Cor.
Length 5 in.

2510—3 Toed Bon Bon
Diameter 7 in.

2510—6½ in. Bon Bon
Width 5 in.

2510—7 in. Oval Tray
Width 5 in.

2510—6 in. Divided Sweetmeat
Width 4 in.

2510—Jelly and Cover
Height 7¼ in.

2510—5 in. Comport
Height 4 in.

2510
Footed Individual
Almond

2510—3 Piece Salad Set
Consisting of
1/12 Doz. 2510—12 in. Salad Bowl
1/12 Doz. 2510—16 in. Flat Plate
1/12 Doz. Salad Fork and Spoon—Wood
Height 4¼ in.

2510—Ice Bucket
Height 4¼ in. Top Diameter 6⅛ in.
Chromium Handle and Tongs
Tongs Priced Separately

SUNRAY PATTERN

No. 2510 LINE
See price list for colors

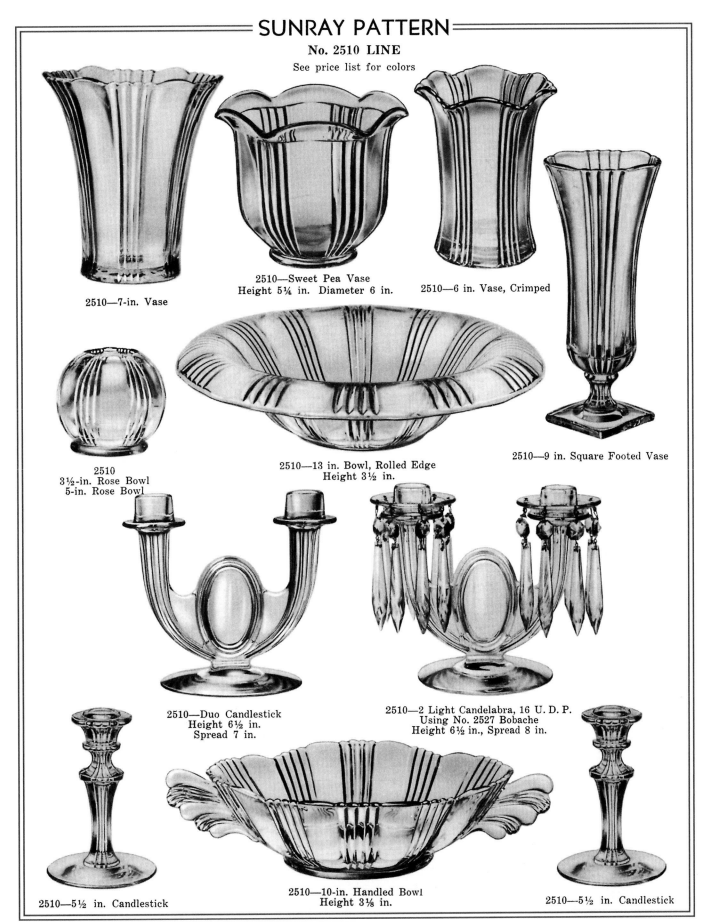

2510—7-in. Vase

2510—Sweet Pea Vase
Height 5¼ in. Diameter 6 in.

2510—6 in. Vase, Crimped

2510
3½-in. Rose Bowl
5-in. Rose Bowl

2510—13 in. Bowl, Rolled Edge
Height 3½ in.

2510—9 in. Square Footed Vase

2510—Duo Candlestick
Height 6½ in.
Spread 7 in.

2510—2 Light Candelabra, 16 U. D. P.
Using No. 2527 Bobache
Height 6½ in., Spread 8 in.

2510—5½ in. Candlestick

2510—10-in. Handled Bowl
Height 3⅛ in.

2510—5½ in. Candlestick

SUNRAY PATTERN

No. 2510 LINE
See price list for colors

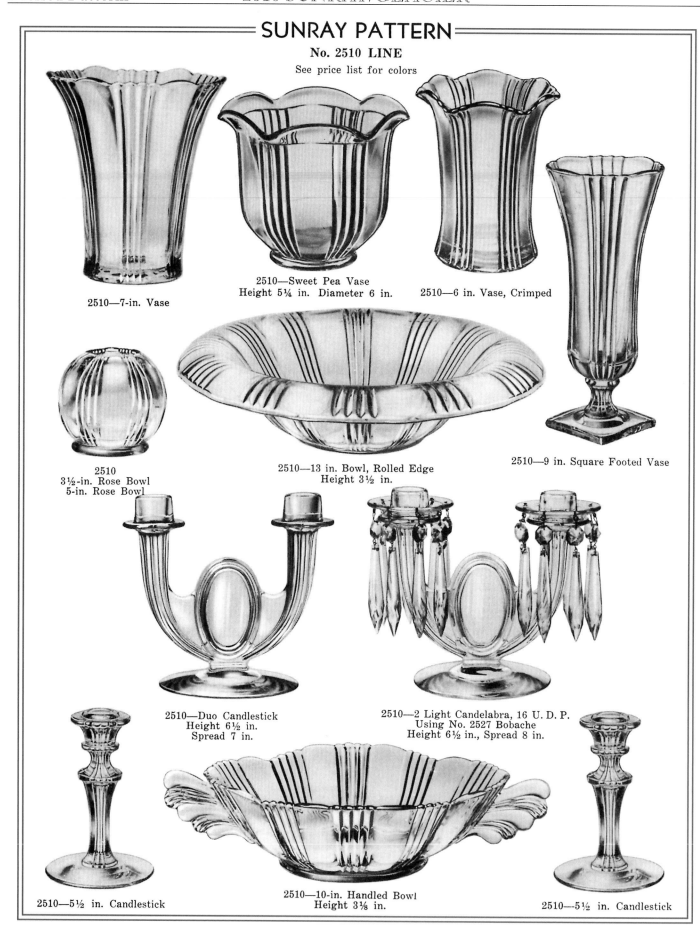

2510—7-in. Vase

2510—Sweet Pea Vase
Height 5¼ in. Diameter 6 in.

2510—6 in. Vase, Crimped

2510
3½-in. Rose Bowl
5-in. Rose Bowl

2510—13 in. Bowl, Rolled Edge
Height 3½ in.

2510—9 in. Square Footed Vase

2510—Duo Candlestick
Height 6½ in.
Spread 7 in.

2510—2 Light Candelabra, 16 U. D. P.
Using No. 2527 Bobache
Height 6½ in., Spread 8 in.

2510—5½ in. Candlestick

2510—10-in. Handled Bowl
Height 3⅛ in.

2510—5½ in. Candlestick

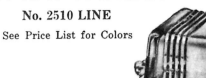

SUN RAY PATTERN

No. 2510 LINE

See Price List for Colors

2510½—Oblong Cigarette Box
and Cover
Length 4¾ in. Width 3⅜ in.

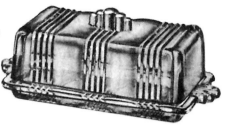

2510—Cheese and Cover
or Butter and Cover
Length 6 in.
Width 3⅜ in.

2510
3 in. Candlestick

2510—8½ in. Condiment Tray

2510—5-Piece Condiment Set
Consisting of:
1/6   Doz. 2510—3 oz. Oil, D/S
1/6   Doz. 2510—Mustard and Cover and Spoon
1/12 Doz. 2510—8½ in. Condiment Tray

2510½—8-Piece Decanter Set
Consisting of:
1/12 Doz. 2510½—Oblong Decanter and Stopper
1/2   Doz. 2510½—2 oz. Whiskey
1/12 Doz. 2510   —10½ in. Oblong Tray

2510½—Oblong Decanter and Stopper
Capacity 26 oz.
Height 9⅛ in.

2513 GRAPE LEAF

Pieces were made later in milk glass.

Almond, Individual
  Crystal, 1935-1943; $8.00
  Regal Blue, 1935-1942; $22.00
  Burgundy, 1935-1942; $22.00
  Empire Green, 1935-1942; $22.00
Candy Jar and Cover
  Crystal, 1935-1938; $40.00
Mayonnaise, Plate, Ladle
  Crystal, 1935-1940; $40.00
Mint, Handled
  Crystal, 1935-1940; $12.00
Plate, 7"
  Crystal, 1935-1940; $20.00
Preserve, 5"
  Crystal, 1935-1939; $22.00
Relish, 2-part
  Crystal, 1935-1939; $22.00
Relish, 3-part
  Crystal, 1935-1940; $24.00

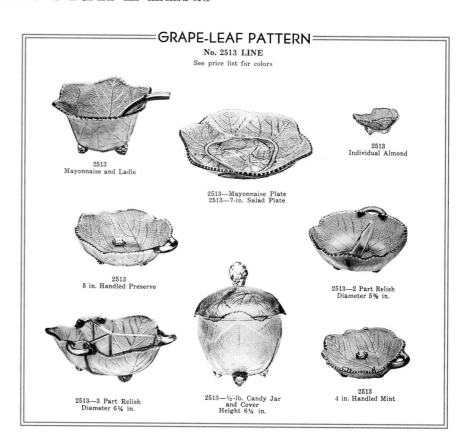

2545 FLAME

Flame followed Baroque in production, and the two designs blend together well. In the etched and cut dinnerware patterns, Fostoria often used pieces from both Baroque and Flame, especially the 12½" Bowl and Baroque candlesticks. That bowl and the 2" Candlestick were the only pieces made after 1943.

Unique to the Flame design is the ball of glass with its crown of spikes. On the Handled Lunch Tray, the ball is suspended above the spikes (or flames), a truly remarkable piece.

Bobaches for the Duo Candelabra seem to be the most difficult items to find. Notice that they used the "B" prism rather than the U-Drop prism, although nowadays all prisms are scarce. The Flame Candle Lamp, like all other Fostoria candle lamps, is seldom seen because the fragile little shade was so easily broken. Like earlier candle lamps, it has three parts: the base, the candle holder, and the shade.

Bowl, 12½" Oval
  Crystal, 1936-1958; $38.00
  Azure, 1936-1940; $52.00
  Gold Tint,1937-1940; $50.00
Candelabra, 2-light (priced each)
  Crystal, 1936-1942; $135.00
  Azure, 1936-1939; $175.00
  Gold Tint, 1937-1940; $175.00
Candle Lamp
  Crystal, 1938-1944; $47.00
Candlestick, 2"
  Crystal, 1937-1958; $12.00
  Azure, 1937-1940; $22.00
  Gold Tint, 1937-1938; $22.00

Gold Tint Duo Candelabra, 8" Lustres

Candlestick, 4½"
    Crystal, 1937-1958; $20.00
    Azure, 1937-1939; $32.00
    Gold Tint, 1937-1943; $30.00
Candlestick, Duo
    Crystal, 1936-1958; $57.00
    Azure, 1936-1939; $65.00
    Gold Tint, 1937-1943; $60.00
Candlestick, Lustre
    Crystal, 1936-1942; $67.50
    Azure, 1937-1942; $80.00
    Gold Tint, 1937-1942; $75.00
Candy Box and Cover
    Crystal, 1937-1938; $36.00
    Azure, 1937-1938; $64.00
    Gold Tint, 1937-1938; $64.00
Sauce Boat and Plate
    Crystal, 1938-1943; $32.00
    Azure, 1937-1938; $60.00
    Gold Tint, 1937-1943; $55.00
Tray, 12" Handled Lunch
    Crystal, 1937-1943; $35.00
    Azure, 1937-1938; $65.00
    Gold Tint, 1937-1938; $65.00
Vase, 10"
    Crystal, 1937-1943; $65.00
    Azure, 1937-1938; $95.00
    Gold Tint, 1937-1938;
    $95.00

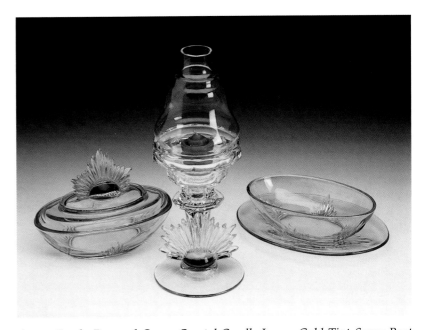

Azure Candy Box and Cover, Crystal Candle Lamp, Gold Tint Sauce Boat and Plate

2545—2 in. "Flame" Candlestick

2545—4½ in. "Flame" Candlestick

Azure 10" Vase

2545—Oval Candy Box and Cover
Capacity ½ lb. Height 4¾ in.
Length 6½ in.

2545—Sauce Boat
2545—Sauce Boat Plate

2545—12 in. Handled Lunch Tray

109

2550 SPOOL

This massive, yet elegant line was introduced to the world during the golden jubilee of the Fostoria Glass Company and was relatively short-lived. Aptly named, the spools, or flutes, may be found either as horizontal or vertical depending on the piece. Although made in Azure for about the same time as Crystal and Gold Tint, the latter colors seem more abundant with the Azure seldom seen. Spool was intended to enhance other lines and was seldom used alone. Vases, Centerpieces, and Candlesticks were most often seen. The Crystal Decanter shown is exceptionally clear crystal, as are all the pieces in this pattern, and would bring pride to anyone displaying it.

Ash Tray, 3¼" Round
　　Crystal, 1937-1943; $8.00
　　Azure, 1937-1942; $10.00
　　Gold Tint, 1937-1940; $10.00
2550½ Ash Tray, Individual
　　Crystal, 1937-1943; $6.00
　　Azure, 1937-1943; $8.00
　　Gold Tint,1937-1943; $8.00
2550½ Ash Tray, 4½"
　　Crystal, 1938-1943; $8.00
2550½ Ash Tray, 5½"
　　Crystal, 1937-1943; $10.00
　　Azure, 1937-1943; $15.00
　　Gold Tint, 1937-1943; $15.00
2550½ Ash Tray Set, 3-piece, Assorted Colors or
　　Crystal, 1938-1943; $24.00
Bowl, 8" Straight
　　Crystal, 1937-1943; $21.00
　　Azure, 1937-1942; $34.00
　　Gold Tint, 1937-1942; $30.00
Bowl, 9½" Flared
　　Crystal, 1937-1943; $28.00
　　Azure, 1937-1942; $38.00
　　Gold Tint, 1937-1940; $34.00
Bowl, 10½" Centerpiece
　　Crystal, 1937-1943; $36.00
　　Azure, 1937-1938; $52.00
　　Gold Tint,1937-1938; $48.00
Bowl, 11" Oval
　　Crystal, 1937-1943; $32.00
　　Azure, 1937-1940; $50.00
　　Gold Tint, 1937-1942; $47.00
Candlestick, 3"
　　Crystal, 1937-1943; $12.00
　　Azure, 1937-1938; $22.00
　　Gold Tint, 1937-1942; $20.00
2550½ Candlestick, 3"
　　Crystal, 1938-1943; $10.00
　　Azure, 1938-1941; $24.00
　　Gold Tint, 1938; $28.00
2550½ Candle Lamp, 3-piece
　　Crystal, 1939-1943; $37.00
Cigarette and Cover
　　Crystal, 1937-1943; $42.00
　　Azure, 1937-1940; $68.00
　　Gold Tint, 1937-1940; $69.00
2550½ Cigarette Box, Oblong, and Cover
　　Crystal, 1937-1943; $44.00
　　Azure, 1937-1939; $70.00

Cigarette Box, Decanter, Cigarette Set, Individual Ash Tray

　　Gold Tint, 1937-1939; $68.00
Coaster, 3⅛"
　　Crystal, 1937-1940; $6.00
　　Azure, 1937-1940; $12.00
　　Gold Tint, 1937-1940; $12.00
Comport, 6" Low
　　Crystal, 1937-1943; $24.00
　　Azure, 1937-1939; $38.00
　　Gold Tint, 1937-1943; $33.00
Decanter and Stopper
　　Crystal, 1937-1938; $110.00
　　Azure, 1937-1938; $175.00
　　Gold Tint, 1937-1938; $175.00
Decanter Set, 7-piece (includes 2518 Tumbler)
　　Crystal, 1937-1938; $175.00
　　Azure, 1937-1938; $225.00
　　Gold Tint, 1937-1938; $200.00
Mayonnaise, Plate, Ladle
　　Crystal, 1938-1943; $45.00
Nappy, 6½"
　　Crystal, 1937-1943; $22.00
　　Azure, 1937-1943; $28.00
　　Gold Tint, 1937-1942; $28.00
Plate, 13"
　　Crystal, 1937-1939; $32.00
　　Azure, 1937-1939; $46.00
　　Gold TInt, 1937-1938; $45.00

Plate, 14" Buffet
    Crystal, 1937-1943; $35.00
    Azure, 1937-1938; $50.00
    Gold Tint, 1937-1940; $47.00
Sweetmeat
    Crystal, 1938-1943; $18.00

Azure Flared Vase, Crystal Flared Vase, Gold Tint 6½" Straight Vase

Spool Candle Lamp

2518 Tumbler, Whiskey Sham
    Crystal, 1937-1942; $10.00
    Azure, 1937-1942; $16.00
    Gold Tint, 1937-1942; $14.00
Vase, 5½" Straight
    Crystal, 1937-1943; $50.00
    Azure, 1937-1940; $75.00
    Gold Tint, 1937-1940; $65.00
Vase, 5½" Flared
    Crystal, 1937-1943; $50.00
    Azure, 1937-1943; $75.00
    Gold Tint,1937-1940; $75.00
Vase, 6" Straight
    Crystal, 1937-1940; $55.00
    Azure, 1937-1939; $85.00
    Gold Tint, 1937-1940; $75.00

Vase, 6" Flared
    Crystal, 1937-1939;
    $50.00
    Azure, 1937-1939;
    $85.00
    Gold Tint, 1937-1939;
    $80.00

2550½—Individual Ash Tray
Diameter 3⅛ in.

2550—Mayonnaise and Plate and Ladle
Mayo Height 2¾ in.
Mayo Diameter 5 in.
Plate Diameter 7½ in.

2550—Sweetmeat
Height 2⅜ in.
Top Diameter 6¼ in.

2550½—3 Pce. Ash Tray Set
Height Nested 1⅞ in.
Set Consisting of:
1/12 Doz. 2550½ Lge. Ash Tray
1/12 Doz. 2550½ Med. Ash Tray
1/12 Doz. 2550½ Ind. Ash Tray

2550½—Medium Ash Tray
Diameter 4¼ in.

2550½—5½ in. Large Ash Tray

SPOOL PATTERN
No. 2550 LINE

See Price List for Colors

2550½—5½ in. Vase, Straight

2550—6½ in. Nappy
Height 1⅜ in.

2550½—5 in. Vase, Flared

2550½—3 in. Candlestick

2550—11 in. Oval Bowl
Height 3¼ in.

2550½—3 in. Candlestick

2550—3 in. Candlestick
Height 2¼ in.

2550—Centerpiece
Height 2 in.—Diameter 10½ in.
DESIGN PATENT NO. 104712

2550—3 in. Candlestick
Height 2¼ in.

SPOOL PATTERN

No. 2550 LINE

See Price List for Colors

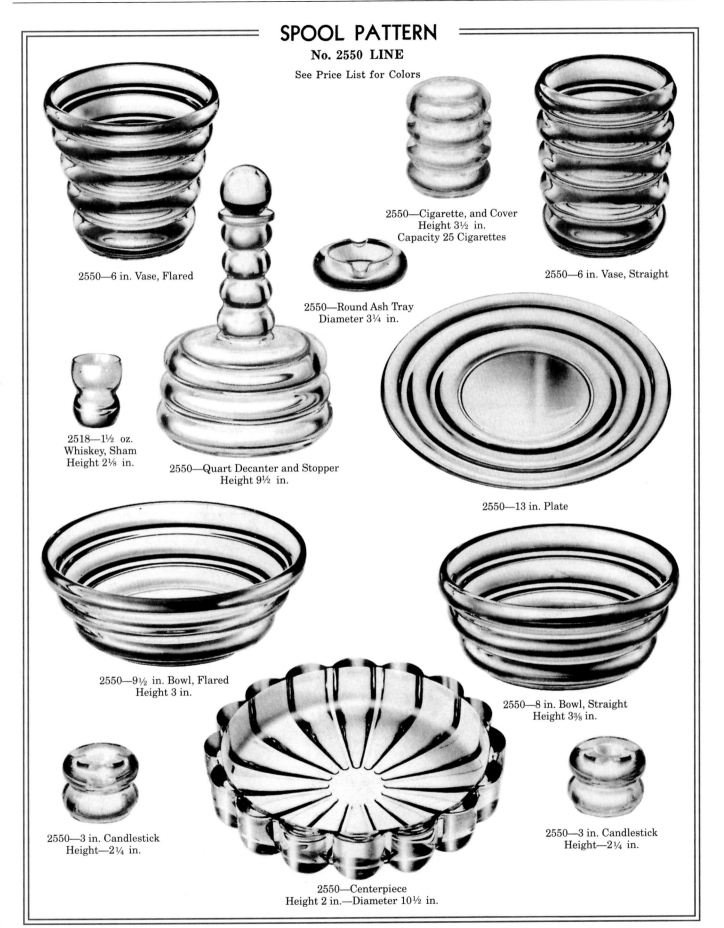

2550—6 in. Vase, Flared

2550—Cigarette, and Cover
Height 3½ in.
Capacity 25 Cigarettes

2550—6 in. Vase, Straight

2550—Round Ash Tray
Diameter 3¼ in.

2518—1½ oz.
Whiskey, Sham
Height 2⅛ in.

2550—Quart Decanter and Stopper
Height 9½ in.

2550—13 in. Plate

2550—9½ in. Bowl, Flared
Height 3 in.

2550—8 in. Bowl, Straight
Height 3⅜ in.

2550—3 in. Candlestick
Height—2¼ in.

2550—3 in. Candlestick
Height—2¼ in.

2550—Centerpiece
Height 2 in.—Diameter 10½ in.

SPOOL PATTERN
No. 2550 LINE
See Price List for Colors

2550½—Oblong Cigarette Box and Cover
Height 2⅛ in. Length 4¾ in.
Width 3⅜ in.

2550½—5½ in. Ash Tray

2550—14 in. Buffet Plate

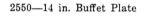

2550½—Individual Ash Tray
Diameter 3⅛ in.

2550—11 in. Oval Bowl Height 3¼ in.

2550—Coaster
Diameter 3⅛ in.

2550—6 in. Low Comport
Height 3⅜ in.

2550½—5½ in. Vase, Straight

2550½—5 in. Vase, Flared

2592 MYRIAD

The Oblong Ashtray and the Cigarette Box and Cover were made in Ebony and in Ebony with gold decoration in the 1950s.

Ash Tray, Individual, 1942-1944; $14.00
Ash Tray, Oblong, 1941-1944; $16.00
Bon Bon, Handled, 1942-1944; $18.00
Bowl, 8½", 1941-1944; $24.00
Bowl, 10½" Lily Pond, 1941-1944; $36.00
Bowl, 11" Fruit, 1941-1944; $36.00
Bowl, 11" Oblong, 1942-1944; $42.00
Candlestick, 4", 1941-1944; $30.00
Candlestick, Duo, 1942-1944; $32.00
Candy Box and Cover, 1941-1943; $64.00
Cigarette Box and Cover, 1941-1943; $64.00
Console Set, 3-piece, 1941-1944; $105.00
Jelly, Handled, 1942-1944; $18.00
Lemon, Handled, 1942-1944; $16.00
Salver, 12", 1941-1944; $45.00
Sweetmeat, Handled, 1942-1944; $18.00
Vase, 7" Oval, 1942-1943; $58.00
Vase, 9" Flared, 1941-1943; $60.00
Whip Cream, Handled, 1942-1944; $18.00

Cigarette Box and Cover, Oblong Ash Tray, Individual Ash Tray

2592—Oblong Cigarette Box and Cover
Length 6 in.   Width 3½ in.
Height with cover 3¼ in.
Capacity 48 Cigarettes

2592—Oblong Ash Tray
Length 3¾ in.   Width 2¾ in.
2592—Individual Ash Tray
Length 3 in.   Width 2¼ in.

2592—Candy Box and Cover
Height with Cover 4⅛ in.
Top Diameter 5⅛ in.

2592—9 in. Vase, Flared

2592—10½ in. Lily Pond
Height 2½ in.

2592—8½ in. Bowl
Height 4¼ in.

2592—11 in. Fruit Bowl
Height 2⅞ in.

2592—4 in. Candlestick

2592—12 in. Salver
Height 1½ in.

MYRIAD PATTERN
No. 2592 LINE

2592—Handled Bon Bon
Length 6⅝ in.
Width 5¾ in.

2592—Handled Lemon
Diameter 6⅝ in.

2592—Handled Sweetmeat
Height 1⅞ in.
Diameter 5⅞ in.

2592—Handled Jelly
Diameter 5½ in.
Height 2 in.

2592—Handled Whip Cream
Diameter 6 in.
Height 1⅞ in.

2592—7 in. Vase, Oval

Showing 2592 11 in. Oblong Bowl and Duo Candlestick in Use.

2592—Duo Candlestick
Height 2¼ in.
Length 6½ in.

2592—11 in. Oblong Bowl
Height 2¼ in.

2620 WISTAR

1942 – 1943

Wistar is a beautiful pressed pattern with large heart-shaped leaves circling every piece. Short-lived in crystal, the pattern was reintroduced in milkglass in the 1950s as Betsy Ross. Stemware is featured in *Fostoria Stemware,* page 48.

Bon Bon, 3-toed; $22.00
Bowl, 3-toed Nut; $22.00
Bowl, 3-toed Tricorne; $22.00
Bowl, 10" Salad; $38.00
Bowl, 12" Lily Pond; $40.00
Bowl, 13" Fruit; $44.00
Candlestick, 4"; $24.00
Celery, 9½"; $24.00

Mayonnaise, Plate and Ladle; $54.00
Nappy, Handled Regular; $15.00
Nappy, Handled Square; $15.00
Nappy, Handled Flared; $15.00
Nappy, 3-cornered; $15.00
Plate, 7"; $8.00
Plate, 14" Torte; $40.00
Sugar and Cream; $45.00

2620—7 in. Plate

2620—Mayonnaise & Plate & Ladle
Mayo. Height 2⅞ in.
Mayo. Diameter 5¼ in.
Plate Diameter 7 in.

2620—Footed Sugar
Height 3½ in.

2620—Handled Nappy, Sq.
Width 4 in.
Height 2 in.

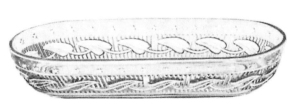

2620—9½ in. Celery

2620—Footed Cream
Height 4 in.
Capacity 7½ oz.

2620—Handled Nappy, Fld.
Diameter 5 in.
Height 1⅞ in.

2620—Handled Nappy, 3 Cor.
Length 4½ in.
Height 2 in.

2620—Handled Nappy, Reg.
Diameter 4¼ in.
Height 2 in.

WISTAR PATTERN

No. 2620 LINE

2620—3 toed Bon Bon
Diameter 6⅝ in.
Height 2¼ in.

2620—3 toed Tricorne
Length 6¾ in.
Width 6 in.
Height 2⅞ in.

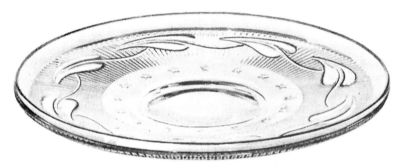

2620—14 in. Torte Plate

2620—3 toed Nut Bowl
Diameter 5½ in.
Height 2¾ in.

2620—13 in. Fruit Bowl
Height 2⅞ in.

2620—10 in. Salad Bowl
Height 3⅞ in.

2620—4 in. Candlestick

2620—12 in. Lily Pond
Height 2⅜ in.

ETCHINGS

NEEDLE ETCHINGS
36 Irish Lace
45 Greek
73 Lenore
74 Richmond
77 Sherman
83 Eilene
84 Camden
    Kingston, Decoration 41

BROCADE ETCHINGS
287 Grape
288 Cupid
289 Paradise
Decoration 71 Victoria
290 Oak Leaf
Decoration 72 Oakwood
Decoration 73 Palm Leaf

PLATE ETCHINGS
237 Garland
241 Lily of the Valley
250 Oriental
264 Woodland
    Goldwood, Decoration 50
266 Washington
267 Virginia
268 Melrose
269 Rogene
270 Mystic
272 Delphian
    Duchess, Decoration 51
273 Royal
274 Seville
275 Vesper
276 Beverly
277 Vernon

MASTER ETCHINGS
278 Versailles
279 June
280 Trojan
281 Verona
    Firenze, Decoration 502
282 Acanthus
283 Kashmir
284 New Garland
285 Minuet
286 Manor
305 Fern
306 Queen Anne
307 Fountain
308 Wildflower
309 Legion
310 Fuchsia
311 Florentine
312 Mayday
313 Morning Glory
315 Chateau
316 Midnight Rose
318 Springtime
319 Flemish
320 Fruit
322 Nectar
323 Rambler
    Rambler, Decoration 615
324 Daisy
325 Corsage
326 Arcady
327 Navarre
328 Meadow Rose
329 Lido
331 Shirley
338 Chintz
339 Rosemary

NEEDLE ETCHINGS

Needle etchings had been the standard design used on glassware, primarily blown ware, for two decades; some of the more popular patterns were made until 1928. Early needle etchings were found on stemware more than on serving pieces and are featured in *Fostoria Stemware*. A few of those early lines had tableware and complementary pieces, mostly jugs, tankards, plates, and comports, but some approached a complete dinner service. We include those patterns here. Many of them shared common tableware pieces, thus, if you cannot find a shape pictured with a pattern, please check other needle etchings, and early cuttings. By 1930, plate etchings far surpassed needle etchings in number and desirability.

IRISH LACE

Needle Etching 36

Pre-1900 – 1928
Optic except for the cover on the 317½ Jug.
Pieces marked with an asterisk (*) were the only pieces still offered in 1928.
Stemware is featured in *Fostoria Stemware*, pages 20 – 22, 34 and 35.

*766 Almond; $12.00
5051 Almond, Small; $12.00
5051 Almond, Large; $15.00
766 Bon Bon; $15.00
766 Comport, 5" Footed; $16.00
* 803 Comport, 5"; $15.00
766 Comport, 6" Footed; $16.00
803 Comport, 6"; $15.00
766 Custard; $6.00
810 Custard, 200-5" Plate; $4.00
*300 Decanter, Quart, Cut Neck; $35.00
*766 Finger Bowl, 2283 6" Plate; $18.00
810 Finger Bowl, 200 6" Plate; $18.00
300/5 Jug, Claret; $65.00
1236/6 Jug; $60.00
*300/7 Jug, Tankard; $60.00
*303/7 Jug; $60.00
317½ /7 Jug and Plain Cover; $75.00
*318/7 Jug; $60.00
724/7 Jug, Tankard; $60.00
766 Nappy, 4½" Footed; $12.00
803 Nappy, 4½" Deep; $10.00
1227 Nappy, 4½"; $10.00

766 Nappy, 5" Footed; $10.00
803 Nappy, 5" Deep; $10.00
*803 Nappy, 5" Footed; $10.00
766 Nappy, 6" Footed; $10.00
803 Nappy, 6" Deep; $10.00
*803 Nappy, 6" Footed; !2.00
766 Nappy, 7" Footed; $12.00
803 Nappy, 7" Deep; $12.00
803 Nappy, 8" Footed; $15.00
1227 Nappy, 8"; $15.00
300½ Oil, Small; $30.00
*300½ Oil, Large; $35.00
1465 Oil, 7 oz., Large, Cut Neck; $35.00
2283 Plate, 5"; $6.00
1897 Plate, 7"; $6.00
*2283 Plate, 7"; $6.00
1165½ Shaker, SPT; pair, $35.00
858 Short Cake; $12.00
*1480 Sugar and Cream; $25.00
858 Sweetmeat; $15.00
*880 Sweetmeat; $15.00
922 Toothpick; $18.00
160½ Water Bottle, Cut Neck; $54.00

GREEK

Needle Etching 45

Pre 1924 – 1928, Crystal
Some pieces made in Rose, Green, and Amber, 1930 – 1932
Stemware is featured in *Fostoria Stemware*, pages 35 and 67.

863 Almond; $18.00
858 Bowl, Finger, and Plate,
 Rose, Green, Amber, 1930-1932; $18.00
803 Comport, 5"; $15.00
481 Custard; $6.00
300 Decanter; $50.00
945½ Grapefruit and Liner; $30.00

303/7 Jug; $50.00
318/7 Jug; $50.00
1236/6 Jug; $50.00
5000 Jug,
 Rose, Green, Amber, 1930-1932; $195.00
803 Nappy, 5" Footed; $15.00
803 Nappy, 6" Footed; $15.00

2283 Plate, 5"; $6.00
2283 Plate, 6"; $6.00
2283 Plate, 7", Rose, Green, Amber, 1930-1932; $8.00
2283 Plate, 8", Rose, Green, Amber, 1930-1932; $8.00

300½ Small Oil; $32.00
1478 Sugar and Cream; $35.00
858 Sweetmeat; $15.00
880 Sweetmeat; $15.00

LENORE

Needle Etching 73

1923 – 1930
Crystal with regular optic.
Stemware is featured in *Fostoria Stemware*, on pages 22 through 26.

880 Bon Bon; $15.00
858 Bowl, Finger, and Underplate; $15.00
5078 Comport, 5" and 6"; $15.00
1236/4 Jug; $45.00
1236/6 Jug; $50.00
300/7 Jug; $50.00
318/7 Jug; $50.00
858 Mayonnaise, Plate, Ladle; $25.00 (same as Finger

Bowl and Underplate)
5078 Nappy, 5"; $15.00
5078 Nappy, 6"; $18.00
5078 Nappy, 7"; $18.00
312 Oil; $32.00
840 Plate, 5" Tumbler; $6.00
2133 Sugar and Cream; $35.00
858 Sweetmeat; $15.00

RICHMOND

Needle Etching 74

1924 – 1928, 1933 – 1943 except where noted.
Richmond was also offered with a Coin Gold Band as Decoration 43, Princess in 1924.
Stemware is featured in *Fostoria Stemware*, pages 64 and 65.

1769 Bowl, Finger, and Plate; $15.00
5078 Comport, 5"; $15.00
303/7 Jug; $50.00
318/7 Jug, 1924-1928; $60.00
2270/7 Jug, 1924-1928, 1933-1934; $65.00
2270 Jug and Cover, 1924-1927; $75.00

5078 Nappy, 5", 1924-1928; 1933-1934; $15.00
5078 Nappy, 6", 1924-1928; $15.00
701 Plate, 5" Tumbler, 1924-1928; $5.00
2283 Plate, 7"; $7.00
858 Sweetmeat, 1924-1928; $18.00

No. 2283 - 7 in. Plate.   No. 5078. 6 in. Nappy.   No. 5078. 5 in. Nappy.   No. 945½ Grape Fruit. No. 945½ Grape Fruit Liner.   No. 858. Sweet Meat.   No. 5078. 5 in. Comport.

SHERMAN

Needle Etching 77

1925 – 1930

Stemware is featured in *Fostoria Stemware*, page 31.

869 Bowl, Finger, and 2283 Plate; $15.00
5078 Comport, 5"; $15.00
945½ Grapefruit and Liner; $20.00
4095/7 Jug; $60.00
2270/7 Jug; $65.00

4095 Nappy, 5"; $10.00
4095 Nappy, 6"; $10.00
4095 Nappy, 7"; $10.00
2283 Plate, 7"; $6.00
2283 Plate, 8"; $7.00

EILENE

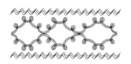

Needle Etching 83

1928 – 1932

Crystal, Green, Rose, and Azure

Stemware is featured in *Fostoria Stemware*, pages 64 and 65.

CAMDEN

Needle Etching 84

1928 – 1929

Green, Amber Bowl with Crystal Foot

Also 5000 Jug in solid color.

Stemware is featured in *Fostoria Stemware*, page 68.

KINGSTON

Decoration 41

Gold Band on Needle Etching 84.

Green only, 1928

Also 5000 Jug.

Kingston, Camden, and Eilene shared these pieces with exceptions noted.

869 Bowl, Finger; $15.00
5098 Comport, 5"; $27.00
4095 Jug, Footed, Solid Color; $135.00
5098 Nappy, 6"; $35.00

2283 Plate, 6"; $8.00
2283 Plate, 7"; $10.00
2283 Plate, 8"; $12.00

THE BROCADES

The word "brocade" evokes images of richly embroidered, woven fabric worn by royalty. Fostoria's line of Brocade etchings in the late 1920s must have reflected the affluence of a segment of the populace prior to the economic crash of 1929. Nothing since has equaled the beautifully executed designs and skillful finish of these Brocade patterns. After 1930 it was not practical to continue such labor-intensive production, and the Brocades disappeared forever.

Three of the Brocade designs appeared simultaneously in 1927. Grape was made in Blue in 1927, in Orchid from 1927 – 1928, and in Green from 1927 – 1929. Cupid was shown in 1927 only in colors of Blue, Green, and Ebony. It is by far the most difficult pattern to find. The boudoir items in Cupid are extremely desirable. Paradise was offered in Green from 1927 – 1929, and in Orchid from 1927 – 1928. It was decorated with the Mother of Pearl iridescent finish as Victoria, Decoration 71, made in 1927 only in crystal. Palm Leaf is unusual as it was offered only as a decoration.

Azure Oakwood 5000 Jug, 877 Goblet, Footed Iced Tea, Footed Juice

In 1928, Oak Leaf was offered in Rose, Green, and Crystal and continued in production through 1930. A few pieces were made in Ebony. Stemware with this etching was offered on the 877 Line and was made in Green and Crystal only. All stemware is shown in *Fostoria Stemware*, page 33. Oak Leaf was an extensive pattern. The 2415 Combination Bowl, 2395 Oval Confection and Cover, 2413 Urn and Cover were not made in Crystal and were only listed in 1929.

When Oak Leaf was decorated with Mother of Pearl iridescence and finished with Gold Bands, it was called Oakwood. Reminiscent of the rich moire taffetas and satins of the period, Oakwood is the prize of all Fostoria's decorations.

When introduced in 1928, it was offered in Azure and Orchid, but in 1929, only the Azure color was made. A complete collection of Oakwood in either color would contain more than 50 pieces.

One wonders at the different choices of color between Oak Leaf and Oakwood. Could it be that Fostoria designers wanted to show off the new Azure color? Perhaps the iridescence on the brocade etching seemed to call for the delicate Orchid color, so short lived. Certainly, Orchid Oakwood would stand well with any crystal made in the world.

The Brocade etchings came at the close of an era in our country's history. Many skilled hands and processes were required to produce these grand creations in crystal. In the final analysis, the brocades represent the penultimate offerings from the Fostoria Glass Company.

Green Grape 4100 8" Vase, 2327 Comport, 2331 Candy Box and Cover, 2297 12½" Deep Bowl "E"

123

GRAPE
Brocade Etching 287

2375 Bon Bon
  Green, 1929; $47.00
2339 Bowl "D", 7½"
  Blue, 1927; $135.00
  Orchid, 1927-1928; $125.00
  Green, 1927-1929; $110.00
2297 Bowl "A", 10½" Shallow
  Blue, 1927; $125.00
  Orchid, 1927; $110.00
  Green, 1927; $110.00
2297 Bowl "C", 10½" Deep
  Blue, 1927; $125.00
  Orchid, 1927; $110.00
  Green, 1927; $110.00
2297 Bowl "A", 12" Deep
  Blue, 1927; $125.00
  Orchid, 1927-1928; $110.00
  Green, 1927-1929; $110.00
2362 Bowl, 12" Low
  Blue, 1927; $135.00
  Orchid, 1927-1928; $125.00
  Green, 1927-1929; $110.00
2297 Bowl "E", 12½" Deep
  Blue, 1927; $135.00
  Orchid, 1927; $110.00
  Green, 1927; $110.00
2372 Candlestick, 2" (pair)
  Blue, 1927; $75.00
  Orchid, 1927-1928; $75.00
  Green, 1927-1929; $65.00
2362 Candlestick, 3" (pair)
  Blue, 1927; $75.00
  Orchid, 1927-1928; $68.00
  Green, 1927-1929; $60.00
2324 Candlestick, 4" (pair)
  Blue, 1927; $75.00
  Orchid, 1927-1928; $75.00
  Green, 1927-1929; $70.00
2331 Candy Box and Cover
  Blue, 1927; $225.00
  Orchid, 1927-1928; $195.00
  Green, 1927-1929; $175.00
2329 Centerpiece, 11" Round
  Blue, 1927; $195.00
  Orchid, 1927-1928; $175.00
  Green, 1927-1929; !65.00
2329 Centerpiece, 13" Round
  Blue, 1927; $225.00
  Orchid, 1927-1928; $210.00
  Green, 1927-1929; $195.00
2371 Centerpiece, 13" Oval, 2371 Flower
  Holder
  Blue, 1927, $295.00

Orchid, 1927; $275.00
  Green, 1927; $225.00
2327 Comport, 7"
  Blue, 1927; $95.00
  Orchid, 1927-1928; $85.00
  Green, 1927-1929; $65.00
2362 Comport, 11" Footed
  Blue, 1927; $150.00
  Orchid, 1927-1928; $135.00
  Green, 1927-1929; $125.00
2378 Ice Bucket, NP Handle
  Blue, 1927; $125.00
  Orchid, 1927; $110.00
  Green, 1927; $110.00
2378 Ice Bucket, NP Handle, Drainer, Tongs
  Blue, 1927; $150.00
  Orchid, 1927; $135.00
  Green, 1927; $135.00
2375 Lemon, Handled
  Green, 1929; $45.00
2375 Sweetmeat, Handled
  Green, 1929; $47.00
2387 Tray, Handled Lunch
  Blue, 1927; $125.00
  Orchid, 1927-1928; $110.00
  Green, 1927-1929; $110.00
2342 Tray, Handled Lunch (2370)
  Blue, 1927; $125.00
  Orchid, 1927-1928; $110.00
  Green, 1927-1929; $110.00
4103 Vase, 3" Regular Optic (RO)
  Blue, 1927; $95.00
  Orchid, 1927-1928; $85.00
  Green, 1927-1929; $75.00
4103 Vase, 4" RO
  Blue, 1927; $95.00
  Orchid, 1927-1928; $85.00
  Green, 1927-1928; $85.00
4103 Vase, 5" RO
  Blue, 1927; $115.00
  Orchid, 1927-1928; $100.00
  Green, 1927-1928; $100.00
4103 Vase, 6" RO
  Blue, 1927; $115.00
  Orchid, 1927-1928; $100.00
  Green, 1927-1928; $100.00
4100 Vase, 6" RO
  Blue, 1927; $115.00
  Orchid, 1927-1928; $100.00
  Green, 1927-1929; $100.00
4100 Vase, 8" RO
  Blue, 1927; $145.00
  Orchid, 1927-1928; $125.00
  Green, 1927-1929; $125.00

2369 Vase, 7" RO
    Blue, 1927; $135.00
    Orchid, 1927-1928; $115.00
    Green, 1927-1929; $115.00
2369 Vase, 9" RO
    Blue, 1927; $165.00
    Orchid, 1927-1928; $150.00

Green, 1927-1928; $150.00
2292 Vase, 8"
    Blue, 1927; $145.00
    Orchid, 1927-1928; $135.00
    Green, 1927-1929; $125.00
2375 Whip Cream, Handled
    Green, 1929; $48.00

Orchid Grape Large Comport,
2362 Console Set

Blue Grape 2329 Oval Center-
piece, 2297 Deep Bowl "E"

"GRAPE" PATTERN, PLATE ETCHING No. 287.
MADE IN BLUE, GREEN AND ORCHID.
PRICED PAGE 36 — No. 2 SUPPLEMENT PRICE LIST.

2327—7 in. Comport.

2297—10½ in. Deep Bowl "C."

2297—12 in. Deep Bowl "A."

2378—Ice Bucket.
With N. P. Handle, Drainer and Tongs.

2297—12½ in. Deep Bowl "E".

"GRAPE" PATTERN, PLATE ETCHING No. 287.
MADE IN BLUE, GREEN AND ORCHID.
PRICED PAGE 36 — No. 2 SUPPLEMENT PRICE LIST.

2292—8 in. Vase.

4100—6 in. Vase
Optic.

4103—5 in. Vase.
Optic.

2372—2 in. Candle.

2371—13 in. Centerpiece (Oval).
2371—Flower Holder.

2372—2 in. Candle.

"GRAPE" PATTERN, PLATE ETCHING No. 287.
MADE IN BLUE, GREEN AND ORCHID.
PRICED PAGE 36 — No. 2 SUPPLEMENT PRICE LIST.

2362—11 in. Comport.

2331—3 Candy Box and Cover

2342—12 in. Hld. Lunch Tray.

2369—7 in. Vase.
Optic.

"GRAPE" PATTERN, PLATE ETCHING No. 287.
MADE IN BLUE, GREEN AND ORCHID.
PRICED PAGE 36 — No. 2 SUPPLEMENT PRICE LIST.

2324—4 in. Candle.

2329—11 in. Centerpiece.
2309—3¾ in. Flower Block.

2324—4 in. Candle.

2287—11 in. Hld. Lunch Tray.

2339—7¼ in. Bowl "D."

2362—3 in. Candle.

2362—12 in. Bowl.
2309—3¾ in. Flower Block.

2362—3 in. Candle.

127

CUPID

Brocade Etching 288

All pieces were made in Blue in 1927, and in Green and Ebony from 1927 – 1928. The Centerpiece and 4" Candles are listed in the catalog but not the price list in Amber.

2297 Bowl "A", 12" Deep
    Blue, $200.00
    Green, $200.00
    Ebony, $200.00
2324 Candlestick, 4" (priced as pair)
    Blue, $125.00
    Green, $125.00
    Ebony, $125.00
2298 Candlestick (priced as pair)
    Blue, $225.00
    Green, $225.00
    Ebony, $225.00
2329 Centerpiece, 11"
    Blue, $250.00
    Green, $250.00
    Ebony, $250.00
2329 Centerpiece, 13"
    Blue, $300.00
    Green, $300.00
    Ebony, $300.00

2298 Clock
    Blue, $250.00
    Green, $250.00
    Ebony, $250.00
2298 Clock Set, Clock and 2 Candlesticks
    Blue, $500.00
    Green, $450.00
    Ebony, $450.00
2322 Cologne
    Blue, $450.00
    Green, $450.00
    Ebony, $450.00
2359½ Puff and Cover
    Blue, $400.00
    Green, $400.00
    Ebony, $400.00
2276 Vanity Set
    Blue, $495.00
    Green, $495.00
    Ebony, $495.00

Blue Cupid 2297 Shallow Bowl "A", 2298 Candlesticks; Green 2297 Shallow Bowl "A"

"CUPID" PATTERN, PLATE ETCHING No. 288.
MADE IN BLUE, GREEN AND EBONY.
PRICED PAGE 36 — No. 2 SUPPLEMENT PRICE LIST.

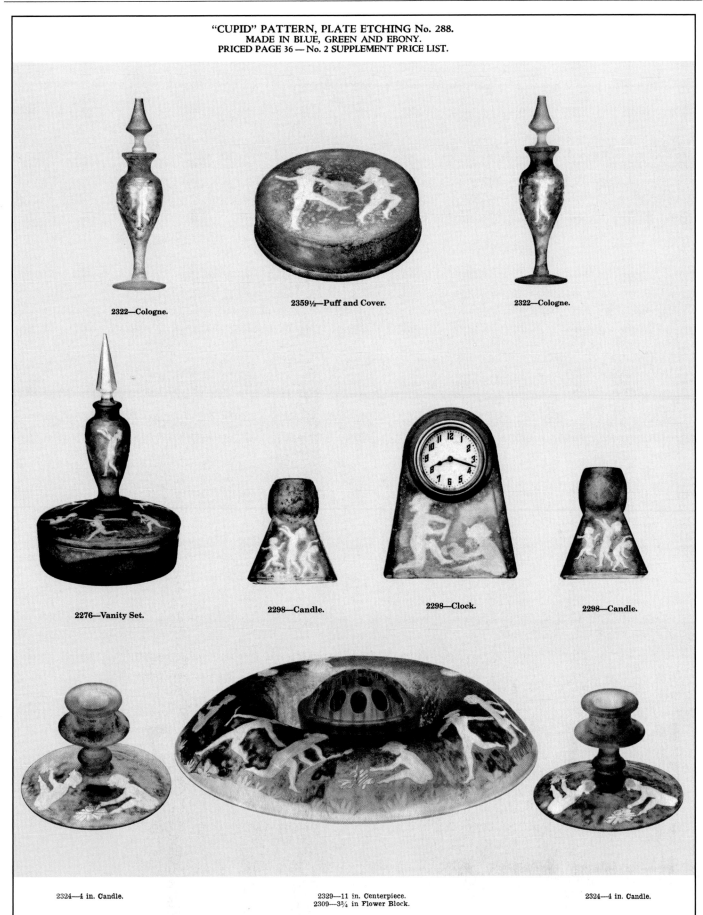

2322—Cologne.

2359½—Puff and Cover.

2322—Cologne.

2276—Vanity Set.

2298—Candle.

2298—Clock.

2298—Candle.

2324—4 in. Candle.

2329—11 in. Centerpiece.
2309—3¾ in Flower Block.

2324—4 in. Candle.

PARADISE

Brocade Etching 289

1927 – 1929, Green
1927 – 1928, Orchid

VICTORIA

Decoration 71

Mother of Pearl Iridescence on Brocade Etching 289, Paradise
1927, Crystal
Prices for pieces in either color or decorated are about the same.

2297 Bowl "A", 10½" Shallow; $125.00
2297 Bowl "A", 12" Deep; $125.00
2315 Bowl "C", 10½" Footed; $125.00
2342 Bowl, 12"; $110.00
2362 Bowl, 12"; $125.00 (not decorated)
2372 Candlestick, 2" Block (pair); $65.00
2362 Candlestick, 3" (pair); $65.00
    (not decorated)
2324 Candlestick, 4" (pair); $65.00
    (not decorated)
2331 Candy Box and Cover; $125.00
2329 Centerpiece, 11"; $125.00
2329 Centerpiece, 13"; $150.00
2371 Centerpiece, 13" Oval, 2371 Flower Holder;
    $175.00

2327 Comport, 7"; $95.00
2350 Comport, 8"; $85.00
2362 Comport, 11"; $125.00
2380 Confection and Cover; $135.00
2378 Ice Bucket, NP Handle, Drainer and Tongs;
    $135.00
2342 Tray, Handled Lunch; $95.00
4100 Vase, 6", Optic; $95.00
4100 Vase, 8", Optic; $125.00
4103 Vase, 3", Optic; $75.00 (not decorated)
4103 Vase, 5", Optic; $75.00
2369 Vase, 7", Optic; $125.00 (not decorated)
2369 Vase, 9", Optic; $125.00 (not decorated)

Green Paradise 4103 Vase, Orchid 2315 Footed Bowl "C", 2378 Ice Bucket

"PARADISE" PATTERN, PLATE ETCHING No. 289.
MADE IN GREEN AND ORCHID.
PRICED PAGE 22-C. No. 2 SUPPLEMENT PRICE LIST.

2380—Confection & Cover.

4103—5 in. Vase.
Optic.

2342—12 in. Lunch Tray.

2362—11 in. Comport.

2362—3 in. Candle.

2362—12 in. Bowl.
2309—3¾ in. Flower Block.

2362—3 in. Candle.

2378—Ice Bucket.
With N. P. Handle, Drainer & Tongs.

4100—8 in. Vase.
Optic.

2369—7 in. Vase.
Optic.

2331—3 Candy Box & Cover.

"PARADISE" PATTERN, PLATE ETCHING No. 289.
MADE IN GREEN AND ORCHID.
PRICED PAGE 22-C. No. 2 SUPPLEMENT PRICE LIST.

2350—8 in. Comport.

2327—7 in. Comport.

2315—Ftd. Bowl "C".

2324—4 in. Candle.

2329—11 in. Centerpiece.
2309—3¾ in. Flower Block.

2324—4 in. Candle.

2372—2 in Candle Block.

2371—13 in. Centerpiece (Oval).
2371—Flower Holder.

2372—2 in Candle Block.

2297—12 in. Deep Bowl "A".

2342—12 in. Bowl.

OAK LEAF
Brocade Etching 290

Stemware is featured in *Fostoria Stemware*, page 33.

2375 Bon Bon
    Crystal, 1928-1930; $42.00
    Green, 1928-1930; $48.00
    Rose, 1928-1930; $48.00
869 Bowl, Finger, and 2283 Plate
    Crystal, July 1928; $67.00
    Green, July 1928; $70.00
2395 Bowl, 10"
    Crystal, 1928-1930; $140.00
    Green, 1928-1930; $150.00
    Rose, 1928-1930; $150.00
    Ebony, 1928-1930; $150.00
2398 Bowl, 11"
    Crystal, 1928-1930; $135.00
    Green, 1928-1930; $145.00
    Rose, 1928-1930; $145.00
2342 Bowl, 12"
    Crystal, 1928-1930; $140.00
    Green, 1928-1930; $150.00
    Rose, 1928-1930; $150.00
2394 Bowl, 12"
    Crystal, 1928-1930; $135.00
    Green, 1928-1930; $145.00
    Rose, 1928-1930; $145.00
2375 Bowl, Large Dessert
    Crystal, 1929-1930; $110.00
    Green, 1929-1930; $120.00
    Rose, 1929-1930; $120.00
2415 Bowl, Combination
    Green, 1929; $150.00
    Rose, 1929; $165.00
    Ebony, 1929; $165.00
2394 Candlestick, 2" (pair)
    Crystal, 1928-1930; $125.00
    Green, 1928-1930; $135.00
    Rose, 1928-1930; $135.00
2375 Candlestick, 3" (pair)
    Crystal, 1928-1930; $95.00
    Green, 1928-1930; $110.00
    Rose, 1928-1930; $110.00
2395 Candlestick, 3" (pair)
    Crystal, 1928-1930; $120.00
    Green, 1928-1930; $130.00
    Rose, 1928-1930; $130.00
    Ebony, 1928-1930; $130.00
2375½ Candlestick (pair)
    Crystal, 1928-1930; $95.00
    Green, 1928-1930; $110.00
    Rose, 1928-1930; $110.00
2331 Candy Box and Cover
    Crystal, 1928-1930; $150.00
    Green, 1928-1930; $175.00
    Rose, 1928-1930; $175.00

Green Oak Leaf 2394 Console Set

    Ebony, 1928-1930; $175.00
2375 Centerpiece, 12"
    Crystal, 1928-1930; $125.00
    Green, 1928-1930; $135.00
    Rose, 1928-1930; $135.00
2375½ Centerpiece, Oval
    Crystal, 1928-1930; $150.00
    Green, 1928-1930; $165.00
    Rose, 1928-1930; $165.00
2368 Cheese and Cracker
    Crystal, 1928-1930; $95.00
    Green, 1928-1930; $110.00
    Rose, 1928-1930; $110.00
2391 Cigarette and Cover, Small
    Crystal, 1928-1930; $95.00

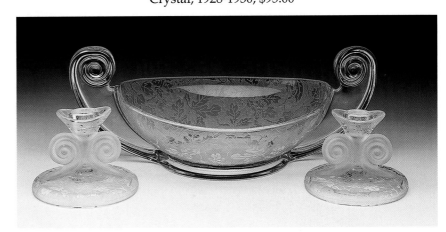

Crystal Oak Leaf 2395 Bowl, 2375½ Candlesticks

Green, 1928-1930; $110.00
Rose, 1928-1930; $110.00
Ebony, 1928-1930; $115.00
2391 Cigarette and Cover, Large
Crystal, 1928-1930; $115.00
Green, 1928-1930; $125.00
Rose, 1928-1930; $125.00
Ebony, 1928-1930; $135.00
2350 Comport, 8"
Crystal, 1928-1930; $68.00
Green, 1928-1930; $77.00
Rose, 1928-1930; $77.00
2400 Comport, 8"
Crystal, 1928-1930; $68.00
Green, 1928-1930; $77.00
Rose, 1928-1930; $77.00
2380 Confection and Cover
Crystal, 1928-1930; $150.00
Green, 1928-1930; $165.00
Rose, 1928-1930; $165.00
2395 Confection and Cover, Oval
Green, 1928-1930; $165.00
Rose, 1928-1930; $165.00
2378 Ice Bucket, NP Handle
Crystal, 1928-1930; $120.00
Green, 1928-1930; $135.00
Rose, 1928-1930; $135.00
5000 Jug
Crystal, July 1928; $775.00
Green, July 1928; $800.00
2375 Lemon Dish
Crystal, 1928-1930; $48.00
Green, 1928-1930; $55.00
Rose, 1928-1930; $55.00
2315 Mayonnaise
Crystal, 1928-1930; $67.00
Green, 1928-1930; $75.00
Rose, 1928-1930; $75.00
2394 Mint
Crystal, 1928-1930; $44.00
Green, 1928-1930; $50.00
Rose, 1928-1930; $50.00
2332 Plate, 7" Mayonnaise
Crystal, 1928-1930; $30.00
Green, 1928-1930; $34.00
Rose, 1928-1930; $34.00
2283 Plate, 7"
Crystal, 1928-1930; $30.00
Green, 1928-1930; $34.00
Rose, 1928-1930; $34.00
2283 Plate, 8"
Crystal, 1928-1930; $30.00
Green, 1928-1930; $35.00
Rose, 1928-1930; $35.00
2375 Plate, 10" Cake

Rose Oak Leaf 2373 Window Box, 2394 Bowl, 2375½ Candlestick, 2378 Whip Cream Pail, 2375 Mayonnaise and Ladle

Crystal, 1929-1920; $85.00
Green, 1929-1930; $95.00
Rose, 1929-1930; $95.00
2315 Plate, 13" Lettuce/Mayonnaise
Crystal, 1928-1930; $95.00
Green, 1928-1930; $110.00
Rose, 1928-1930; $110.00
2315 Salver, 12"
Crystal, 1928-1930; $135.00
Green, 1928-1930; $150.00

Orchid Oakwood 2283 7" Plate, 2387 8" Vase, 2375 Round Centerpiece, 3" Candlestick

Rose, 1928-1930; $150.00
2378 Sugar Pail
   Crystal, 1928-1930; $135.00
   Green, 1928-1930; $175.00
   Rose, 1928-1930; $175.00
2375 Sweetmeat
   Crystal, 1928-1930; $47.00
   Green, 1928-1930; $50.00
   Rose, 1928-1930; $50.00
2342 Tray, Handled Lunch
   Crystal, 1928-1930; $110.00
   Green, 1928-1930; $125.00
   Rose, 1928-1930; $125.00
2413 Urn and Cover
   Green, 1929-1930; $225.00
   Rose, 1929-1930; $225.00
4103 Vase, 3" Optic
   Crystal, 1928-1930; $58.00
   Green, 1928-1930; $65.00
   Rose, 1928-1930; $75.00
4105 Vase, 6" Optic
   Crystal, 1928-1930; $75.00
   Green, 1928-1930; $95.00
   Rose, 1928-1930; $95.00
4105 Vase, 8" Optic
   Crystal, 1928-1930; $95.00
   Green, 1928-1930; $110.00
   Rose, 1928-1930; $110.00
2369 Vase, 7" Optic
   Crystal, 1928-1930; $95.00
   Green, 1928-1930; $125.00
   Rose, 1928-1930; $125.00
2369 Vase, 9" Optic
   Crystal, 1928-1930; $125.00
   Green, 1928-1930; $145.00
   Rose, 1928-1930; $150.00
2292 Vase, 8"
   Crystal, 1928-1930; $100.00
   Green, 1928-1930; $125.00
   Rose, 1928-1930; $125.00
   Ebony, 1928-1930; $125.00
2387 Vase, 8"
   Crystal, 1928-1930; $100.00
   Green, 1928-1930; $125.00

Crystal Oak Leaf 2292 8" Vase, 2385 Fan Vase, 2373 Window Box, 2378 Whip Cream Pail; Ebony 2373 Window Box, 2395 Candlesticks

Rose, 1928-1930; $125.00
2385 Vase, 8½" Fan
   Crystal, 1928-1930; $200.00
   Green, 1928-1930; $250.00
   Rose, 1928-1930; $250.00
   Ebony, 1928-1930; $250.00
2373 Vase, Small Window Box, and Cover
   Crystal, 1928-1930; $200.00
   Green, 1928-1930; $250.00
   Rose, 1928-1930; $250.00
   Ebony, 1928-1930; $250.00
2373 Vase, Large Window Box, and Cover
   Crystal, 1928-1930; $225.00
   Green, 1928-1930; $275.00
   Rose, 1928-1930; $275.00
   Ebony, 1928-1930; $275.00
2375 Whip Cream
   Crystal, 1928-1930; $47.00
   Green, 1928-1930; $50.00
   Rose, 1928-1930; $50.00
2375 Whip Cream Pail
   Crystal, 1928-1930; $135.00

OAKWOOD

Decoration 72

Mother of Pearl Iridescence and Gold Trim on Brocade Etching 290, Oak Leaf.
Stemware is featured in *Fostoria Stemware*, page 33.

2375 Bon Bon
   Orchid, 1928; $55.00
   Azure, 1928-1929; $55.00
869 Bowl, Finger, and Plate

   Orchid, 1928; $110.00
   Azure, 1928-1929; $110.00
2375 Bowl, Large Dessert
   Azure, 1929; $175.00

2398 Bowl, 11"
Orchid, 1928; $175.00
Azure, 1928-1929; $175.00
2342 Bowl, 12"
Orchid, 1928; $175.00
Azure, 1928-1929; $175.00
2394 Bowl, 12"
Orchid, 1928; $175.00
Azure, 1928-1929; $175.00
2415 Bowl, Combination
Azure, 1929; $300.00
2375 Candlestick, 3" (pair)
Orchid, 1928; $145.00
Azure, 1928-1929; $145.00
2375½ Candlestick, Mushroom (pair)
Orchid, 1928; $150.00
Azure, 1928-1929; $150.00
2394 Candlestick, 2" (pair)
Orchid, 1928; $140.00
Azure, 1928-1929; $140.00
2331 Candy Box and Cover
Orchid, 1928; $325.00
Azure, 1928-1929; $325.00
2375 Centerpiece, 11"
Orchid, 1928; $225.00
Azure, 1928-1929; $225.00
2375½ Centerpiece, 13" Oval; 2371 Flower Holder
Orchid, 1928; $500.00
Azure, 1928-1929; $500.00
2391 Cigarette and Cover, Small
Orchid, 1928; $175.00
Azure, 1928-1929; $175.00
2391 Cigarette and Cover, Large
Orchid, 1928; $225.00
Azure, 1928-1929; $225.00
2400 Comport, 8"
Orchid, 1928; $150.00
Azure, 1928-1929; $150.00
2380 Confection and Cover
Orchid, 1928; $225.00
Azure, 1928-1929; $225.00
2395 Confection and Cover
Azure, 1929; $250.00
2378 Ice Bucket, GF Handle
Orchid, 1928; $195.00
Azure, 1928-1929; $195.00
5000 Jug
Orchid, 1928; $1,200.00 to market
Azure, 1928-1929; $1,100.00 to market
2375 Lemon, Handled
Orchid, 1928; $55.00
Azure, 1928-1929; $55.00
2315 Mayonnaise, Plate, Ladle
Orchid, 1928; $195.00
Azure, 1928-1929; $195.00

Azure Oakwood 2385 Fan Vase, 2378 Ice Bucket and Tongs, 2400 8" Comport, 2380 Confection and Cover

2315 Plate, 13" Lettuce (used with Mayonnaise)
Orchid, 1928; $135.00
Azure, 1928-1929; $135.00
2332 Plate, 7" Mayonnaise
Orchid, 1928; $35.00
Azure, 1928-1929; $35.00
2283 Plate, 7"
Orchid, 1928; $35.00
Azure, 1928-1929; $35.00
2283 Plate, 8"
Orchid, 1928; $40.00
Azure, 1928-1929; $40.00
2375 Plate, 10" Cake
Azure, 1929; $135.00
2315 Salver, Cake
Orchid, 1928; $175.00
Azure, 1928-1929; $175.00
2378 Sugar Pail, GF Handle
Orchid, 1928; $425.00
Azure, 1928-1929; $425.00
2375 Sweetmeat
Orchid, 1928; $60.00
Azure, 1928-1929; $60.00
2342 Tray, Handled Lunch
Orchid, 1928; $195.00
Azure, 1928-1929; $195.00
2413 Urn and Cover
Azure, 1929; $500.00 to market
4105 Vase, 6"
Orchid, 1928; $150.00
Azure, 1928-1929; $150.00
4105 Vase, 8"
Orchid, 1928; $245.00
Azure, 1928-1929; $225.00
2387 Vase, 8"
Orchid, 1928; $450.00
Azure, 1928-1929; $450.00

2385 Vase, 8½" Fan
    Orchid, 1928; $550.00
    Azure, 1928-1929; $550.00
2373 Vase, Small Window and Cover
    Orchid, 1928; $500.00
    Azure, 1928-1929; $500.00
2373 Vase, Large Window and Cover
    Orchid, 1928; $525.00
    Azure, 1928-1929; $525.00
2375 Whip Cream
    Orchid, 1928; $65.00
    Azure, 1928-1929; $65.00
2378 Whip Cream Pail, GF Handle
    Orchid, 1928; $425.00
    Azure, 1928-1929; $425.00

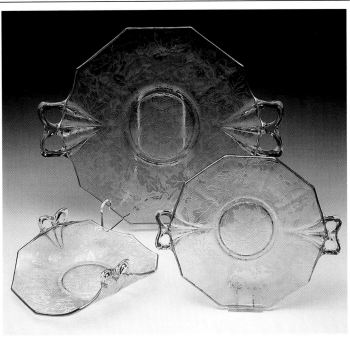

*Azure Oakwood 2375 Handled Cake
Plate, Bon Bon, Lemon Dish*

PALM LEAF

Decoration 73

Mother of Pearl Iridescence and Gold on Brocade Etching 291.
Rose and Green
1929

2375 Bon Bon; $60.00
2375 Bowl, Large Dessert; $195.00
2395 Bowl, 10"; $350.00
2394 Bowl, 12"; $250.00
2415 Bowl, Combination; $350.00
2394 Candlestick, 2" (pair); $165.00
2375 Candlestick, 3" (pair); $165,00
2395½ Candlestick, 5" (pair); $300.00
2383 Candlestick, Trindle (pair); $400.00
2375 Centerpiece, 11"; $245.00
2400 Comport, 6"; $145.00
2395 Confection and Cover, Oval; $275.00
2378 Ice Bucket, GF Handle; $195.00
2375 Lemon Dish; $60.00
2419 Plate, 8" Square; $40.00
2375 Plate, 10" Cake; $195.00
2378 Sugar Pail, GF Handle; $435.00
2375 Sweetmeat; $65.00
2342 Tray, Handled Lunch; $200.00
2413 Urn and Cover; $500.00 to market
2408 Vase, 8"; $300.00
4105 Vase, 8"; $300.00
2385 Vase, 8½" Fan; $575.00
2373 Vase, Small Window and Cover; $500.00
2373 Vase, Large Window and Cover; $525.00

Palm Leaf 2395½ Candlesticks, 2408 Vase, 2395 Bowl, 2394 Candlesticks, 2375 Bon Bon

2421 Vase, 10½" Footed; $500.00 to market
2375 Whip Cream; $70.00
2378 Whip Cream Pail; $450.00

PLATE ETCHINGS

The page below was taken from a booklet published by the Fostoria Glass Company to commemorate the American Bicentennial in 1976. Not only were plate etchings "immensely popular," the patterns from the late twenties and early thirties were enormous, offering everything from cups and saucers to decanters and tiny almond dishes, all in the finest crystal and colors. To show all the pieces in every pattern would take many more volumes than this one. Thus, the reader is encouraged to check the number which precedes the name of the piece. That number refers to the pattern blank on which the etching was placed, i.e., 2375, which was Fairfax. Garland through Mystic plate etchings were from an earlier period and had many shapes in common. These predate the complete dinner service which began with Royal.

Hands and tools, old friends with a thorough understanding of their job and each other.

After gradual cooling in large tunnel ovens called "lehrs" (a process which tempers the glass and makes it less breakable), much of Fostoria blown crystal goes on to other departments for decoration. Acid-etched designs, handcut patterns, and handpainted, fired-on gold and platinum bands are typical decorations.

Etching is a complicated process resulting in a delicate lacy pattern penetrated into the surface of the glass. Immensely popular from the late twenties through the early fifties, etched patterns have enjoyed renewed popularity in recent years. Fostoria offers a greater selection of etched ware than any other glass house in America.

Handcutting crystal is one of the most highly skilled jobs in the industry. The educated hands of Fostoria cutters create delicate patterns by guiding crystal "blanks" along the single cutting edge of a lubricated abrasive wheel.

Gold and platinum bands are applied by steady hands and carefully "trained" brushes. More than a dozen Fostoria patterns are available with gold or platinum trim.

Each decorated piece is carefully hand-checked for uniformity of design. In fact, inspection occurs at every phase in the production of every single item, enabling Fostoria to maintain the high level of quality it is famous for.

Metamorphosis
The Fostoria etching process. This complex operation actually required 10 separate steps to transform a crystal "blank" into a delicately patterned goblet.

Blown crystal blank to which a tissue will be applied, transferring the etching pattern in wax from an engraved plate.

Tissue has been removed, leaving pattern "printed" on the glass.

Stem and rim and inside of glass are coated with a wax masking composition.

After an acid bath, a delicate beauty emerges from its waxy cocoon.

GARLAND

Plate Etching 237

1915 – 1928, Crystal
Stemware is featured in *Fostoria Stemware,* pages 20 – 22, 26 – 30 and 35 – 36.

766 Almond; $20.00
863 Almond; $20.00
5051 Almond, Small; $18.00
5051 Almond, Large; $22.00
1918 Bar Bottle, Cut Neck; $57.00
1918 Bitters Bottle, Tube, Cut Neck; $57.00
880 Bon Bon, 4½ oz.; $20.00
2219 Candy Jar and Cover, ¼ pound; $58.00
2219 Candy Jar and Cover, ½ pound; $65.00
2219 Candy Jar and Cover, pound; $75.00
1697 Carafe Set; $65.00
766 Comport, 5"; $20.00
803 Comport and Cover, 5" Footed; $26.00
766 Comport, 6"; $22.00
803 Comport, 5" Footed; $20.00
803 Comport, 6" Footed; $22.00
481 Custard and Plate; $18.00
766 Custard and Plate; $18.00
300 Decanter, Quart, Cut Neck; $50.00
1918 Decanter, Handled, Cut Neck; $65.00
766 Finger Bowl and Plate; $20.00
1769 Finger Bowl and Plate; $20.00
979 Horseradish; $45.00
1718 Ice Tub, 6"; $35.00
1918 Jar, Cherry, Cut Neck; $65.00
825 Jelly and Cover; $30.00
300/7 Jug, Plain or Cut Flute, Star Bottom extra; $65.00
303/7 Jug; $65.00
317½ Jug and Cover; $85.00
724/7 Jug; $70.00
1236/6 Jug; $65.00
1236/7 Jug; $70.00
1761 Jug, Claret; $75.00
1787/6 Jug; $65.00
2018 Jug, Cut Neck; $70.00
2104 Jug and Tumbler; $75.00
1281 Lemon Dish; $15.00
1968 Marmalade and Cover; $25.00
2138 Mayonnaise, Plate, Ladle; $35.00
2017 Molasses Can, Nickel Handle; $75.00
831 Mustard and Cover; $22.00

766 Nappy, 4½" Footed; $20.00
1227 Nappy, 4½"; $12.00
803 Nappy, 4½" Deep Footed; $20.00
766 Nappy, 5" Footed; $20.00
803 Nappy and Cover, 5" Footed; $25.00
803 Nappy, 5" Deep Footed; $25.00
766 Nappy, 6" Footed; $22.00
803 Nappy, 6" Deep Footed; $22.00
766 Nappy, 7" Footed; $22.00
803 Nappy, 7" Deep Footed; $22.00
1227 Nappy, 8"; $25.00
1465 Oil, Small, Plain or Cut Neck; $38.00
1465 Oil, Large, Plain or Cut Neck; $45.00
200 Plate, 5"; $4.00
200 Plate, 6"; $4.00
701 Plate, 5"; $4.00
840 Plate, 5"; $4.00
932 Plate, 6"; $4.00
1499 Plate, 6"; $4.00
1897 Plate, 7"; $5.00
2238 Plate, 8½" Salad; $6.00
1848 Plate, 9" Sandwich; $10.00
1719 Plate, 10½" Sandwich; $10.00
2238 Plate, 11" Salad; $12.00
1227 Punch Bowl and Foot, Beveled Edge Optional; $125.00
2083 Salad Dressing Bottle; $60.00
2169 Salad Dressing Bottle; $60.00
880 Salt, Footed; $20.00
1165 Shaker, SPT (pair); $28.00
1165½ Shaker, Pearl Top (pair); $35.00
2022 Shaker, FGT (pair); $35.00
2223 Shaker, FGT (pair); $35.00
1478 Sugar and Cream; $27.00
1480 Sugar and Cream; $27.00
2017 Sugar Duster (Shaker) Nickel Top; $50.00
2194 Syrup, 8 oz. Nickel Top; $50.00
2194 Syrup, 12 oz. Nickel Top; $55.00
922 Toothpick, Plain or Cut 19; $23.00
160½ Water Bottle, Cut Neck ; $45.00

LILY OF THE VALLEY

Plate Etching 241

1915 – 1928, Crystal

Stemware is featured in *Fostoria Stemware*, pages 22 – 26 and 34.

810 Bowl, Finger, and Plate; $22.00
858 Bowl, Finger, and Plate; $22.00
1697 Carafe; $60.00
4023 Carafe Tumbler, 6 oz.; $10.00
803 Comport, 5"; $20.00
803 Comport, 6"; $20.00
300/7 Jug; $75.00
303/7 Jug; $75.00
318/7 Jug; $75.00
1968 Marmalade and Cover, Plain; $42.00
1831 Mustard and Cover, Plain; $35.00
1227 Nappy, 4½"; $15.00

803 Nappy, 5"; $15.00
803 Nappy, 6"; $15.00
803 Nappy, 7"; $18.00
1227 Nappy, 8"; $18.00
300½ Oil, Small; $38.00
1465 Oil, 7 oz., Cut Neck; $45.00
1848 Plate, 9" Sandwich; $15.00
1719 Plate, 10½" Sandwich Plain; $18.00
2083 Salad Dressing Bottle; $65.00
1480 Sugar and Cream; $45.00
858 Sweetmeat; $22.00
922 Toothpick, Cut 19, Pty.; $25.00

Garland 2083 Salad Dressing Bottle, 1236 Jug

Oriental 4061 Handled Lemonade, 300 Jug

ORIENTAL

Plate Etching 250

1918 – 1928, Crystal

The Oriental design is possibly the most elaborate of all the Fostoria etchings. One wishes it could have come into being a decade later so that it would have been offered as a complete dinner service. The crystal is of the finest, thin-blown glass, with each piece a marvel of delicacy. Although Oriental is not from the era of Master Etchings, to the eye there is no doubt that it was designed by a master. Other pieces may have been made in this pattern. Stemware is featured in *Fostoria Stemware*, page 20.

766 Almond; $25.00
880 Bon Bon, 4½"; $28.00
766 Bowl, Finger, and 1736 Plate; $25.00
1697 Carafe, and 4023, 6 oz. Tumbler; $75.00

1691 Carafe, Whiskey, 981, 2½ oz.; $75.00
2618 Cigarette Box and Cover; $62.00
803 Comport, 5"; $28.00
803 Comport, 6"; $30.00

766 Cup, 4 oz. Custard; $15.00
300 Decanter, Cut Neck, Quart; $75.00
979 Horseradish; $50.00
300/7 Jug; $225.00
303/7 Jug; $200.00
317½ Jug and Cover; $245.00
724/7 Jug; $225.00
1761 Jug, Claret; $250.00
2105 Jug and Tumbler; $125.00
1968 Marmalade and Cover; $45.00
2138 Mayonnaise, Plate, Ladle; $50.00
1831 Mustard and Cover; $38.00
803 Nappy, 5"; $20.00
803 Nappy, 6"; $20.00
803 Nappy, 7"; $22.00
1227 Nappy, 4½"; $20.00
1227 Nappy, 8"; $25.00
1465 Oil, 5 oz., Cut Neck; $65.00
1465 Oil, 7 oz., Cut Neck; $75.00
701 Plate, 5" Tumbler; $7.00
1897 Plate, 7" Salad; $8.00
1848 Plate, 9" Sandwich; $14.00
1719 Plate, 10½" Sandwich; $25.00
1227 Punch Bowl and Foot; $395.00
2083 Salad Dressing Bottle; $75.00
2169 Salad Dressing Bottle; $75.00
2022 Shaker, FGT (pair); $50.00
2133 Sugar and Cream; $48.00
858 Sweetmeat; $28.00
2194 Syrup, 8 oz.; $125.00

Oriental Grapefruit and Liner, 833 Whiskey, 303 Jug

Oriental 2618 Cigarette Box and Cover

Oriental design

Oriental Sugar, Syrup, and Goblet (Photograph by Milbra Long)

WOODLAND

Plate Etching 264

1922 – 1928, Crystal

GOLDWOOD

Decoration 50

Coin Gold on Plate Etching 264, Woodland
1922 – 1928
Stemware for both patterns is featured in *Fostoria Stemware*, pages 17 and 18.

766 Bowl, Finger, and 1736 Plate; $22.00
   Goldwood Decoration 50; $22.00
2250 Candy Jar and Cover, ¼ pound; $45.00
2250 Candy Jar and Cover, ½ pound; $55.00
2250 Candy Jar and Cover, pound; $58.00
1697 Carafe; $55.00
   Goldwood Decoration 50; $55.00
4023 Carafe, 6 oz. Tumbler; $10.00
803 Comport, 5"; $22.00
803 Comport, 6"; $22.00
300 Decanter, Quart, Cut Neck; $65.00
825 Jelly and Cover; $28.00
300/7 Jug; $150.00
   Goldwood Decoration 50; $150.00
303/7 Jug; $150.00
1743/4 Jug, Grape Juice and Cover; $150.00
1743/7 Jug; $150.00
4089 Marmalade and Cover; $42.00
2138 Mayonnaise, Plate, Ladle; $50.00
1831 Mustard and Cover; $35.00
803 Nappy, 5"; $15.00
803 Nappy, 6"; $15.00
803 Nappy, 7"; $18.00
1465 Oil, 5 oz., Cut Neck; $38.00
1465 Oil, 7 oz., Cut Neck; $45.00
701 Plate, 5" Tumbler; $4.00
   Goldwood Decoration 50; $4.00
840 Plate, 5" Sherbet; $4.00
   Goldwood Decoration 50; $4.00
1897 Plate, 7" Salad; $5.00
   Goldwood Decoration 50; $5.00

2238 Plate, 8¼"; $6.00
   Goldwood Decoration 50; $6.00
2238 Plate, 11"; $12.00
2083 Salad Dressing Bottle; $60.00
   Goldwood Decoration 50; $60.00
2022 Shaker, FGT (pair); $35.00
766 Sweetmeat; $28.00
2194 Syrup, 8 oz., Nickel Top; $100.00

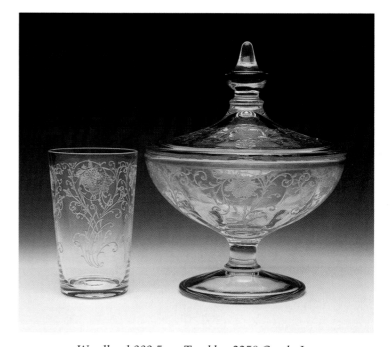

Woodland 889 5 oz. Tumbler, 2250 Candy Jar

WASHINGTON

Plate Etching 266

1923 – 1928
Stemware is featured in *Fostoria Stemware*, pages 17 and 18.

766 Bon Bon (Sweetmeat); $18.00
766 Bowl, Finger, and 2283 Plate; $15.00
2267 Bowl, 9" Console; $25.00
2275 Candlestick, 9½", Plain (pair); $38.00
2250 Candy Jar and Cover, ¼ pound, Optic; $42.00

2250 Candy Jar and Cover, ½ pound, Optic; $45.00
1697 Carafe; $50.00
4023 Carafe Tumbler, 6 oz.; $10.00
5078 Comport, 5"; $18.00
5078 Comport, 6"; $20.00

5078 Comport and Cover, 5"; $22.00
5078 Comport and Cover, 6"; $25.00
300 Decanter, Quart, Cut Neck; $47.00
825 Jelly and Cover; $22.00
300/7 Jug, Tankard, Optic; $75.00
303/7 Jug; $75.00
318/7 Jug; $75.00
318½/3½ Jug; $45.00
2270 Jug and Cover; $75.00
4087 Marmalade and Cover, Optic; $25.00
766 Mayonnaise/Plate/Spoon; $32.00
2138 Mayonnaise, Plate, and Ladle, Plain; $32.00
5078 Nappy, 5"; $15.00
5078 Nappy, 6"; $15.00
5078 Nappy, 7"; $18.00
5078 Nappy, 8"; $18.00
5078 Nappy and Cover, 5"; $20.00
5078 Nappy and Cover, 6"; $20.00
5078 Nappy and Cover, 7"; $25.00
5078 Nappy and Cover, 8"; $25.00
1465 Oil, 5 oz., Cut Neck; $38.00
1465 Oil, 7 oz., Cut Neck; $45.00
2283 Plate, 5" Sherbet; $4.00
2283 Plate, 7" Salad; $5.00
2238 Plate, 8¼" Optic; $6.00
1848 Plate, 9", Cut Matt Star, Optic; $10.00

2238 Plate, 11" Cut Matt Star; $15.00
2083 Salad Dressing Bottle; $58.00
2235 Shaker, FGT, Plain (pair); $38.00
2234 Shaker, Pearl Top, Plain (pair); $45.00
1851 Sugar and Cream, Optic; $28.00
2194 Syrup, 8 oz., Nickel Top, Plain; $50.00
4095 Toothpick (2½ oz. Footed Tumbler); $15.00

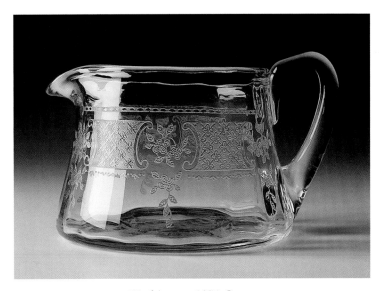

Washington 1851 Cream

No. 1831 Mustard and Cover.

No. 766 Finger Bowl.
No. 1736 Finger Bowl Plate.

No. 2138. Mayonnaise Plate and Ladle.

No. 318-3½ Jug.

No. 1851 Sugar

No. 1851 Cream

No. 2235 Shaker, Pearl Top.

No. 4089. Marmalade and Cover.

No. 2194-8 oz. Syrup, N. T.

No. 1465-7 oz. Oil, C/N.

No. 2083. Salad Dressing Bottle

VIRGINIA
Plate Etching 267
1923 – 1928, Crystal
Stemware is featured in *Fostoria Stemware*, pages 18 and 19.

880 Bon Bon; $18.00
1769 Bowl, Finger, and 2283 Plate; $18.00
2267 Bowl, 9" Console; $25.00
2275 Candlestick, 9½"; $38.00
2250 Candy Jar and Cover, ¼ pound, Optic; $42.00
2250 Candy Jar and Cover, ½ pound, Optic; $45.00
1697 Carafe, and 4023 Tumbler; $60.00
2241 Cologne; $65.00
5078 Comport, 5"; $18.00
5078 Comport, 6"; $20.00
300 Decanter, Quart, CN, Optic; $47.00
825 Jelly and Cover; $22.00
303/3 Jug, Optic; $75.00
303/7 Jug, Optic; $75.00
318/7 Jug, Optic; $75.00
1852/6 Jug, Optic; $70.00
2270 Jug and Cover, Optic; $78.00
4089 Marmalade and Cover, Optic; $36.00
1769 Mayonnaise, Plate, Ladle; $32.00
2138 Mayonnaise, Plate, Ladle; $32.00
1831 Mustard and Cover, Optic; $28.00
5078 Nappy, 5"; $15.00
5078 Nappy, 6'"; $15.00
5078 Nappy, 7"; $18.00
5078 Nappy, 8"; $18.00
5078 Nappy and Cover, 5"; $20.00
5078 Nappy and Cover, 6"; $20.00
5078 Nappy and Cover, 7"; $25.00
5078 Nappy and Cover, 8"; $25.00
1465 Oil, 5 oz., CN, Optic; $38.00
1465 Oil, 7 oz., CN, Optic; $45.00
2283 Plate, 5" Sherbet, Optic; $4.00
2283 Plate, 7", Optic; $5.00

2238 Plate, 8¼" Salad, Optic; $6.00
1848 Plate, 9" Sandwich, Cut Matt Star, Optic; $10.00
2238 Plate, 11", Cut Matt Star, Optic; $15.00
2083 Salad Dressing Bottle, Optic; $58.00
2235 Shaker, FGT (pair); $38.00
2235 Shaker, Pearl Top (pair); $45.00
2133 Sugar and Cream, Optic; $28.00
2194 Syrup, 8 oz. Nickel Top; $50.00
4055 Vase D, Optic; $65.00

Virginia 4085 8 oz. Tumbler, 2270 Jug

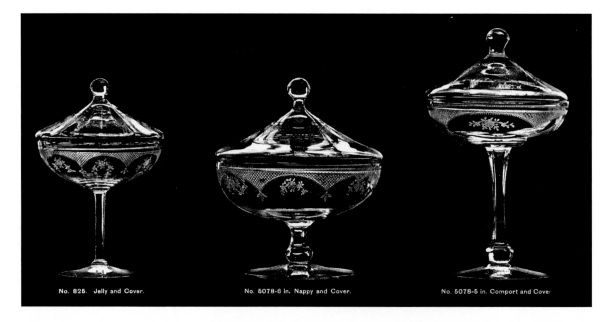

No. 825. Jelly and Cover.   No. 5078-6 in. Nappy and Cover.   No. 5078-5 in. Comport and Cover

Blown Ware, Deep Etched No. 267, "Virginia"

No. 2250 - ½ Lb. Candy Jar and Cover.

No. 2250 - ¼ Lb. Candy Jar and Cover.

No. 880. Bon Bon.

No. 303-3. Jug.

No. 1852-6. Jug.

No. 2238-8¼ in. Plate,

No. 1848-9 in. Plate, Matt Star.

Blown Ware, Deep Etched No. 267, "Virginia"

No. 2133 Sugar.

No. 2133 Cream.

No. 4087 Marmalade and Cover.

No. 1697. 2 Piece Bed Room Set.

No. 2235 Shaker, F.G.T.

No. 2241. Cologne, Drip Stopper.

No. 300. Quart Decanter, C/N.

No. 4055-D. Vase.

No. 2275. 9½ in. Candle

No. 2267. 9 in. Console Bowl.

No. 2275. 9½ in. Candle.

MELROSE

Plate Etching 268

1924 – 1928, Crystal, Optic unless marked Plain.
Stemware is featured in *Fostoria Stemware*, page 19.

1769 Bowl, Finger, and 2283 Plate; $18.00
1697 Carafe and Tumbler; $60.00
803 Comport, 5"; $20.00
803 Comport, 6"; $20.00
300 Decanter, Quart, Cut Neck; $50.00
825 Jelly and Cover; $20.00
303/7 Jug; $75.00
1852/6 Jug; $75.00
4095/4 Jug; $65.00
4095/7 Jug; $85.00
4087 Marmalade and Cover; $36.00
2138 Mayonnaise, Plate/Ladle, Plain; $36.00

803 Nappy, 5"; $15.00
803 Nappy, 6"; $15.00
803 Nappy, 7"; $18.00
1465 Oil, 5 oz., Cut Neck; $38.00
2238 Plate, 7"; $5.00
2238 Plate, 8¼"; $6.00
2238 Plate, 11"; $10.00
2238 Plate, 11", Cut Matt Star; $14.00
2235 Shaker, FGT or Pearl Top,
    Plain (pair); $40.00
1480 Sugar and Cream; $28.00
2287 Tray, Lunch, Plain; $32.00

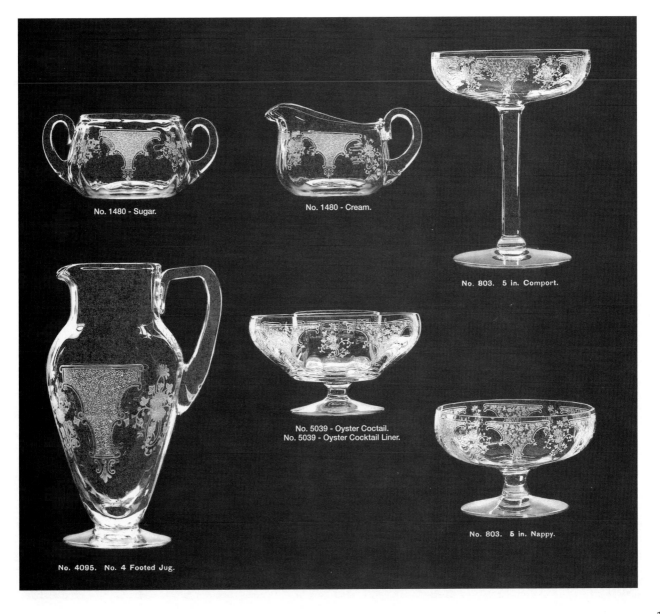

No. 1480 - Sugar.

No. 1480 - Cream.

No. 803.   5 in. Comport.

No. 5039 - Oyster Coctail.
No. 5039 - Oyster Cocktail Liner.

No. 4095.   No. 4 Footed Jug.

No. 803.   6 in. Nappy.

ROGENE

Plate Etching 269

1924 – 1928, Crystal, Regular Optic unless noted.
Stemware is featured in *Fostoria Stemware*, pages 64 and 65.

766 Bowl, Finger, and 2283 Plate; $22.00
1697 Carafe and Tumbler; $75.00
5078 Comport, 5"; $22.00
5078 Comport, 6"; $24.00
300 Decanter, Quart, Cut Neck; $64.00
825 Jelly and Cover; $28.00
4095/4 Jug; $95.00
1852/6 Jug; $110.00
318/7 Jug; $125.00
2270/7 Jug; $125.00
2270/7 Jug and Cover; $150.00
4095/7 Jug; $135.00
1968 Marmalade and Cover; $47.00
766 Mayonnaise, Plate, Ladle; $47.00
2138 Mayonnaise, Plate, Ladle, Plain;
   $48.00
5078 Nappy, 5"; $18.00
5078 Nappy, 6"; $18.00
5078 Nappy, 7"; $22.00
4095 Nut; $25.00
1465 Oil, 5 oz., Cut Neck; $48.00

2238 Plate, 7"; $6.00
2238 Plate, 8¼"; $8.00
2238 Plate, 11"; $12.00
2238 Plate, 11", Cut Matt Star; $15.00
2235, Shaker, FGT or Pearl Top,
   Plain (pair); $54.00
1851 Sugar and Cream; $35.00
4095 Vase, Medium Rolled Edge, Plain; $85.00

No. 766 Finger Bowl
No. 2283 - 6 in. Plate

No. 1968 - Marmalade and Cover

Rogene 887 2 oz. Tumbler, 1697 Carafe

Rogene 2138 Mayonnaise and Ladle

MYSTIC

Plate Etching 270, 270½

Plate Etching 270, Crystal
1925 – 1928
Plate Etching 270½, Green, Spiral Optic
1925 – 1929

4095 Bowl, Finger, and Plate
Crystal, $28.00
Green, $34.00
4095/4 Jug, 1925-1926
Crystal, $295.00
4095/7 Jug
Crystal, $295.00
Green, $330.00
2283 Plate, 6"
Crystal, $12.00

2283 Plate, 7", 8"
Crystal, $16.00
Green, $18.00
2283 Plate, 13"
Crystal, $48.00
Green, $67.00
4095 Vase, 8½", Crystal, $165.00

Crystal 660 Champagne, Green Mystic 5082 Goblet

DELPHIAN

Plate Etching 272

DUCHESS

Decoration 51

Coin Gold Band on Plate Etching 272, Delphian
1925 – 1927, Crystal with Blue Foot
Stemware is featured in *Fostoria Stemware*, pages 64 and 65.

4095 Bowl, Finger; $22.00
4095½ Candy Jar and Cover; $50.00
4095 Nappy, 4½", Decoration 51 only; $22.00
4095 Nappy, 5", $24.00
4095 Nappy, 6"; $24.00
4095 Nappy, 7"; $28.00
4095 Nappy and Cover, 5"; $30.00

4095 Nappy and Cover, 6", $34.00
4095 Nappy and Cover, 7"; $40.00
4095/7 Jug; $295.00
    Decoration 51; $295.00
4095½ Vase, 8"; $275.00
2283 Plate, 6"; $8.00
    Decoration 51; $10.00

149

2283 Plate, 7"; $10.00   2283 Plate 8"; $10.00
    Decoration 51; $12.00   Decoration 51; $12.00

No.4095-2½ oz. Tumbler.
No.4095-5 oz. Tumbler.
No.4095½ Candy Jar and Cover
No.4095-6 in. Nappy and Cover
No.4095 Finger Bowl
No.2283-6 in. Plate
No. 4095½-8 in. Vase.   No. 4095-10 oz. Tumbler.   No. 4095-13 oz. Tumbler.   No. 4095. No. 7 Jug.

ROYAL

Plate Etching 273

The first complete, etched dinnerware service in crystal and colors offered by the Fostoria Glass Company. Stemware is featured in *Fostoria Stemware*, page 31.

2350 Ash Tray, Small
    Crystal, 1928-1933; $12.00
    Amber, 1929-1933; $15.00
    Green, 1929-1933; $15.00
2350½ Bouillon
    Crystal 1926-1933; $12.00
    Amber, 1926-1933; $18.00
    Green, 1926-1933; $18.00
    Blue, 1926-1927; $20.00
869 Bowl, Finger, and Plate
    Crystal, 1925-1933; $18.00
    Amber, 1925-1933; $20.00
    Green, 1925-1933; $20.00
    Blue, 1925-1927; $28.00
2350 Bowl, 5" Fruit
    Crystal, 1926-1933; $14.00
    Amber, 1926-1933; $18.00
    Green 1926-1933; $18.00
    Blue, 1926-1927; $26.00
2350 Bowl, 6" Cereal
    Crystal, 1926-1933; $16.00
    Amber, 1926-1933; $18.00

    Green, 1926-1933; $18.00
    Blue, 1926-1927; $27.00
2350 Bowl, 7" Soup
    Crystal, 1926-1933; $18.00
    Amber, 1926-1933; $22.00
    Green, 1926-1933; $22.00
    Blue, 1926-1927; $28.00
2267 Bowl, 7" Low Foot
    Crystal, 1925-1929; $18.00
    Amber, 1925-1929; $22.00
    Green, 1925-1929; $24.00
    Blue, 1925-1927; $30.00
    Ebony, 1925-1926; $25.00
2350 Bowl, 8" Nappy
    Crystal, 1927; $20.00
    Amber, 1927; $25.00
    Green, 1927; $25.00
    Blue, 1927; $30.00
2350 Bowl, 9" Nappy
    Crystal, 1927; $20.00
    Amber, 1927; $25.00
    Green, 1927; $25.00

Blue, 1927; $32.00
2350 Bowl, 9" Oval Baker
    Crystal, 1926-1933; $20.00
    Amber, 1926-1933; $28.00
    Green, 1926-1933; $28.00
    Blue, 1926-1927; $35.00
2324 Bowl, 10" Footed
    Crystal, 1925-1927; $37.00
    Amber, 1925-1927; $42.00
    Green, 1925-1927; $45.00
    Blue, 1925-1927; $54.00
2350 Bowl, 12" Salad
    Crystal, 1927; $35.00
    Amber, 1927; $50.00
    Green, 1927; $50.00
    Blue, 1927; $65.00
2350 Bowl, 10½" Oval Baker
    Crystal, 1926-1927; $30.00
    Amber, 1926-1927; $38.00
    Green, 1926-1927; $38.00
    Blue, 1926-1927; $45.00
2315 Bowl "A", 10½" Footed, Flared
    Crystal, 1925-1929; $34.00
    Amber, 1925-1929; $40.00
    Green, 1925-1927; $40.00
2297 Bowl "A", 12" Deep
    Crystal, 1925-1933; $35.00
    Amber, 1925-1933; $42.00
    Green, 1925-1933; $42.00
    Blue, 1925-1927; $65.00
    Ebony, 1925-1926; $45.00
2324 Bowl, 13" Footed
    Crystal, 1926-1927; $52.00
    Amber, 1926-1927; $72.00
    Green, 1926-1927; $72.00
    Blue, 1926-1927; $95.00
2350 Butter and Cover
    Crystal, 1927-1929; $95.00
    Amber, 1927-1929; $125.00
    Green, 1927-1929; $135.00
    Blue, 1927; $200.00
2324 Candlestick, 2" (pair)
    Crystal, 1926-1927; $35.00
    Amber, 1926-1927; $45.00
    Green, 1926-1927; $45.00
    Blue, 1926-1927; $56.00
2324 Candlestick, 4" (pair)
    Crystal, 1925-1933; $38.00
    Amber, 1925-1933; $47.00
    Green, 1925-1933; $47.00
    Blue, 1925-1927; $60.00
    Ebony, 1925-1926; $55.00
2324 Candlestick, 9" (pair)
    Crystal, 1925-1927; $55.0
    Amber, 1925-1927; $75.00
    Green, 1925-1927; $85.00

Blue Royal 2331 Candy Box and Cover, 2350 Cereal, 2287 Handled Lunch Tray, 1861 Jelly

    Blue, 1925-1927; $95.00
2324 Candlestick, 12" (pair)
    Crystal, 1926-1927; $95.00
    Amber, 1926-1927; $125.00
    Green, 1926-1927; $135.00
    Blue, 1926-1927; $160.00
2331 Candy Box and Cover
    Crystal, 1925-1933; $55.00
    Amber, 1925-1933; $68.00
    Green, 1925-1933; $70.00
    Blue, 1925-1927; $95.00
    Ebony, 1925-1926; $75.00
2250 Candy and Cover, ½ pound
    Crystal, 1925-1927; $65.00
    Amber, 1925-1927; $75.00
    Green, 1925-1927; $75.00
    Blue, 1925-1927; $95.00
2350 Celery
    Crystal, 1926-1933; $20.00
    Amber, 1926-1933; $22.00
    Green, 1926-1933; $22.00
    Blue, 1926-1927; $30.00
2329 Centerpiece, 11"
    Crystal, 1925-1931; $50.00
    Amber, 1925-1931; $55.00
    Green, 1925-1931; $58.00
    Blue, 1925-1927; $67.00
    Ebony, 1925-1926; $60.00
2329 Centerpiece, 13"
    Crystal, 1926-1931; $65.00
    Amber, 1926-1931; $75.00
    Green, 1926-1931; $75.00
    Blue, 1926-1927; $95.00
2371 Centerpiece, 13" Oval
    Crystal, 1927; $85.00
    Amber, 1927; $95.00
    Green, 1927; $95.00
    Blue, 1927; $125.00

2276 Cheese (Cover) and Cracker
Amber, 1925-1927; $125.00
Green, 1925-1927; $125.00
2322 Cologne, Tall
Crystal, 1926-1927; $95.00
Amber, 1926-1927; $125.00
Green, 1926-1927; $125.00
Blue, 1926-1927; $175.00
2323 Cologne, Squat
Crystal, 1926-1927; $95.00
Amber, 1926-1927; $125.00
Green, 1926-1927; $125.00
Blue, 1926-1927; $175.00
2327 Comport, 7"
Crystal, 1925-1933; $30.00
Amber, 1925-1933; $34.00
Green, 1925-1933; $34.00
Blue, 1925-1927; $45.00
Ebony, 1925-1926; $40.00
2350 Comport, 8"
Crystal, 1927; $45.00
Amber, 1927; $50.00
Green, 1927; $55.00
Blue, 1927; $75.00
2350 Cream Soup
Crystal, 1926-1933; $20.00
Amber, 1926-1933; $22.00
Green, 1926-1933; $24.00
Blue, 1926-1927; $28.00
2350 Cup and Saucer
Crystal, 1926-1927; $16.00
Amber, 1926-1927; $20.00
Green, 1926-1927; $22.00
Blue, 1926-1927; $32.00
2350 Cup and Saucer, After Dinner
Crystal, 1927-1933; $16.00
Amber, 1927-1933; $22.00
Green, 1927-1933; $24.00
Blue, 1927; $35.00
2350½ Cup and Saucer
Crystal, 1926-1933; $16.00
Amber, 1926-1933; $20.00
Green, 1926-1933; $22.00
Blue, 1926-1927; $34.00
2378 Ice Bucket
Crystal, 1927-1931; $54.00
Amber, 1927-1931; $58.00
Green, 1927-1931; $58.00
Blue, 1927; $75.00
1861½ Jelly, 6"
Crystal, 1925-1929; $27.00
Amber, 1925-1929; $34.00
Green, 1925-1929; $34.00
Blue, 1925-1927; $48.00
1236 Jug, Optic
Crystal, 1925-1930; $225.00

Amber, 1925-1930; $295.00
Green, 1925-1930; $325.00
Blue, 1925-1927; $700.00
5000 Jug
Crystal, 1926-1933; $225.00
Amber, 1926-1933; $295.00
Green, 1926-1933; $325.00
Blue, 1926-1927; $750.00
2315 Mayonnaise (Grapefruit)
Crystal, 1925-1929; $28.00
Amber, 1925-1929; $34.00
Green, 1925-1929; $36.00
Blue, 1925-1927; $42.00
2350 Pickle
Crystal, 1926-1933; $16.00
Amber, 1926-1933; $18.00
Green, 1926-1933; $18.00
Blue, 1926-1927; $28.00
2283 Plate, 6"
Crystal, 1925-1933; $10.00
Amber, 1925-1933; $12.00
Green, 1925-1933; $12.00
Blue, 1925-1927; $15.00
2350 Plate, 6"
Crystal, 1926-1933; $10.00
Amber, 1926-1933; $12.00
Green, 1926-1933; $12.00
Blue, 1926-1927; $15.00
2290 Plate, 7"
Crystal, 1925-1929; $10.00
Amber, 1925-1929; $14.00
Green, 1925-1929; $14.00
Blue, 1925-1927; $18.00
2283 Plate, 7"
Crystal, 1925-1933; $10.00
Amber, 1925-1933; $12.00
Green, 1925-1933; $12.00
Blue, 1925-1927; $18.00
2350 Plate, 7"
Crystal, 1926-1933; $10.00
Amber, 1926-1933; $12.00
Green, 1926-1933; $12.00
Blue, 1926-1927; $18.00
2290 Plate, 8"
Crystal, 1925-1929; $12.00
Amber, 1925-1929; $14.00
Green, 1925-1929; $14.00
Blue, 1925-1927; $18.00
2283 Plate, 8"
Crystal, 1925-1933; $12.00
Amber, 1925-1933; $14.00
Green, 1925-1933; $14.00
Blue, 1925-1927; $18.00
2350 Plate, 8"
Crystal, 1926-1933; $12.00
Amber, 1926-1933; $14.00

Green, 1926-1933; $14.00
Blue, 1926-1927; $18.00
2283 Plate, 9"
Crystal, 1925-1933; $14.00
Amber, 1925-1933; $18.00
Green, 1925-1933; $18.00
Blue, 1925-1927; $22.00
2350 Plate, 9"
Crystal, 1926-1933; $24.00
Amber, 1926-1933; $30.00
Green, 1926-1933; $32.00
Blue, 1926-1927; $50.00
2283 Plate, 10"
Crystal, 1925-1933; $35.00
Amber, 1925-1933; $50.00
Green, 1925-1933; $55.00
Blue, 1925-1927; $75.00
2350 Plate, 10"
Crystal, 1926-1933; $35.00
Amber, 1926-1933; $50.00
Green, 1926-1933; $55.00
Blue, 1926-1927; $75.00
2290 Plate, 13"
Crystal, 1925-1929; $30.00
Amber, 1925-1929; $34.00
Green, 1925-1929; $38.00
Blue, 1925-1927; $68.00
2321 Plate, 8" Salad
Crystal, 1926-1930; $12.00
Amber, 1926-1930; $14.00
Green, 1926-1930; $14.00
Blue, 1926-1927; $18.00
2316 Plate, 8" Soup
Crystal, 1925-1926; $12.00
Amber, 1925-1926; $14.00
Green, 1925-1926; $14.00
Blue, 1925-1926; $18.00
2350 Plate, 13" Chop
Crystal, 1927-1933; $24.00
Amber, 1927-1933; $34.00
Green, 1927-1933; $35.00
Blue, 1927; $68.00
2350 Plate, 15" Chop
Crystal, 1926-1927; $35.00
Amber, 1926-1927; $40.00
Green, 1926-1927; $45.00
Blue, 1926-1927; $68.00
2350 Platter, 10½"
Crystal, 1926-1927; $24.00
Amber, 1926-1927; $35.00
Green, 1926-1927; $38.00
Blue, 1926-1927; $54.00
2350 Platter, 12"
Crystal, 1926-1933; $25.00
Amber, 1926-1933; $35.00

Green Royal Grapefruit/Mayonnaise; Amber Royal 945½ Grapefruit and Liner

Green, 1926-1933; $38.00
Blue, 1926-1927; $54.00
2350 Platter, 15"
Crystal, 1926-1927; $30.00
Amber, 1926-1927; $42.00
Green, 1926-1927; $45.00
Blue, 1926-1927; $75.00
2350 Sauce Boat and Plate
Crystal, 1927-1933; $36.00
Amber, 1927-1933; $48.00
Green, 1927-1933; $50.00
Blue, 1927; $95.00
5000 Shaker, FGT (pair)
Crystal, 1926-1930; $85.00
Amber, 1926-1930; $95.00
Green, 1926-1930; $100.00
Blue, 1926-1927; $150.00
2315 Sugar and Cream
Crystal, 1925-1927; $35.00
Amber, 1925-1927; $40.00
Green, 1925-1927; $40.00
Blue, 1925-1927; $58.00
2350 Sugar and Cream
Crystal, 1926-1933; $34.00
Amber, 1926-1933; $40.00
Green, 1926-1933; $40.00
Blue, 1926-1927; $58.00
2350½ Sugar, Cover, Cream
Crystal, 1926-1930; $35.00
Amber, 1926-1930; $45.00
Green, 1926-1930; $45.00
Blue, 1926-1927; $64.00
2287 Tray, Handled Lunch
Crystal, 1925-1931; $35.00
Amber, 1925-1931; $45.00
Green, 1925-1931; $48.00

Blue, 1925-1927; $65.00
2324 Urn, Small
    Crystal, 1925-1927; $42.00
    Amber, 1925-1927; $65.00
    Green, 1925-1927; $70.00
    Blue, 1925-1927; $125.00
2276 Vanity Set
    Crystal, 1925-1927; $58.00
    Amber, 1925-1927; $74.00

Green, 1925-1927; $77.00
Blue, 1925-1927; $125.00
Ebony, 1925-1926; $75.00
2292 Vase, 8" Footed, Flared
    Crystal, 1925-1930; $37.00
    Amber, 1925-1930; $45.00
    Green, 1925-1930; $45.00
    Blue, 1925-1927; $85.00

2350—Pickle.

2315—Sugar

2315½—Cream.

2350—Butter and Cover.

2350—Cream Soup.
2332—7 in. Cream Soup Plate.

2367—7 in. Bowl.

5100—Ftd. Shaker.
Optic. F. G. Top.

2350—6 in. Cereal.

2350—8 in. Salad Plate.

869—Finger Bowl.
2283—6 in. Finger Bowl Plate.
Optic.

2350½—Ftd. Tea Cup.
2350—Saucer.

1236—No. 6 Jug.
Optic.

Royal Pattern, Plate Etching No. 273
Made in Crystal, Amber, Blue and Green.

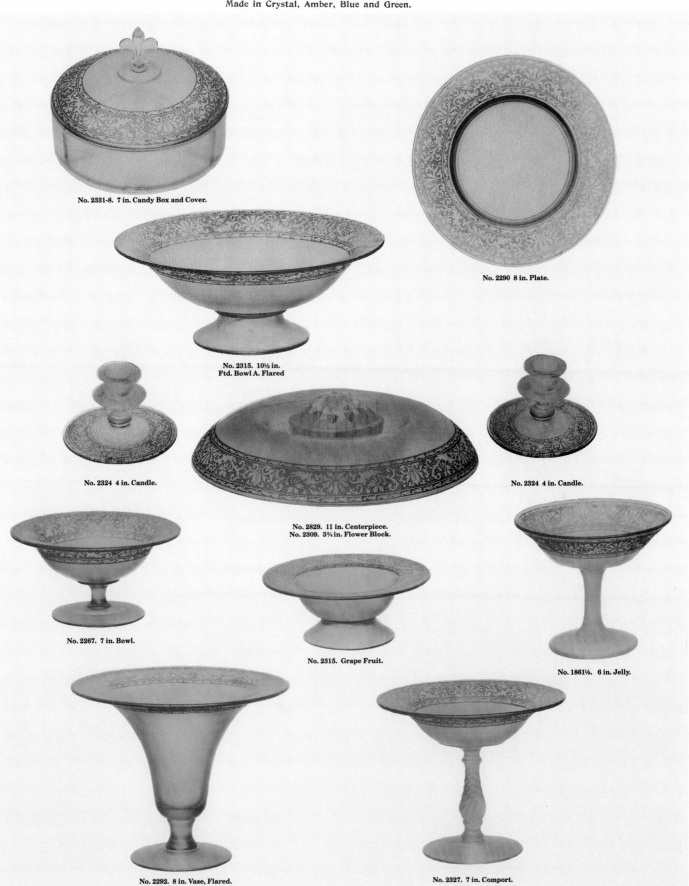

No. 2331-8. 7 in. Candy Box and Cover.

No. 2290 8 in. Plate.

No. 2315. 10½ in.
Ftd. Bowl A. Flared

No. 2324 4 in. Candle.

No. 2324 4 in. Candle.

No. 2829. 11 in. Centerpiece.
No. 2309. 3¾ in. Flower Block.

No. 2267. 7 in. Bowl.

No. 2315. Grape Fruit.

No. 1861½. 6 in. Jelly.

No. 2292. 8 in. Vase, Flared.

No. 2327. 7 in. Comport.

SEVILLE

Plate Etching 274

Stemware is featured in *Fostoria Stemware,* page 32.

2350 Ash Tray, Small
  Crystal, 1929-1932; $10.00
  Amber, 1929-1932; $12.00
  Green, 1929-1932; $12.00
2350½ Bouillon
  Crystal, 1927-1933; $12.00
  Amber, 1927-1933; $15.00
  Green, 1927-1933; $15.00
2350 Bowl, 5" Fruit
  Crystal, 1927-1933; $12.00
  Amber, 1927-1933; $15.00
  Green, 1927-1933; $15.00
2350 Bowl, 6" Cereal
  Crystal, 1927-1933; $12.00
  Amber, 1927-1933; $15.00
  Green, 1927-1933; $15.00
2350 Bowl, 7" Soup
  Crystal, 1927-1933; $14.00
  Amber, 1927-1933; $18.00
  Green, 1927-1933; $18.00
2350 Bowl, 8" Nappy
  Crystal, 1927-1928; $20.00
  Amber, 1927-1928; $25.00
  Green 1927-1928; $25.00
2350 Bowl, 9" Nappy
  Crystal, 1927-1928; $20.00
  Amber, 1927-1928; $25.00
  Green, 1927-1928; $25.00
2350 Bowl, 9" Oval Baker
  Crystal, 1927-1933; $20.00
  Amber, 1927-1933; $28.00
  Green, 1927-1933; $28.00
869 Bowl, Finger, and 2283 Plate
  Crystal, 1927-1933; $15.00

  Amber, 1927-1933; $18.00
  Green, 1927-1933; $18.00
2267 Bowl, 7" Low Footed
  Crystal, 1927-1928; $18.00
  Amber, 1927-1928; $22.00
  Green, 1927-1928; $22.00
2324 Bowl, 10" Footed
  Crystal, 1927-1929; $35.00
  Amber, 1927-1929; $40.00
  Green, 1927-1929; $40.00
2350 Bowl, 10" Salad
  Crystal, 1927-1929; $35.00
  Amber, 1927-1929; $40.00
  Green, 1927-1929; $40.00
2315 Bowl, 10½" Flared
  Crystal, 1927-1928; $34.00
  Amber, 1927-1928; $38.00
  Green, 1927-1928; $38.00
2350 Bowl, 10½" Oval Baker
  Crystal, 1927-1929; $30.00
  Amber, 1927-1929; $34.00
  Green, 1927-1929; $34.00
2297 Bowl, 12" "A"
  Crystal, 1927-1933; $34.00
  Amber, 1927-1933; $38.00
  Green, 1927-1933; $38.00
2350 Butter and Cover
  Crystal, 1927-1930; $85.00
  Amber, 1927-1930; $95.00
  Green, 1927-1930; $110.00
2324 Candlestick, 2" (pair)
  Crystal, 1927-1929; $32.00
  Amber, 1927-1929; $37.00
  Green, 1927-1929; $37.00

2324 Candlestick, 4" (pair)
Crystal, 1927-1933; $35.00
Amber, 1927-1933; $40.00
Green, 1927-1933; $40.00

2324 Candlestick, 9" (pair)
Crystal, 1927-1929; $52.00
Amber, 1927-1929; $58.00
Green, 1927-1929; $58.00

2250 Candy Jar and Cover, ½ pound
Crystal, 1927-1929; $60.00
Amber, 1927-1929; $65.00
Green, 1927-1929; $65.00

2329 Centerpiece, 11" Round
Crystal, 1927-1930; $50.00
Amber, 1927-1930; $55.00
Green, 1927-1930; $57.00

2329 Centerpiece, 13" Round
Crystal, 1927-1932; $60.00
Amber, 1927-1932; $65.00
Green, 1927-1932; $65.00

2371 Centerpiece, 13" Oval, and Flower Holder
Crystal, 1927-1929; $60.00
Amber, 1927-1929; $65.00
Green, 1927-1929; $70.00

2350 Celery
Crystal, 1927-1933; $18.00
Amber, 1927-1933; $22.00
Green, 1927-1933; $22.00

2368 Cheese and Cracker
Crystal, 1927-1932; $45.00
Amber, 1927-1932; $50.00
Green, 1927-1932; $50.00

2327 Comport, 7"
Crystal, 1927-1932; $26.00
Amber, 1927-1932; $28.00
Green, 1927-1932; $30.00

2350 Comport, 8"
Crystal, 1927-1930; $40.00
Amber, 1927-1930; $45.00
Green, 1927-1930; $50.00

2350 Cream Soup and Plate
Crystal, 1927-1933; $25.00
Amber, 1927-1933; $28.00
Green, 1927-1933; $30.00

2350 Cup and Saucer
Crystal, 1927-1929; $14.00
Amber, 1927-1929; $17.00
Green, 1927-1929; $18.00

2350 Cup and Saucer, After Dinner
Crystal, 1927-1933; $14.00
Amber, 1927-1933; $17.00
Green, 1927-1933; $18.00

2350½ Cup and Saucer
Crystal, 1927-1933; $14.00
Amber, 1927-1933; $17.00
Green, 1927-1933; $18.00

2315 Grapefruit (Same as Mayonnaise)
Crystal, 1927-1930; $20.00
Amber, 1927-1930; $22.00
Green, 1927-1930; $22.00

2378 Ice Bucket, Nickel Plated Handle
Crystal, 1927-1932; $50.00
Amber, 1927-1932; $54.00
Green, 1927-1932; $54.00

5084 Jug
Crystal, 1927-1933; $110.00
Amber, 1927-1933; $125.00
Green, 1927-1933; $135.00

2315 Mayonnaise (Same as Grapefruit)
Crystal, 1927-1930; $20.00
Amber, 1927-1930; $22.00
Green, 1927-1930; $22.00

2350 Pickle
Crystal, 1927-1933; $16.00
Amber, 1927-1933; $18.00
Green, 1927-1933; $18.00

2350 Plate, 6"
Crystal, 1927-1933; $8.00
Amber, 1927-1933; $10.00
Green, 1927-1933; $12.00

2350 Plate, 7"
Crystal, 1927-1933; $8.00
Amber, 1927-1933; $10.00
Green, 1927-1933; $12.00

2350 Plate, 8"
Crystal, 1927-1933; $9.00
Amber, 1927-1933; $10.00
Green, 1927-1933; $12.00

2350 Plate, 9"
Crystal, 1927-1933; $10.00
Amber, 1927-1933; $14.00
Green, 1927-1933; $14.00

2350 Plate, 10"
Crystal, 1927-1933; $15.00
Amber, 1927-1933; $20.00
Green, 1927-1933; $22.00

2350 Plate, 13" Chop
Crystal, 1927-1933; $20.00
Amber, 1927-1933; $27.00
Green, 1927-1933; $30.00

2350 Plate, 15" Round
Crystal, 1927-1929; $20.00
Amber, 1927-1929; $27.00
Green, 1927-1929; $30.00

2350 Platter, 10½"
 Crystal, 1927-1928; $22.00
 Amber, 1927-1928; $28.00
 Green, 1927-1928; $30.00
2350 Platter, 12"
 Crystal, 1927-1933; $22.00
 Amber, 1927-1933; $30.00
 Green, 1927-1933; $32.00
2350 Platter, 15"
 Crystal, 1927-1928; $24.00
 Amber, 1927-1928; $30.00
 Green, 1927-1928; $35.00
2350 Sauce Boat and Plate
 Crystal, 1927-1933; $35.00
 Amber, 1927-1933; $45.00
 Green, 1927-1933; $45.00
5000 Shaker, FGT (pair)
 Crystal, 1927-1930; $65.00
 Amber, 1927-1930; $75.00
 Green, 1927-1930; $85.00
2315½ Sugar and Cream
 Crystal, 1927-1928; $30.00
 Amber, 1927-1928; $35.00
 Green, 1927-1928; $35.00
2350½ Sugar and Cream
 Crystal, 1927-1933; $30.00
 Amber, 1927-1933; $35.00
 Green, 1927-1933; $35.00
2350½ Sugar and Cover
 Crystal, 1927-1928; $18.00

2350—After Dinner Cup
2350—A. D. Saucer

2350—Bouillon
2350—Saucer

 Amber, 1927-1928; $22.00
 Green, 1927-1928; $22.00
2287 Tray, Handled Lunch
 Crystal, 1927-1932; $34.00
 Amber, 1927-1932; $38.00
 Green, 1927-1932; $42.00
2324 Urn, Small
 Crystal 1927-1929; $42.00
 Amber, 1927-1929; $45.00
 Green, 1927-1929; $47.00
2292 Vase, 8"
 Crystal, 1927-1930; $44.00
 Amber, 1927-1930; $48.00
 Green, 1927-1930; $50.00

VESPER

Plate Etching 275

For pieces not shown, consult similar patterns and the pressed patterns of Pioneer and 2315. Stemware is featured in *Fostoria Stemware*, page 66.

2350 Ash Tray
 Amber, 1929-1933; $15.00
 Green, 1929-1933; $15.00
2350 Bouillon and Saucer
 Amber, 1926-1929; $18.00
 Green, 1926-1929; $18.00
 Blue, 1926-1927; $24.00
2350½ Bouillon, Footed
 Amber, 1929-1933; $18.00
 Green, 1929-1933; $18.00
869 Bowl, Finger, and 2283 Plate
 Amber, 1926-1933; $20.00
 Green, 1926-1933; $20.00
 Blue, 1926-1927; $28.00
2350 Bowl, 5 " Fruit
 Amber, 1926-1933; $18.00
 Green, 1926-1933; $18.00

 Blue, 1926-1927; $26.00
2350 Bowl, 6" Cereal
 Amber, 1926-1933; $18.00
 Green, 1926-1933; $18.00
 Blue, 1926-1927; $27.00
2350 Bowl, 7" Soup
 Amber, 1926-1933; $22.00
 Green, 1926-1933; $22.00
 Blue, 1926-1927; $38.00
2267 Bowl, 7" Low Foot
 Amber, 1926-1927; $22.00
 Green, 1926-1927; $24.00
 Blue, 1926-1927; $30.00
2350 Bowl, 8" Nappy
 Amber, 1926-1927; $24.00
 Green, 1926-1927; $24.00
 Blue, 1926-1927; $35.00

2350 Bowl, 9" Nappy
    Amber, 1926-1927; $24.00
    Green, 1926-1927; $24.00
    Blue, 1926-1927; $35.00
2350 Bowl, 9" Oval Baker
    Amber, 1926-1933; $30.00
    Green, 1926-1933; $30.00
    Blue, 1926-1927; $42.00
2324 Bowl, 10" Footed
    Amber, 1926-1927; $65.00
    Green, 1926-1927; $75.00
    Blue, 1926-1927; $95.00
2350 Bowl, 10" Salad
    Amber, 1926-1927; $38.00
    Green, 1926-1927; $38.00
    Blue, 1926-1927; $50.00
2315 Bowl, 10½" Footed, Flared
    Amber, 1926-1927; $58.00
    Green, 1926-1927; $67.00
    Blue, 1926-1927; $87.00
2350 Bowl, 10½" Oval Baker
    Amber, 1926-1928; $52.00
    Green, 1926-1928; $54.00
    Blue, 1926-1927; $65.00
2297 Bowl "A", 12" Deep
    Amber, 1926-1933; $55.00
    Green, 1926-1933; $60.00
    Blue, 1926-1927; $95.00
2350 Butter and Cover
    Amber, 1926-1927; $345.00
    Green, 1926-1927; $345.00
    Blue, 1926-1927; $465.00
2324 Candlestick, 2" (pair)
    Amber, 1926-1927; $48.00
    Green, 1926-1927; $50.00
    Blue, 1926-1927; $60.00
2324 Candlestick, 4" (pair)
    Amber, 1926-1933; $48.00
    Green, 1926-1933; $50.00
    Blue, 1926-1927; $60.00
2324 Candlestick, 9" (pair)
    Amber, 1926-1927; $125.00
    Green, 1926-1927; $150.00
    Blue, 1926-1927; $195.00
2250 Candy Jar and Cover
    Amber, 1926-1927; $75.00
    Green, 1926-1927; $75.00
    Blue, 1926-1927; $110.00
2331 Candy Box and Cover
    Amber, 1926-1933; $125.00
    Green, 1926-1933; $125.00
    Blue, 1926-1927; $195.00
2350 Celery
    Amber, 1926-1933; $24.00
    Green, 1926-1933; $24.00
    Blue, 1926-1927; $30.00

2329 Centerpiece, 11"
    Amber, 1926-1932; $58.00
    Green, 1926-1932; $58.00
    Blue, 1926-1927; $65.00
2329 Centerpiece, 13"
    Amber, 1926-1932; $75.00
    Green, 1926-1932; $75.00
    Blue, 1926-1927; $125.00
2371 Centerpiece, 13" Oval
    Amber, 1926; $95.00
    Green, 1926; $95.00
    Blue, 1926; $125.00
2368 Cheese and Cracker
    Amber, 1926-1933; $65.00
    Green, 1926-1933; $65.00
    Blue, 1926-1927; $95.00
2327 Comport, 7"
    Amber, 1926-1933; $34.00
    Green, 1926-1933; $38.00
    Blue, 1926-1927; $50.00
2350 Comport, 8"
    Amber, 1926-1927; $50.00
    Green, 1926-1927; $55.00
    Blue, 1926-1927; $75.00
2315½ Cream
    Amber, 1926; $20.00

Green, 1926; $20.00
2350 Cream Soup and Plate
    Amber, 1926-1929; $26.00
    Green, 1926-1929; $26.00
    Blue, 1926-1927; $32.00
2350½ Cream Soup and Plate
    Amber, 1929-1933; $28.00
    Green, 1929-1933; $28.00
2350 Cup and Saucer, AD
    Amber, 1926-1933; $20.00
    Green, 1926-1933; $22.00
    Blue, 1926-1927; $34.00
2350 Cup and Saucer
    Amber, 1926-1930; $20.00
    Green, 1926-1930; $22.00
    Blue, 1926-1927; $32.00
2350½ Cup and Saucer
    Amber, 1926-1933; $22.00
    Green, 1926-1933; $24.00
    Blue, 1926-1927; $35.00
2378 Ice Bucket, NPH
    Amber, 1926-1932; $58.00
    Green, 1926-1932; $58.00
    Blue, 1926-1927; $75.00
5000 Jug
    Amber, 1926-1933; $325.00
    Green, 1926-1933; $350.00
    Blue, 1926-1927; $1,200.00 to market
2315 Mayonnaise/Grapefruit
    Amber, 1926-1927; $35.00
    Green, 1926-1927; $35.00
    Blue, 1926-1926; $42.00
2350 Pickle
    Amber, 1926-1933; $20.00
    Green, 1926-1933; $20.00
    Blue, 1926-1927; $28.00
2350 Plate, 6"
    Amber, 1926-1933; $12.00
    Green, 1926-1933; $12.00
    Blue, 1926-1927; $15.00
2350 Plate, 7"
    Amber, 1926-1933; $12.00
    Green, 1926-1933; $12.00
    Blue, 1926-1927; $16.00
2350 Plate, 8"
    Amber, 1926-1933; $14.00
    Green, 1926-1933; $14.00
    Blue, 1926-1927; $18.00
2350 Plate, 9"
    Amber, 1926-1933; $30.00
    Green, 1926-1933; $35.00
    Blue, 1926-1927; $50.00
2350 Plate, 10"
    Amber, 1926-1933; $50.00
    Green, 1926-1933; $55.00
    Blue, 1926-1927; $75.00

Blue Vesper 5000 Jug (Photograph by Bert Kennedy)

2321 Plate, 6"
    Amber, 1926-1933; $12.00
    Green, 1926-1933; $12.00
    Blue, 1926-1927; $15.00
2321 Plate, 7"
    Amber, 1926-1933; $12.00
    Green, 1926-1933; $12.00
    Blue, 1926-1927; $15.00
2321 Plate, 8"
    Amber, 1926-1933; $14.00
    Green, 1926-1933; $14.00
    Blue, 1926-1927; $18.00
2321 Plate 9"
    Amber, 1926-1933; $30.00
    Green, 1926-1933; $35.00
    Blue, 1926-1927; $50.00
2321 Plate, 10"
    Amber, 1926-1933; $50.00
    Green, 1926-1933; $55.00
    Blue, 1926-1927; $75.00
2350 Plate, 12" Chop
    Amber, 1926-1933; $34.00
    Green, 1926-1933; $38.00
    Blue, 1926-1927; $68.00
2350 Plate, 15" Round
    Amber, 1926-1927; $45.00
    Green, 1926-1927; $48.00
    Blue, 1926-1927; $77.00
2350 Platter, 10½"
    Amber, 1926-1927; $35.00

Green, 1926-1927; $38.00
Blue, 1926-1927; $54.00
2350 Platter, 12"
  Amber, 1926-1933; $35.00
  Green, 1926-1933; $38.00
  Blue, 1926-1927; $54.00
2350 Platter, 15"
  Amber, 1926-1933; $42.00
  Green, 1926-1933; $45.00
  Blue, 1926-1927; $75.00
2350 Sauce Boat and Plate
  Amber, 1926-1933; $48.00
  Green, 1926-1933; $50.00
  Blue, 1926-1927; $85.00
5000 Shaker, Footed, FGT (pair)
  Amber, 1926-1930; $95.00
  Green, 1926-1930; $100.00
  Blue, 1926-1927; $150.00
2315 Sugar and Cream
  Amber, 1926-1927; $37.00
  Green, 1926-1927; $40.00
  Blue, 1926-1927; $65.00
2350 Sugar and Cover, Cream
  Amber, 1926; $60.00
  Green, 1926; $60.00
  Blue, 1926; $85.00
2350½ Sugar and Cream
  Amber, 1927-1933; $64.00
  Green, 1927-1933; $67.00
  Blue, 1927; $85.00
2350½ Sugar and Cover
  Amber, 1927-1930; $50.00
  Green, 1927-1930; $54.00
  Blue, 1927; $75.00

Green Vesper 5000 Jug, Amber Vesper Jug

2287 Tray, Handled Lunch
  Amber, 1926-1932; $45.00
  Green, 1926-1932; $48.00
  Blue, 1926-1927; $65.00
2276 Vanity Set
  Amber, 1926-1927; $135.00
  Green, 1926-1927; $150.00
  Blue, 1926-1927; $225.00
2292 Vase, 8"
  Amber, 1926-1927; $95.00
  Green, 1926-1927; $95.00
  Blue, 1926-1927; $125.00
2324 Vase, Small Urn
  Amber, 1926-1927; $95.00
  Green, 1926-1927; $110.00
  Blue, 1926-1927; $150.00

2350—Cream Soup.

2350—Celery.

2368—Ftd. Cheese.
2368—11 in. Cracker Plate.

BEVERLY

Plate Etching 276

For pieces not shown, consult similar patterns and the pressed patterns of Pioneer and 2315. Stemware is featured in *Fostoria Stemware*, page 67.

2350 Ash Tray, Small, 1931-1932
  Crystal, $10.00
  Amber, $12.00
  Green, $12.00
2350½ Bouillon, Footed, 1927-1933
  Crystal, $12.00
  Amber, $14.00
  Green, $14.00
869 Bowl, Finger, and 2283
  6" Plate, 1931-1933
  Crystal, $15.00
  Amber, $18.00
  Green, $18.00
2350 Bowl, 5" Fruit, 1927-1933
  Crystal, $15.00
  Amber, $18.00
  Green, $18.00
2350 Bowl, 6" Cereal, 1931-1933
  Crystal, $16.00
  Amber, $20.00
  Green, $20.00
2350 Bowl, 7" Soup, 1931-1933
  Crystal, $18.00
  Amber, $22.00
  Green, $22.00
2350 Bowl, 8" Nappy, 1927-1929
  Crystal, $24.00
  Amber, $26.00
  Green, $28.00
2350 Bowl, 9" Baker, 1927-1933
  Crystal, $28.00
  Amber, $30.00
  Green, $32.00
2297 Bowl "A", Deep, 1931-1933
  Crystal, $35.00
  Amber, $40.00
  Green, $42.00
2324 Bowl, 10" Footed, 1927-1929
  Crystal, $55.00
  Amber, $64.00
  Green, $75.00
2350 Bowl, 10" Salad, 1927-1929
  Crystal, $40.00
  Amber, $42.00
  Green, $44.00
2329 Bowl, 11" Centerpiece, 1931-1932
  Crystal, $50.00
  Amber, $52.00
  Green, $55.00
2329 Bowl, 13" Centerpiece, 1931-1932
  Crystal, $55.00

  Amber, $58.00
  Green, $60.00
2324 Candlestick, 4", 1931-1933 (pair)
  Crystal, $40.00
  Amber, $42.00
  Green, $44.00
2331 Candy Box and Cover, 1931-1933
  Crystal, $57.00
  Amber, $59.00
  Green, $60.00
2350 Celery, 1931-1933
  Crystal, $22.00
  Amber, $24.00
  Green, $24.00
2368 Cheese and Cracker, 1931-1933
  Crystal, $50.00
  Amber, $52.00
  Green, $55.00
2327 Comport, 7", 1931-1933
  Crystal, $28.00
  Amber, $30.00
  Green, $32.00
2350 Cream Soup, 1927-1930
  Crystal, $20.00
  Amber, $22.00
  Green, $22.00
2350½ Cream Soup, Footed, 1931-1933
  Crystal, $26.00
  Amber, $28.00
  Green, $30.00
2350 Cream Soup Plate, 1931-1933
  Crystal, $7.00
  Amber, $9.00
  Green, $10.00
2350 Cup and Saucer, 1927-1930
  Crystal, $16.00

Green Beverly Cheese and Cracker, Sugar and Cream

Amber, $18.00
Green, $20.00
2350½ Cup and Saucer, 1927-1933
Crystal, $18.00
Amber, $20.00
Green, $22.00
2350 Cup and Saucer, AD, 1927-1933
Crystal, $18.00
Amber, $20.00
Green, $22.00
2315 Grapefruit, 1927-1929
Crystal, $24.00
Amber, $26.00
Green, $28.00
2378 Ice Bucket, 1931-1932
Crystal, $50.00
Amber, $52.00
Green, $55.00
5000 Jug, 1931-1933
Crystal, $150.00
Amber, $175.00
Green, $195.00
2350 Pickle, 1931-1933
Crystal, $20.00
Amber, $22.00
Green, $24.00
2350 Plate, 6", 1927-1933
Crystal, $6.00
Amber, $8.00
Green, $8.00
2350 Plate, 7", 1927-1933
Crystal, $8.00
Amber, $10.00
Green, $10.00
2350 Plate, 8", 1927-1933
Crystal, $8.00
Amber, $10.00

Green, $10.00
2350 Plate, 9", 1927-1933
Crystal, $24.00
Amber, $26.00
Green, $28.00
2350 Plate, 10", 1927-1933
Crystal, $30.00
Amber, $32.00
Green, $34.00
2350 Plate, 13" Chop, 1931-1933
Crystal, $37.00
Amber, $40.00
Green, $42.00
2350 Platter, 10½", 1927-1929
Crystal, $38.00
Amber, $40.00
Green, $40.00
2350 Platter, 12", 1931-1933
Crystal, $40.00
Amber, $42.00
Green, $42.00
2350 Platter, 15", 1931-1933
Crystal, $44.00
Amber, $46.00
Green, $46.00
2350 Sauce Boat and Plate, 1931-1933
Crystal, $50.00
Amber, $52.00
Green, $54.00
2350½ Sugar and Cream, Footed, 1927-1933
Crystal, $35.00
Amber, $38.00
Green, $40.00
2292 Vase, 8", 1927
Crystal, $44.00
Amber, $48.00
Green, $50.00

2324—10 in. Bowl.   2350—10 in. Salad Bowl.

2350—Cream Soup.

2315—Grape Fruit.

2350—After Dinner Cup.
2350—A. D. Saucer.

2350½—Ftd. Tea Cup.
2350—Saucer.

2350—7 in. Salad Plate.

2350—Cup.
2350—Saucer.

VERNON

Plate Etching 277

Stemware is featured in *Fostoria Stemware,* page 33.

2350 Ash Tray, Small
    Azure, 1928-1932; $22.00
    Green, 1927-1932; $18.00
    Amber, 1927-1932; $18.00
    Orchid, 1927-1928; $24.00
2375 Bon Bon
    Azure, 1928-1933; $26.00
    Green, 1927-1933; $24.00
    Amber, 1927-1933; $22.00
2375 Bouillon
    Azure, 1928-1933; $18.00
    Green, 1927-1933; $16.00
    Amber, 1927-1933; $16.00
    Orchid, 1927-1928; $18.00
869 Bowl, Finger, and 2283 Plate
    Crystal, 1927-1933; $20.00
    Azure, 1928-1933; $25.00
    Green, 1927-1933; $24.00
    Amber, 1927-1933; $20.00
    Orchid, 1927-1928; $25.00
2375 Bowl, 5" Fruit
    Azure, 1928-1933; $18.00
    Green, 1927-1933; $16.00
    Amber, 1927-1932; $14.00
    Orchid, 1927-1928; $18.00
2375 Bowl, 6" Cereal
    Azure, 1928-1933; $20.00

    Green, 1927-1933; $18.00
    Amber, 1927-1933; $16.00
    Orchid, 1927-1928; $20.00
2375 Bowl, 7" Soup
    Azure, 1928-1933; $22.00
    Green, 1927-1933; $20.00
    Amber, 1927-1933; $18.00
    Orchid, 1927-1928; $22.00
2375 Bowl, 9" Baker
    Azure, 1928-1933; $47.00
    Green, 1927-1933; $42.00
    Amber, 1927-1933; $40.00
    Orchid, 1927-1928; $47.00
2375 Bowl, 12"
    Azure, 1928-1933; $65.00
    Green, 1927-1933; $57.00
    Amber, 1927-1933; $52.00
    Orchid, 1927-1928; $65.00
2384 Bowl "A", 12"
    Azure, 1928-1933; $65.00
    Green, 1928-1933; $55.00
    Amber, 1928-1933; $52.00
    Orchid, 1928; $65.00
2415 Bowl, Combination
    Azure, 1929; $85.00
    Green, 1929; $75.00
    Amber, 1929; $70.00

2394 Candlestick, 2" (pair)
    Azure, 1928-1933; $75.00
    Green, 1928-1933; $65.00
    Amber, 1928-1933; $60.00
    Orchid, 1928; $75.00
2375 Candlestick, 3" (pair)
    Azure, 1928-1933; $65.00
    Green, 1927-1933; $58.00
    Amber, 1927-1933; $54.00
    Orchid, 1927-1928; $60.00
2375½ Candlestick (pair)
    Azure, 1928-1932; $95.00
    Green, 1927-1932; $85.00
    Amber, 1927-1932; $80.00
    Orchid, 1927-1928; $95.00
2331 Candy Box and Cover
    Azure, 1928-1932; $95.00
    Green, 1927-1932; $85.00
    Amber, 1927-1932; $80.00
    Orchid, 1927-1928; $95.00
2375½ Celery, 11½"
    Azure, 1928-1933; $30.00
    Green, 1927-1933; $28.00
    Amber, 1927-1933; $28.00
    Orchid, 1927-1928; $30.00
2375½ Centerpiece, 13" Oval, Flower Holder
    Azure, 1928-1932; $300.00
    Green, 1927-1932; $250.00
    Amber, 1927-1932; $200.00
    Orchid, 1927; $350.00
2368 Cheese and Cracker
    Azure, 1928-1932; $90.00
    Green, 1927-1932; $75.00
    Amber, 1927-1932; $70.00
2375 Comport, 7"
    Azure, 1928-1932; $42.00
    Green, 1927-1932; $37.00
    Amber, 1927-1932; $35.00
2400 Comport, 8"
    Crystal, 1928-1932; $54.00
    Azure, 1928-1932; $65.00
    Green, 1928-1932; $60.00
    Amber, 1928-1932; $57.00
    Orchid, 1928; $65.00
2375 Cream Soup and Plate
    Azure, 1928-1933; $50.00
    Green, 1927-1933; $45.00
    Amber, 1927-1933; $40.00
    Orchid, 1927-1928; $50.00
2375 Cup and Saucer, After Dinner
    Azure, 1928-1933; $32.00
    Green, 1927-1933; $28.00
    Amber, 1928-1933; $26.00
    Orchid, 1927-1928; $32.00

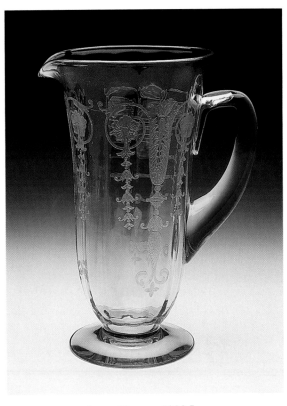

Azure Vernon 5000 Jug

2375½ Cup and Saucer
    Crystal, 1928-1933; $24.00
    Azure, 1928-1933; $23.00
    Green, 1927-1933; $28.00
    Amber, 1927-1933; $26.00
    Orchid, 1927-1928; $32.00
2375 Ice Bucket
    Azure, 1930-1933; $100.00
    Green, 1930-1933; $85.00
    Amber, 1930-1933; $75.00
2378 Ice Bucket
    Azure, 1928-1929; $100.00
    Green, 1927-1929; $85.00
    Amber, 1927-1929; $75.00
    Orchid, 1927-1928; $100.00
5000 Jug
    Crystal, 1930-1933; $175.00
    Azure, 1928-1933; $295.00
    Green, 1927-1933; $250.00
    Amber, 1927-1933; $250.00
    Orchid, 1927-1928; $295.00
2375 Lemon
    Azure, 1928-1933; $24.00
    Green, 1928-1933; $22.00
    Amber, 1928-1933; $22.00
    Orchid, 1927-1928; $24.00

2375 Oil, Footed
    Azure, 1929-1932; $75.00
    Green, 1929-1932; $55.00
    Amber, 1929-1932; $55.00
2375 Plate, 6"
    Azure, 1928-1933; $10.00
    Green, 1927-1933; $8.00
    Amber, 1928-1933; $8.00
    Orchid, 1927-1928; $10.00
2375 Plate, 7"
    Crystal, 1931-1933; $10.00
    Azure, 1928-1933; $12.00
    Green, 1927-1933; $10.00
    Amber, 1927-1933; $10.00
    Orchid, 1927-1928; $12.00
2375 Plate, 8"
    Crystal, 1931-1933; $10.00
    Azure, 1928-1933; $14.00
    Green, 1927-1933; $12.00
    Amber, 1927-1933; $10.00
    Orchid, 1927-1928; $14.00
2375 Plate, 9"
    Azure, 1928-1933; $20.00
    Green, 1927-1933; $18.00
    Amber, 1927-1933; $16.00
    Orchid, 1927-1928; $20.00
2375 Plate, 10"
    Azure, 1928-1933; $60.00
    Green, 1927-1933; $45.00
    Amber, 1927-1933; $40.00
    Orchid, 1927-1928; $52.00
2375 Plate, 13" Chop
    Azure, 1928-1933; $50.00
    Green, 1927-1933; $45.00
    Amber, 1927-1933; $40.00
    Orchid, 1927-1928; $45.00
2375 Platter, 12"
    Azure, 1928-1933; $48.00
    Green, 1927-1933; $45.00
    Amber, 1927-1933; $42.00
    Orchid, 1927-1928; $48.00
2375 Platter, 15"
    Azure, 1929-1933; $67.00
    Green, 1929-1933; $60.00
    Amber, 1929-1933; $55.00
2375 Relish, 8½"
    Azure, 1928-1933; $35.00
    Green, 1927-1933; $32.00
    Amber, 1927-1933; $30.00
    Orchid, 1927-1928; $35.00

Orchid Vernon 2375½ 13" Oval Centerpiece, 2375 Candlesticks

2375 Sauce Boat and Plate
    Azure, 1929-1932; $65.00
    Green, 1929-1932; $60.00
    Amber, 1929-1932; $58.00
2375 Shaker, FGT (pair)
    Azure, 1929-1933; $95.00
    Green, 1929-1933; $85.00
    Amber, 1929-1933; $85.00
5000 Shaker, FGT (pair)
    Green, 1927-1928; $85.00
    Amber, 1927-1928; $85.00
    Orchid, 1927-1928; $95.00
2375½ Sugar and Cream
    Crystal, 1929-1933; $40.00
    Azure, 1928-1933; $55.00
    Green, 1927-1933; $50.00
    Amber, 1927-1933; $45.00
    Orchid, 1927-1928; $54.00
2375½ Sugar and Cover
    Azure, 1928-1929; $47.00
    Green, 1927-1929; $45.00
    Amber, 1927-1929; $40.00
    Orchid, 1927-1928; $47.00
2375 Tray, Handled Lunch
    Azure, 1928-1932; $85.00
    Green, 1927-1932; $75.00
    Amber, 1927-1932; $65.00
    Orchid, 1927-1928; $85.00
2375 Whip Cream
    Azure, 1929-1933; $32.00
    Green, 1929-1933; $28.00
    Amber, 1929-1933; $28.00

"VERNON" PATTERN, PLATE ETCHING No. 277.
MADE IN AMBER, GREEN AND ORCHID.
PRICED PAGE 22-B — No. 2 SUPPLEMENT PRICE LIST.

2375—3 in. Candle.

2375—12 in. Bowl.
2309—3¾ in. F. Block.

2375—3 in. Candle.

2331—3 Candy Box & Cover.

2375½—Ftd. Cup.
2375—Saucer.

2368—Footed Cheese.
2368—11 in. Cracker Plate.

2375½—Candle.

2375½—13 in. Oval Centerpiece.
2371—Flower Holder.

2375½—Candle.

2375—5 in. Fruit.

2375—Ftd. Cream Soup.
2375—Cream Soup Plate.

2375—7 in. Soup.

2375—6 in. Cereal.

2375—Ftd. Mayonnaise.
2375—Mayonnaise Plate.

2375—7 in. Comport.

MASTER ETCHINGS

As a prelude to its fiftieth anniversary, Fostoria announced "New Master Etchings" in the 1936 catalog. From the page below, it is evident that Fostoria planned to make the most of this announcement. In the Jubilee year, not only were plate etchings now Master Etchings, but the color Topaz was renamed "Gold Tint." Also in 1937, the company employed the services of Elizabeth Lounsbery to formulate a wonderful booklet entitled "Modern Decorative Tables for All Occasions." On the next to last page of that booklet is the only reference we have found to Azure-Tint: "These pieces are available in clearest crystal, Azure-Tint or Gold-Tint." Possibly, Fostoria considered changing Azure to Azure-Tint at the same time Topaz was renamed Gold Tint, but if so, the idea did not last long enough to be incorporated into a catalog or price list.

WE'RE TELLING
OVER 4 MILLION FAMILIES:
"See These New MASTER-ETCHINGS"*

The new Fostoria "Master-Etched" Lines are going to sell . . . and sell plenty!

. . . Not only because we've produced the most beautiful etchings in Fostoria history

. . . Not only because there's a definite trend toward more delicate glassware decoration

. . . But because we're getting behind these etchings with a powerful advertising program.

The market is ripe for something new . . . and with these lovely patterns and a driving advertising campaign whipping up interest, easy sales are going to be made by dealers who stock Fostoria "Master-Etchings".

Leading magazines will carry the sales story to over 4,000,000 glass-buying homes. There'll be radio broadcasts by "Jean Abbey" in the major cities. You'll have special window displays, counter cards, leaflets and mats for newspaper advertising.

*"MASTER-ETCHING"

A name given by Fostoria to etchings on glass that have been created by master designers, executed with rare skill and applied with unusual care. The perfection of this mechanical reproduction of "Master-Etchings" requires the unequaled equipment and facilities of Fostoria.

VERSAILLES
Plate Etching 278
Stemware is featured in *Fostoria Stemware*, pages 68 – 70.

2350 Ash Tray, Small
  Rose, 1928-1934; $48.00
  Azure, 1928-1934; $48.00
  Green, 1928-1934; $36.00
  Topaz, 1929-1934; $36.00

2375 Bon Bon
  Rose, 1928-1940; $50.00
  Azure, 1928-1934; $54.00
  Green, 1928-1934; $50.00
  Topaz/Gold Tint, 1929-1940; $40.00

2375 Bouillon
  Rose, 1928-1934; $48.00
  Azure, 1928-1934; $52.00
  Green, 1928-1934; $48.00
  Topaz, 1929-1935; $35.00

869 Bowl, Finger, and 2283 Plate
  Rose, 1928-1940; $85.00
  Azure, 1928-1943; $95.00
  Green, 1928-1936; $100.00
  Topaz/Gold Tint, 1929-1943; $85.00

2375 Bowl, 5" Fruit
  Rose, 1928-1940; $35.00
  Azure, 1928-1943; $37.00
  Green, 1928-1934; $42.00
  Topaz/Gold Tint, 1929-1943; $32.00

2375 Bowl, 6" Cereal
  Rose, 1928-1934; $57.00
  Azure, 1928-1934; $62.00
  Green, 1928-1934; $57.00
  Topaz, 1929-1934; $48.00

2394 Bowl, 6"
  Topaz, 1931-1934; $45.00

2375 Bowl, 7" Soup
  Rose, 1931-1934; $125.00
  Azure, 1931-1934; $145.00
  Green, 1931-1934; $145.00
  Topaz, 1931-1935; $125.00

2375 Bowl, 9" Baker
  Rose, 1928-1940; $135.00
  Azure, 1928-1943; $135.00
  Green, 1928-1936; $140.00
  Topaz/Gold Tint, 1929-1940; $110.00

2375 Bowl, Large Dessert
  Rose, 1931-1934; $135.00
  Azure, 1931-1934; $150.00
  Green, 1931-1934; $135.00
  Topaz, 1931-1934; $125.00

2395 Bowl, 10"
  Rose, 1928-1938; $175.00
  Azure, 1928-1938; $250.00
  Green, 1928-1934; $250.00
  Topaz/Gold Tint, 1929-1939; $140.00

2394 Bowl "A", 12"
  Rose, 1928-1938; $95.00
  Azure, 1928-1939; $125.00
  Green, 1928-1934; $95.00
  Topaz/Gold Tint, 1929-1939; $95.00

2394 Candlestick, 2" (pair)
  Rose, 1928-1939; $48.00
  Azure, 1928-1939; $56.00
  Green, 1928-1934; $56.00
  Topaz/Gold Tint, 1929-1940; $48.00

2375 Candlestick, 3" (pair)
  Rose, 1928-1939; $52.00
  Azure, 1928-1939; $58.00
  Green, 1928-1934; $52.00
  Topaz, 1929-1939; $52.00

2375½ Candlestick (pair)
  Rose, 1928-1934; $125.00
  Azure, 1928-1934; $125.00
  Green, 1928-1934; $125.00
  Topaz, 1929-1934; $120.00

2395 Candlestick, 3" (pair)
  Rose, 1928-1930; $165.00
  Azure, 1928-1930; $185.00
  Green, 1928-1930; $165.00

2395½ Candlestick, 5" (pair)
  Rose, 1931-1939; $140.00
  Azure, 1931-1939; $150.00
  Green, 1931-1934; $165.00
  Topaz/Gold Tint, 1931-1939; $135.00

2331 Candy Box and Cover
  Rose, 1928-1934; $250.00
  Azure, 1928-1934; $270.00
  Green, 1928-1934; $250.00

2394 Candy Jar and Cover, ½ pound
  Topaz, 1929-1932; $275.00

2375 Celery, 11½"
  Rose, 1931-1934; $125.00
  Azure, 1931-1934; $135.00
  Green, 1931-1934; $125.00
  Topaz/Gold Tint, 1939-1938; $95.00

2375 Centerpiece, 11"
  Rose, 1928-1929; $175.00
  Azure, 1928-1929; $195.00
  Green, 1928-1929; $195.00

2375 Centerpiece, 12"
  Rose, 1930-1934; $125.00
  Azure, 1930-1934; $135.00
  Green, 1930-1934; $125.00
  Topaz, 1930-1935; $125.00

2375½ Centerpiece, 13" Oval, and Flower Holder
  Rose, 1928-1932; $350.00
  Azure, 1928-1932; $350.00

Green, 1928-1932; $350.00
2368 Cheese and Cracker
  Rose, 1928-1934; $95.00
  Azure, 1928-1934; $125.00
  Green, 1928-1934; $95.00
  Topaz, 1929-1934; $95.00
2375 Cheese and Cracker
  Rose, 1931-1934; $125.00
  Azure, 1931-1934; $150.00
  Green, 1931-1934; $125.00
  Topaz, 1931-1934; $125.00
5098 Comport, 5"
  Rose, 1928-1934; $75.00
  Azure, 1928-1934; $85.00
  Green, 1928-1934; $75.00
2400 Comport, 6"
  Rose, 1931-1934; $85.00
  Azure, 1931-1934; $95.00
  Green, 1931-1934; $85.00
  Topaz, 1931-1934; $75.00
5099 Comport, 6"
  Topaz, 1929-1934; $75.00
2375 Comport, 7"
  Rose, 1928-1934; $95.00
  Azure, 1928-1934; $110.00
  Green, 1928-1934; $95.00
2400 Comport, 8"
  Rose, 1928-1932; $125.00
  Azure, 1928-1932; $150.00
  Green, 1928-1932; $125.00
2375 Cream Soup and Plate
  Rose, 1928-1940; $85.00
  Azure, 1928-1943; $95.00
  Green, 1928-1936; $95.00
  Topaz/Gold Tint, 1929-1943; $85.00
2375 Cup and Saucer, After Dinner
  Rose, 1928-1934; $125.00
  Azure, 1928-1934; $135.00
  Green, 1928-1934; $125.00
  Topaz, 1929-1935; $115.00
2375½ Cup and Saucer
  Rose, 1928-1940; $40.00
  Azure, 1928-1943; $45.00
  Green, 1928-1936; $48.00
  Topaz/Gold Tint, 1929-1943; $40.00
2439 Decanter and Stopper
  Rose, July 1930-1932; market
  Azure, July 1930-1932; market
  Green, July 1930-1932; market
2375 Ice Bucket
  Rose, 1929-1932; $150.00
  Azure, 1929-1932; $175.00
  Green, 1929-1932; $150.00
  Topaz/Gold Tint, 1930-1943; $125.00

Green Versailles 2378 Whip Cream Pail, 2375 12" Centerpiece, 2375½ Candlesticks

2378 Ice Bucket
  Rose, 1928; $150.00
  Azure, 1928; $175.00
  Green, 1928; $150.00
2451 Ice Dish, Plate, Liners
  Rose, 1931-1934; $95.00
  Azure, 1931-1934; $125.00
  Green, 1931-1934; $95.00
  Topaz, 1931-1934; $95.00
5000 Jug
  Rose, 1928-1939; $800.00
  Azure, 1928-1939; $800.00
  Green, 1928-1936; $900.00
  Topaz/Gold Tint, 1929-1943; $575.00
2375 Lemon Dish
  Rose, 1928-1934; $34.00
  Azure, 1928-1934; $38.00
  Green, 1928-1934; $34.00
  Topaz/Gold Tint, 1929-1943; $32.00
2375 Mayonnaise, Plate, Ladle
  Rose, 1928-1934; $125.00
  Azure, 1928-1934; $135.00
  Green, 1928-1934; $125.00
  Topaz, 1929-1934; $125.00
2394 Mint
  Rose, 1928-1934; $34.00
  Azure, 1928-1934; $38.00
  Green, 1928-1934; $34.00
  Topaz, 1929-1934; $34.00
5098 Nappy, 6" Footed
  Rose, 1928-1930; $75.00
  Azure, 1928-1930; $85.00
  Green, 1928-1930; $75.00
2375 Oil, Footed
  Rose, 1930-1934; $395.00
  Azure, 1930-1934; $580.00

Green, 1930-1934; $395.00
Topaz, 1930-1934; $395.00
2375 Plate, 6"
 Rose, 1928-1940; $12.00
 Azure, 1928-1943; $14.00
 Green, 1928-1936; $12.00
 Topaz, 1929-1943; $10.00
2375 Plate, 7"
 Rose, 1928-1940; $15.00
 Azure, 1928-1943; $15.00
 Green, 1928-1936; $18.00
 Topaz, 1929-1943; $14.00
2375 Plate, 8"
 Rose, 1928-1940; $20.00
 Azure, 1928-1943; $20.00
 Green, 1928-1936; $22.00
 Topaz, 1929-1943; $18.00
2375 Plate, 9"
 Rose, 1928-1940; $45.00
 Azure, 1928-1943; $45.00
 Green, 1928-1936; $50.00
 Topaz, 1929-1943; $40.00
2375 Plate, 10"
 Rose, 1928-1940; $95.00
 Azure, 1928-1943; $120.00
 Green, 1928-1936; $110.00
 Topaz, 1929-1943; $95.00
2375 Plate, Canape
 Rose, 1929-1930; $25.00
 Azure, 1929-1930; $25.00
 Green, 1929-1930; $25.00
 Topaz, 1929-1930; $20.00
2375 Plate, 10" Grill
 Rose, 1930; $85.00
 Azure, 1930; $85.00
 Green, 1930; $85.00
2375 Plate, 10" Cake
 Rose, 1931-1934; $85.00
 Azure, 1931-1934; $95.00
 Green, 1931-1934; $85.00
 Topaz/Gold Tint, 1931-1939; $78.00
2375 Plate, 13" Chop
 Rose, 1928-1936; $125.00
 Azure, 1928-1936; $150.00
 Green, 1928-1936; $!25.00
 Topaz, 1929-1936; $125.00
2375 Platter, 12"
 Rose, 1928-1940; $165.00
 Azure, 1928-1943; $175.00
 Green, 1928-1936; $175.00
 Topaz/Gold Tint, 1929-1943; $165.00
2375 Platter, 15"
 Rose, 1931-1940; $250.00
 Azure, 1931-1940; $275.00
 Green, 1931-1936; $300.00

Rose Versailles 2385 Fan Vase, 4100 8" Vase, 5000 Jug, 2375 Comport, 2375 Shakers

Topaz/Gold Tint, 1931-1938; $250.00
2375 Relish, 8½"
 Rose, 1928-1940; $42.00
 Azure, 1928-1940; $48.00
 Green, 1928-1934; $48.00
 Topaz, 1929-1943; $42.00
2083 Salad Dressing Bottle
 Rose, July 1930-1932; $900.00/market
 Azure, July 1930-1932; $1,100.00/market
 Green, July 1930-1932; $800.00/market
 Topaz, July 1930-1932; $800.00/market
2375 Salad Dressing Bottle
 Rose, 1933-1934; $900.00/market
 Azure, 1933-1934; $1000.00/market
 Green, 1933-1934; $900.00/market
 Topaz, 1933-1934; $650.00/market
2375 Sauce Boat and Plate
 Rose, 1930-1935; $425.00
 Azure, 1930-1935; $550.00
 Green, 1930-1934; $525.00
 Topaz, 1930-1935; $400.00
2375 Shaker, FGT (pair)
 Rose, 1928-1940; $225.00
 Azure, 1928-1943; $225.00
 Green, 1928-1936; $300.00
 Topaz, 1929-1940; $225.00
2375½ Sugar and Cover
 Rose, 1928-1934; $235.00
 Azure, 1928-1934; $250.00
 Green, 1928-1934; $235.00
 Topaz, 1929-1934; $225.00
2375½ Sugar and Cream, Tea
 Rose, 1929-1934; $165.00
 Azure, 1929-1934; $175.00

VERSAILLES

DESIGN PATENT NOS. 76372 AND 76454

VERSAILLES DESIGN

PLATE ETCHING No. 278   *Priced on pages 20 and 21—1931 Price List*

STEMWARE

Made in Crystal Base with Rose Bowl—Crystal Base with Azure Bowl—
Crystal Base with Green Bowl

1.	5098	Goblet	6.	5098	Cocktail	10.	5098	12-oz. Footed Tumbler
2.	5098	High Sherbet	5.	5098	Cordial	10.	5098	9-oz. Footed Tumbler
3.	5098	Low Sherbet	7.	5098	Oyster Cocktail	10.	5098	5-oz. Footed Tumbler
4.	5098	Parfait	8.	5082½	Grape Fruit	10.	5098	2½-oz. Footed Tumbler
5.	5098	Claret	8.	945½	Grape Fruit Liner	11.	5098	5-in. Comport
5.	5098	Wine	9.	869	Finger Bowl	12.	5000-7	Footed Jug
			9.	2283	6-in. Plate, Reg. Opt.			

Made in Crystal Base with Topaz Bowl

13.	5099	Goblet	18.	5099	Cocktail	20.	5099	12-oz. Footed Tumbler
14.	5099	High Sherbet	17.	5099	Cordial	20.	5099	9-oz. Footed Tumbler
15.	5099	Low Sherbet	19.	5099	Oyster Cocktail	20.	5099	5-oz. Footed Tumbler
16.	5099	Parfait	8.	5082½	Grape Fruit	20.	5099	2½-oz. Footed Tumbler
17.	5099	Claret	8.	945½	Grape Fruit Liner	21.	5099	6-in. Comport
17.	5099	Wine	9.	869	Finger Bowl	12.	5000-7	Footed Jug
			9.	2283	6-in. Plate, Reg. Opt.			

[18]

DESIGN PATENT NOS. 76372 AND 76454

VERSAILLES DESIGN

PLATE ETCHING No. 278   *Priced on pages 20 and 21 —1931 Price List*

DINNERWARE

Made in Rose, Azure, Green and Topaz

22.	2375	Footed Shaker	29.	2375	After Dinner Saucer	44.	2375	Bon Bon
	2439	Decanter	30.	2375	Footed Bouillon	45.	2375	Lemon Dish
	2429	Service Tray	31.	2375	Cream Soup	46.	2375	10-in. Cake Plate
	2429	Service and Lemon Tray	31.	2375	Cream Soup Plate	47.	2375	Large Dessert
23.	2451	Ice Dish	32.	2375	9-in. Baker	48.	2375	Ice Bucket
23.	2451	T. J. Liner (not etched)	33.	2375	12-in. Platter	49.	2375	Cheese and Cracker
23.	2451	C. M. Liner (not etched)	33.	2375	15-in. Platter	50.	2368	Cheese and Cracker
24.	2375	7-in. Comport	34.	2375	Sauce Boat	51.	2394	½-lb. Candy Jar and Cover
25.	2400	6-in. Comport	34.	2375	Sauce Boat Plate	52.	2331-3	Candy Box and Cover
25.	2400	8-in. Comport	35.	2375	8½-in. Relish	53.	2394	Mint
	2350	Small Ash Tray	36.	2375	11½-in. Celery	53.	2394	6-in. Bowl
26.	2375	6-in. Bread and Butter Plate		2375½	Footed Sugar and Cover	53.	2394	12-in. Bowl
26.	2375	7-in. Salad Plate	37.	2375½	Footed Sugar	54.	2394	2-in. Candlestick
26.	2375	8-in. Luncheon Plate	38.	2375½	Footed Cream	55.	2375	12-in. Centerpiece
26.	2375	9-in. Dinner Plate	37.	2375½	Tea Sugar	55.	2375½	13-in. Oval Centerpiece
26.	2375	10-in. Dinner Plate	38.	2375½	Tea Cream	56.	2375½	Candlestick
26.	2375	13-in. Chop Plate	39.	2375	Mayonnaise	57.	2375	12-in. Bowl
27.	2375	5-in. Fruit	39.	2375	Mayonnaise Plate	58.	2375	3-in. Candlestick
27.	2375	6-in. Cereal	40.	2375	Footed Oil	59.	2395	10-in. Bowl
27.	2375	7-in. Soup		2083	Salad Dressing Bottle	60.	2395½	5-in. Candlestick
28.	2375½	Footed Cup	41.	2375	Handled Lunch Tray		2385	8½-in. Footed Fan Vase
28.	2375	Saucer	42.	2375	Whip Cream		4100	8-in. Vase, Reg. Opt.
29.	2375	After Dinner Cup	43.	2375	Sweetmeat	61.	2417	8-in. Vase, Reg. Opt.

[19]

Green, 1929-1934; $165.00
Topaz, 1929-1934; $165.00
2375½ Sugar and Cream
Rose, 1928-1940; $110.00
Azure, 1928-1943; $125.00
Green, 1928-1936; $125.00
Topaz, 1929-1934; $125.00
2378 Sugar Pail, NP Handle
Rose, 1928-1929; $365.00
Azure, 1928-1929; $395.00
Green, 1928-1929; $365.00
Topaz, 1929; $365.00
2375 Sweetmeat
Rose, 1928-1939; $34.00
Azure, 1928-1939; $38.00
Green, 1928-1934; $38.00
Topaz, 1929-1943; $34.00
2375 Tray, Handled Lunch
Rose, 1928-1934; $145.00
Azure, 1928-1934; $165.00
Green, 1928-1934; $135.00
Topaz/Gold Tint, 1929-1943; $125.00
2429 Tray, Service, and Lemon
Rose, 1929-1932; $300.00

Azure, 1929-1932; $350.00
Green, 1929-1932; $300.00
Topaz, 1929-1932; $300.00
2417 Vase, 8" R.O.
Topaz, 1930-1932; $300.00
4100 Vase, 8" R.O.
Rose, 1928-1934; $150.00
Azure, 1928-1934; $200.00
Green, 1928-1934; $175.00
2385 Vase, 8½" Fan
Rose, 1928-1932; $300.00
Azure, 1928-1932; $365.00
Green, 1928-1932; $300.00
2375 Whip Cream
Rose, 1928-1935; $38.00
Azure, 1928-1934; $45.00
Green, 1928-1934; $45.00
Topaz, 1929-1935; $40.00
2378 Whip Cream Pail, NP Handle
Rose, 1928-1930; $320.00
Azure, 1928-1930; $365.00
Green, 1928-1930; $350.00
Topaz, 1929-1930; $350.00

JUNE

Plate Etching 279

One of the most beautiful and extensive patterns offered by the Fostoria Glass Company. Stemware is featured in *Fostoria Stemware*, pages 68 and 69.

2350 Ash Tray, Small
Crystal, 1929-1943; $40.00
Rose, 1928-1934; $56.00
Azure, 1928-1934; $60.00
Topaz, 1929-1935; $48.00
2375 Bon Bon
Crystal, 1929-1943; $38.00
Rose, 1928-1934; $46.00
Azure, 1928-1934; $54.00
Topaz/Gold Tint, 1929-1943; $40.00
2375 Bouillon
Crystal, 1929-1943; $30.00
Rose, 1928-1940; $44.00
Azure, 1928-1940; $44.00
Topaz/Gold Tint, 1929-1943; $34.00
869 Bowl, Finger, and 2283 Plate
Crystal, 1928-1943; $75.00
Rose, 1928-1940; $95.00
Azure, 1928-1940; $100.00
Topaz/Gold Tint, 1929-1943; $85.00
2375 Bowl, 5" Fruit
Crystal, 1929-1943; $32.00
Rose, 1928-1940; $37.00
Azure, 1928-1943; $38.00

Topaz/Gold Tint, 1929-1943; $34.00
2375 Bowl, 6" Cereal
Crystal, 1929-1943; $40.00
Rose, 1928-1934; $58.00
Azure, 1928-1943; $58.00
Topaz, 1929-1935; $50.00
2394 Bowl, 6" (Same as Mint)
Rose, 1928-1934; $45.00
Azure, 1928-1934; $45.00
Topaz, 1929-1934; $45.00
2375 Bowl, 7" Soup
Crystal, 1931-1942; $52.00
Rose, 1931-1934; $125.00
Azure, 1931-1934; $145.00
Topaz, 1931-1934; $125.00
2375 Bowl, 7" Round Nappy
Crystal, 1933-1941; $50.00
Rose, 1933-1934; $150.00
Azure, 1933-1934; $150.00
Topaz, 1933-1934; $150.00
2375 Bowl, 9" Baker/Vegetable
Crystal, 1929-1943; $65.00
Rose, 1928-1940; $135.00
Azure, 1928-1943; $135.00

Topaz/Gold Tint, 1929-1940; $110.00
2395 Bowl, 10" ("Grecian")
    Crystal, 1929-1939; $175.00
    Rose, 1928-1938; $225.00
    Azure, 1928-1938; $225.00
    Topaz/Gold Tint, 1929-1939; $200.00
2375 Bowl, Large Dessert
    Crystal, 1931-1940; $95.00
    Rose, 1931-1934; $135.00
    Azure, 1931-1934; $150.00
    Topaz, 1931-1934; $125.00
2375 Bowl, 12"
    Crystal, 1929-1943; $75.00
    Rose, 1928-1940; $95.00
    Azure, 1928-1940; $95.00
    Topaz/Gold Tint, 1929-1939; $85.00
2394 Bowl "A", 12"
    Crystal, 1929-1943; $87.00
    Rose, 1928-1939; $95.00
    Azure, 1928-1939; $125.00
    Topaz/Gold Tint, 1929-1940; $95.00
2394 Candlestick, 2" (pair)
    Crystal, 1929-1943; $45.00
    Rose, 1928-1939; $50.00
    Azure, 1928-1939; $54.00
    Topaz/Gold Tint, 1929-1940; $50.00
2375½ Candlestick, Mushroom (pair)
    Crystal, 1931-1942; $75.00
    Rose, 1928-1934; $125.00
    Azure, 1928-1934; $135.00
    Topaz, 1931-1934; $125.00
2375 Candlestick, 3" (pair)
    Crystal, 1929-1943; $45.00
    Rose, 1928-1940; $52.00
    Azure, 1928-1940; $55.00
    Topaz/Gold Tint, 1929-1939; $52.00
2395 Candlestick, 3" ("Grecian") (pair)
    Rose, 1928-1929; $175.00
    Azure, 1928-1929; $195.00
    Topaz, 1929 (May not have been made); $225.00
2395½ Candlestick, 5" ("Grecian") (pair)
    Crystal, 1930-1939; $125.00
    Rose, 1930-1939; $140.00
    Azure, 1930-1939; $$145.00
    Topaz/Gold Tint, 1930-1939; $125.00
2394 Candy and Cover, ½ lb.
    Crystal, 1931-1934; $200.00
    Rose, 1931-1934; $300.00
    Azure, 1931-1934; $350.00
    Topaz, 1931-1934; $300.00
2331 Candy Box and Cover, 3-part
    Rose, 1928-1934; $250.00
    Azure, 1928-1934; $275.00
    Topaz, 1929-1934; $275.00
2375 Celery, 11½"
    Crystal, 1931-1943; $95.00

Azure June 5000 Jug, 2375 Large Dessert, 2385 Fan Vase, 2378 Sugar Pail, 2375 Shakers

    Rose, 1931-1936; $137.00
    Azure, 1931-1942; $125.00
    Topaz/Gold Tint, 1931-1939; $110.00
2375 Centerpiece, 11"
    Rose, 1928-1929; $175.00
    Azure, 1928-1929; $195.00
2375 Centerpiece, 12"
    Crystal, 1930-1942; $125.00
    Rose, 1930-1934; $175.00
    Azure, 1930-1934; $195.00
    Topaz, 1930-1934; $175.00
2375½ Centerpiece, 13" Oval and Flower Holder
    Crystal, 1929-1932; $295.00
    Rose, 1928-1932; $350.00
    Azure, 1928-1932; $350.00
2375 Cheese and Cracker
    Crystal, 1931-1942; $110.00
    Rose, 1931-1934; $135.00
    Azure, 1931-1934; $150.00
    Topaz/Gold Tint, 1931-1939; $125.00
2368 Cheese and Cracker
    Crystal, 1929-1934; $110.00
    Rose, 1928-1934; $125.00
    Azure, 1928-1934; $150.00
    Topaz, 1929-1934; $125.00
5098 Comport, 5"
    Crystal, 1929-1934; $70.00
    Rose, 1928-1934; $75.00
    Azure, 1928-1934; $85.00
    Topaz, 1929-1934; $75.00
2400 Comport, 6"
    Crystal, 1931-1943; $68.00
    Rose, 1931-1935; $95.00
    Azure, 1931-1938; $100.00
    Topaz/Gold Tint, 1931-1943; $85.00
2375 Comport, 7"
    Rose, 1928-1934; $95.00
    Azure, 1928-1934; $110.00
    Topaz, 1929-1934; $95.00

2400 Comport, 8"
    Rose, 1928-1932; $125.00
    Azure, 1928-1932; $150.00
    Topaz, 1929-1932; $135.00
2375 Cream Soup and Plate
    Crystal, 1929-1943; $70.00
    Rose, 1928-1940; $85.00
    Azure, 1928-1940; $95.00
    Topaz/Gold Tint, 1929-1940; $85.00
2375 Cup and Saucer, After Dinner
    Crystal, 1929-1943; $95.00
    Rose, 1928-1940; $125.00
    Azure, 1928-1942; $125.00
    Topaz/Gold Tint, 1929-1938; $125.00
2375½ Cup and Saucer
    Crystal, 1929-1951; $35.00
    Rose, 1928-1940; $45.00
    Azure, 1928-1943; $50.00
    Topaz/Gold Tint, 1929-1942; $45.00
2439 Decanter
    Crystal, July 1930-1932; market
    Rose, July 1930-1932; market
    Azure, July 1930-1932; market
    Topaz, July 1930-1932; market
2375 Ice Bucket, NP Handle
    Crystal, 1930-1942; $110.00
    Rose, 1930-1940; $165.00
    Azure, 1930-1942; $165.00
    Topaz/Gold Tint, 1930-1942; $125.00
2378 Ice Bucket, NP Handle
    Crystal, 1929; $110.00
    Rose, 1928-1929; $165.00
    Azure, 1928-1929; $165.00
    Topaz, 1929; $125.00
2451 Ice Dish, Unetched Liners
    Crystal, 1931-1951; $65.00
    Rose, 1931-1934; $125.00
    Azure, 1931-1940; $125.00
    Topaz/Gold Tint, 1931-1940; $95.00
2451 Ice Dish Plate
    Crystal, 1934; $20.00
    Rose, 1934; $25.00
    Azure, 1934; $25.00
    Topaz, 1934; $25.00
5000 Jug
    Crystal, 1928-1943, 1947-1951; $495.00
    Rose, 1928-1940; $800.00
    Azure, 1928-1939; $825.00
    Topaz/Gold Tint, 1929-1940; $575.00
2375 Lemon Dish
    Crystal, 1929-1943; $32.00
    Rose, 1928-1934; $35.00
    Azure, 1928-1934; $38.00
    Topaz/Gold Tint, 1929-1943; $34.00
2375 Mayonnaise, Plate, and Ladle
    Crystal, 1934-1945; $78.00

    Rose, 1928-1934; $125.00
    Azure, 1928-1934; $135.00
    Topaz/Gold Tint, 1929-1939; $125.00
2394 Mint
    Rose, 1928-1934; $45.00
    Azure, 1928-1934; $45.00
    Topaz, 1929-1934; $45.00
5098 Nappy, 6" Footed
    Crystal, 1928-1930; $75.00
    Rose, 1928-1930; $75.00
    Azure, 1928-1930; $85.00
2375 Oil, Footed
    Crystal, 1931-1943; $450.00
    Rose, 1931-1934; $800.00/market
    Azure, 1931-1934; $1000.00/market
    Topaz, 1931-1934; $795.00
2375 Plate, 6"
    Crystal, 1929-1951; $10.00
    Rose, 1928-1940; $12.00
    Azure, 1928-1943; $14.00
    Topaz/Gold Tint, 1929-1943; $12.00
2375 Plate, 7"
    Crystal, 1928-1951; $11.00
    Rose, 1928-1940; $15.00
    Azure, 1928-1943; $15.00
    Topaz/Gold Tint, 1929-1943; $12.00
2375 Plate, 8"
    Crystal, 1928-1951; $18.00
    Rose, 1928-1940; $20.00
    Azure, 1928-1943; $20.00
    Topaz/Gold Tint, 1929-1943; $20.00
2375 Plate, 9"
    Crystal, 1929-1944; $32.00
    Rose, 1928-1940; $45.00
    Azure, 1928-1943; $45.00
    Topaz/Gold Tint, 1929-1943; $42.00
2375 Plate, 10"
    Crystal, 1929-1944; $68.00
    Rose, 1928-1940; $125.00
    Azure, 1928-1943; $150.00
    Topaz/Gold Tint, 1929-1943; $95.00
2375 Plate, 10" Grill
    Crystal, 1930-1934; $55.00
    Rose, 1930-1934; $75.00
    Azure, 1930-1934; $75.00
    Topaz, 1930-1934; $65.00
2375 Plate, 10" Cake
    Crystal, 1930-1939; $72.00
    Rose, 1930-1939; $85.00
    Azure, 1930-1937; $95.00
    Topaz/Gold Tint, 1930-1939; $75.00
2375 Plate, 13" Chop
    Crystal, 1928-1940; $95.00
    Rose, 1928-1940; $125.00
    Azure, 1928-1935; $200.00
    Topaz/Gold Tint, 1929-1943; $95.00

2440 Plate, 13" Torte
    Crystal, 1934-1942; $95.00
    Rose, 1934-1940; $150.00
    Azure, 1934-1937; $200.00
    Topaz, 1934; $200.00
2375 Platter, 12"
    Crystal, 1929-1943; $110.00
    Rose, 1928-1940; $165.00
    Azure, 1928-1942; $175.00
    Topaz/Gold Tint, 1929-1939; $165.00
2375 Platter, 15"
    Crystal, 1931-1940; $175.00
    Rose, 1931-1940; $250.00
    Azure, 1931-1940; $275.00
    Topaz/Gold Tint, 1931-1939; $250.00
2375 Relish, 8½"
    Crystal, 1929-1943; $37.00
    Rose, 1928-1940; $42.00
    Azure, 1928-1936; $48.00
    Topaz/Gold Tint, 1929-1942; $42.00
2083 Salad Dressing Bottle
    Crystal, July 1930-1932; $700.00/market
    Rose, July 1930-1932; $900.00/market
    Azure, July 1930-1932; $1,100.00/market
    Topaz/Gold Tint, July 1930-1932; $800.00/market
2375 Salad Dressing Bottle
    Crystal, 1933-1943; $650.00
    Rose, 1933-1934; $900.00/market
    Azure, 1933-1934; $1,000.00/market
    Topaz/Gold Tint, 1933-1943; $695.00
2375 Sauce Boat and Plate
    Crystal, 1931-1936; $300.00
    Rose, 1931-1936; $425.00
    Azure, 1931-1936; $550.00
    Topaz, 1931-1936; $425.00
2375 Shaker, Footed, FGT (pair)
    Crystal, 1928-1943; $165.00
    Rose, 1928-1940; $225.00
    Azure, 1928-1943; $225.00
    Topaz/Gold Tint, 1929-1940; $200.00
2375½ Sugar and Cream
    Crystal, 1928-1944; $85.00
    Rose, 1928-1940; $110.00
    Azure, 1928-1943; $125.00
    Topaz/Gold Tint, 1929-1943; $110.00
2375½ Sugar and Cover
    Crystal, 1928-1936; $200.00
    Rose, 1928-1934; $250.00
    Azure, 1928-1936; $250.00
    Topaz, 1929-1936; $225.00
2375½ Sugar and Cream, Tea
    Crystal, 1931-1943; $95.00
    Rose, 1931-1934; $165.00
    Azure, 1931-1934; $175.00
    Topaz/Gold Tint, 1931-1940; $135.00

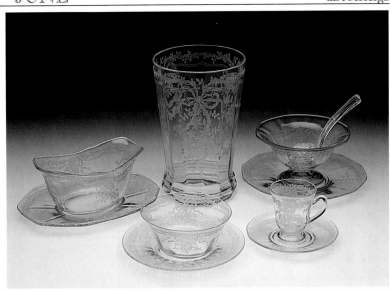

Topaz June 4117 8" Vase, 2375 Finger Bowl and Plate, Sauce Boat and Plate, After Dinner Cup and Saucer, Mayonnaise and Plate

2378 Sugar Pail, NP Handle
    Rose, 1928-1930; $365.00
    Azure, 1928-1930; $395.00
    Topaz, 1929-1930; $365.00
2375 Sweetmeat
    Crystal, 1929-1943; $30.00
    Rose, 1928-1935; $35.00
    Azure, 1928-1935; $40.00
    Topaz/Gold Tint, 1929-1943; $35.00
2375 Tray, Handled Lunch
    Crystal, 1929-1951; $95.00
    Rose, 1928-1940; $145.00
    Azure, 1928-1934; $165.00
    Topaz/Gold Tint, 1929-1943; $125.00
2429 Tray, Service, and Lemon Insert
    Crystal, 1929-1930; $300.00
    Rose, 1929-1930; $350.00
    Azure, 1929-1930; $400.00
    Topaz, 1929-1930; $350.00
2417 Vase, 8", R.O.
    Topaz, 1931-1932; $450.00
4100 Vase, 8" R.O.
    Crystal, 1932-1934; $195.00
    Rose, 1928-1934; $225.00
    Azure, 1928-1934; $225.00
2385 Vase, 8½" Fan
    Rose, 1928-1932; $330.00
    Azure, 1928-1932; $365.00
2375 Whip Cream
    Crystal, 1929-1943; $34.00
    Rose, 1928-1934; $38.00
    Azure, 1928-1934; $45.00
    Topaz/Gold Tint, 1929-1942; $36.00
2378 Whip Cream Pail, NP Handle
    Crystal, 1928-1930; $275.00
    Rose, 1928-1930; $325.00
    Azure, 1928-1930; $365.00

JUNE

DESIGN PATENT NOS. 76373 AND 76455

JUNE DESIGN

Plate Etching No. 279

STEMWARE

Made in Solid Crystal — Crystal Base with Rose Bowl — Crystal Base with Azure Bowl
Crystal Base with Topaz Bowl

1. 5098 9-oz. Goblet	6. 5098 3-oz. Cocktail	10. 5098 12-oz. Footed Tumbler
2. 5098 6-oz. High Sherbet	5. 5098 ¾-oz. Cordial	10. 5098 9-oz. Footed Tumbler
3. 5098 6-oz. Low Sherbet	7. 5098 5-oz. Oyster Cocktail	10. 5098 5-oz. Footed Tumbler
4. 5098 6-oz. Parfait	8. 869 Finger Bowl	10. 5098 2½-oz. Footed Tumbler
5. 5098 4-oz. Claret	8. 2283 6-in. F. B. Plate, R/O	11. 5098 5-in. Comport
5. 5098 2½-oz. Wine	9. 5082½ Grape Fruit	12. 5000 7 Footed Jug
	9. 945½ Grape Fruit Liner	

DINNERWARE

Made in Rose, Azure, Crystal and Topaz

13. 2375 6-in. Bread and Butter Plate	13. 2375 9-in. Dinner Plate	14. 2375 6-in. Cereal
13. 2375 7-in. Salad Plate	13. 2375 10-in. Dinner Plate	14. 2375 7-in. Soup
13. 2375 8-in. Luncheon Plate	13. 2375 13-in. Chop Plate	15. 2375½ Footed Cup
	2375 10-in. Grill Plate	15. 2375 Saucer
	14. 2375 5-in. Fruit	

50

32

42   36   39

DESIGN PATENT NOS. 76373 AND 76455

JUNE DESIGN

DINNERWARE—Continued

Made in Rose, Azure, Crystal and Topaz — Items marked * not made in Crystal

16.	2375	After Dinner Cup	26.	2375	Mayonnaise Plate		2451	C. M. Liner (Not Etched)
16.	2375	After Dinner Saucer	27.	2375	Handled Lunch Tray		2451	F. C. Liner (Not Etched)
17.	2375	Footed Bouillon	28.	2375	Whip Cream	40.	2350	Small Ash Tray
18.	2375	Footed Cream Soup	29.	2375	Sweetmeat	41.	*2375	7-in. Comport
18.	2375	Cream Soup Plate	30.	2375	Bon Bon	42.	2400	6-in. Comport
19.	2375	9-in. Baker	31.	2375	Lemon Dish	43.	*2331	3 Candy Box & Cover
14.	2375	7-in. Round Nappy	32.	2375	10-in. Cake Plate	44.	2394	½ Lb. Candy Jar and
20.	2375	12-in. Platter	33.	2375	Large Dessert			Cover
20.	2375	15-in. Platter	34.	2375	Ice Bucket	45.	*2394	Mint
21.	2375	Sauce Boat	35.	2375	Footed Oil	45.	2394	6-in. Bowl
21.	2375	Sauce Boat Plate		2375	Salad Dressing Bottle	45.	2394	12-in. Bowl "A"
22.	2375	8½-in. Relish	36.	2375	Footed Shaker	46.	2394	2-in. Candlestick
23.	2375	11½-in. Celery	37.	2375	Footed Cheese	47.	2395	10-in. Bowl
	2375½	Footed Sugar & Cover	37.	2375	Cracker Plate	48.	2395½	5-in. Candlestick
24.	2375½	Footed Sugar	37.	2375	Cheese and Cracker	49.	2375	12-in. Centerpiece
25.	2375½	Footed Cream	38.	2368	Cheese and Cracker	50.	2375½	Candlestick
24.	2375½	Tea Sugar	39.	2451	Ice Dish	51.	2375	12-in. Bowl
25.	2375½	Tea Cream		2451	Ice Dish Plate	52.	2375	3-in. Candlestick
26.	*2375	Mayonnaise	39.	2451	T. J. Liner (Not Etched)	53.	4100	8-in. Vase, R/O

TROJAN
Plate Etching 280
Stemware is featured in *Fostoria Stemware*, page 70.

2350 Ash Tray, Small
    Topaz, 1929-1934; $47.00
    Rose, 1929-1934; $47.00
2350 Ash Tray, Large
    Topaz, 1929-1934; $50.00
    Rose, 1929-1934; $50.00
2375 Bon Bon
    Topaz, 1929-1936; $42.00
    Rose, 1929-1934; $48.00
2375 Bouillon
    Topaz, 1929-1936; $32.00
    Rose, 1929-1934; $38.00
869 Bowl, Finger, and 2283 Plate, 6"
    Topaz, 1929-1943; $75.00
    Rose, 1929-1934; $85.00
2375 Bowl, 5" Fruit
    Topaz, 1929-1943; $32.00
    Rose, 1929-1934; $37.00
2375 Bowl, 6" Cereal
    Topaz, 1929-1934; $46.00
    Rose, 1929-1934; $46.00
2394 Bowl, 6"
    Topaz, 1931-1934; $45.00
    Rose, 1931-1934; $45.00
2375 Bowl, 7" Soup
    Topaz, 1929-1934; $95.00
    Rose, 1929-1934; $110.00
2375 Bowl, 7" Round Nappy
    Topaz, 1933-1934; $140.00
    Rose, 1933-1934; $140.00
2375 Bowl, 9" Baker
    Topaz, 1929-1940; $95.00
    Rose, 1929-1934; $125.00
2395 Bowl, 10"
    Topaz, 1931-1939; $200.00
    Rose, 1931-1934; $275.00
2375 Bowl, Large Dessert
    Topaz, 1929-1936; $95.00
    Rose, 1929-1934; $110.00
2415 Bowl, Combination
    Topaz, 1929; $225.00
    Rose, 1929; $235.00
2375 Bowl, 12"
    Topaz, 1929-1939; $85.00
    Rose, 1929-1934; $115.00
2394 Bowl "A", 12"
    Topaz, 1931-1940; $95.00
    Rose, 1931-1934; $115.00
2394 Candlestick, 2" (pair)
    Topaz, 1931-1940; $50.00
    Rose, 1931-1934; $65.00
2375 Candlestick, 3" (pair)
    Topaz, 1929-1939; $50.00

    Rose, 1929-1934; $60.00
2375½ Candlestick (pair)
    Topaz, 1929-1934; $100.00
    Rose, 1929-1934; $100.00
2395½ Candlestick, 5" (pair)
    Topaz, 1931-1939; $125.00
    Rose, 1931-1934; $150.00
2394 Candy Jar and Cover
    Topaz, 1929-1932; $300.00
    Rose, 1929-1932; $350.00
2375 Celery, 11½"
    Topaz, 1929-1939; $85.00
    Rose, 1929-1934; $110.00
2375 Centerpiece, 12"
    Topaz, 1929-1934; $150.00
    Rose, 1929-1934; $165.00
2368 Cheese and Cracker
    Topaz, 1929-1934; $125.00
    Rose, 1929-1934; $140.00
2375 Cheese and Cracker
    Topaz, 1931-1935; $135.00
    Rose, 1931-1934; $150.00
2400 Comport, 6"
    Topaz, 1929-1936; $85.00
    Rose, 1929-1934; $100.00
5099 Comport, 6"
    Topaz, 1929-1934; $87.00
    Rose, 1929-1934; $100.00
2375 Cream Soup and Plate
    Topaz, 1929-1943; $75.00
    Rose, 1929-1934; $125.00

Rose Trojan Lemon Dish, 7" Plate, 2429 Service Tray, 5000 Jug, Oval Baker, 2375 Cream Soup and Plate, Two-part Relish

2375 Cup and Saucer, After Dinner
    Topaz, 1929-1936; $125.00
    Rose, 1929-1934; $150.00
2375½ Cup and Saucer
    Topaz, 1929-1943; $45.00
    Rose, 1929-1934; $57.00
2375 Ice Bucket, NP Handle
    Topaz, 1929-1936; $125.00
    Rose, 1929-1934; $175.00
2451 Ice Dish and Liner
    Topaz, 1929-1934; $85.00
    Rose, 1929-1934; $95.00
5000 Jug
    Topaz, 1929-1939; $575.00
    Rose, 1929-1934; $800.00/market
2375 Lemon
    Topaz, 1929-1936; $34.00
    Rose, 1929-1934; $40.00
2375 Mayonnaise, Plate, and Ladle
    Topaz, 1929-1934; $125.00
    Rose, 1929-1934; $135.00
2394 Mint
    Topaz, 1929-1932; $38.00
    Rose, 1929-1932; $38.00
2375 Oil
    Topaz, 1929-1934; $395.00
    Rose, 1929-1934; $450.00
2375 Plate, 6"
    Topaz, 1929-1943; $12.00
    Rose, 1929-1934; $16.00
2375 Plate, 7"
    Topaz, 1929-1943; $12.00
    Rose, 1929-1934; $16.00
2375 Plate, 8"
    Topaz, 1929-1943; $18.00
    Rose, 1929-1934; $22.00
2375 Plate, 9"
    Topaz, 1929-1943; $40.00
    Rose, 1929-1934; $55.00
2375 Plate, 10" Dinner
    Topaz, 1929-1943; $85.00
    Rose, 1929-1934; $100.00
2375 Plate, 10" Cake
    Topaz, 1929-1939; $75.00
    Rose, 1929-1934; $87.00
2375 Plate, 10" Grill
    Topaz, 1929-1939; $68.00
    Rose, 1929-1934; $76.00
2375 Plate, Canape
    Topaz, 1929-1930; $40.00
    Rose, 1929-1930; $50.00
2375 Plate, 13" Chop
    Topaz, 1929-1942; $95.00
    Rose, 1929-1934; $125.00
2375 Platter, 12"
    Topaz, 1929-1939; $155.00

Topaz Trojan 2378 Sugar Pail, Footed Oil, 2817 8" Vase, Cup and Saucer, Celery, 2394 Candlestick, 2375 Handled Lunch Tray, Bon Bon

    Rose, 1929-1934; $170.00
2375 Platter, 15"
    Topaz, 1929-1938; $225.00
    Rose, 1929-1934; $250.00
2375 Relish, 8½"
    Topaz, 1929-1943; $42.00
    Rose, 1929-1934; $50.00
2350 Relish, 3-part
    Topaz, 1929-1932; $55.00
    Rose, 1929-1932; $60.00
2375 Sauce and Plate
    Topaz, 1929-1936; $295.00
    Rose, 1929-1934; $325.00
2375 Shaker, FGT (pair)
    Topaz, 1929-1940; $195.00
    Rose, 1929-1934; $250.00
2375½ Sugar and Cream, Tea
    Topaz, 1929-1936; $125.00
    Rose, 1929-1934; $135.00
2375½ Sugar and Cream
    Topaz, 1929-1943; $4,100.00
    Rose, 1929-1934; $115.00
2375½ Sugar and Cover
    Topaz, 1929-1934; $150.00
    Rose, 1929-1934; $165.00
2378 Sugar Pail, NP Handle
    Topaz, 1929-1930; $350.00
    Rose, 1929-1930; $365.00
2375 Sweetmeat
    Topaz, 1929-1936; $38.00
    Rose, 1929-1934; $42.00
2375 Tray, Handled Lunch
    Topaz, 1929-1936; $115.00
    Rose, 1929-1934; $135.00

DESIGN PATENT NOS. 79226 AND 79227

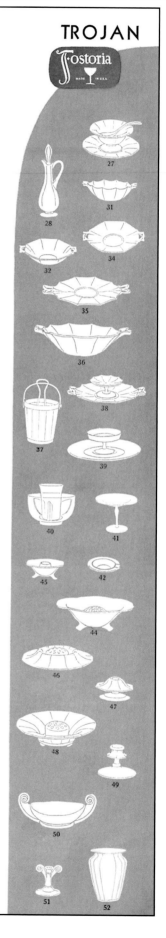

TROJAN DESIGN

Plate Etching No. 280   *Priced on pages 16 and 17 — 1931 Price List*

DINNERWARE—Continued
Made in Rose and Topaz

18.	2375	Footed Cream Soup
18.	2375	Cream Soup Plate
19.	2375	9-in. Baker
20.	2375	12-in. Platter
20.	2375	15-in. Platter
21.	2375	Sauce Boat
21.	2375	Sauce Boat Plate
22.	2375	8½-in. Relish
23.	2375	11½-in. Celery
24.	2350	3-Compartment Relish
	2375½	Sugar and Cover
25.	2375½	Footed Sugar
26.	2375½	Footed Cream
25.	2375½	Tea Sugar
26.	2375½	Tea Cream
27.	2375	Mayonnaise
27.	2375	Mayonnaise Plate
28.	2375	Footed Oil

29.	2375	Footed Shaker
30.	2375	Handled Lunch Tray
31.	2375	Whip Cream
32.	2375	Sweetmeat
33.	2375	Bon Bon
34.	2375	Lemon Dish
35.	2375	10-in. Cake Plate
36.	2375	Large Dessert
37.	2375	Ice Bucket
38.	2375	Footed Cheese
38.	2375	Cracker Plate
38.	2375	Cheese and Cracker
39.	2368	Footed Cheese
39.	2368	Cracker Plate
39.	2368	Cheese and Cracker
	2429	Service Tray
	2429	Service and Lemon Tray
40.	2451	Ice Dish

40.	2451	T. J. Liner (not etched)
40.	2451	C. M. Liner (not etched)
41.	2400	6-in. Comport
42.	2350	Small Ash Tray
42.	2350	Large Ash Tray
43.	2394	½-lb. Candy Jar and Cover
44.	2394	6-in. Bowl
44.	2394	Mint
44.	2394	12-in. Bowl "A"
45.	2394	2-in. Candlestick
46.	2375	12-in. Centerpiece
47.	2375½	Candlestick
48.	2375	12-in. Bowl
49.	2375	3-in. Candlestick
50.	2395	10-in. Bowl
51.	2395½	5-in. Candlestick
52.	4105	8-in. Vase
53.	2417	8-in. Vase

[15]

2429 Tray, Service, and Lemon Insert
    Topaz, 1929-1932; $295.00
    Rose, 1929-1932; $320.00
2417 Vase, 8" R.O.
    Topaz, 1929-1932; $275.00
    Rose, 1929-1932; $325.00
4105 Vase, 8" R.O.
    Topaz, 1929-1932; $275.00

    Rose, 1929-1932; $325.00
2375 Whip Cream
    Topaz, 1929-1934; $48.00
    Rose, 1929-1934; $54.00
2378 Whip Cream Pail, NP Handle
    Topaz, 1929-1930; $350.00
    Rose, 1929-1930; $365.00

VERONA

Plate Etching 281

1929 – 1930
Crystal, Rose and Green
Stemware is featured in *Fostoria Stemware*, page 38.

890 Bowl, Finger, 2283 Plate; $68.00
2394 Bowl, 12"; $95.00
2394 Candlestick, 2" (pair); $75.00
2400 Comport, 8"; $115.00
2375½ Cup and Saucer; $40.00
890 Jug; $600.00

2375 Plate, 6"; $12.00
2375 Plate, 7"; $14.00
2375 Plate, 8"; $18.00
2375 Plate, 13"; $110.00
2375½ Sugar and Cover, and Cream; $145.00

FIRENZE

Decoration 502

Gold edge on Plate Etching 281 Verona.
July 1929 – 1932
Topaz

2375 Bon Bon; $48.00
2395 Bowl, 10"; $145.00
2394 Bowl, 12"; $125.00
2394 Candlestick, 2" (pair); $95.00
2395½ Candlestick, 5" (pair); $125.00
2375 Cheese and Cracker; $125.00
2427 Cigarette Box and Cover; $125.00
2415 Combination Bowl, July 1929; $250.00
2400 Comport, 6"; $85.00
2375 Ice Bucket, Gold Plated Handle and Tongs; $135.00
2375 Lemon Dish; $48.00
2375 Plate, 10" Cake; $95.00
2375 Tray, Handled Lunch; $110.00

2417 Vase, 8"; $375.00
4105 Vase, 8"; $375.00

Firenze 2375 Bon Bon, 2315 Combination Bowl

ACANTHUS
Plate Etching 282
1930 – 1932
Amber and Green
Stemware is featured in *Fostoria Stemware,* pages 68 and 69.

4095 Almond, regular optic; $40.00
2350 Ash Tray, Small; $38.00
2375 Bon Bon; $44.00
2375 Bouillon; $35.00
869 Bowl, Finger, and 2283
    Plate 6", Regular Optic; $48.00
2375 Bowl, 5" Fruit; $24.00
2375 Bowl, 6" Cereal; $26.00
2375 Bowl, 7" Soup; $35.00
2394 Bowl, 6"; $32.00
2375 Bowl, 9" Baker; $77.00
2375 Bowl, Large Dessert; $85.00
2395 Bowl, 10"; $125.00
2430 Bowl, 11"; $95.00
2375 Bowl, 12"; $95.00
2394 Bowl "A", 12"; $95.00
2394 Candlestick, 2" (pair); $95.00
2375 Candlestick, 3" (pair); $85.00
2375½ Candlestick (pair); $95.00
2395½ Candlestick, 5" (pair); $125.00
2430 Candlestick, 9½" (pair); $195.00
2430 Candy Jar and Cover, ½ pound; $100.00
2375 Celery, 11½"; $52.00
2375 Centerpiece, 12"; $125.00
2375 Cheese and Cracker; $115.00
5098 Comport, 6"; $72.00
2375 Cream Soup and Plate; $85.00
2375½ Cup and Saucer; $40.00
2375 Cup and Saucer, After Dinner; $65.00
5082½ Grapefruit and Liner; $85.00
2375 Ice Bucket; $115.00
2430 Jelly, 7"; $35.00
5000 Jug; $450.00
2375 Lemon Dish; $42.00
2375 Mayonnaise, Plate and Ladle; $110.00
2430 Mint, 5½"; $28.00
2375 Oil, Footed; $400.00
2375 Pickle, 8½"; $30.00
2375 Plate, 6"; $12.00
2375 Plate, 7"; $14.00
2375 Plate, 8"; $20.00
2375 Plate, 9"; $28.00
2375 Plate, 10"; $65.00
2375 Plate, 10" Grill; $60.00

2375 Plate, 10" Cake; $75.00
2375 Plate, 13" Chop; $95.00
2375 Platter, 12"; $125.00
2375 Platter, 15"; $150.00
2375 Relish, 8½"; $42.00
2083 Salad Dressing Bottle; $400.00
2375 Sauce Boat and Plate; $295.00
2375 Shaker, Footed, FGT (pair); $200.00
2375½ Sugar and Cover; $150.00
2375½ Sugar and Cream; $110.00
2375½ Sugar and Cream, Tea; $115.00
2375 Sweetmeat; $46.00
2375 Tray, Handled Lunch; $115.00
2417 Vase, 8 ", Regular Optic; $300.00
2430 Vase, 8"; $275.00
4105 Vase, 8", Regular Optic; $295.00

Amber Acanthus Sweetmeat, Tea Sugar

ACANTHUS DESIGN

PLATE ETCHING No. 282   *Priced on pages 14 and 15—1931 Price List*

STEMWARE

Made in Crystal Base with Green Bowl—Crystal Base with Amber Bowl

1.	5098	Goblet	4.	5098	Cordial	8.	5098	9-oz. Footed Tumbler
2.	5098	High Sherbet	6.	5098	Oyster Cocktail	8.	5098	5-oz. Footed Tumbler
3.	5098	Low Sherbet	7.	869	Finger Bowl	8.	5098	2½-oz. Footed Tumbler
4.	5098	Claret	7.	2283	6-in. Plate, Reg. Opt.		5098	6-in. Comport
4.	5098	Wine	8.	5098	12-oz. Footed Tumbler		5000-7	Footed Jug
5.	5098	Cocktail					4095	Individual Almond, R/O

DINNERWARE

Made in Green and Amber

9.	2375	6-in. Bread and Butter Plate	15.	2375	Sauce Boat	24.	2375	10-in. Cake Plate
9.	2375	7-in. Salad Plate	15.	2375	Sauce Boat Plate	25.	2375	Large Dessert
9.	2375	8-in. Luncheon Plate	16.	2375	8½-in. Relish	25.	2375	Ice Bucket
9.	2375	9-in. Dinner Plate	17.	2375	8½-in. Pickle	26.	2375	Footed Cheese
9.	2375	10-in. Dinner Plate	17.	2375	11½-in. Celery	26.	2375	Cracker Plate
9.	2375	13-in. Chop Plate		2375½	Sugar and Cover	27.	2394	6-in. Bowl
10.	2375	5-in. Fruit	18.	2375½	Footed Sugar	27.	2394	12-in. Bowl "A"
10.	2375	6-in. Cereal	19.	2375½	Footed Cream	28.	2394	2-in. Candlestick
10.	2375	7-in. Soup	18.	2375½	Tea Sugar		2430	11-in. Bowl
11.	2375½	Footed Cup	19.	2375½	Tea Cream		2430	9½-in. Candlestick
11.	2375	Saucer		2375	Mayonnaise	29.	2430	8-in. Vase
	2375	After Dinner Cup		2375	Mayonnaise Plate	30.	2430	½-lb. Candy Jar and Cover
	2375	After Dinner Saucer		2375	Footed Oil		2375	12-in. Centerpiece
12.	2375	Bouillon	20.	2375	Footed Shaker		2375½	Candlestick
12.	2375	Cream Soup	21.	2375	Handled Lunch Tray		2375	12-in. Bowl
12.	2375	Cream Soup Plate	22.	2375	Sweetmeat		2375	3-in. Candlestick
13.	2375	9-in. Baker	23.	2375	Bon Bon	31.	2395	10-in. Bowl
14.	2375	12-in. Platter	24.	2375	Lemon Dish	32.	2395½	5-in. Candlestick
14.	2375	15-in. Platter					2417	8-in. Vase, Reg. Opt.

{ 13 }

KASHMIR
Plate Etching 283

This unusual pattern was one of the first to use pieces from the new Mayfair dinner service as well as Fairfax. Stemware in Kashmir is featured in *Fostoria Stemware,* pages 57 – 59 and 70.

2375 Bon Bon
  Azure, 1930-1933; $48.00
  Topaz, 1930-1933; $42.00
869 Bowl, Finger, and 2283 6"Plate
  Azure, 1930-1933; $85.00
  Topaz, 1930-1933; $75.00
4021 Bowl, Finger
  Green Base, 1930-1933; $65.00
2375 Bowl, Fruit, 5"
  Azure, 1930-1933; $40.00
  Topaz, 1930-1933; $36.00
2375 Bowl, 6" Cereal
  Azure, 1930-1933; $42.00
  Topaz, 1930-1933; $38.00
2394 Bowl, 6"
  Azure, 1930-1933; $45.00
  Topaz, 1930-1933; $42.00
2375 Bowl, 7" Soup
  Azure, 1930-1933; $75.00
  Topaz, 1930-1933; $65.00
2375 Bouillon
  Azure, 1930-1933; $38.00
  Topaz, 1930-1933; $32.00
2375 Bowl, Large Dessert
  Azure, 1930-1933; $110.00
  Topaz, 1930-1933; $95.00
2375 Bowl, 9" Baker
  Azure, 1930-1933; $115.00
  Topaz, 1930-1933; $95.00
2395 Bowl, 10"
  Azure, 1930-1933; $250.00
  Topaz, 1930-1933; $200.00
2430 Bowl, 11"
  Azure, 1930-1932; $165.00
  Topaz, 1930-1932; $150.00
2394 Bowl "A", 12"
  Azure,1930-1933; $165.00
  Topaz, 1930-1933; $145.00
2375 Bowl, 12"
  Azure, 1930-1933; $165.00
  Topaz, 1930-1933; $145.00
2394 Candlestick, 2" (pair)
  Azure, 1930-1933; $85.00
  Topaz, 1930-1933; $64.00
2375½ Candlestick (pair)
  Azure, 1930-1933; $125.00
  Topaz, 1930-1933; $95.00
2375 Candlestick, 3" (pair)
  Azure, 1930-1933; $68.00
  Topaz, 1930-1933; $50.00
2395½ Candlestick, 5"(pair)
  Azure, 1930-1933; $150.00

Topaz, 1930-1933; $115.00
2430 Candlestick, 9½" (pair)
  Azure, 1930-1932; $250.00
  Topaz, 1930-1932; $195.00
2430 Candy Jar and Cover
  Azure, 1930-1932; $165.00
  Topaz, 1930-1932; $125.00
2375 Celery, 11½"
  Azure, 1930-1933; $110.00
  Topaz, 1930-1933; $85.00
2375 Centerpiece, 12"
  Azure, 1930-1933; $200.00
  Topaz, 1930-1933; $150.00
2375 Cheese and Cracker
  Azure, 1930-1933; $165.00
  Topaz, 1930-1933; $110.00
5099 Comport, 6"
  Azure, 1930-1933; $95.00
  Topaz, 1930-1933; $75.00
2375 Cream Soup and Plate
  Azure, 1930-1933; $125.00
  Topaz, 1930-1933; $75.00
2375 Cup and Saucer, After Dinner
  Azure, 1930-1933; $150.00
  Topaz, 1930-1933; $110.00
2375½ Cup and Saucer
  Azure, 1930-1933; $52.00
  Topaz, 1930-1933; $40.00
2350½ Cup and 2419 Saucer
  Green, 1930-1933; $48.00
2350 Cup and 2419 Saucer, After Dinner
  Green, 1930-1933; $95.00
2375 Ice Bucket, NP Handle
  Azure, 1930-1933; $175.00
  Topaz, 1930-1933; $110.00
2430 Jelly, 7"
  Azure, 1930-1932; $50.00
  Topaz, 1930-1932; $32.00
4020 Jug
  Green Base, 1930-1933; $425.00
5000 Jug
  Azure, 1930-1933; $800.00/market
  Topaz, 1930-1933; $495.00
2375 Lemon Dish
  Azure, 1930-1933; $48.00
  Topaz, 1930-1933; $34.00
2430 Mint, 5½"
  Azure, 1930-1932; $45.00
  Topaz, 1930-1932; $32.00
2375 Oil, Footed
  Azure, 1930-1933; $575.00
  Topaz, 1930-1933; $475.00

2375 Pickle, 8½"
    Azure, 1930-1933; $48.00
    Topaz, 1930-1933; $42.00
2375 Plate, 6"
    Azure, 1930-1933; $16.00
    Topaz, 1930-1933; $12.00
2375 Plate, 7"
    Azure, 1930-1933; $18.00
    Topaz, 1930-1933; $12.00
2375 Plate, 8"
    Azure, 1930-1933; $24.00
    Topaz, 1930-1933; $16.00
2375 Plate, 9"
    Azure, 1930-1933; $55.00
    Topaz, 1930-1933; $40.00
2375 Plate, 10"
    Azure, 1930-1933; $115.00
    Topaz, 1930-1933; $85.00
2419 Plate, 6"
    Green, 1930-1933; $14.00
2419 Plate, 7"
    Green, 1930-1933; $14.00
2419 Plate, 8"
    Green, 1930-1933; $18.00
2375 Plate, 10" Cake
    Azure, 1930-1933; $95.00
    Topaz, 1930-1933; $75.00
2375 Plate, 13" Chop
    Azure, 1930-1933; $125.00
    Topaz, 1930-1933; $85.00
2375 Platter, 12"
    Azure, 1930-1933; $165.00
    Topaz, 1930-1933; $125.00
2375 Platter, 15"
    Azure, 1930-1933; $250.00
    Topaz, 1930-1933; $195.00
2375 Relish, 8½"
    Azure, 1930-1933; $50.00
    Topaz, 1930-1933; $42.00
2375 Sauce Boat and Plate
    Azure, 1930-1933; $350.00
    Topaz, 1930-1933; $250.00
2375 Shaker, FGT (pair)
    Azure, 1930-1933; $250.00
    Topaz, 1930-1933; $195.00
2375 Sugar and Cream, Tea
    Azure, 1930-1933; $140.00
    Topaz, 1930-1933; $120.00
2375½ Sugar and Cream
    Azure, 1930-1933; $125.00
    Topaz, 1930-1933; $95.00
2375 Sweetmeat
    Azure, 1930-1933; $50.00
    Topaz, 1930-1933; $37.00
2375 Tray, Handled Lunch

Topaz Kashmir 2430 8" Vase, Cocktail, Grill Plate, Cream Soup and Plate, Green 2375 After Dinner Cup and Saucer, Handled Lunch Tray

    Azure, 1930-1933; $150.00
    Topaz, 1930-1933; $100.00
2417 Vase, 8"
    Azure, 1930-1932; $400.00
    Topaz, 1930-1932; $325.00
2430 Vase, 8"
    Azure, 1930-1932; $300.00
    Topaz, 1930-1932; $250.00
4105 Vase, 8"
    Azure, 1930-1933; $325.00
    Topaz, 1930-1933; $265.00

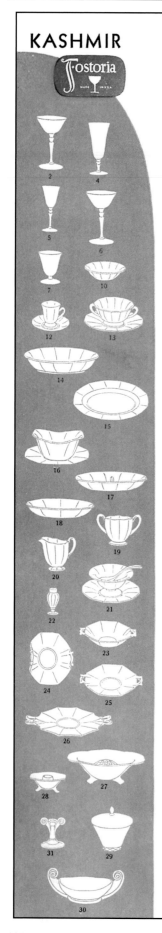

KASHMIR DESIGN

PLATE ETCHING No. 283   *Priced on pages 12 and 13 —1931 Price List*

STEMWARE

Made in Crystal Base with Azure Bowl—Crystal Base with Topaz Bowl

1.	5099	Goblet	6.	5099	Cocktail	8. 5099	12-oz. Footed Tumbler
2.	5099	High Sherbet	5.	5099	Cordial	8. 5099	9-oz. Footed Tumbler
3.	5099	Low Sherbet	7.	5099	Oyster Cocktail	8. 5099	5-oz. Footed Tumbler
4.	5099	Parfait		869	Finger Bowl	8. 5099	2½-oz. Footed Tumbler
5.	5099	Claret		2283	6-in. Plate, Reg. Opt.	5000-7	Footed Jug
5.	5099	Wine				5099	6-in. Comport

DINNERWARE

Made in Azure and Topaz

9.	2375	6-in. Bread and Butter Plate	15.	2375	15-in. Platter	25.	2375	Lemon Dish
9.	2375	7-in. Salad Plate	16.	2375	Sauce Boat	26.	2375	10-in. Cake Plate
9.	2375	8-in. Luncheon Plate	16.	2375	Sauce Boat Plate		2375	Large Dessert
9.	2375	9-in. Dinner Plate	17.	2375	8½-in. Relish		2375	Ice Bucket
9.	2375	10-in. Dinner Plate	18.	2375	8½-in. Pickle		2375	Footed Cheese
9.	2375	13-in. Chop Plate	18.	2375	11½-in. Celery		2375	Cracker Plate
10.	2375	5-in. Fruit	19.	2375½	Footed Sugar	27.	2394	6-in. Bowl
10.	2375	6-in. Cereal	20.	2375½	Footed Cream	27.	2394	12-in. Bowl "A"
10.	2375	7-in. Soup	19.	2375½	Tea Sugar	28.	2394	2-in. Candlestick
11.	2375½	Footed Cup	20.	2375½	Tea Cream		2430	11-in. Bowl
11.	2375	Saucer	21.	2375	Mayonnaise		2430	9½-in. Candlestick
12.	2375	After Dinner Cup	21.	2375	Mayonnaise Plate		2430	8-in. Vase
12.	2375	After Dinner Saucer		2375	Footed Oil	29.	2430	½-lb. Candy Jar and Cover
13.	2375	Bouillon	22.	2375	Footed Shaker		2375	12-in. Bowl
13.	2375	Cream Soup		2375	Handled Lunch Tray		2375	3-in. Candlestick
13.	2375	Cream Soup Plate	23.	2375	Sweetmeat	30.	2395	10-in. Bowl
14.	2375	9-in. Baker	24.	2375	Bon Bon	31.	2395½	5-in. Candlestick
15.	2375	12-in. Platter					4105	8-in. Vase

[12]

NEW GARLAND

Plate Etching 284

One of the few patterns to use the Mayfair dinner service. Stemware is featured in *Fostoria Stemware,* pages 57 – 59 and 73.

4020 Almond
    Amber, 1930-1933; $28.00
    Rose, 1931-1933; $32.00
    Topaz, 1931-1933; $32.00
2419 Bon Bon
    Amber, 1930-1933; $28.00
    Rose, 1931-1933; $32.00
    Topaz, 1931-1933; $30.00
4020 Bowl, Finger
    Amber Base, 1930-1933; $36.00
    Rose Bowl, 1931-1933; $40.00
    Topaz Bowl, 1931-1933; $37.00
6002 Bowl, Finger
    Rose Bowl, 1931-1933; $45.00
2419 Bowl, 5" Fruit,
    Amber,1930-1933; $18.00
    Rose, 1931-1933; $24.00
    Topaz, 1931-1933; $22.00
2419 Bowl, 6" Cereal
    Amber, 1930-1933; $20.00
    Rose, 1931-1933; $26.00
    Topaz, 1931-1933; $24.00
2419 Bowl, 7" Soup
    Amber, 1930-1933; $24.00
    Rose, 1931-1933; $30.00
    Topaz, 1931-1933; $26.00
2394 Bowl "D", 7½"
    Amber, 1930-1933; $70.00
    Rose, 1931-1933; $110.00
    Topaz, 1931-1933; $100.00
2433 Bowl "D", 7½"
    Amber, 1930-1932; $110.00
    Rose, 1931-1932; $125.00
    Topaz, 1931-1932; $110.00
2419 Bowl, 10" Baker
    Amber, 1930-1933; $48.00
    Rose, 1931-1933; $55.00
    Topaz, 1931-1933; $50.00
2430 Bowl, 11"
    Amber, 1930-1933; $65.00
    Rose, 1931-1933; $85.00
    Topaz, 1931-1933; $75.00
2394 Bowl "A", 12"
    Amber, 1930-1933; $65.00
    Rose, 1931-1933; $80.00
    Topaz, 1931-1933; $75.00
2433 Bowl "A", 12"
    Amber, 1930-1932; $70.00
    Rose, 1931-1932; $110.00
    Topaz, 1931-1932; $88.00
2441 Bowl, 12"
    Amber, 1930-1933; $70.00

    Rose, 1931-1933; $90.00
    Topaz, 1931-1933; $85.00
2394 Candlestick, 2" (pair)
    Amber, 1930-1933; $65.00
    Rose, 1931-1933; $75.00
    Topaz, 1931-1933; $70.00
2375 Candlestick, 3" (pair)
    Amber, 1930-1933; $60.00
    Rose, 1931-1933; $70.00
    Topaz, 1931-1933; $65.00
2433 Candlestick, 3" (pair)
    Amber, 1930-1932; $65.00
    Rose, 1931-1932; $75.00
    Topaz, 1931-1932; $70.00
2430 Candlestick, 9½" (pair)
    Amber, 1930-1932; $175.00
    Rose, 1931-1932; $195.00
    Topaz, 1931-1932; $195.00
2430 Candy Jar and Cover
    Amber, 1930-1933; $100.00
    Rose, 1931-1933; $125.00
    Topaz, 1931-1933; $125.00
2419 Celery, 11"
    Amber, 1930-1933; $50.00
    Rose, 1931-1933; $57.00
    Topaz, 1931-1933; $55.00
2400 Comport, 6"
    Amber, 1930-1933; $60.00
    Rose, 1931-1933; $65.00
    Topaz, 1931-1933; $65.00
2433 Comport, Low
    Amber, 1930-1932; $38.00
    Rose, 1931-1932; $45.00
    Topaz, 1931-1932; $45.00
2433 Comport, Tall
    Amber, 1930-1932; $75.00
    Rose, 1931-1932; $95.00
    Topaz, 1931-1932; $85.00
2419 Cream Soup
    Amber, 1930-1933; $54.00
    Rose, 1931-1933; $58.00
    Topaz, 1931-1933; $58.00
2419 Cup and Saucer, After Dinner
    Amber, 1930-1933; $50.00
    Rose, 1931-1933; $60.00
    Topaz, 1931-1933; $55.00
2419 Cup and Saucer
    Amber, 1930-1933; $38.00
    Rose, 1931-1933; $45.00
    Topaz, 1931-1933; $40.00
2439 Decanter
    Amber, 1930-1932; $600.00

NEW GARLAND

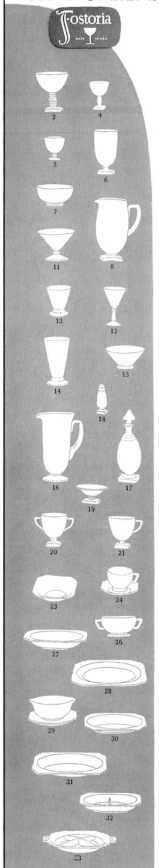

DESIGN PATENT NOS. 83493 AND 83893

NEW GARLAND DESIGN

PLATE ETCHING No. 284   *Priced on pages 10 and 11—1931 Price List*

STEMWARE

Made in Amber Base with Crystal Bowl—Crystal Base with Rose Bowl—Crystal Base with Topaz Bowl

1.	4020	Goblet	4.	4020½	4-oz. Cocktail	6.	4020	10-oz. Footed Tumbler
2.	4020	High Sherbet	5.	4020	3½-oz. Cocktail	6.	4020	5-oz. Footed Tumbler
3.	4020	7-oz. Low Sherbet	5.	4020	2-oz. Whiskey	7.	4021	Finger Bowl
3.	4020	5-oz. Low Sherbet	6.	4020	16-oz. Footed Tumbler	8.	4020	Footed Jug
			6.	4020	13-oz. Footed Tumbler			

Crystal Base with Rose Bowl

9.	6002	Goblet	12.	6002	Wine	14.	6002	5-oz. Footed Tumbler
10.	6002	High Sherbet	12.	6002	Cordial	14.	6002	2-oz. Footed Tumbler
11.	6002	Low Sherbet	13.	6002	Oyster Cocktail	15.	6002	Finger Bowl
12.	6002	Claret	14.	6002	13-oz. Footed Tumbler	16.	5000-7	Footed Jug
			14.	6002	10-oz. Footed Tumbler			

DINNERWARE

Made in Rose, Amber and Topaz

17.	4020	Footed Decanter	19.	4020	Individual Almond	21.	4020	Footed Cream
18.	4020	Footed Shaker	20.	4020	Footed Sugar	22.	2419	6-in. Bread and Butter Plate

[10]

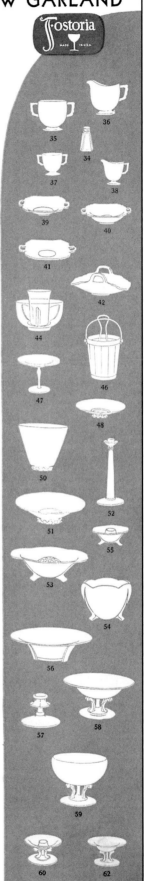

DESIGN PATENT NOS. 83493 AND 83893

NEW GARLAND DESIGN

PLATE ETCHING No. 284   *Priced on pages 10 and 11—1931 Price List*

DINNERWARE—Continued

Made in Rose, Amber and Topaz

22. 2419 7-in. Salad Plate	33. 2419 4-Part Relish	47. 2400 6-in. Comport
22. 2419 8-in. Luncheon Plate	34. 2419 Shaker	48. 2430 5½-in. Mint
22. 2419 9-in. Dinner Plate	35. 2419 Sugar	48. 2430 7-in. Jelly
23. 2419 5-in. Fruit	36. 2419 Cream	49. 2430 ½-lb. Candy Jar and Cover
23. 2419 6-in. Cereal	37. 2419 Tea Sugar	50. 2430 8-in. Vase
23. 2419 7-in. Soup	38. 2419 Tea Cream	51. 2430 11-in. Bowl
24. 2419 Footed Cup	39. 2419 Jelly—2 Handles	52. 2430 9½-in. Candlestick
24. 2419 Saucer	40. 2419 Mayonnaise—2 Handles	53. 2394 12-in. Bowl "A"
25. 2419 After Dinner Cup	41. 2419 Lemon Dish—2 Handles	54. 2394 7½-in. Bowl "D"
25. 2419 After Dinner Saucer	42. 2419 Bon Bon—2 Handles	55. 2394 2-in. Candlestick
26. 2419 Cream Soup	43. 2419 10-in. Cake Plate—2 H'dles	56. 2441 12-in. Bowl
27. 2419 10-in. Baker	44. 2451 Ice Dish	57. 2375 3-in. Candlestick
28. 2419 12-in. Platter	44. 2451 T. J. Liner (not etched)	58. 2433 12-in. Bowl "A"
28. 2419 15-in. Platter	44. 2451 C. M. Liner (not etched)	59. 2433 7½-in. Bowl "D"
29. 2419 Sauce Bowl and Stand	2083 Salad Dressing Bottle	60. 2433 3-in. Candlestick
30. 2419 8½-in. Pickle	45. 2375 Footed Oil	61. 2433 6-in. Tall Comport
31. 2419 11-in. Celery	2439 Decanter	62. 2433 6-in. Low Comport
32. 2419 8½-in. Relish	46. 2375 Ice Bucket	

[11]

Rose, 1931-1932; $700.00/market
Topaz, 1931-1932; $650.00/market

4020 Decanter
Amber, 1930-1932; $600.00
Rose, 1931-1932; $700.00/market
Topaz, 1931-1932; $650.00/market

2375 Ice Bucket
Amber, 1930-1933; $100.00
Rose, 1931-1933; $120.00
Topaz, 1931-1933; $110.00

2451 Ice Dish and Liner
Amber, 1930-1933; $64.00
Rose, 1931-1933; $68.00
Topaz, 1931-1933; $65.00

2419 Jelly, 2-Handled
Amber, 1930-1933; $38.00
Rose, 1931-1933; $45.00
Topaz, 1931-1933; $42.00

2430 Jelly, 7"
Amber, 1930-1932; $35.00
Rose, 1931-1932; $45.00
Topaz, 1931-1932; $40.00

4020 Jug
Amber Base, 1930-1933; $325.00
Rose Bowl, 1931-1933; $450.00
Topaz Bowl, 1931-1933; $400.00

5000 Jug
Rose, 1931-1933; $600.00

2419 Lemon
Amber, 1930-1933; $35.00
Rose, 1931-1933; $42.00
Topaz, 1931-1933; $40.00

2419 Mayonnaise
Amber, 1930-1933; $38.00
Rose, 1931-1933; $45.00
Topaz, 1931-1933; $42.00

2430 Mint, 5½"
Amber, 1930-1932; $30.00
Rose, 1931-1932; $34.00
Topaz, 1931-1932; $32.00

2375 Oil, Footed
Amber, 1930-1933; $295.00
Rose, 1931-1933; $350.00
Topaz, 1931-1933; $325.00

2419 Pickle, 8½"
Amber, 1930-1933; $38.00
Rose, 1931-1933; $44.00
Topaz, 1931-1933; $40.00

2419 Plate, 6"
Amber, 1930-1933; $5.00
Rose, 1931-1933; $8.00
Topaz, 1931-1933; $6.00

2419 Plate, 7"
Amber, 1930-1933; $6.00
Rose, 1931-1933; $8.00
Topaz, 1931-1933; $7.00

2419 Plate, 8"
Amber, 1930-1933; $10.00
Rose, 1931-1933; $15.00
Topaz, 1931-1933; $12.00

2419 Plate, 9"
Amber, 1930-1933; $15.00
Rose, 1931-1933; $25.00
Topaz, 1931-1933; $20.00

2419 Plate, 10" Cake
Amber, 1930-1933; $68.00
Rose, 1931-1933; $75.00
Topaz, 1931-1933; $70.00

2419 Platter, 12"
Amber, 1930-1933; $68.00
Rose, 1931-1933; $75.00
Topaz, 1931-1933; $70.00

2419 Relish, 8½"
Amber, 1930-1933; $42.00
Rose, 1931-1933; $47.00
Topaz, 1931-1933; $44.00

2419 Relish, 4-part
Amber, 1930-1933; $55.00
Rose, 1931-1933; $67.00
Topaz, 1931-1933; $64.00

2083 Salad Dressing Bottle
Amber, 1930-1933; $295.00
Rose, 1931-1933; $350.00
Topaz, 1931-1933; $325.00

2419 Sauce and Stand
Amber, 1930-1933; $65.00
Rose, 1931-1933; $95.00
Topaz, 1931-1933; $85.00

2419 Shaker, FGT (pair)
Amber, 1930-1933; $87.00
Rose, 1931-1933; $110.00
Topaz, 1931-1933; $95.00

4020 Shaker, FGT (pair)
Amber, 1930-1932; $97.00
Rose, 1931-1932; $125.00
Topaz, 1931-1932; $110.00

2419 Sugar and Cream, Tea
Amber, 1930-1933; $48.00
Rose, 1931-1933; $57.00
Topaz, 1931-1933; $52.00

2419½ Sugar and Cream
Amber, 1932-1933; $54.00
Rose, 1932-1933; $65.00
Topaz, 1932-1933; $60.00

4020 Sugar and Cream
Amber, 1930-1933; $68.00
Rose, 1931-1933; $75.00
Topaz, 1931-1933; $75.00

2430 Vase, 8"
Amber, 1930-1933; $195.00
Rose, 1931-1933; $275.00
Topaz, 1931-1933; $250.00

New Garland 2433 Low Comport, 7" Plate, 2433 Candlestick

MINUET

Plate Etching 285

Stemware is featured in *Fostoria Stemware*, pages 57 – 59 and 73.

2419 Bon Bon
  Green, 1931-1933; $36.00
  Topaz, 1931-1933; $32.00
4020 Bowl, Finger
  Green Base, 1931-1933; $40.00
6002 Bowl, Finger
  Topaz, 1931-1933; $45.00
2419 Bowl, 5" Fruit
  Green, 1931-1933; $30.00
  Topaz, 1931-1933; $28.00
2419 Bowl, 6" Cereal
  Green, 1931-1933; $40.00
  Topaz, 1931-1933; $35.00
2419 Bowl, 7" Soup
  Green, 1931-1933; $55.00
  Topaz, 1931-1933; $50.00
2394 Bowl "D", 7½"
  Green, 1931-1933; $110.00
  Topaz, 1931-1933; $100.00
2433 Bowl "D", 7½"
  Green, 1931-1932; $175.00
  Topaz, 1931-1932; $125.00
2419 Bowl, 10" Baker
  Green, 1931-1933; $65.00
  Topaz, 1931-1933; $60.00
2430 Bowl, 11"
  Green, 1931-1933; $125.00
  Topaz, 1931-1933; $100.00

2394 Bowl "A", 12"
  Green, 1931-1933; $125.00
  Topaz, 1931-1933; $100.00
2433 Bowl "A", 12"
  Green, 1931-1932; $225.00

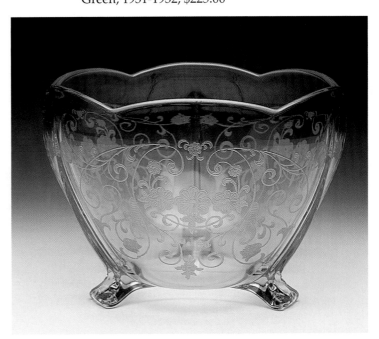

Topaz Minuet Bowl D

193

MINUET

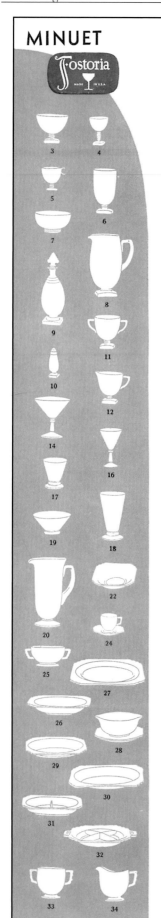

DESIGN PATENT NOS. 83788 AND 83492

MINUET DESIGN

Plate Etching No. 285

Priced on pages 8 and 9—1931 Price List

STEMWARE

Made in Green Base with Crystal Bowl

1.	4020	Goblet	5.	4020	2-oz. Whiskey	8.	4020	Footed Jug
2.	4020	High Sherbet	6.	4020	16-oz. Footed Tumbler	9.	4020	Footed Decanter
3.	4020	7-oz. Low Sherbet	6.	4020	13-oz. Footed Tumbler	10.	4020	Footed Shaker
3.	4020	5-oz. Low Sherbet	6.	4020	10-oz. Footed Tumbler	11.	4020	Footed Sugar
4.	4020½	4-oz. Cocktail	6.	4020	5-oz. Footed Tumbler	12.	4020	Footed Cream
5.	4020	3½-oz. Cocktail	7.	4021	Finger Bowl			

Crystal Base with Topaz Bowl

13.	6002	Goblet	17.	6002	Oyster Cocktail	20.	5000-7	Footed Jug
14.	6002	High Sherbet	18.	6002	13-oz. Footed Tumbler	9.	4020	Footed Decanter
15.	6002	Low Sherbet	18.	6002	10-oz. Footed Tumbler	10.	4020	Footed Shaker
16.	6002	Claret	18.	6002	5-oz. Footed Tumbler	11.	4020	Footed Sugar
16.	6002	Wine	18.	6002	2-oz. Footed Tumbler	12.	4020	Footed Cream
16.	6002	Cordial	19.	6002	Finger Bowl			

DINNERWARE

Made in Green and Topaz

21.	2419	6-in. Bread and Butter Plate	21.	2419	8-in. Luncheon Plate	22.	2419	5-in. Fruit
21.	2419	7-in. Salad Plate	21.	2419	9-in. Dinner Plate	22.	2419	6-in. Cereal

{ 8 }

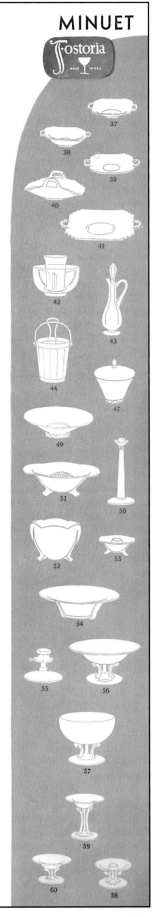

DESIGN PATENT NOS. 83788 AND 84492

MINUET DESIGN

PLATE ETCHING No. 285   *Priced on pages 8 and 9—1931 Price List*

DINNERWARE—Continued

Made in Green and Topaz

22. 2419 7-in. Soup	35. 2419 Tea Sugar	46. 2430 7-in. Jelly
23. 2419 Footed Cup	36. 2419 Tea Cream	47. 2430 ½-lb. Candy Jar and Cover
23. 2419 Saucer	37. 2419 Jelly—2 Handles	48. 2430 8-in. Vase
24. 2419 After Dinner Cup	38. 2419 Mayonnaise—2 Handles	49. 2430 11-in. Bowl
24. 2419 After Dinner Saucer	39. 2419 Lemon Dish—2 Handles	50. 2430 9½-in. Candlestick
25. 2419 Cream Soup	40. 2419 Bon Bon—2 Handles	51. 2394 12-in. Bowl "A"
26. 2419 10-in. Baker	41. 2419 Cake Plate—2 Handles	52. 2394 7½-in. Bowl "D"
27. 2419 12-in. Platter	42. 2451 Ice Dish	53. 2394 2-in. Candlestick
27. 2419 15-in. Platter	42. 2451 T. J. Liner (not etched)	54. 2441 12-in. Bowl
28. 2419 Sauce Bowl and Stand	42. 2451 C. M. Liner (not etched)	55. 2375 3-in. Candlestick
29. 2419 8½-in. Pickle	2083 Salad Dressing Bottle	56. 2433 12-in. Bowl "A"
30. 2419 11-in. Celery	43. 2375 Footed Oil	57. 2433 7½-in. Bowl "D"
31. 2419 8½-in. Relish	2439 Decanter	58. 2433 3-in. Candlestick
32. 2419 4-Part Relish	44. 2375 Ice Bucket	59. 2433 6-in. Tall Comport
33. 2419 Sugar	45. 2400 6-in. Comport	60. 2433 6-in. Low Comport
34. 2419 Cream	46. 2430 5½-in. Mint	

[9]

Topaz, 1931-1932; $200.00
2441 Bowl, 12"
Green, 1931-1933; $125.00
Topaz, 1931-1933; $100.00
2394 Candlestick, 2" (pair)
Green, 1931-1933; $100.00
Topaz, 1931-1933; $85.00
2375 Candlestick, 3" (pair)
Green, 1931; $100.00
Topaz, 1931; $85.00
2433 Candlestick, 3" (pair)
Green, 1931-1932; $150.00
Topaz, 1931-1932; $135.00
2430 Candlestick, 9½" (pair)
Green, 1931-1932; $225.00
Topaz, 1931-1932; $225.00
2430 Candy Jar and Cover
Green, 1931-1933; $125.00
Topaz, 1931-1933; $110.00
2419 Celery, 11"
Green 1931-1933; $57.00
Topaz, 1931-1933; $55.00
2400 Comport, 6"
Green, 1931-1933; $65.00
Topaz, 1931-1933; $60.00
2433 Comport, Low
Green, 1931-1932; $45.00
Topaz, 1931-1932; $40.00
2433 Comport, Tall
Green, 1931-1932; $125.00
Topaz, 1931-1932; $125.00
2419 Cream Soup
Green, 1931-1933; $58.00
Topaz, 1931-1933; $55.00
2419 Cup and Saucer, After Dinner
Green, 1931-1933; $65.00
Topaz, 1931-1933; $58.00
2419 Cup and Saucer
Green, 1931-1933; $45.00
Topaz, 1931-1933; $40.00
2439 Decanter
Green, 1931-1932; $700.00/market
Topaz, 1931-1932; $650.00/market
4020 Decanter
Green Foot, 1931-1932; $600.00/market
Topaz Bowl, 1931-1932; $550.00/market
2375 Ice Bucket, NP Handle
Green, 1931-1933; $125.00
Topaz, 1931-1933; $115.00
2451 Ice Dish and Liner
Green, 1931-1933; $70.00
Topaz, 1931-1933; $65.00
2419 Jelly, 2 Handles
Green, 1931-1933; $45.00
Topaz, 1931-1933; $42.00

Green Minuet 2419 Handled Cake, 2451 Ice Dish and Liner, 2375 Candlestick, After Dinner Cup and Saucer

2430 Jelly, 7"
Green, 1931-1932; $45.00
Topaz, 1931-1932; $42.00
4020 Jug
Green Base, 1931-1933; $550.00
5000 Jug
Topaz, 1931-1933; $600.00
2419 Lemon, 2 Handles
Green, 1931-1933; $45.00
Topaz, 1931-1933; $42.00
2419 Mayonnaise, 2 Handles
Green, 1931-1933; $47.00
Topaz, 1931-1933; $45.00
2430 Mint, 5½"
Green, 1931-1932; $38.00
Topaz, 1931-1932; $34.00
2375 Oil, Footed
Green, 1931-1933; $375.00
Topaz, 1931-1933; $350.00
2419 Pickle, 8½"
Green, 1931-1933; $44.00
Topaz, 1931-1933; $40.00
2419 Plate, 6"
Green, 1931-1933; $12.00
Topaz, 1931-1933; $12.00
2419 Plate, 7"
Green, 1931-1933; $15.00
Topaz, 1931-1933; $15.00
2419 Plate, 8"

Green, 1931-1933; $25.00
Topaz, 1931-1933; $20.00
2419 Plate, 9"
  Green, 1931-1933; $45.00
  Topaz, 1931-1933; $40.00
2419 Plate, Handled Cake
  Green, 1931-1933; $85.00
  Topaz, 1931-1933; $75.00
2419 Platter, 12"
  Green, 1931-1933; $85.00
  Topaz, 1931-1933; $80.00
2419 Platter, 15"
  Green, 1931-1933; $145.00
  Topaz, 1931-1933; $125.00
2419 Relish, 8½"
  Green, 1931-1933; $48.00
  Topaz, 1931-1933; $45.00
2419 Relish, 4-part
  Green, 1931-1933; $67.00
  Topaz, 1931-1933; $64.00
2083 Salad Dressing Bottle
  Green, 1931-1933; $350.00
  Topaz, 1931-1933; $325.00
2419 Sauce and Stand
  Green, 1931-1933; $95.00
  Topaz, 1931-1933; $85.00
4020 Shaker, FGT (pair)
  Green, 1931-1932; $135.00
  Topaz, 1931-1932; $125.00
2419 Sugar and Cream
  Green, 1931-1933; $75.00

Green Minuet Vase, 4020 Goblet, Candy and Cover

Topaz, 1931-1933; $70.00
2419 Sugar and Cream, Tea
  Green, 1931-1933; $75.00
  Topaz, 1931-1933; $70.00
2419½ Sugar and Cream
  Green, 1932-1933; $85.00
  Topaz, 1932-1933; $80.00
4020 Sugar and Cream
  Green Base, 1931-1933; $75.00
  Topaz Bowl, 1931-1933; $70.00
2430 Vase, 8"
  Green, 1931-1933; $275.00
  Topaz, 1931-1933; $250.00

MANOR

Plate Etching 286

This incredibly beautiful etching used Crystal, Green, and Topaz, combining color and crystal for many pieces. A few pieces had the Wisteria base but not a Wisteria bowl since the Wisteria color was never etched by Fostoria. Stemware is featured in Fostoria *Stemware*, pages 74 and 77.

4020 Almond, Individual
  Crystal, 1931-1942; $32.00
  Green, 1931-1934; $36.00
  Topaz , 1931-1934; $32.00
2419 Ash Tray
  Crystal, 1931-1943; $42.00
  Green, 1931-1934; $48.00
  Topaz, 1931-1934; $45.00
2419 Bon Bon
  Crystal, 1931-1940; $32.00
  Green, 1931-1934; $36.00
  Topaz, 1931-1934; $32.00
4020 Bowl, Finger
  Crystal, 1931-1943; $35.00

  Green, 1931-1934; $50.00
  Topaz, 1931-1935; $45.00
  Wisteria, 1931-1936; $75.00
2419 Bowl, 5" Fruit
  Crystal, 1931-1943; $28.00
  Green, 1931-1934; $32.00
  Topaz, 1931-1934; $30.00
2419 Bowl, 6" Cereal
  Crystal, 1931-1939; $32.00
  Green, 1931-1934; $40.00
  Topaz, 1931-1934; $35.00
2419 Bowl, 7" Soup
  Crystal, 1931-1936; $45.00
  Green, 1931-1934; $55.00

Topaz, 1931-1934; $50.00
2419 Bowl, 10" Baker
    Crystal, 1931-1940; $55.00
    Green, 1931-1934; $65.00
    Topaz, 1931-1934; $60.00
2443 Bowl, 10" Oval
    Crystal, 1931-1939; $120.00
    Green, 1931-1934; $145.00
    Topaz, 1931-1934; $135.00
2470½ Bowl, 10½"
    Crystal, 1933-1943; $150.00
    Green, 1933; $185.00
    Topaz, 1933; $175.00
2394 Bowl "A," 12"
    Crystal, 1931-1943; $95.00
    Green, 1931-1934; $125.00
    Topaz, 1931-1934; $125.00
2433 Bowl "A," 12"
    Crystal, 1931-1932; $195.00
    Green, 1931-1932; $225.00
    Topaz, 1931-1932; $225.00
2394 Candlestick, 2" (pair)
    Crystal, 1931-1943; $75.00
    Green, 1931-1934; $100.00
2443 Candlestick, 3" (pair)
    Crystal, 1931-1939; $87.00
    Green, 1931-1934; $125.00
    Topaz, 1931-1934; $115.00
2433 Candlestick, 3" (pair)
    Crystal, 1931-1932; $125.00
    Green, 1931-1932; $145.00
    Topaz, 1931-1932; $135.00
2470½ Candlestick, 5½" (pair)
    Crystal, 1933-1943; $135.00
    Green, 1933; $165.00
    Topaz, 1933; $150.00
2430 Candy Jar and Cover, ½ pound
    Crystal, 1931-1935; $110.00
    Green, 1931-1934; $125.00
    Topaz, 1931-1934; $125.00
2419 Celery, 11"
    Crystal, 1931-1940; $52.00
    Green, 1931-1934; $57.00
    Topaz, 1931-1934; $54.00
2419 Comport, 6"
    Crystal, 1931-1940; $55.00
    Green, 1931-1934; $65.00
    Topaz, 1931-1934; $60.00
2433 Comport, 6" Low
    Crystal, 1931-1932; $58.00
    Green, 1931-1932; $67.00
    Topaz, 1931-1932; $65.00
2433 Comport, 6" Tall
    Crystal, 1931-1932; $125.00

Crystal Manor 4108 5" Vase, Green 12" Bowl "A"

    Green, 1931-1932; $135.00
    Topaz, 1931-1932; $135.00
2419 Cream Soup
    Crystal, 1931-1936; $50.00
    Green, 1931-1934; $58.00
    Topaz, 1931-1934; $56.00
2419 Cup and Saucer, After Dinner
    Crystal, 1931-1938; $55.00
    Green, 1931-1934; $65.00
    Topaz, 1931-1934; $60.00
2419 Cup and Saucer
    Crystal, 1931-1943; $35.00
    Green, 1931-1934; $45.00
    Topaz, 1931-1934; $40.00
4020 Decanter, Footed
    Crystal, 1931-1932; $500.00/market
    Green, 1931-1932; $600.00/market
    Topaz, 1931-1932; $550.00/market
2451 Ice Dish and Liner
    Crystal, 1931-1943; $58.00
    Green, 1931-1934; $70.00
    Topaz, 1931-1934; $65.00
2451 Ice Dish Plate
    Crystal, 1933-1935; $12.00
    Green, 1933-1934; $15.00
    Topaz, 1933-1934; $15.00
2443 Ice Tub, 6"
    Crystal, 1931-1942; $110.00
    Green, 1931-1934; $125.00
    Topaz, 1931-1934; $125.00
4020 Jug (foot in colors)
    Crystal, 1931-1940; $450.00
    Green, 1931-1934; $550.00
    Topaz, 1931-1935; $500.00
    Wisteria, 1931-1934; $1,000.00/market
2419 Jelly
    Crystal, 1931-1939; $40.00

Green, 1931-1934; $45.00
Topaz,1931-1934; $42.00
2419 Lemon Dish
Crystal, 1931-1939; $40.00
Green, 1931-1934; $45.00
Topaz, 1931-1934; $42.00
2419 Mayonnaise
Crystal, 1931-1943; $42.00
Green, 1931-1934; $47.00
Topaz, 1931-1934; $45.00
2419 Pickle, 8½"
Crystal, 1931-1942; $38.00
Green, 1931-1934; $44.00
Topaz, 1931-1934; $40.00
2419 Plate, 6"
Crystal, 1931-1943; $12.00
Green, 1931-1934; $14.00
Topaz, 1931-1934; $14.00
2419 Plate, 7"
Crystal, 1931-1934; $12.00
Green, 1931-1934; $15.00
Topaz, 1931-1934; $15.00
2419 Plate, 8"
Crystal, 1931-1934; $18.00
Green, 1931-1934; $25.00
Topaz, 1931-1934; $25.00
2419 Plate, 9"
Crystal, 1931-1934; $35.00
Green, 1931-1934; $45.00
Topaz, 1931-1934; $40.00
2419 Plate, Cake
Crystal, 1931-1943; $65.00
Green, 1931-1934; $85.00
Topaz,1931-1934; $70.00
2440 Plate, 13" Torte
Crystal, 1935-1943; $95.00
2419 Platter, 12"
Crystal, 1931-1940; $85.00
Green, 1931-1934; $95.00
Topaz, 1931-1934; $90.00
2419 Platter, 15"
Crystal, 1931-1938; $110.00
Green, 1931-1934; $135.00
Topaz, 1931-1934; $125.00
2419 Relish, 8½"
Crystal, 1931-1943; $40.00
Green, 1931-1934; $48.00
Topaz, 1931-1934; $45.00
2419 Relish, 4-part
Crystal, 1931-1943; $59.00
Green, 1931-1934; $67.00
Topaz, 1931-1934; $64.00
2419 Sauce Bowl and Stand
Crystal, 1931-1937; $85.00

Topaz Manor 2419 Cream Soup, Shakers, Sauce Bowl and Stand

Green, 1931-1937; $95.00
Topaz, 1931-1937; $90.00
2419 Shaker, FGT (pair)
Crystal, 1931-1943; $110.00
Green, 1931-1934; $135.00
Topaz, 1931-1934; $125.00
4020 Shaker, Footed, FGT (pair)
Crystal, 1931-1932; $125.00
Green, 1931-1932; $150.00
Topaz, 1931-1932; $135.00
2419 Sugar and Cream, Tea
Crystal, 1931-1943; $65.00
Green, 1931-1934; $85.00
Topaz, 1931-1934; $75.00
2419 Sugar and Cream
Crystal, 1931-1939; $65.00
Green, 1931-1934; $85.00
Topaz, 1931-1934; $75.00
2419½ Sugar and Cream, Footed
Crystal, 1933-1943; $75.00
Green, 1933-1934; $85.00
Topaz, 1933-1934; $80.00
2419 Syrup, Cover, Saucer

Manor Crystal 2443 Ice Tub, 4107 9" Vase, Wisteria 4020 Jug

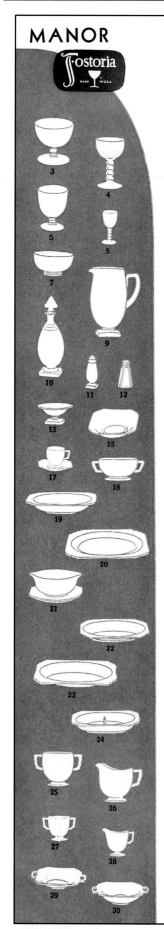

MANOR

DESIGN PATENT APPLIED FOR

MANOR DESIGN

PLATE ETCHING No. 286
Priced on pages 6 and 7 — 1931 Price List

STEMWARE

*Made in Solid Crystal—Crystal Base with Green Bowl—Crystal Base with Topaz Bowl—
Wisteria Base with Crystal Bowl*

1.	6003	Goblet	5.	6003	Cordial	8.	6003	9-oz. Footed Tumbler
2.	6003	High Sherbet	6.	6003	Oyster Cocktail	8.	6003	5-oz. Footed Tumbler
3.	6003	Low Sherbet	7.	4021	Finger Bowl	8.	6003	2½-oz. Footed Tumbler
4.	6003	Cocktail	8.	6003	12-oz. Footed Tumbler	9.	4020	Footed Jug

DINNERWARE

Made in Crystal, Green and Topaz

10.	4020	Footed Decanter	14.	2419	8-in. Luncheon Plate	16.	2419	Saucer
11.	4020	Footed Shaker	14.	2419	9-in. Dinner Plate	17.	2419	After Dinner Cup
12.	2419	Shaker	15.	2419	5-in. Fruit	17.	2419	After Dinner Saucer
13.	4020	Individual Almond	15.	2419	6-in. Cereal	18.	2419	Cream Soup
14.	2419	6-in. Bread and Butter Plate	15.	2419	7-in. Soup	19.	2419	10-in. Baker
14.	2419	7-in. Salad Plate	16.	2419	Footed Cup			

{ 6 }

MANOR

DESIGN PATENT APPLIED FOR

MANOR DESIGN

PLATE ETCHING No. 286

Priced on pages 6 and 7—1931 Price List

DINNERWARE—Continued
Made in Crystal, Green and Topaz

20.	2419	12-in. Platter	32.	2419	Bon Bon	42.	2443	10-in. Oval Bowl
20.	2419	15-in. Platter	33.	2419	Cake Plate	43.	2443	3-in. Candlestick
21.	2419	Sauce Bowl and Stand	34.	2419	Handled Lunch Tray	44.	2394	12-in. Bowl "A"
22.	2419	8½-in. Pickle	35.	2419	4-Part Relish	45.	2394	2-in. Candlestick
23.	2419	11-in. Celery	36.	2419	Syrup	46.	2433	12-in. Bowl "A"
24.	2419	8½-in. Relish	36.	2419	Syrup and Cover	47.	2433	3-in. Candlestick
25.	2419	Sugar	36.	2419	Syrup Saucer	48.	2433	6-in. Tall Comport
26.	2419	Cream	37.	2419	Ash Tray	49.	2433	6-in. Low Comport
27.	2419	Tea Sugar	38.	2419	Comport	50.	4106	7-in. Vase
28.	2419	Tea Cream	39.	2430	½-lb. Candy Jar and Cover	51.	4107	9-in. Vase
29.	2419	Jelly	40.	2451	Ice Dish	52.	4108	5-in. Vase
30.	2419	Mayonnaise	40.	2451	5-oz. T. J. Liner (not etched)	52.	4108	6-in. Vase
31.	2419	Lemon Dish	40.	2451	4-oz. C. M. Liner (not etched)	52.	4108	7-in. Vase
			41.	2443	6-in. Ice Tub			

[7]

Crystal, 1931-1940; $200.00
Green, 1931-1934; $250.00
Topaz, 1931-1934; $225.00
2419 Tray, Handled Lunch
Crystal, 1931-1939; $110.00
Green, 1931-1934; $125.00
Topaz, 1931-1934; $125.00
4108 Vase, 5"
Crystal, 1931-1942; $125.00
Green, 1931-1934; $140.00
Topaz, 1931-1934; $135.00
4108 Vase, 6"
Crystal, 1931-1932; $135.00
Green, 1931-1932; $165.00

Topaz, 1931-1932; $150.00
4108 Vase, 7"
Crystal, 1931-1932; $175.00
Green, 1931-1932; $195.00
Topaz, 1931-1932; $185.00
4106 Vase, 7"
Crystal, 1931-1934; $165.00
Green, 1931-1934; $185.00
Topaz, 1931-1934; $175.00
4107 Vase, 9"
Crystal, 1931-1933; $265.00
Green, 1931-1933; $325.00
Topaz, 1931-1933; $300.00

FERN

Plate Etching 305

Stemware is featured in *Fostoria Stemware*, pages 57 – 59 and 68 – 69.

FERN

Decoration 501

Gold edge on Ebony glass, Plate Etching 305.

2375 Bon Bon
Crystal, 1930-1933; $34.00
Rose, 1930-1933; $40.00
Decoration 501, 1930-1932; $38.00
869 Bowl, Finger
Crystal, 1929-1933; $32.00
Rose, 1930-1933; $38.00
4021 Bowl, Finger,
Crystal, 1929-1933; $32.00
2395 Bowl, 10"
Crystal, 1929-1933; $135.00
Rose, 1930-1933; $175.00
Decoration 501, 1929-1932; $225.00
2315 Bowl, Combination
Crystal, 1929; $165.00
Decoration 501, 1929; $250.00
2497 Bowl, 12" Deep "A"
Crystal, 1929-1933; $95.00
Rose, 1930-1933; $125.00
Decoration 501, 1929-1932; $135.00
2324 Candlestick, 4" (pair)
Crystal, 1929-1933; $75.00
Rose, 1930-1933; $95.00
Decoration 501, 1929-1932; $110.00

2395½ Candlestick, 5" (pair)
Crystal, 1929-1933; $115.00
Rose, 1930-1933; $135.00
Decoration 501, 1929-1932; $145.00
2427 Cigarette Box and Cover
Decoration 501, 1929-1932; $150.00
2400 Comport, 6"
Crystal, 1929-1933; $62.00
Rose, 1930-1933; $75.00
Decoration 501, 1929-1932; $75.00
2350½ Footed Cup,
Crystal, 1929-1933; $26.00

Fern 2315 Combination Bowl, 2395½ Candlesticks

2419 Saucer
   Crystal, 1929-1933; $9.00
   Rose, 1930-1933; $12.00
2419 Cup
   Rose, 1930-1933; $33.00
2350 After Dinner Cup and Saucer,
   Crystal, 1929-1933; $45.00
2375 Lemon Dish
   Crystal, 1929-1933; $34.00
   Rose, 1930-1933; $40.00
   Decoration 501, 1929-1932; $38.00
4020 Jug
   Crystal, 1929-1933; $325.00
   Ebony Base, 1929-1933; $365.00
5000 Jug
   Crystal, 1929-1933; $365.00
   Rose, 1930-1933; $425.00
2283 Plate, 6" Finger Bowl R.O.
   Crystal, 1929-1933; $12.00
   Rose,   1930-1933;
   $15.00
2419 Plate, 6",
   Crystal,   1929-1933;
   $9.00
2419 Plate, 7"
   Crystal,   1929-1933;
   $12.00
   Rose, 1930-1933; $15.00
2419 Plate, 8"
   Crystal, 1929-1933; $20.00
   Rose, 1930-1933; $25.00
2375 Plate, 10" Cake
   Crystal, 1929-1933; $72.00
   Rose, 1930-1933; $85.00

Decoration 501, 1929-1932; $85.00
4020 Sugar and Cream
   Crystal, 1929-1933; $75.00
   Ebony Base, 1929-1933; $85.00
2409 Vase, 7½"
   Decoration 501, 1929-1932; $195.00
4105 Vase, 8" Regular Optic
   Crystal, 1929-1932; $195.00
   Rose 1930-1932; $235.00
   Decoration 501, No Optic,
   1929-1932; $200.00
2373 Vase, Large Window and Cover
   Decoration 501, 1929-1932; $265.00
2385 Vase, 8½" Fan
   Decoration 501, 1929-1932; $265.00

QUEEN ANNE

Plate Etching 306

Stemware is featured in *Fostoria Stemware,* pages 57 – 59.

4020 Bowl, Finger
Crystal, 1929-1933; $32.00
Amber Base, 1929-1933; $37.00
2350 Cream Soup and Plate
Crystal, 1929-1933; $48.00
Amber, 1933; $55.00
2350 Cup and Saucer, After Dinner
Crystal, 1929-1933; $48.00
Amber, 1933; $55.00
2350½ Cup and 2350 Saucer
Crystal, 1929-1933; $32.00
Amber, 1933; $38.00
4020 Jug
Crystal, 1929-1933; $325.00
Amber Base, 1929-1933; $350.00
2350 Plate, 6"
Crystal, 1929-1933; $9.00
Amber, 1933; $12.00
2350 Plate, 7"
Crystal, 1929-1933; $12.00
Amber, 1933; $16.00
2350 Plate, 9"
Crystal, 1929-1933; $40.00
Amber, 1933; $45.00
2419 Plate, 6"
Crystal, 1933; $10.00
Amber, 1933; $12.00
2419 Plate, 7"
Crystal, 1933; $15.00
Amber, 1933; $20.00
2419 Plate, 8"
Crystal, 1933; $18.00
Amber, 1933; $22.00
2419 Saucer, After Dinner
Crystal, 1933; $10.00

Queen Anne 4020 Amber Footed Ice Tea, 2419 After Dinner Cup and Saucer

Amber, 1933; $12.00
2419 Saucer
Crystal, 1933; $9.00
Amber, 1933; $12.00
4020 Shaker, FGT (pair)
Crystal, 1929-1932; $95.00
Amber Base, 1929-1932; $110.00
4020 Sugar and Cream
Crystal, 1929-1933; $64.00
Amber Base, 1929-1933; $70.00

FOUNTAIN

Plate Etching 307

1929 – 1930

Although there are few pieces in this pattern, it does qualify as a complete dinner service since it has both a cup and sauce and a 9" dinner plate. Stemware is featured in *Fostoria Stemware,* page 58.

4021 Bowl, Finger
Crystal, $25.00
Green Base, $32.00
2350½ Cup and Saucer, $28.00
2350 After Dinner Cup and Saucer, $30.00
2350 Cream Soup, $22.00

2350 Plate, 6", $6.00
2350 Plate, 7", $8.00
2350 Plate, 9", $28.00
2419 Plate, 6", $6.00
2419 Plate, 7", $8.00
2419 Plate, 8", $24.00

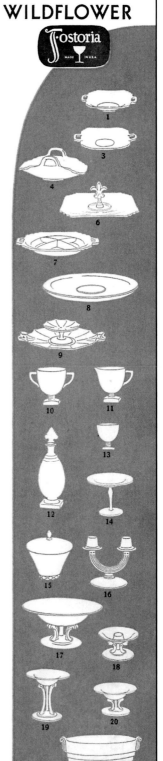

WILDFLOWER

WILDFLOWER DESIGN

PLATE ETCHING No. 308

Priced on page 31—1931 Price List

Made in Green and Amber

1. 2419 Jelly	12. 4020 Footed Decanter	23. 2443 4-in. Candlestick
2. 2419 Mayonnaise	13. 4020 2-oz. Whiskey	24. 2419 Syrup
3. 2419 Lemon Dish	14. 2400 6-in. Comport	24. 2419 Syrup and Cover
4. 2419 Bon Bon	15. 2430 ½-lb. Candy Jar and Cover	24. 2419 Syrup Saucer
5. 2419 Cake Plate	16. 2447 Duo Candlestick	25. 4106 7-in. Vase
6. 2419 Handled Lunch Tray	17. 2433 12-in. Bowl "A"	26. 4107 9-in. Vase
7. 2419 4-Part Relish	18. 2433 3-in. Candlestick	26. 4107 12-in. Vase
8. 2364 16-in. Plate	19. 2433 6-in. Tall Comport	26. 4107 15-in. Vase
9. 2375 Cheese and Cracker	20. 2433 6-in. Low Comport	27. 4108 5-in. Vase
10. 4020 Footed Sugar	21. 2443 6-in. Ice Tub	27. 4108 6-in. Vase
11. 4020 Footed Cream	22. 2443 10-in. Oval Bowl	27. 4108 7-in. Vase

[27]

WILDFLOWER

Plate Etching 308

1931 – 1932
Green and Amber

2419 Bon Bon; $38.00
2443 Bowl, 10" Oval; $150.00
2433 Bowl "A", 12"; $225.00
2433 Candle, 3" (pair); $145.00
2443 Candle, 4" (pair); 125.00
2447 Candle, Duo (pair); $225.00
2430 Candy Jar and Cover, ½ pound; $175.00
2375 Cheese and Cracker; $150.00
2400 Comport, 6"; $75.00
2433 Comport, 6" Low; $85.00
2433 Comport, 6" Tall; $250.00
4020 Decanter and 2 oz.
 Whiskey; $800.00/market
2443 Ice Tub, 6"; $135.00
2419 Jelly; $47.00

2419 Lemon; $38.00
2419 Mayonnaise; $48.00
2419 Plate, Cake; $95.00
2364 Plate, 16"; $200.00
2419 Relish, 4-part; $75.00
4020 Sugar and Cream; $95.00
2419 Syrup and Cover and Saucer; $200.00
2419 Tray, Handled Lunch; $125.00
4106 Vase, 7"; $250.00
4107 Vase, 9"; $275.00
4107 Vase, 12"; $400.00
4107 Vase, 15"; $500.00/market
4108 Vase, 5"; $125.00
4108 Vase, 6"; $150.00
4108 Vase, 7"; $195.00

LEGION

Plate Etching 309

Stemware is featured in *Fostoria Stemware,* page 72.

2470 Bon Bon
 Crystal, 1933-1935; $37.00
 Rose, 1933-1934; $45.00
 Topaz, 1933-1934; $40.00
2424 Bowl, 8"
 Crystal, 1933-1935; $42.00
 Rose, 1933-1934; $48.00
 Topaz, 1933-1934; $45.00
2440 Bowl, 10½"
 Crystal, 1933-1939; $58.00
 Rose, 1933-1934; $67.00
 Topaz, 1933-1934; $65.00
2440 Bowl, 12" Salad
 Crystal, 1933-1939; $65.00
 Rose, 1933-1934; $85.00
 Topaz, 1933-1934; $75.00
2470 Bowl, 12"
 Crystal, 1933-1936; $125.00
 Rose, 1933-1934; $150.00
 Topaz, 1933-1934; $135.00
2375 Candlestick, 3" (pair)
 Crystal, 1933-1939; $55.00
 Rose, 1933-1934; $67.00
 Topaz, 1933-1934; $62.00
2470 Candlestick, 5½" (pair)
 Crystal, 1933-1936; $135.00
 Rose, 1933-1934; $165.00
 Topaz, 1933-1934; $150.00

2456 Candy Jar and Cover, ½ lb.
 Crystal, 1933-1934; $125.00
 Rose, 1933-1934; $150.00
 Topaz, 1933-1934; $135.00
2470 Comport, 6" Low
 Crystal, 1933-1934; $45.00
 Rose, 1933-1934; $56.00
 Topaz, 1933-1934; $50.00
2470 Comport, 6" Tall
 Crystal, 1933-1934; $125.00
 Rose, 1933-1934; $145.00
 Topaz, 1933-1934; $135.00
2419 Comport, 6"
 Crystal, 1933-1934; $95.00
 Rose, 1933-1934; $125.00
 Topaz, 1933-1934; $110.00
2375½ Cup and Saucer
 Crystal, 1933-1939; $32.00
2470 Lemon Dish
 Crystal, 1933-1936; $37.00
 Rose, 1933-1934; $45.00
 Topaz, 1933-1934; $40.00
2375 Plate, 6"
 Crystal, 1933-1939; $8.00
2375 Plate, 7"
 Crystal, 1933-1939; $9.00
2375 Plate, 8"
 Crystal, 1933-1939; $12.00

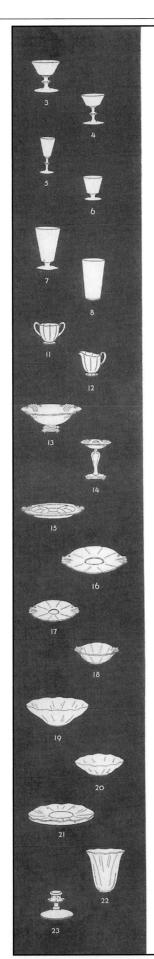

LEGION DESIGN

PLATE ETCHING No. 309

STEMWARE AND DINNERWARE

1.	6000	10-oz. Goblet
2.	6000	6-oz. Saucer Champagne
3.	6000	6-oz. Low Sherbet
4.	6000	3½-oz. Cocktail
5.	6000	3-oz. Wine
6.	6000	4-oz. Oyster Cocktail
7.	6000	13-oz. Footed Tumbler
7.	6000	5-oz. Footed Tumbler
8.	4076	9-oz. Tumbler

9.	2375	6-in. Bread and Butter Plate
9.	2375	7-in. Salad Plate
9.	2375	8-in. Luncheon Plate
9.	2375	9-in. Dinner Plate
10.	2375½	Footed Cup
10.	2375	Saucer
11.	2375½	Footed Sugar
12.	2375½	Footed Cream

TABLEWARE

13.	2470	12-in. Bowl
14.	2470	5½-in. Candlestick
15.	2470	4-Part Oval Relish
16.	2470	10-in. Cake Plate
17.	2470	Lemon Dish
18.	2470	Sweetmeat

19.	2440	12-in. Salad Bowl
20.	2440	10½-in. Bowl, "B"
21.	2440	13-in. Torte Plate
22.	2440	7-in. Vase
23.	2375	3-in. Candlestick

96

2375 Plate, 9"
    Crystal, 1933-1936; $30.00
2470 Plate, 10" Cake
    Crystal, 1933-1936; $60.00
    Rose, 1933-1934; $68.00
    Topaz, 1933-1934; $65.00
2440 Plate, 13" Torte
    Crystal, 1933-1939; $65.00
    Rose, 1933-1934; $75.00
    Topaz, 1933-1934; $70.00
2470 Relish, 3-part Round
    Crystal, 1933-1934; $57.00
    Rose, 1933-1934; $68.00
    Topaz, 1933-1934; $65.00
2470 Service Dish, 9"
    Crystal, 1933-1934; $60.00
    Rose, 1933-1934; $68.00
    Topaz, 1933-1934; $65.00

2375½ Sugar and Cream
    Crystal, 1933-1936; $65.00
2470 Sweetmeat
    Crystal, 1933-1936; $38.00
    Rose, 1933-1934; $45.00
    Topaz, 1933-1934; $40.00
2470 Tray, Sugar and Cream
    Crystal, 1933-1934; $38.00
    Rose, 1933-1934; $48.00
    Topaz, 1933-1934; $45.00
2440 Vase, 7"
    Crystal, 1933-1939; $95.00
    Rose, 1933-1934; $150.00
    Topaz, 1933-1934; $125.00
2454 Vase, 8"
    Crystal, 1933-1935; $125.00
    Rose, 1933-1934; $150.00
    Topaz, 1933-1934; $125.00

FUCHSIA

Plate Etching 310

One of the loveliest of all Fostoria's etchings. We have often wished more pieces had been made in this pattern. Stemware is featured in *Fostoria Stemware,* page 75.

2470 Bon Bon, 1933-1939; $38.00
869 Bowl, Finger, 1933-1943; $30.00
2395 Bowl, 10", 1933-1938; $125.00
2470½ Bowl, 10½", 1933-1943; $87.00
2440 Bowl "B", 10½", 1933-1940; $95.00
2470 Bowl, 12"
    Crystal, 1933-1940; $125.00
    Wisteria Base, 1933-1935; $225.00
2375 Candlestick, 3", 1933-1943 (pair); $75.00
2395½ Candlestick, 5", 1933-1940 (pair); $120.00
2470 Candlestick, 5½" (pair)
    Crystal, 1933-1940; $165.00
    Wisteria Base, 1933-1935; $495.00
2470½ Candlestick, 5½", 1933-1943 (pair); $150.00
2470 Comport, 6" Low
    Crystal, 1933-1943; $45.00
    Wisteria Base, 1933-1935; $75.00
2470 Comport, 6" Tall
    Crystal, 1933-1934; $95.00
    Wisteria Base, 1933-1934; $195.00
2440 Cup and Saucer, 1933-1943; $32.00

2470 Lemon Dish, 1933-1939; $35.00
2440 Plate, 6", 1933-1943; $12.00
2440 Plate, 7", 1933-1943; $15.00
2440 Plate, 8", 1933-1943; $20.00
2440 Plate, 9", 1933-1943; $60.00
2470 Plate, 10" Cake, 1933-1943; $68.00
2440 Sugar and Cream, 1933-1943; $75.00
2470 Sweetmeat, 1933-1939; $38.00

Rose Legion 2470 Sweetmeat, Fuchsia 2440 Sugar and Cream, Champagne with Wisteria Base

FUCHSIA

FUCHSIA DESIGN

Plate Etching No. 310

STEMWARE

Made in Solid Crystal — Wisteria Base with Crystal Bowl

1.	6004	9-oz. Goblet	6.	6004	2½-oz. Wine	9.	6004	2½-oz. Footed Tumbler	
2.	6004	5½-oz. High Sherbet	7.	6004	¾-oz. Cordial	10.	869	Finger Bowl (Crystal Only)	
3.	6004	5½-oz. Low Sherbet	8.	6004	4½-oz. Oyster Cocktail	11.	833	12-oz. Tumbler (Crystal Only)	
4.	6004	5½-oz. Parfait	9.	6004	12-oz. Footed Tumbler	11.	833	8-oz. Tumbler (Crystal Only)	
5.	6004	3-oz. Cocktail	9.	6004	9-oz. Footed Tumbler	11.	833	5-oz. Tumbler (Crystal Only)	
6.	6004	4-oz. Claret	9.	6004	5-oz. Footed Tumbler	11.	833	2-oz. Tumbler (Crystal Only)	

DINNERWARE

Made in Solid Crystal. Items marked * also made in Wisteria

12.	2440	6-in. Bread and Butter Plate	15.	2440	Footed Cream	22.	*2470	12-in. Bowl
12.	2440	7-in. Salad Plate	16.	2440	10½-in. Bowl "B"	23.	*2470	5½-in. Candlestick
12.	2440	8-in. Luncheon Plate	17.	2375	3-in. Candlestick	24.	*2470	6-in. Tall Comport
12.	2440	9-in. Dinner Plate	18.	2395	10-in. Bowl	25.	*2470	6-in. Low Comport
13.	2440	Cup	19.	2395½	5-in. Candlestick	26.	2470	10-in. Cake Plate
13.	2440	Saucer	20.	2470½	10½-in. Bowl	27.	2470	Lemon Dish
14.	2440	Footed Sugar	21.	2470½	5½-in. Candlestick	28.	2470	Bon Bon
						29.	2470	Sweetmeat

FLORENTINE
Plate Etching 311

This extraordinarily delicate pattern is seldom seen, but certainly, a table set with Florentine would be a sight to behold. Stemware is featured in *Fostoria Stemware*, page 76.

2470 Bon Bon
    Crystal, 1933-1939; $38.00
    Topaz/Gold Tint, 1933-1939; $42.00
869 Bowl, Finger
    Crystal, 1933-1943; $28.00
    Topaz/Gold Tint, $30.00
2470½ Bowl, 10½"
    Crystal, 1933-1943; $87.00
    Topaz/Gold Tint, 1933-1940; $95.00
2470 Bowl, 12"
    Crystal, 1933-1940; $125.00
    Topaz/Gold Tint, 1933-1940; $150.00
2470 Candlestick, 5½" (pair)
    Crystal, 1933-1943; $135.00
    Topaz, 1933-1936; $165.00
2470½ Candlestick, 5½" (pair)
    Crystal, 1933-1943; $125.00
    Topaz/Gold Tint, 1933-1940; $150.00
2470 Comport, Low
    Crystal, 1933-1940; $45.00
    Topaz, 1933-1934; $52.00
2470 Comport, Tall
    Crystal, 1933-1939; $95.00
    Topaz, 1933-1934; $135.00
2440 Cup and Saucer
    Crystal, 1933-1943; $37.00
    Topaz/Gold Tint, 1933-1940; $44.00
2470 Lemon Dish
    Crystal, 1933-1939; $36.00
    Topaz, 1933-1934; $40.00
2440 Plate, 6"
    Crystal, 1933-1943; $12.00
    Topaz/Gold Tint, 1933-1940; $14.00
2440 Plate, 7"
    Crystal, 1933-1943; $14.00
    Topaz/Gold Tint, 1933-1940; $16.00
2440 Plate, 8"
    Crystal, 1933-1943; $20.00
    Topaz/Gold Tint, 1933-1940; $23.00

2440 Plate, 9"
    Crystal, 1933-1943; $60.00
    Topaz, 1933-1934; $70.00
2440 Plate, 10" Cake
    Crystal, 1933-1940; $68.00
    Topaz/Gold Tint, 1933-1940; $77.00
2440 Plate, 13" Torte
    Crystal, 1935-1943; $90.00
2470 Relish, 3-part Round
    Crystal, 1933-1939; $64.00
    Topaz/Gold Tint, 1933-1937; $68.00
2440 Sugar and Cream
    Crystal, 1933-1943; $75.00
    Topaz/Gold Tint, 1933-1940; $85.00
2470 Sweetmeat
    Crystal, 1933-1939; $38.00
    Topaz, 1933-1934; $45.00
2470 Tray, Sugar and Cream
    Crystal, 1933-1940; $38.00
    Topaz, 1933-1934; $45.00

Topaz Florentine 2470 5" Candlesticks

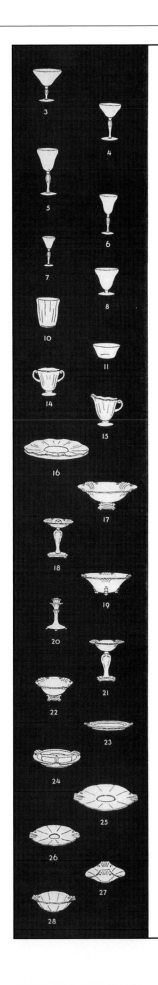

FLORENTINE DESIGN

PLATE ETCHING No. 311

STEMWARE

1.	6005	9-oz. Goblet
2.	6005	5½-oz. Saucer Champagne
3.	6005	7-oz. Low Sherbet
4.	6005	4-oz. Cocktail
5.	6005	5-oz. Claret
6.	6005	3-oz. Wine
7.	6005	1-oz. Cordial
8.	6005	6-oz. Oyster Cocktail
9.	6005	12-oz. Footed Tumbler
9.	6005	9-oz. Footed Tumbler
9.	6005	5-oz. Footed Tumbler
9.	6005	2½-oz. Footed Tumbler
10.	4005	12-oz. Tumbler
10.	4005	9-oz. Tumbler
10.	4005	5-oz. Tumbler
10.	4005	2½-oz. Tumbler
11.	869	Finger Bowl

DINNERWARE

12.	2440	6-in. Bread and Butter Plate
12.	2440	7-in. Salad Plate
12.	2440	8-in. Luncheon Plate
12.	2440	9-in. Dinner Plate
13.	2440	Cup
13.	2440	Saucer
14.	2440	Footed Sugar
15.	2440	Footed Cream
16.	2440	13-in. Torte Plate
17.	2470	12-in. Bowl
18.	2470	5½-in. Candlestick
19.	2470½	10½-in. Bowl
20.	2470½	5½-in. Candlestick
21.	2470	6-in. Tall Comport
22.	2470	6-in. Low Comport
23.	2470	Sugar and Cream Tray
24.	2470	3-Part Round Relish
25.	2470	10-in. Cake Plate
26.	2470	Lemon Dish
27.	2470	Bon Bon
28.	2470	Sweetmeat

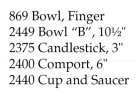

MAYDAY

Plate Etching 312

July 1931 Supplement

Since this pattern only appeared one time, it was probably never made. Prices would be similar to the Manor pattern if a piece were ever found. Stemware is featured in *Fostoria Stemware,* page 76.

869 Bowl, Finger
2449 Bowl "B", 10½"
2375 Candlestick, 3"
2400 Comport, 6"
2440 Cup and Saucer

2440 Plate, 6"
2440 Plate, 7"
2440 Plate, 8"
2440 Plate, 9"
2440 Sugar and Cream

MORNING GLORY

Plate Etching 315

Stemware is featured in *Fostoria Stemware,* page 77.

2470 Bon Bon
  Crystal, 1933-1939; $37.00
869 Bowl, Finger
  Crystal, 1933-1943; $30.00
2440 Bowl, 5" Fruit
  Crystal, 1933-1934; $30.00
2440 Bowl, 6" Cereal
  Crystal, 1933-1934; $34.00
2440 Bowl, 10" Baker
  Crystal, 1933-1934; $58.00
2470½ Bowl, 10"
  Crystal, 1933-1943; $85.00
2470 Bowl, 12"
  Crystal, 1933-1934; $95.00
  Amber Base, 1933-1934; $125.00
2470 Candlestick, 5½" (pair)
  Crystal, 1933-1934; $125.00
  Amber Base, 1933-1934; $150.00
2470½ Candlestick, 5½" (pair)
  Crystal, 1933-1943; $95.00
2440 Celery, 11½"
  Crystal, 1933-1943; $50.00
2470 Comport, Low
  Crystal, 1933-1934; $50.00
  Amber Base, 1933-1934; $57.00
2440 Cream Soup
  Crystal, 1933-1934; $50.00
2440 Cup and Saucer
  Crystal, 1933-1943; $37.00
2440 Cup and Saucer, After Dinner
  Crystal, 1933-1938; $45.00
2451 Ice Dish and Liner
  Crystal, 1933-1934; $58.00
2451 Ice Dish Plate
  Crystal, 1933-1934; $18.00
2270 Jug
  Crystal, 1933-1939; $265.00
2470 Lemon
  Crystal, 1933-1939; $36.00

2440 Olive, 6½"
  Crystal, 1933-1943; $30.00
2440 Pickle, 8½"
  Crystal, 1933-1943; $37.00
2440 Plate, 6"
  Crystal, 1933-1943; $6.00
2440 Plate, 7"
  Crystal, 1933-1943; $9.00
2440 Plate, 8"
  Crystal, 1933-1943; $12.00
2440 Plate, 9"
  Crystal, 1933-1943; $32.00
2440 Plate, 10"
  Crystal, 1933-1942; $45.00
2470 Plate, 10" Cake
  Crystal, 1933-1943; $70.00

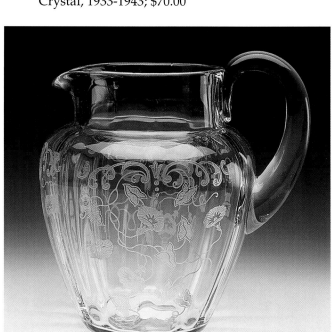

Morning Glory 2270 Jug

MORNING GLORY

MORNING GLORY DESIGN

Plate Etching No. 313

STEMWARE

Made in Solid Crystal — Amber Base with Crystal Bowl

(See Price List for Complete Line)

1. 6007 10-oz. Goblet	5. 6007 3-oz. Wine	7. 6007 5-oz. Footed Tumbler
2. 6007 5½-oz. High Sherbet	5. 6007 1-oz. Cordial	7. 6007 2-oz. Footed Tumbler
3. 6007 5½-oz. Low Sherbet	6. 6007 4½-oz. Oyster Cocktail	8. 2470 6-in. Low Comport
4. 6007 3½-oz. Cocktail	7. 6007 12-oz. Footed Tumbler	9. 2470 12-in. Bowl
5. 6007 4-oz. Claret	7. 6007 9-oz. Footed Tumbler	10. 2470 5½-in. Candlestick

DINNERWARE

Made in Solid Crystal Only

11. 869 Finger Bowl	2440 After Dinner Cup	20. 2451 7-in. Ice Dish Plate
12. 2440 6-in. Bread and Butter Plate	2440 After Dinner Saucer	21. 2419 4 Part Relish
12. 2440 7-in. Salad Plate	15. 2440 Footed Sugar	22. 2470 3 Part Relish
12. 2440 8-in. Luncheon Plate	16. 2440 Footed Cream	23. 2470 Lemon Dish
12. 2440 9-in. Dinner Plate	17. 2440 6½-in. Olive	24. 2470 Sweetmeat
12. 2440 10-in. Dinner Plate	17. 2440 8½-in. Pickle	25. 2470 Bon Bon
13. 2440 5-in. Fruit	17. 2440 11½-in. Celery	26. 2470 Cake Plate
13. 2440 6-in. Cereal	18. 2440 13-in. Torte Plate	27. 2470 Sugar and Cream Tray
14. 2440 Cup	19. 2440 7-in. Vase	28. 2470½ 10½-in. Bowl
14. 2440 Saucer	20. 2451 Ice Dish	29. 2470½ 5½-in. Candlestick
		30. 2467 7½-in. Vase

57

2440 Plate, 13" Torte
    Crystal, 1933-1943; $85.00
2440 Platter, 12"
    Crystal, 1933-1938; $77.00
2470 Relish, 3-part
    Crystal, 1933-1939; $54.00
2419 Relish, 4-part
    Crystal, 1933-1943; $54.00
2440 Sugar and Cream
    Crystal, 1933-1943; $64.00

2470 Sugar and Cream Tray
    Crystal, 1933-1938; $36.00
2470 Sweetmeat
    Crystal, 1933-1939; $38.00
2440 Vase, 7"
    Crystal, 1933-1940; $100.00
2467 Vase, 7½"
    Crystal, 1933-1938; $135.00

CHATEAU

Plate Etching 315

Stemware is featured in *Fostoria Stemware*, page 78.

2470 Bon Bon, 1933-1935; $38.00
1769 Bowl, Finger, 1933-1934; $38.00
2470½ Bowl, 10½", 1933-1939; $85.00
2481 Bowl, Oblong, 1933-1934; $125.00
2481 Candlestick, 5", 1933-1934 (pair); $125.00
2470½ Candlestick, 5½", 1933-1939
    (pair); $120.00
2472 Candlestick, Duo, 1933-1935 (pair); $135.00
2482 Candlestick, Trindle, 1933-1939
    (pair); $145.00
2440 Celery, 11½", 1933-1939; $50.00
2470 Comport, 6" Low, 1933-1934; $52.00
2440 Cream Soup, 1933-1935; $50.00
2440 Cup and Saucer, 1933-1939; $35.00

2451 Ice Dish, Liner and Plate, 1933-1934; $65.00
2470 Lemon, 1933-1935; $36.00
2440 Olive, 6½", 1933-1939; $35.00
2440 Pickle, 8½" , 1933-1939; $40.00
2440 Plate, 6", 1933-1936; $12.00
2440 Plate, 7", 1933-1939; $14.00
2440 Plate, 8", 1933-1939; $18.00
2440 Plate, 9", 1933-1939; $45.00
2470 Plate, Cake, 1933-1939; $68.00
2440 Plate, 13" Torte, 1933-1939; $95.00
2419 Relish, 4-part, 1933-1939; $60.00
2440 Sugar and Cream, 1933-1939; $67.00
2470 Sweetmeat, 1933-1935; $38.00
2467 Vase, 7½", 1933-1935; $125.00

MIDNIGHT ROSE

Plate Etching 316

This pattern has some very unusual pieces which are unique to the pattern, especially the 2464 Jug and the 2485 and 2486 Square and Crescent Vases. Stemware is featured in *Fostoria Stemware*, page 79.

2440 Bon Bon, 5", 1934-1942; $38.00
869 Bowl, Finger, and Plate, 1933-1943; $37.00
2470½ Bowl, 7", 1933-1943; $38.00
2470½ Bowl, 10½", 1933-1957; $95.00
2481 Bowl, 11", 1933-1939; $145.00
2481 Candlestick, 5", 1933-1938 (pair); $145.00
2470½ Candlestick, 5½", 1933-1945
    (pair); $125.00
2472 Candlestick, Duo, 1933-1957 (pair); $135.00
2482 Candlestick, Trindle, 1933-1957
    (pair); $150.00
4099 Candy Jar and Cover, 1934-1938; $125.00
2440 Celery, 11½", 1933-1944; $50.00
2440 Cup and Saucer, 1933-1957; $35.00
2440 Lemon, 5", 1934-1943; $36.00
2464 Jug, Ice, 1933-1943; $400.00

2464 Tumbler, 10 oz., 1933-1943; $35.00
2440 Mayonnaise, 2-part, 1934-1943; $35.00
2440 Olive, 7½", 1933-1944; $25.00
2440 Pickle, 8½", 1933-1944; $30.00
2440 Plate, 6", 1933-1957; $7.00
2440 Plate, 7", 1933-1957; $9.00
2440 Plate, 8", 1933-1957; $15.00
2440 Plate, 9", 1933-1957; $45.00
2375 Plate, Cake, 1933-1943; $65.00
2440 Plate, 10½" Cake, 1934-1946; $65.00
2496 Plate, Handled Cake, 1947-1957; $60.00
2440 Plate, 13" Torte, 1933-1957; $85.00
2440 Relish, 2-part, 1934-1943; $32.00
2440 Relish, 3-part, 1934-1943; $37.00
2419 Relish, 4-part, 1933-1943; $40.00
2470 Relish, 4-part, 1933-1939; $42.00

CHATEAU

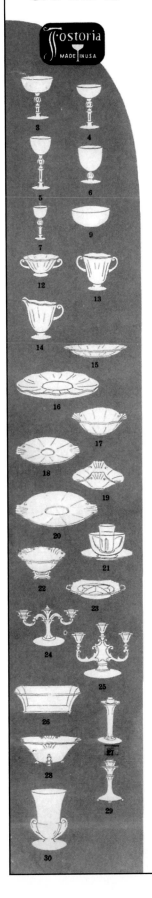

CHATEAU DESIGN

Plate Etching No. 315

STEMWARE AND DINNERWARE

Made in Solid Crystal

1.	6008	10-oz. Goblet
2.	6008	5½-oz. High Sherbet
3.	6008	5½-oz. Low Sherbet
4.	6008	3¼-oz. Cocktail
5.	6008	4-oz. Wine
6.	6008	5-oz. Oyster Cocktail
7.	6008	1-oz. Cordial
8.	6008	12-oz. Footed Tumbler
8.	6008	9-oz. Footed Tumbler
8.	6008	5-oz. Footed Tumbler
9.	1769	Finger Bowl
10.	2440	6-in. Bread and Butter Plate
10.	2440	7-in. Salad Plate
10.	2440	8-in. Luncheon Plate
10.	2440	9-in. Dinner Plate
11.	2440	Cup
11.	2440	Saucer
12.	2440	Cream Soup
13.	2440	Footed Sugar
14.	2440	Footed Cream
15.	2440	6½-in. Olive
15.	2440	8½-in. Pickle
15.	2440	11½-in. Celery
16.	2440	13-in. Torte Plate
17.	2470	Sweetmeat
18.	2470	Lemon
19.	2470	Bon Bon
20.	2470	Cake Plate
21.	2451	Ice Dish
21.	2451	Ice Dish Plate
22.	2470	6-in. Low Comport
23.	2419	4 Part Relish
24.	2472	Duo Candlestick
25.	2482	Trindle Candlestick
26.	2481	Oblong Bowl
27.	2481	5-in. Candlestick
28.	2470½	10½-in. Bowl
29.	2470½	5½-in. Candlestick
30.	2467	7½-in. Vase

2419 Relish, 5-part, 1933-1943; $70.00
2462 Relish, Metal Handle, 1934-1938; $75.00
2462 Relish, 5-part, 1933-1939; $85.00
2440 Sauce and Tray, 1934-1943; $85.00
2440 Sugar and Cream, 1933-1957; $65.00
2470 Sugar and Cream Tray, 1934-1942
2440 Sweetmeat, 4½", 1934-1942; $48.00
2485 Vase, 5" Crescent, 1933-1934; $175.00
2486 Vase, 7" Square, 1933-1934; $195.00
2485 Vase, 7" Crescent, 1933-1934; $200.00
2486 Vase, 9" Square, 1933-1934; $250.00
4111 Vase, 6½", 1933-1940; $175.00
4110 Vase, 7½", 1933-1942; $160.00
2467 Vase, 7½", 1933-1946; $95.00
4112 Vase, 8½", 1933-1940; $200.00
2470 Vase, 10", 1933-1943; $195.00

Midnight Rose 4110 Vase, 2464 Jug

SPRINGTIME

Plate Etching 318

Stemware is featured in *Fostoria Stemware*, pages 39, and 83 – 84.

2440 Bon Bon, 5"
    Crystal, 1934-1940; $36.00
869 Bowl, Finger
    Crystal, 1934-1943; $25.00
    Topaz, 1934; $35.00
2440 Bowl, 5" Fruit
    Crystal, 1934-1943; $22.00
    Topaz, 1934-1935; $30.00
2440 Bowl, 6" Cereal
    Crystal, 1934-1939; $25.00
    Topaz, 1934; $35.00
2470½ Bowl, 7"
    Crystal, 1934-1943; $28.00
    Topaz, 1934; $38.00
2470½ Bowl, 10½"
    Crystal, 1934-1943; $85.00
    Topaz, 1934-1935; $97.00
2481 Bowl, 11" Oblong
    Crystal, 1934-1938; $90.00
    Topaz, 1934; $125.00
2481 Candlestick, 5" (pair)
    Crystal, 1934-1938; $95.00
    Topaz, 1934; $125.00
2470½ Candlestick, 5½" (pair)
    Crystal, 1934-1943; $95.00
    Topaz, 1934-1935; $135.00
2482 Candlestick, Trindle (pair)
    Crystal, 1934-1943; $145.00
    Topaz, 1934-1935; $175.00

2440 Celery, 11½"
    Crystal, 1934-1943; $52.00
    Topaz, 1934; $65.00
2400 Comport, 6"
    Crystal, 1934-1943; $64.00
    Topaz, 1934; $75.00
2440 Cream Soup
    Crystal, 1934-1940; $60.00
    Topaz, 1934; $72.00
2440 Cup and Saucer
    Crystal, 1934-1943; $35.00
    Topaz, 1934-1935; $47.00
6011 Jug
    Crystal, 1934-1943; $375.00
2440 Lemon, 5"
    Crystal, 1934-1939; $35.00
2470 Lemon
    Crystal, 1934-1939; $35.00
    Topaz, 1934; $44.00
2440 Mayonnaise, 2-part
    Crystal, 1934-1943; $40.00
2440 Olive, 6½"
    Crystal, 1934-1943; $28.00
    Topaz, 1934; $44.00
2440 Pickle, 8½"
    Crystal, 1934-1943; $42.00
    Topaz, 1934; $48.00
2440 Plate, 6"
    Crystal, 1934-1943; $7.00

MIDNIGHT ROSE

MIDNIGHT ROSE DESIGN

Plate Etching No. 316

STEMWARE AND DINNERWARE

Made in Solid Crystal

1.	6009	9-oz. Goblet
2.	6009	5½-oz. High Sherbet
3.	6009	5½-oz. Low Sherbet
4.	6009	3¾-oz. Cocktail
5.	6009	3¾-oz. Claret-Wine
6.	6009	1-oz. Cordial
7.	6009	4¾-oz. Oyster Cocktail
8.	6009	12-oz. Footed Tumbler
8.	6009	9-oz. Footed Tumbler
8.	6009	5-oz. Footed Tumbler
	869	Finger Bowl
9.	2440	6-in. Bread and Butter Plate
9.	2440	7-in. Salad Plate
9.	2440	8-in. Luncheon Plate
9.	2440	9-in. Dinner Plate

10.	2440	Cup
10.	2440	Saucer
	2440	Footed Sugar
	2440	Footed Cream
11.	2440	6½-in. Olive
11.	2440	8½-in. Pickle
11.	2440	11½-in. Celery
12.	2440	13-in. Torte Plate
	2375	Cake Plate
13.	2419	4 Part Relish
14.	2419	5 Part Relish
15.	2462	5 Part Relish
16.	2470	4 Part Relish
	2462	Metal Handled Relish
17.	2464	Ice Jug
18.	2464	Tumbler

19.	2470½	10½-in. Bowl
20.	2470½	5½-in. Candlestick
19.	2470½	7-in. Bowl
21.	2481	11-in. Oblong Bowl
22.	2481	5-in. Candlestick
23.	2482	Trindle Candlestick
24.	2472	Duo Candlestick
25.	2467	7½-in. Vase
26.	2470	10-in. Vase
27.	2485	7-in. Crescent Vase
27.	2486	9-in. Square Vase
27.	2485	5-in. Crescent Vase
27.	2486	7-in. Square Vase
28.	4110	7½-in. Vase
29.	4111	6½-in. Vase
30.	4112	8½-in. Vase

59

Topaz, 1934-1935; $9.00
2440 Plate, 7"
   Crystal, 1934-1943; $12.00
   Topaz, 1934-1935; $16.00
2440 Plate, 8"
   Crystal, 1934-1943; $24.00
   Topaz, 1934-1935; $42.00
2440 Plate, 9"
   Crystal, 1934-1943; $48.00
   Topaz, 1934-1935; $67.00
2470 Plate, Cake
   Crystal, 1934-1943; $62.00
   Topaz, 1934; $77.00
2440 Plate, 13" Torte
   Crystal, 1934-1943; $88.00
   Topaz, 1934-1935; $120.00
2440 Relish, 2-part
   Crystal, 1934-1943; $37.00
2440 Relish, 3-part
   Crystal, 1934-1943; $43.00
2470 Relish, 4-part Oval
   Crystal, 1934-1940; $58.00
   Topaz, 1934; $68.00
2419 Relish, 4-part
   Crystal, 1934-1943; $54.00
   Topaz, 1934; $65.00
2419 Relish, 5-part
   Crystal, 1934-1943; $68.00
2440 Sauce and Tray
   Crystal, 1934-1943; $75.00
2440 Sugar and Cream
   Crystal, 1934-1943; $67.00
   Topaz, 1934; $78.00
2440 Sweetmeat, 4½"
   Crystal, 1934-1940; $25.00
2470 Sweetmeat
   Crystal, 1934-1939; $28.00

Topaz Springtime 2482 Trindle Candlestick

Topaz, 1934; $37.00
4111 Vase, 6½"
   Crystal, 1934-1940; $165.00
   Topaz, 1934; $195.00
4111 Vase, 8½"
   Crystal, 1934-1938; $200.00
   Topaz, 1934; $235.00
2470 Vase, 10"
   Crystal, 1934-1943; $225.00
   Topaz, 1934; $265.00

FLEMISH

Plate Etching 319

2440 Bon Bon, 5" Handled, 1933-1936; $15.00
4099 Candy Jar and Cover, 1933-1936; $62.00
2440 Lemon, 5" Handled, 1933-1936; $15.00
2440 Mayonnaise, 2-part, 1933-1936; $32.00
2440 Plate, 10½" Cake, 1933-1936; $55.00

2440 Relish, 2-part, 1933-1938; $28.00
2440 Relish, 3-part, 1933-1938; $35.00
2440 Sauce and Tray, 1933-1938; $54.00
2440 Sugar, Cream, Tray, 1933-1938; $65.00
2440 Sweetmeat, 4½", 1933-1938; $15.00

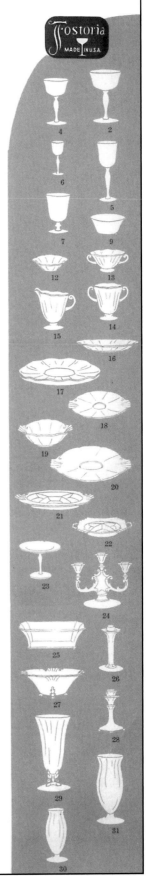

SPRINGTIME DESIGN

Plate Etching No. 318

STEMWARE AND DINNERWARE

Made in Solid Crystal and Topaz

1.	891	9-oz. Goblet
2.	891	6½-oz. High Sherbet
3.	891	6½-oz. Low Sherbet
4.	891	4-oz. Cocktail
5.	891	4-oz. Claret-Wine
6.	891	1-oz. Cordial
7.	891	5-oz. Oyster Cocktail
8.	891	12-oz. Footed Tumbler
8.	891	9-oz. Footed Tumbler
8.	891	5-oz. Footed Tumbler
9.	869	Finger Bowl
10.	2440	6-in. Bread and Butter Plate
10.	2440	7-in. Salad Plate
10.	2440	8-in. Luncheon Plate
10.	2440	9-in. Dinner Plate
11.	2440	Cup
11.	2440	Saucer
12.	2440	Fruit
12.	2440	Cereal
13.	2440	Cream Soup
14.	2440	Footed Sugar
15.	2440	Footed Cream
16.	2440	6½-in. Olive
16.	2440	8½-in. Pickle
16.	2440	11½-in. Celery
17.	2440	13-in. Torte Plate
18.	2470	Lemon
19.	2470	Sweetmeat
20.	2470	Cake Plate
21.	2470	4 Part Oval Relish
22.	2419	4 Part Relish
23.	2400	6-in. Comport
24.	2482	Trindle Candlestick
25.	2481	11-in. Oblong Bowl
26.	2481	5-in. Candlestick
27.	2470½	10½-in. Bowl
28.	2470½	5½-in. Candlestick
27.	2470½	7-in. Bowl
29.	2470	10-in. Vase
30.	4111	6½-in. Vase
31.	4112	8½-in. Vase

61

FLEMISH DESIGN
PLATE ETCHING No. 319
Made in Solid Crystal Only.

2440—6½ in. Oval
Sauce Dish

2440—5 in. Handled
Bon Bon

2440—5 in.
Handled Lemon

2440—4½ in. Handled
Sweetmeat

2440—8½ in. Oval Tray

2440—6½ in. 2 Part
Mayonnaise

2440
Footed Sugar

2440
Footed Cream

2470—Sugar and Cream Tray

2440—2 Part Handled
Relish

2440—3 Part Handled Relish

4099—Candy Jar
and Cover

FRUIT

Plate Etching 320

2440 Bon Bon, 1933-1938; $18.00
2499 Candy Jar and Cover, 1933-1938; $85.00
2440 Lemon, Handled, 1933-1938; $18.00
2440 Mayonnaise, 2-part, 1933-1938; $37.00
2397 Plate, 8", 1933-1938; $15.00
2449½ Plate, Crescent Salad, 1933-1938; $35
2440 Plate, 10½" Cake, 1933-1936; $68.00
2440 Plate, 13" Torte, 1933-1938; $85.00

2440 Relish, 2-part, 1933-1938; $42.00
2440 Relish, 3-part, 1933-1938; $48.00
2419 Relish, 5-part, 1933-1938; $75.00
2440 Sauce and Tray, 1933-1938; $75.00
2440 Sugar and Cream, 1933-1938; $65.00
2440 Sweetmeat, 4½", 1933-1938; $18.00
2440 Tray, Sugar and Cream, 1933-1938; $25.00

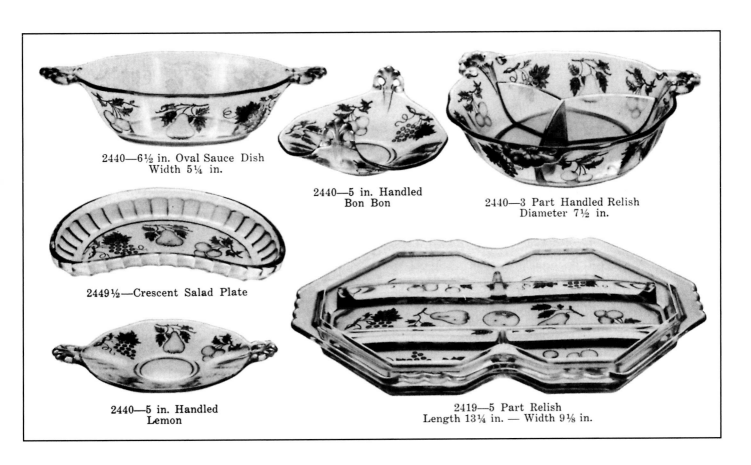

2440—6½ in. Oval Sauce Dish
Width 5¼ in.

2440—5 in. Handled
Bon Bon

2440—3 Part Handled Relish
Diameter 7½ in.

2449½—Crescent Salad Plate

2440—5 in. Handled
Lemon

2419—5 Part Relish
Length 13¼ in. — Width 9⅛ in.

NECTAR

Plate Etching 322

Stemware is featured in *Fostoria Stemware*, pages 81 – 82.

1769 Bowl, Finger, 1936-1942; $18.00
4024 Bowl, 10" Footed, 1936-1938; $55.00
4024 Candlestick, 6", 1936-1938 (pair); $55.00
4024 Comport, 5", 1936-1942; $28.00
2350 Cup and Saucer, After Dinner, 1936; $30.00
2350½ Cup and Saucer, 1936-1942; $22.00
6011 Decanter, 1936-1940; $195.00
6011 Jug, 1936-1942; $195.00

2337 Plate, 6", 1936-1942; $10.00
2337 Plate, 7", 1936-1942; $10.00
2337 Plate, 8", 1936-1942; $12.00
2337 Plate, 11", 1936; $30.00
2440 Plate, 13" Torte, 1936-1942; $40.00
2235 Shaker (pair); $37.00
2350½ Sugar and Cream; $42.00

2   24   1   7   13

NECTAR DESIGN
PLATE ETCHING No. 322

1.	6011	10-oz. Goblet
2.	6011	5½-oz. Saucer Champagne
3.	6011	5½-oz. Low Sherbet
4.	6011	3-oz. Cocktail
5.	6011	4½-oz. Rhine Wine
6.	6011	4½-oz. Claret
7.	6011	3-oz. Wine
8.	6011	2-oz. Sherry
9.	6011	2-oz. Creme de Menthe
10.	6011	1-oz. Cordial
11.	6011	1-oz. Brandy
12.	6011	4-oz. Oyster Cocktail
13.	6011	13-oz. Footed Tumbler
13.	6011	10-oz. Footed Tumbler
13.	6011	5-oz. Footed Tumbler
14.	6011	2-oz. Footed Whiskey
15.	6011	Footed Jug
16.	6011	Footed Decanter
17.	795	5½-oz. Hollow Stem Champagne
18.	906	Brandy Inhaler
19.	701	10-oz. Tumbler, Sham, Plain
19.	701	12-oz. Tumbler, Sham, Plain
19.	4122	1½-oz. Whiskey, Sham, Plain
20.	1184	Old Fashioned Cocktail, Sham, Plain
21.	1769	Finger Bowl
22.	2235	Shaker
23.	4024	5-in. Comport
24.	2337	6-in. Plate
24.	2337	7-in. Plate
24.	2337	8-in. Plate
24.	2337	11-in. Plate
25.	2350½	Footed Cup
25.	2350	Saucer
26.	2350	After Dinner Cup
26.	2350	After Dinner Saucer
27.	2350½	Footed Sugar
28.	2350½	Footed Cream
29.	2440	13-in. Torte Plate
30.	4024	10½-in. Footed Bowl
31.	4024	6-in. Candlestick

RAMBLER

Plate Etching 323

Decoration 615

Gold on Plate Etching 323

Stemware is featured in *Fostoria Stemware*, pages 83 – 84.

2440 Bon Bon, 1935-1942; $30.00
1769 Bowl, Finger, 1935-1943; $25.00
2484 Bowl, 10" Handled, 1935-1957; $110.00
2470½ Bowl, 10½", 1935-1957; $85.00
    Decoration 615, 1935-1949; $85.00
2470½ Candlestick, 5½",
    1935-1943 (pair); $95.00
2472 Candlestick, Duo,
    1935-1957 (pair); $145.00
    Decoration 615, 1935-1949; $145.00
2482 Candlestick, Trindle,
    1935-1957 (pair); $165.00
    Decoration 615, 1935-1949; $165.00
2496 Candlestick, Trindle,
    1935-1957 (pair); $150.00
4117 Candy Jar, Bubble, 1935-1938; $135.00
    Decoration 615, 1942; $175.00
2524 Cocktail Mixer, 1935-1943; $140.00
2525 Cocktail Shaker, Gold Top,
    1935-1938; $250.00
2525½ Cocktail Shaker, Gold Top,
    1935; $295.00
2350½ Cup and Saucer, 1936-1957; $32.00
6011 Decanter, 1935-1939; $275.00
6011 Jug, 1935-1943; 1947-1957; $265.00
    Decoration 615, 1942; $275.00
2440 Lemon, 5", 1935-1943; $32.00

2440 Mayonnaise, 2-part, 1935-1943; $40.00
    Decoration 615, 1942; $45.00
2337 Plate, 6", 1935-1957; $7.00
    Decoration 615, 1935-1949; $7.00
2337 Plate, 7", 1935-1957; $12.00
    Decoration 615, 1935-1949; $12.00
2337 Plate, 8", 1935-1957; $16.00
    Decoration 615, 1935-1949; $16.00
2440 Plate, 13" Torte, 1935-1957; $85.00
    Decoration 615, 1935-1949; $85.00
2440 Relish, 2-part, 1935-1943; $37.00
    Decoration 615, 1942; $37.00
2440 Relish, 3-part, 1935-1943; $43.00
    Decoration 615, 1942; $47.00
2419 Relish, 4-part, 1935-1943; $54.00
    Decoration 615, 1942; $58.00
2419 Relish, 5-part, 1935-1943; $68.00
    Decoration 615, 1942; $75.00
2514 Relish, 5-part, 1935-1939; $75.00
2440 Sauce and Tray, 1935-1943; $75.00
    Decoration 615, 1942; $80.00
2235 Shaker, FGT, 1935-1943 (pair); $95.00
2350½ Sugar and Cream, 1935-1957; $60.00
    Decoration 615, 1935-1949; $60.00
2440 Sweetmeat, 4½", 1935-1942; $28.00
2470 Vase, 11½", 1935-1943; $250.00
    Decoration 615, 1942; $275.00

DAISY

Plate Etching 324

Stemware is featured in *Fostoria Stemware*, page 85.

766 Bowl, Finger, 1935-1943; $28.00
2533 Bowl, 9" Handled, 1935-1943; $165.00
2536 Bowl, 9" Handled, 1935-1942; $125.00
2535 Candlestick, 5½", 1935-1943 (pair); $135.00
2533 Candlestick, Duo, 1935-1943 (pair); $135.00
2535 Cheese and Cracker, 1935-1942; $75.00
6013 Comport, 5", 1935-1940; $56.00
2550½ Cup and Saucer, 1936-1943; $34.00
5000 Jug, 1935-1943; $340.00
2375 Mayonnaise, Plate, Ladle, 1935-1943; $75.00
2440 Mayonnaise, 2-part, 1935-1943; $52.00
2337 Plate, 6", 1935-1943; $7.00
2337 Plate, 7", 1935-1943; $12.00
2337 Plate, 8", 1935-1943; $16.00

2440 Plate, 10½" Oval Cake, 1935-1943; $65.00
2440 Plate, 13" Torte, 1935-1943; $85.00
2364 Plate, 16", 1935-1943; $110.00
2440 Sauce, 6½" Oval, 1935-1943; $42.00
2350½ Sugar and Cream, 1935-1943; $65.00
2419 Relish, 4-part, 1935-1938; $54.00
2528 Tray, Cocktail, 1935-1936; $125.00
2440 Tray, 8½" Oval, 1935-1943; $35.00
2470 Vase, 8", 1935-1943; $137.00
5090 Vase, 8" Bud, 1935-1939; $75.00
5092 Vase, 8" Bud, 1935-1943; $75.00
2470 Vase, 10", 1935-1943; $200.00
760 Vase, 12", 1935-1938; $240.00

13   24   1   7   2

RAMBLER DESIGN
PLATE ETCHING No. 323

1.	6012	10-oz. Goblet
2.	6012	5½-oz. Saucer Champagne
3.	6012	5½-oz. Low Sherbet
4.	6012	4½-oz. Rhine Wine
5.	6012	3-oz. Cocktail
6.	6012	4½-oz. Claret
7.	6012	3-oz. Wine
8.	6012	2-oz. Sherry
9.	6012	2-oz. Creme de Menthe
10.	6012	1-oz. Cordial
11.	6012	1-oz. Brandy
12.	6012	4-oz. Footed Cocktail, Oyster
13.	6012	13-oz. Footed Tumbler
13.	6012	10-oz. Footed Tumbler
13.	6012	5-oz. Footed Tumbler
14.	795	Hollow Stem Champagne
15.	701	12-oz. Tumbler, Sham
15.	701	10-oz. Tumbler, Sham
15.	4122	1½-oz. Whiskey, Sham
16.	1184	Old Fashioned Cocktail, Sham
17.	1769	Finger Bowl
18.	6011	Footed Jug
19.	6011	Footed Decanter
20.	2525	Decanter
21.	2525	42-oz. Cocktail Shaker
22.	2524	Cocktail Mixer
23.	2235	Shaker
24.	2337	6-in. Plate
24.	2337	7-in. Plate
24.	2337	8-in. Plate
25.	2350½	Footed Cup
25.	2350	Saucer
26.	2350½	Footed Sugar
27.	2350½	Footed Cream
28.	2440	4½-in. Handled Sweetmeat
29.	2440	5-in. Handled Bon Bon
30.	2440	5-in. Handled Lemon
31.	2440	8½-in. Oval Tray
32.	2440	6½-in. Sauce Dish
33.	2440	2-Part Oval Mayonnaise
34.	2440	2-Part Handled Relish
35.	2440	3-Part Handled Relish
36.	2440	13-in. Torte Plate
37.	2514	5-Part Square Relish
38.	2419	4-Part Relish
39.	2419	5-Part Relish
40.	4117	Bubble Candy Jar and Cover
41.	2484	10-in. Handled Bowl
42.	2496	Trindle Candlestick
43.	2470½	10½-in. Bowl
44.	2470½	5½-in. Candlestick
45.	2472	Duo Candlestick
46.	2482	Trindle Candlestick
47.	2470	11½-in. Vase

5   3   1

DAISY DESIGN

PLATE ETCHING No. 324 — MADE IN SOLID CRYSTAL

1.	6013	10-oz. Goblet
2.	6013	9-oz. Low Goblet
3.	6013	6-oz. Saucer Champagne
4.	6013	5-oz. Low Sherbet
5.	6013	3½-oz. Cocktail
6.	6013	4-oz. Claret
7.	6013	3-oz. Wine
8.	6013	1-oz. Cordial
9.	6013	4-oz. Oyster Cocktail
10.	6013	13-oz. Footed Tumbler
10.	6013	5-oz. Footed Tumbler
11.	6013	5-in. Comport
12.	766	Finger Bowl, Narrow Optic
13.	701	12-oz. Tumbler, Narrow Optic, Sham
13.	701	10-oz. Tumbler, Narrow Optic, Sham
14.	1184	7-oz. Old Fashioned Cocktail, Narrow Optic
15.	5000	Footed Jug
16.	2337	6-in. Plate
16.	2337	7-in. Plate
16.	2337	8-in. Plate
17.	2350½	Footed Sugar
18.	2350½	Footed Cream

19.	2419	4-Part Relish
20.	2514	5-Part Relish
21.	2440	2-Part Relish
22.	2440	3-Part Relish
23.	2440	2-Part Oval Mayonnaise
24.	2440	6½-in. Oval Sauce Dish
25.	2440	8½-in. Oval Tray
26.	2440	10½-in. Oval Cake Plate
27.	2440	13-in. Torte Plate
28.	2364	16-in. Plate
29.	2528	Cocktail Tray
30.	2375	Mayonnaise and Plate and Ladle
30.	2375	Mayonnaise
30.	2375	Mayonnaise Plate
30.	2375	Mayonnaise Ladle, Plain
31.	2535	Cheese and Cracker
32.	2470	8-in. Vase
32.	2470	10-in. Vase
33.	760	12-in. Vase
34.	5090	8-in. Bud Vase
35.	5092	8-in. Bud Vase
36.	2536	9-in. Handled Bowl
37.	2535	5½-in. Candlestick
38.	2533	9-in. Handled Bowl
39.	2533	Duo Candlestick

123

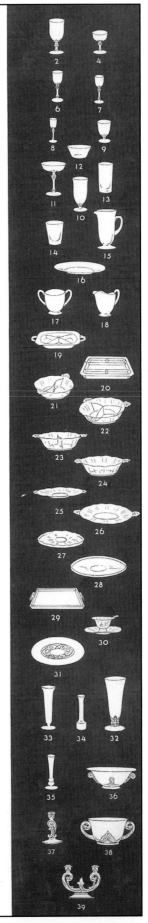

CORSAGE
Plate Etching 325
Stemware is featured in *Fostoria Stemware*, page 86.

2496 Bon Bon, 3-toed, 1938-1959
869 Bowl, Finger, 1935-1943; $45.00
2527 Bowl, 9" Footed, 1935-1938; $75.00
2536 Bowl, 9" Handled, 1935-1942; $87.00
6023 Bowl, 9" Footed, 1939-1943; $85.00
2484 Bowl, 10" Handled, 1935-1959; $85.00
2496 Bowl, 12" Flared, 1936-1959; $77.00
2545 Bowl, 12½" Oval, 1938-1959; $75.00
2527 Candelabra, 2-light,
    1935-1942 (pair); $250.00
2545 Candelabra, 2-light,
    1938-1942 (pair); $250.00
2496 Candlestick, 5½",
    1936-1959 (pair); $95.00
2535 Candlestick, 5½",
    1935-1943 (pair); $100.00
2496 Candlestick, Duo, 1935-1959 (pair); $100.00
2545 Candlestick, Duo, 1938-1959 (pair); $150.00
2496 Candlestick, Trindle,
    1935-1959 (pair); $125.00
2545 Candlestick, Lustre,
    1938-1942 (pair); $175.00
2496 Candy, 3-part and Cover,
    1938-1959; $125.00
2440 Celery, 1935-1944; $48.00
2496 Cheese and Cracker, 1938-1959; $95.00
2496 Comport, 5½", 1938-1959; $67.00
2440 Cup and Saucer, 1936-1959; $32.00
2496 Ice Bucket, Chrome Handle,
    1938-1959; $110.00
5000 Jug, 1935-1957; $325.00
2440 Mayonnaise, 2-part, 1935-1943; $48.00
2496½ Mayonnaise, Plate, Ladle,
    1938-1959' $78.00
2496 Nappy, Regular Han-
    dled, 1938-1944; $26.00
2496 Nappy, Flared Han-
    dled, 1938-1959; $20.00
2496 Nappy, Square Han-
    dled, 1938-1944; $26.00
2496 Nappy, 3-cornered,
    Handled, 1938-1959;
    $20.00
4119 Nappy, 4" Footed, 1935-
    1939; $34.00
2496 Nut Bowl, 3-toed, 1938-
    1944; $57.00
2440 Pickle, 1936-1944;
    $42.00

2666 Pitcher, Quart, 1958-1959; $250.00
2337 Plate, 6", 1935-1959; $10.00
2337 Plate, 7", 1935-1959; $15.00
2337 Plate, 8", 1935-1959; $20.00
2337 Plate, 9", 1938-1959; $40.00
2496 Plate, 10" Handled Cake,
    1947-1959; $58.00
2440 Plate, 10½" Handled Cake,
    1935-1946; $65.00
2440 Plate, 13" Torte, 1935-1959; $84.00
2364 Plate, 16", 1935-1959; $95.00
2440 Relish, 2-part, 1935-1943; $40.00
2440 Relish, 3-part, 1935-1943; $58.00
2419 Relish, 4-part, 1935-1943; $60.00
2419 Relish, 5-part, 1935-1943; $68.00
2496 Relish, 2-part, 1936-1959; $40.00
2496 Relish, 3-part, 1936-1959; $60.00
2496 Relish, 4-part, 1936-1943; $60.00
2440 Sauce, 6½" Oval,
    1935-1943; $45.00
2375 Shaker, Footed, "F" Top,
    1942-1943 (pair); $150.00
2440 Sugar and Cream, 1935-1959; $65.00
2496 Sugar and Cream, Individual,
    1938-1959; $65.00
2496 Sugar, Cream, Tray, 1947-1959; $115.00
2496 Tid Bit, 3-toed, 1938-1959; $42.00
2440 Tray, 8½" Oval, 1935-1943; $32.00
2496½" Tray, Individual Sugar
    and Cream, 1947-1959; $48.00
5092 Vase, 8" Bud, 1935-1943; $75.00
2470 Vase, 10" 1935-1943; $200.00

Corsage 2484 10" Handled Bowl, 2536 9" Handled Bowl

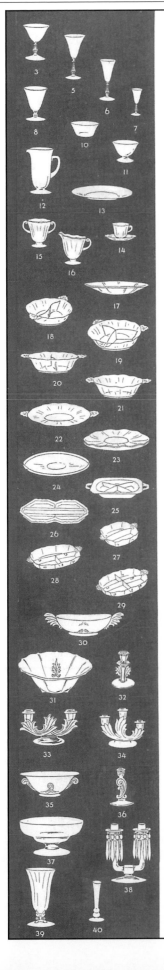

2   1   4   9

CORSAGE DESIGN
PLATE ETCHING No. 325

1.	6014	9-oz. Goblet
2.	6014	5½-oz. Saucer Champagne
3.	6014	5½-oz. Low Sherbet
4.	6014	3½-oz. Cocktail
5.	6014	4-oz. Claret
6.	6014	3-oz. Wine
7.	6014	1-oz. Cordial
8.	6014	4-oz. Oyster Cocktail
9.	6014	12-oz. Footed Tumbler
9.	6014	9-oz. Footed Tumbler
9.	6014	5-oz. Footed Tumbler
10.	869	Finger Bowl
11.	4119	4-in. Footed Nappy
12.	5000	7 Footed Jug
13.	2337	6-in. Plate
13.	2337	7-in. Plate
13.	2337	8-in. Plate
14.	2440	Cup
14.	2440	Saucer
15.	2440	Sugar
16.	2440	Cream
17.	2440	Pickle
17.	2440	Celery
18.	2440	2-Part Relish
19.	2440	3-Part Relish
20.	2440	2-Part Mayonnaise
21.	2440	6½-in. Oval Sauce Dish
22.	2440	8½-in. Oval Tray
22.	2440	10½-in. Cake Plate
23.	2440	13-in. Torte Plate
24.	2364	16-in. Plate
25.	2419	4-Part Relish
26.	2419	5-Part Relish
27.	2496	2-Part Relish
28.	2496	3-Part Relish
29.	2496	4-Part Relish
30.	2484	10-in. Handled Bowl
31.	2496	12-in. Bowl, Flared
32.	2496	5½-in. Candlestick
33.	2496	Duo Candlestick
34.	2496	Trindle Candlestick
35.	2536	9-in. Handled Bowl
36.	2535	5½-in. Candlestick
37.	2527	9-in. Footed Bowl
38.	2527	2-Light Candelabra, U. D. P.
39.	2470	10-in. Vase
40.	5092	8-in. Bud Vase

108

ARCADY

Plate Etching 326

Note that some pieces were discontinued during World War II. Stemware is featured in *Fostoria Stemware*, page 86.

869 Bowl, Finger, 1936-1943; $30.00
2496 Bowl, 10½" Handled,1936-1954; $68.00
2470½ Bowl, 10½",1936-1953; $72.00
2496 Bowl, 12" Flared,1936-1954; $65.00
2496 Candlestick, 5½",
    1936-1954 (pair); $95.00
2496 Candlestick, Duo,
    1936-1954 (pair); $110.00
2496 Candlestick, Trindle,
    1936-1954 (pair); $135.00
2472 Candlestick, Duo,
    1936-1954 (pair); $110.00
2482 Candlestick, Trindle,
    1936-1954 (pair); $145.00
2440 Celery, 11½", 1936-1944; $48.00
2400 Comport, 6", 1936-1954; $50.00
2440 Cup and Saucer, 1936-1954; $35.00
2375 Ice Bucket, 1936-1942; $125.00
5000 Jug, 1936-1954; $325.00
2375 Mayonnaise, Plate, Ladle,
    1936-1945; $75.00

2496 Mayonnaise, 2-part, 1936-1944; $48.00
2440 Pickle, 6½", 1936-1944; $42.00
2440 Plate, 6", 1936-1954; $12.00
2440 Plate, 7", 1936-1954; $20.00
2440 Plate, 8", 1936-1954; $22.00
2440 Plate, 9", 1936-1954; $40.00
2440 Plate, 10" Cake, 1936-1954; $58.00
2496 Plate, 14" Torte, 1936-1954; $75.00
2496 Relish, 2- and 3-part, 1936-1954; $50.00
2496 Relish, 4-part, 1936-1943; $60.00
2419 Relish, 5-part, 1936-1943; $68.00
2496 Sauce, 6½" Oblong, 1936-1944; $45.00
2375 Shaker, Footed, FGT, 1936-1943 (pair); $150.00
2440 Sugar and Cream, 1936-1954; $65.00
2496 Sweetmeat, 1936-1944; $38.00
2496 Tray, 8½" Oblong, 1936-1944; $32.00
4121 Vase, 5", 1936-1943; $137.00
4128 Vase, 5", 1936-1943; $135.00
2470 Vase, 10", 1936-1943; $200.00

2440—Cup
2440—Saucer

2375—Footed Shaker
Height 3½ in.

2440—Footed Cream
Height 4¼ in.
Capacity 6¼ oz.

2440—6 in. Plate   2440—8 in. Plate
2440—7 in. Plate   2440—9 in. Plate

2440—Footed Sugar
Height 3¾ in.

5000—7 Footed Jug
Height 9¾ in.
Capacity 3 Pints

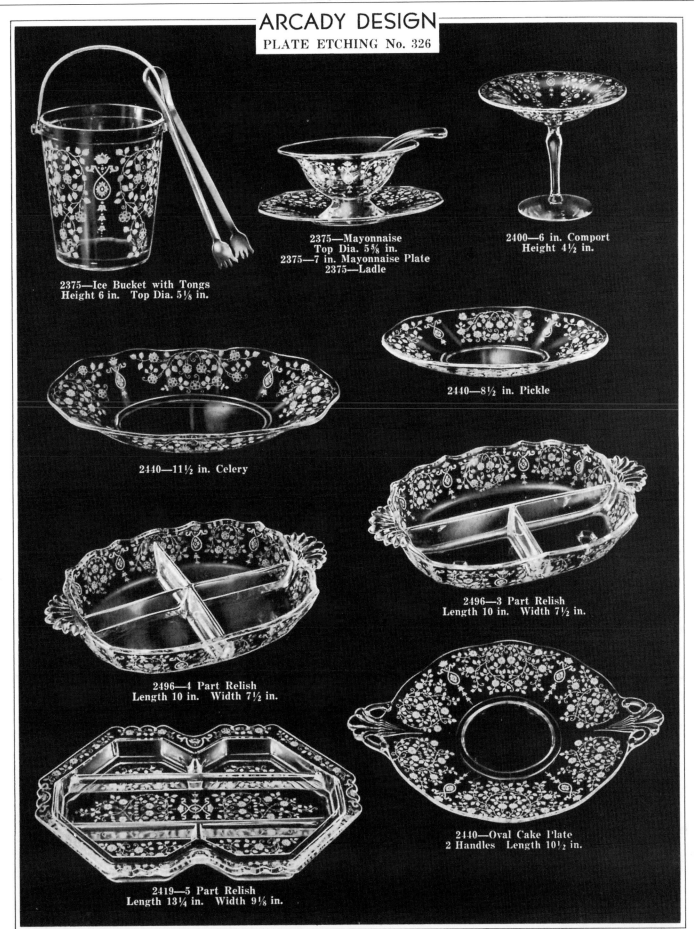

ARCADY DESIGN
PLATE ETCHING No. 326

2375—Ice Bucket with Tongs
Height 6 in.   Top Dia. 5⅛ in.

2375—Mayonnaise
Top Dia. 5⅝ in.
2375—7 in. Mayonnaise Plate
2375—Ladle

2400—6 in. Comport
Height 4½ in.

2440—11½ in. Celery

2440—8½ in. Pickle

2496—3 Part Relish
Length 10 in.   Width 7½ in.

2496—4 Part Relish
Length 10 in.   Width 7½ in.

2440—Oval Cake Plate
2 Handles   Length 10½ in.

2419—5 Part Relish
Length 13¼ in.   Width 9⅛ in.

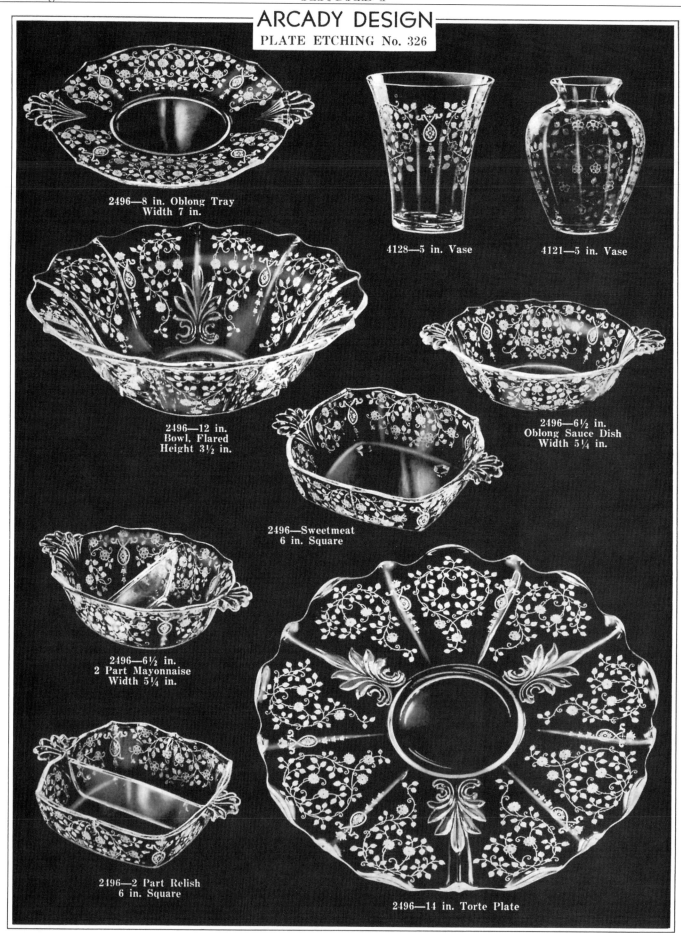

ARCADY DESIGN
PLATE ETCHING No. 326

2496—8 in. Oblong Tray
Width 7 in.

4128—5 in. Vase

4121—5 in. Vase

2496—12 in.
Bowl, Flared
Height 3½ in.

2496—6½ in.
Oblong Sauce Dish
Width 5¼ in.

2496—Sweetmeat
6 in. Square

2496—6½ in.
2 Part Mayonnaise
Width 5¼ in.

2496—2 Part Relish
6 in. Square

2496—14 in. Torte Plate

ARCADY DESIGN
PLATE ETCHING No. 326

2172—Duo Candlestick
Height 5 in. Spread 8¼ in.

2496—5½ in. Candlestick

2496—Duo Candlestick
Height 4½ in. Spread 8 in.

2470½—10½ in. Bowl

2496—10½ in. Handled Bowl
Height 3⅜ in.

2482—Trindle Candlestick
Height 6¾ in. Spread 8½ in.

2470—10 in. Vase

2496—Trindle Candlestick
Height 6 in. Spread 8¼ in.

NAVARRE
Plate Etching 327

The Navarre pattern is the best known and longest lived of any of the etched patterns. As such, Navarre employed pieces from many different dinnerware patterns including Baroque, Lafayette, Sonata, Contour, and Fairfax, as well as some pieces that had only numbers. It was sold to the Lenox Company in 1983, and some stems continued to be made by that company for a few more years. Introduced in 1936, pieces were still being added to the line in 1982, and colors in stemware were added in the late 1970s. Pieces introduced after 1943 will be covered in a following volume. Stemware is featured in *Fostoria Stemware*, pages 87 – 88.

2496 Bon Bon, 1938-1982; $48.00

869 Bowl, Finger, 1936-1943; $40.00

2496 Bowl, Regular Nappy, 1938-1944; $32.00

2496 Bowl, Flared Nappy, 1938-1982; $25.00

2496 Bowl, Square Nappy, 1938-1944; $32.00

2496 Bowl, 3-cornered Nappy,
    1938-1970; $27.00

2496 Bowl, 3-toed Nut, 1938-1944; $58.00

2496 Bowl, 10" Floating Garden,
    1936-1959; $150.00

2470½ Bowl, 10½", 1936-1963; $95.00

2496 Bowl, 12" Flared, 1936-1970; $95.00

2545 Bowl, 12½" Flame, 1936-1959; $110.00

2496 Candlestick, 4",
    1936-1979 (pair); $70.00

2496 Candlestick, 5½",
    1936-1959 (pair); $85.00

2496 Candlestick, Duo,
    1936-1970 (pair); $95.00

2496 Candlestick, Trindle,
    1936-1959 (pair); $135.00

2472 Candlestick, Duo,
    1936-1959 (pair); $150.00

2482 Candlestick, Trindle,
    1936-1970; $175.00

2545 Candlestick, Duo,
    1936-1959 (pair); $200.00

2545 Candelabra, 2-light,
    1936-1943 (pair); $450.00

2545 Candlestick, Lustre,
    1938-1943 (pair); $200.00

2496 Candy and Cover, 1938-1962; $125.00

2440 Celery, 11½", 1936-1944; $58.00

2496 Cheese and Cracker, 1938-1959; $115.00

2496 Comport, 5½", 1937-1959; $50.00

2400 Comport, 6", 1936-1959; $55.00

2440 Cup and Saucer, 1936-1970; $34.00

2496 Ice Bucket and Tongs, 1936-1959; $130.00

2375 Ice Bucket and Tongs, 1936-1943; $175.00

5000 Jug, 1936-1959; $495.00

2375 Mayonnaise, Plate, Ladle,
    1936-1945; $85.00

2496 Mayonnaise, 2-part, 1936-1944; $50.00

2440 Pickle, 8½", 1936-1944; $42.00

2440 Plate, 6", 1936-1967; $14.00

2440 Plate, 7", 1936-1982; $18.00

2440 Plate, 8" 1936-1982; $23.00

2440 Plate, 9", 1936-1959; $68.00

2496 Plate, 10" Cake, 1937-1982; $75.00

2440 Plate, Oval Cake, 1936-1946; $95.00

2496 Plate, 14" Torte, 1936-1982; $95.00

2364 Plate, 16" Torte, 1936-1970; $150.00

2496 Relish, 2-part, 1936-1982; $37.00

2496 Relish, 3-part, 1936-1982; $68.00

2496 Relish, 4-part, 1936-1943; $165.00

2419 Relish, 5-part, 1936-1947; $125.00

2083 Salad Dressing Bottle,
    1936-1943; $500.00/market

2586 Sani-Cut Syrup,
    1940-1943; $700.00/market

2375 Shaker, Footed, FGT,
    1936-1943 (pair); $200.00

2496 Sauce, 6½" Oval, 1936-1944; $120.00

2496 Sugar and Cream, Individual,
    1938-1970; $56.00

2440 Sugar and Cream, 1936-1967,
    1974-1982; $62.00

2496 Sweetmeat, 6", 1936-1944; $50.00

2496 Tid Bit, 3-toed, 1938-1982; $48.00

2496 Tray, 8½" Oval, 1936-1944; $55.00

4121 Vase, 5", 1936-1944, 1952-1959; $125.00

4128 Vase, 5", 1936-1943; $150.00

2470 Vase, 10", 1936-1943, 1952-1959; $295.00

NAVARRE—Henry the Fourth of Navarre and France founded the Bourbon dynasty which inspired this lovely design: an unusually fine *Master-Etching* of aristocratic charm.

Navarre Ice Bucket, 2083 Salad Dressing Bottle, 2482 Candelabra, 2496 3-part Candy and Cover

2440—Cup
2440—Saucer

2375—Footed Shaker
Height 3½ in.

2440—Footed Cream
Height 4¼ in.
Cap. 6¾ oz.

2440—Footed Sugar
Height 3¾ in.

2440—6 in. Plate   2440—8 in. Plate
2440—7 in. Plate   2440—9 in. Plate

5000—7 Footed Jug
Height 9¾ in.
Capacity 3 Pints

NAVARRE DESIGN
PLATE ETCHING No. 327

2375—Ice Bucket with Tongs
Height 6 in.   Top Dia. 5⅛ in.

2375—Mayonnaise
Top Dia. 5⅝ in.
2375—7 in. Mayonnaise Plate
2375—Ladle

2400—6 in. Comport
Height 4½ in.

2440—8½ in. Pickle

2440—11½ in. Celery

2496—3 Part Relish
Length 10 in.   Width 7½ in.

2496—4 Part Relish
Length 10 in.   Width 7½ in.

2440—Oval Cake Plate
2 Handles   Length 10½ in.

2419—5 Part Relish
Length 13¼ in.   Width 9⅛ in.

NAVARRE DESIGN
PLATE ETCHING No. 327

2496—8 in. Oblong Tray
Width 7 in.

4128—5 in. Vase

4121—5 in. Vase

2496—12 in.
Bowl, Flared
Height 3½ in.

2496—6½ in.
Oblong Sauce Dish
Width 5¼ in.

2496—Sweetmeat
6 in. Square

2496—6½ in.
2 Part Mayonnaise
Width 5¼ in.

2496—2 Part Relish
6 in. Square

2496—14 in. Torte Plate

NAVARRE DESIGN
PLATE ETCHING No. 327

2472—Duo Candlestick
Height 5 in.   Spread 8¼ in.

2496—5½ in. Candlestick

2496—Duo Candlestick
Height 4½ in.   Spread 8 in.

2470½—10½ in. Bowl

2496—10½ in. Handled Bowl
Height 3⅜ in.

2482—Trindle Candlestick
Height 6¾ in.   Spread 8½ in.

2470—10 in. Vase

2496—Trindle Candlestick
Height 6 in. Spread 8¼ in.

NAVARRE DESIGN
PLATE ETCHING No. 327

869—Finger Bowl

2083—Salad Dressing Bottle
and Stopper
Height 6½ in.
Capacity 7 oz.

2496—Ice Bucket
Height 4⅜ in. Top Diameter 6½ in.
Chromium Handle and Tongs
Tongs Priced Separately

2496—10 in. Floating Garden
Width 7½ in.

2364—16 in. Plate

NAVARRE DESIGN
PLATE ETCHING No. 327

2545—"Flame" Duo Candlestick
Height 6¾ in. Spread 10¼ in.

2545—2 Light "Flame" Candelabra, Using 12 B Prisms
Height 6¾ in. Spread 11 in.

2545
12½ in. "Flame" Oval Bowl
Height 2⅞ in.

2496
4 in. Candlestick

2496
4 in. Candlestick

NAVARRE DESIGN
PLATE ETCHING No. 327

2496—Individual Sugar
Height 2⅜ in.

2496—Individual Cream
Height 3⅛ in.
Capacity 4 oz.

2496—10 in. Cake Plate. 2 Handles

2545—"Flame" Lustre
Using 8 U. D. P.
Height 7½ in.

2496—Handled Nappy, Reg.
Diameter 4⅜ in.

2496—Handled Nappy, Sq.
4 in. Square

2496—3-Toed Tid Bit
Diameter 8¼ in.

2496—Handled Nappy, Fld.
Diameter 5 in.

2496—3-Part Candy Box and Cover
Height 2½ in. Width 6¼ in.

2496—Handled Nappy, 3-Cor.
Length 4⅝ in.

2496—3-Toed Bon Bon
Diameter 7⅜ in.

2496—5½ in. Comport
Height 4¾ in.

2496—Cheese and Cracker
Diameter of Plate 11 in. Diameter of Cheese 5¼ in. Height 3¼ in.

2496—3-Toed Nut Bowl, Cupped
Diameter 6¼ in.

MEADOW ROSE
Plate Etching 328

A close cousin of Navarre, the Meadow Rose pattern used many of the same pieces. One major difference exists between the two patterns: much of the Meadow Rose pattern was made in Azure through 1943. Another difference is that Meadow Rose included the stunning 2510 Candelabra in its host of candlestick offerings. Stemware is featured in *Fostoria Stemware*, pages 87 – 88.

2496 Bon Bon, 3-toed
    Crystal, 1937-1970; $48.00
    Azure, 1937-1943; $75.00
869 Bowl, Finger
    Crystal, 1936-1943; $30.00
    Azure, 1936-1943; $47.00
2496 Bowl, 8½" Serving
    Crystal, 1936-1961; $64.00
    Azure, 1936-1943; $95.00
2496 Bowl, 10" Floating Garden
    Crystal, 1936-1948; $125.00
    Azure, 1936-1943; $150.00
2496 Bowl, 10½" Handled
    Crystal, 1936-1958; $110.00
    Azure, 1936-1943; $175.00
2496 Bowl, 12" Flared
    Crystal, 1936-1970; $95.00
    Azure, 1936-1943; $135.00
2545 Bowl, 12½" Oval
    Crystal, 1936-1958; $110.00
    Azure, 1936-1940; $165.00
2510 Candelabra, 2-light, UDP (pair)
    Crystal, 1937-1942; $500.00/market
2545 Candelabra, 2-light, B Prisms (pair)
    Crystal, 1936-1942; $350.00
    Azure, 1936-1942; $475.00
2496 Candlestick, 4" (pair)
    Crystal, 1936-1970; $75.00
    Azure, 1936-1943; $135.00
2496 Candlestick, 5½" (pair)
    Crystal, 1936-1958; $87.00
    Azure, 1936-1943; $145.00
2496 Candlestick, Duo (pair)
    Crystal, 1936-1970; $250.00
    Azure, 1936-1943; $375.00
2545 Candlestick, Duo (pair)
    Crystal, 1936-1958; $135.00
    Azure, 1936-1943; $275.00
2496 Candlestick, Trindle (pair)
    Crystal, 1936-1958; $135.00
    Azure, 1936-1943; $250.00
2496 Candy, 3-part and Cover
    Crystal, 1937-1962; $125.00
    Azure, 1937-1943; $200.00
2496 Celery
    Crystal, 1936-1958; $50.00
    Azure, 1936-1942; $85.00
2496 Cheese and Cracker
    Crystal, 1937-1958; $115.00
    Azure, 1937-1940; $175.00

2496 Comport, 5½"
    Crystal, 1936-1958; $50.00
    Azure, 1936-1943; $85.00
2496 Cup and Saucer
    Crystal, 1936-1970; $34.00
    Azure, 1936-1943; $52.00
2496 Ice Bucket, Metal Handle
    Crystal 1936-1958; $130.00
    Azure, 1936-1943; $195.00
2496 Jelly and Cover
    Crystal, 1936-1958; $110.00
    Azure, 1936-1943; $145.00
5000 Jug
    Crystal 1938-1957; $495. 00
    Azure, 1938-1939; $1,200.00/market
2375 Mayonnaise, Plate, Ladle
    Crystal 1939-1945; $95.00
    Azure, 1939-1942; $150.00
2496 Mayonnaise, 2-part
    Crystal, 1936-1944; $55.00
    Azure, 1936-1942; $78.00
2496½ Mayonnaise, Plate, Ladle
    Crystal, 1936-1958; $95.00
    Azure, 1936-1943; $150.00
2496 Nappy, 3-cornered Handled
    Crystal, 1937-1970; $27.00
    Azure, 1937-1943; $45.00
2496 Nappy, Handled, Flared
    Crystal, 1937-1970; $27.00
    Azure, 1937-1943; $45.00

Azure Meadow Rose Jelly and Cover, 2496 Celery, Flared Comport, Sugar, Pickle, and Cream

2496 Pickle
    Crystal, 1936-1958; $32.00
    Azure, 1936-1942; $54.00
2666 Pitcher, Quart
    Crystal, 1958-1970; $325.00
2337 Plate, 7"
    Crystal, 1938-1971; $18.00
2496 Plate, 6"
    Crystal, 1936-1974; $14.00
    Azure, 1936-1943; $26.00
2496 Plate, 7"
    Crystal, 1936-1974; $18.00
    Azure, 1936-1943; $30.00
2496 Plate, 8"
    Crystal, 1936-1974; $23.00
    Azure, 1936-1943; $36.00
2496 Plate, 9"
    Crystal, 1936-1974; $60.00
    Azure, 1936-1943; $97.00
2496 Plate, 10" Cake
    Crystal, 1936-1970; $80.00
    Azure, 1936-1943; $125.00
2496 Plate, 14" Torte
    Crystal, 1936-1970; $110.00
    Azure, 1936-1943; $175.00
2364 Plate, 16"
    Crystal, 1936-1970; $150.00
    Azure, 1936-1940; $225.00
2496 Relish, 2-part
    Crystal, 1936-1970; $42.00
    Azure, 1936-1943; $68.00
2496 Relish, 3-part
    Crystal, 1936-1970; $68.00
    Azure, 1936-1943; $100.00
2440 Relish, 3-part
    Crystal, 1937-1943; $75.00
2419 Relish, 5-part
    Crystal, 1936-1946; $125.00
2083 Salad Dressing Bottle
    Crystal, 1936-1970; $500.00
2586 SaniCut Server
    Crystal, 1940-1943; $700.00/market
2496 Sauce and Tray
    Crystal, 1936-1944; $175.00
    Azure, 1936-1939; $335.00
2364 Shaker, Chrome Top C (pair)
    Crystal, 1950-1970; $75.00
2375 Shaker, Footed, FGT (pair)
    Crystal, 1936-1943; $195.00
    Azure, 1936-1943; $325.00
2496 Sugar and Cream
    Crystal, 1936-1970; $60.00
    Azure, 1936-1943; $125.00
2496 Sugar and Cream, Individual
    Crystal, 1936-1970; $65.00

Azure Meadow Rose, 2545 12½" Bowl and Candelabra, 2496 4" Candlesticks

        Azure, 1936-1943; $125.00
2496 Sugar and Cream Tray
        Crystal, 1943-1970; $55.00
2496 Sweetmeat
        Crystal, 1936-1944; $50.00
        Azure, 1936-1942; $78.00
2496 Tid Bit, 3-toed
        Crystal, 1937-1970; $52.00
        Azure, 1937-1943; $85.00

Azure Meadow Rose 5000 Jug, 4128 5" Vase, Sauce and Plate, 2375 Mayonnaise, Plate and Ladle

2375 Tray, Handled Lunch
    Crystal, 1936-1970; $115.00
    Azure, 1936-1943; $165.00
4128 Vase, 5"
    Crystal, 1936-1943; $150.00
    Azure, 1936-1942; $225.00
2470 Vase, 10"
    Crystal, 1936-1943; $325.00
    Azure, 1936-1942; $475.00

MEADOW ROSE—an intricately etched design of primrose delicacy. It is perfectly executed on crystal with the softness and beauty of an art etching on paper.

2496—Footed Cup
2496—Saucer

2375
Footed Shaker
Height 3½ in.

2496—Footed Cream
Height 3¾ in.
Capacity 7½ oz.

2496—6, 7, 8, 9 in. Plate

2496—Footed Sugar
Height 3½ in.

5000—7 Footed Jug
Height 9¾ in. Capacity 3 Pints

MEADOW ROSE DESIGN
PLATE ETCHING No. 328

2496—Individual Sugar
Height 2⅞ in.

2496—Individual Cream
Height 3⅛ in.
Capacity 4 oz.

2496—5½ in. Comport
Height 4¾ in.

2496—11 in. Celery

2496—Jelly and Cover
Height 7½ in.

2375—11 in. Handled Lunch Tray

2496—8 in. Pickle

2496—10 in. Cake Plate, 2 Handles

2496—Ice Bucket
Height 4⅜ in. Top Diameter 6½ in.
Chromium Handle and Tongs—Tongs Priced Separately

2496—8½ in. Serving Dish, 2 Handles

MEADOW ROSE DESIGN
PLATE ETCHING No. 328

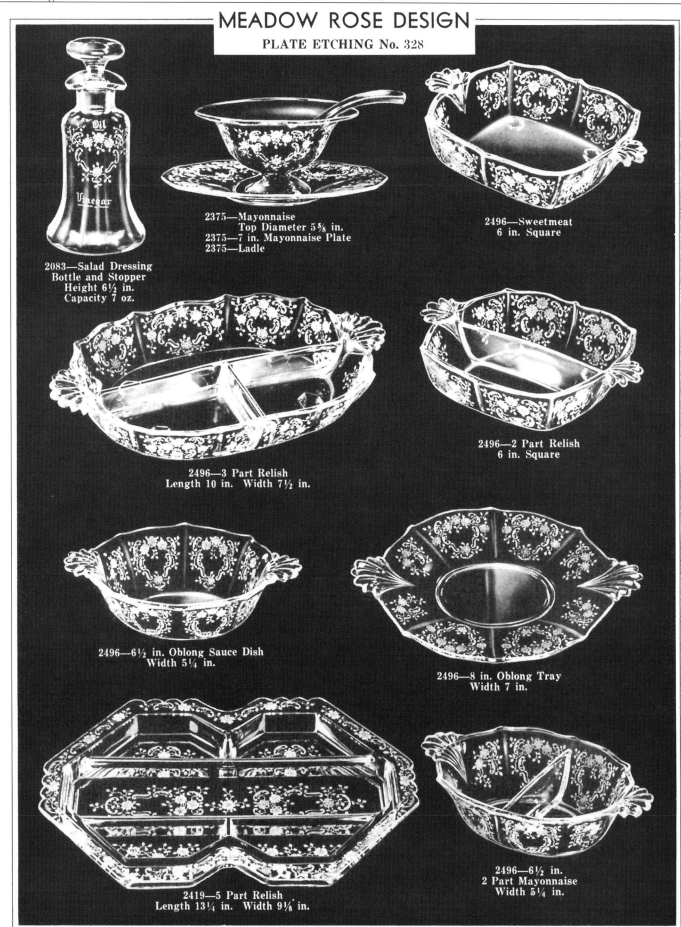

2083—Salad Dressing
Bottle and Stopper
Height 6½ in.
Capacity 7 oz.

2375—Mayonnaise
Top Diameter 5⅝ in.
2375—7 in. Mayonnaise Plate
2375—Ladle

2496—Sweetmeat
6 in. Square

2496—3 Part Relish
Length 10 in. Width 7½ in.

2496—2 Part Relish
6 in. Square

2496—6½ in. Oblong Sauce Dish
Width 5¼ in.

2496—8 in. Oblong Tray
Width 7 in.

2419—5 Part Relish
Length 13¼ in. Width 9⅛ in.

2496—6½ in.
2 Part Mayonnaise
Width 5¼ in.

MEADOW ROSE DESIGN
PLATE ETCHING No. 328

2496
5½ in. Candlestick

2496—12 in. Bowl Flared
Height 3½ in.

2496
5½ in. Candlestick

2496
4 in. Candlestick

2496—10 in. Floating Garden
Width 7½ in.

2496
4 in. Candlestick

2496—14 in. Torte Plate

MEADOW ROSE DESIGN
PLATE ETCHING No. 328

2496—10½ in. Handled Bowl
Height 3⅜ in.

2496—Trindle Candlestick
Height 6 in.   Spread 8¼ in.

2496—Duo Candlestick
Height 4½ in.   Spread 8 in.

2364—16 in. Plate

MEADOW ROSE DESIGN
PLATE ETCHING No. 328

2545—2 Light "Flame" Candelabra
Using 12 B Prisms
Height 6¾ in.   Spread 11 in.

4128
5 in. Vase

2545
12½ in. "Flame" Oval Bowl
Height 2⅞ in.

2470
10 in. Vase

2545—"Flame" Duo Candlestick
Height 6¾ in.   Spread 10¼ in.

MEADOW ROSE DESIGN
PLATE ETCHING No. 328

2496—3 Toed Tid Bit, Flat
Diameter 8¼ in.

2496—3 Toed Bon Bon
Diameter 7⅜ in.

2440—3 Part Handled Relish
Diameter 7½ in.

2496—3 Part Candy Box and Cover
Height 2½ in.   Width 6¼ in.

2496½—Mayonnaise and Plate
and Ladle
Height 3½ in.

2496—Handled Nappy, 3 Cor.
Length 4⅝ in.

2496—Handled Nappy, Flared
Diameter. 5 in.

2510—2 Light Candelabra, 16 U. D. P.
Using No. 2527 Bobache
Height 6½ in.   Spread 9 in.

2496—Cheese and Cracker
Diameter Plate 11 in.
Diameter Cheese 5¼ in.   Height 3¼ in.

LIDO
Plate Etching 329

For pieces not shown in Lido, refer to Navarre or Baroque. Lido was one of the first etched patterns to use the sugar and cream tray for the individual sugar and cream. Stemware is featured in *Fostoria Stemware*, pages 89 – 90.

2486 Bon Bon
  Crystal, 1937-1954; $48.00
  Azure, 1937-1942; $75.00
766 Bowl, Finger
  Crystal, 1937-1943; $40.00
  Azure, 1937-1942; $57.00
2496 Bowl, Regular Handled Nappy
  Crystal, 1937-1944; $34.00
  Azure, 1937-1940; $45.00
2496 Bowl, Flared Handled Nappy
  Crystal, 1937-1954; $30.00
  Azure, 1937-1940; $45.00
2496 Bowl, Square Handled Nappy
  Crystal, 1937-1944; $34.00
  Azure, 1937-1940; $45.00
2496 Bowl, 3-cornered Handled Nappy
  Crystal, 1937-1954; $30.00
  Azure, 1937-1940; $45.00
2496 Bowl, 3-toed Nut
  Crystal, 1937-1944; $50.00
  Azure, 1937-1940; $75.00
2496 Bowl, 8½" Handled Serving
  Crystal, 1937-1953; $68.00
  Azure, 1937-1940; $85.00
2496 Bowl, 10½" Handled
  Crystal 1937-1954; $115.00
  Azure, 1937-1940; $145.00
2496 Bowl, 12" Flared
  Crystal, 1937-1954; $95.00
  Azure, 1937-1942; $125.00
2545 Bowl, 12½" (Flame)
  Crystal, 1937-1954; $115.00
  Azure, 1937-1940; $150.00
2496 Candlestick, 4" (pair)
  Crystal, 1937-1954; $75.00
  Azure, 1937-1942; $100.00
2496 Candlestick, 5½" (pair)
  Crystal, 1937-1954; $85.00
  Azure, 1937-1942; $115.00
2496 Candlestick, Duo (pair)
  Crystal, 1937-1954; $95.00
  Azure, 1937-1942; $125.00
2545 Candlestick, Duo (pair)
  Crystal, 1937-1954; $150.00
  Azure, 1937-1940; $225.00
2545 Candlestick, Lustre (pair)
  Crystal, 1937-1942; $135.00
  Azure, 1937-1942; $180.00
2545 Candelabra, 2-light, B Prisms (pair)
  Crystal, 1937-1942; $395.00
  Azure, 1937-1942; $450.00
2496 Candy Box, 3-part, and Cover

  Crystal, 1937-1954; $125.00
  Azure, 1937-1942; $200.00
2496 Celery, 11"
  Crystal, 1937-1954; $50.00
  Azure, 1937-1940; $85.00
2496 Cheese and Cracker
  Crystal, 1937-1954; $115.00
  Azure, 1937-1940; $165.00
2496 Comport, 5½"
  Crystal, 1937-1954; $50.00
  Azure, 1937-1940; $75.00
2496 Comport, 6½"
  Crystal, 1937-1943; $60.00
  Azure, 1937-1940; $85.00
2496 Cup and Saucer
  Crystal, 1937-1954; $32.00
  Azure, 1937-1942; $45.00
2496 Ice Bucket, Metal Handle
  Crystal, 1937-1954; $115.00
  Azure, 1937-1942; $145.00
2496 Jelly and Cover
  Crystal, 1937-1953; $75.00
  Azure, 1937-1940; $125.00
6011 Jug
  Crystal, 1937-1954; $350.00
  Azure, 1937-1940; $725.00
2496 Mayonnaise, 2-part
  Crystal, 1937-1944; $50.00
  Azure, 1937-1940; $75.00
2496½ Mayonnaise, Plate, Ladle
  Crystal, 1937-1954; $75.00
  Azure, 1937-1940; $95.00
2496 Oil, 3½ oz.
  Crystal, 1937-1953; $110.00
  Azure, 1937-1940; $175.00
2496 Pickle, 8"
  Crystal, 1937-1954; $40.00
  Azure, 1937-1940; $54.00
2496 Plate, 6"
  Crystal, 1937-1954; $14.00
  Azure, 1937-1942; $20.00
2496 Plate, 7"
  Crystal, 1937-1954; $18.00
  Azure, 1937-1942; $30.00
2496 Plate, 8"
  Crystal, 1937-1954; $22.00
  Azure, 1937-1942; $32.00
2496 Plate, 9"
  Crystal, 1937-1954; $58.00
  Azure, 1937-1942; $75.00
2496 Plate, 10" Handled Cake
  Crystal, 1937-1954; $75.00

Azure, 1937-1940; $110.00
2496 Plate, 14" Torte
　Crystal, 1937-1954; $95.00
　Azure, 1937-1940; $135.00
2496 Relish, 2-part
　Crystal, 1937-1954; $40.00
　Azure, 1937-1940; $62.00
2496 Relish, 3-part
　Crystal, 1937-1954; $67.00
　Azure, 1937-1942; $85.00
2419 Relish, 5-part
　Crystal, 1937-1943; $115.00
2496 Sauce Dish, 6½" Oval
　Crystal, 1937-1944; $95.00
　Azure, 1937-1939; $125.00
2496 Shaker, FGT (pair)
　Crystal, 1937-1943; $150.00
　Azure, 1937-1942; $225.00
2496 Sugar and Cream
　Crystal, 1937-1954; $58.00
　Azure, 1937-1942; $110.00
2496 Sugar and Cream, Individual
　Crystal, 1937-1954; $55.00

Azure, 1937-1942; $110.00
2496 Sweetmeat
　Crystal, 1937-1944; $45.00
　Azure, 1937-1940; $68.00
2496 Tid Bit, 3-toed
　Crystal, 1937-1954; $48.00
　Azure, 1937-1940; $72.00
2496½ Tray, 6½", Individual Sugar
　and Cream
　Crystal, 1937-1954; $35.00
　Azure, 1937-1940; $55.00
2496 Tray, 8" Oblong
　Crystal, 1937-1944; $48.00
　Azure, 1937-1939; $65.00
4128 Vase, 5"
　Crystal, 1937-1943; $135.00
　Azure, 1937-1940; $175.00
2496 Vase, 8"
　Crystal, 1937-1939; $145.00
　Azure, 1937-1939; $175.00
2470 Vase, 10"
　Crystal, 1937-1943; $295.00
　Azure, 1937-1942; $400.00

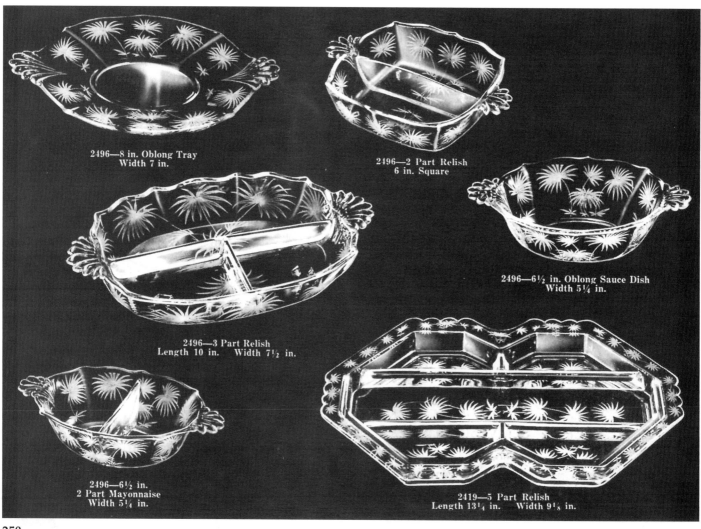

2496—8 in. Oblong Tray
Width 7 in.

2496—2 Part Relish
6 in. Square

2496—3 Part Relish
Length 10 in.　Width 7½ in.

2496—6½ in. Oblong Sauce Dish
Width 5¼ in.

2496—6½ in.
2 Part Mayonnaise
Width 5¼ in.

2419—5 Part Relish
Length 13¼ in.　Width 9⅛ in.

LIDO DESIGN
PLATE ETCHING No. 329

766—Finger Bowl

2496—6 in. Plate
2496—7 in. Plate
2496—8 in. Plate
2496—9 in. Plate

2496—Footed Cup
2496—Saucer

2496—Footed Sugar
Height 3½ in.

2496—Footed Cream
Height 3¾ in.
Capacity 7½ oz.

2496—Individual Sugar
Height 2⅞ in.

2496—Individual Cream
Height 3⅛ in.
Capacity 4 oz.

2496—8 in. Pickle

2496—Shaker
Height 2¾ in.

2496—6½ in. Sugar and Cream Tray
Width 3¾ in.

2496—11 in. Celery

2496½—Mayonnaise and
Plate and Ladle
Height 3½ in.

LIDO DESIGN
PLATE ETCHING No. 329

2496—5½ in. Comport
Height 4¾ in.

2496—Sweetmeat
6 in. Square

2496—Jelly and Cover
Height 7½ in.

2496—3½ oz.
Oil and Stopper
Height 5½ in.

2496—6½ in. Comport
Height 5¾ in.

2496—10 in. Cake Plate, 2 Handles

2496—Ice Bucket
Height 4⅜ in.   Top Diameter 6½ in.
Metal Handle and Tongs. Tongs priced separately

2496—8½ in. Serving Dish, 2 Handles

LIDO DESIGN
PLATE ETCHING No. 329

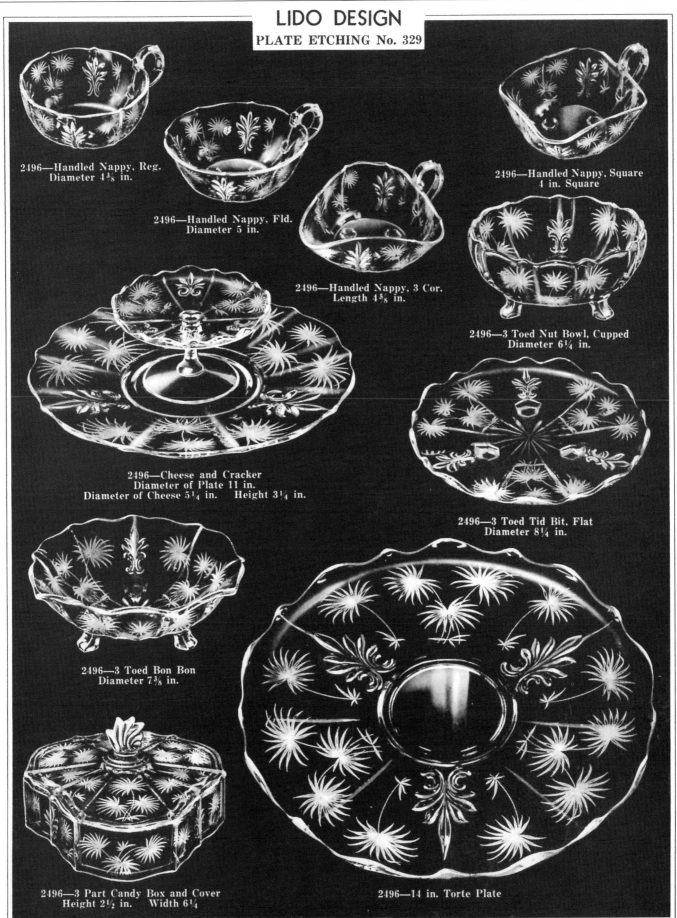

2496—Handled Nappy, Reg.
Diameter 4⅜ in.

2496—Handled Nappy, Fld.
Diameter 5 in.

2496—Handled Nappy, 3 Cor.
Length 4⅝ in.

2496—Handled Nappy, Square
4 in. Square

2496—3 Toed Nut Bowl, Cupped
Diameter 6¼ in.

2496—Cheese and Cracker
Diameter of Plate 11 in.
Diameter of Cheese 5¼ in.   Height 3¼ in.

2496—3 Toed Tid Bit, Flat
Diameter 8¼ in.

2496—3 Toed Bon Bon
Diameter 7⅜ in.

2496—3 Part Candy Box and Cover
Height 2½ in.   Width 6¼

2496—14 in. Torte Plate

SHIRLEY

Plate Etching 331

The Shirley pattern used both Baroque and 2337 plates. Refer to Navarre and Baroque for pieces in this pattern. Stemware is featured in *Fostoria Stemware,* pages 89 – 90.

2496 Bon Bon, 1937-1956; $52.00
766 Bowl, Finger, 1937-1943; $40.00
2496 Bowl, 5" Fruit, 1937-1944; $32.00
2496 Bowl, 3-toed Nut, 1937-1944; $60.00
2496 Bowl, 9½" Oval Vegetable,
    1937-1944; $60.00
2496 Bowl, 10½" Handled,
    1937-1956; $85.00
2496 Bowl, 12" Flared, 1937-1956; $80.00
2545 Bowl, 12½" Oval,
    1937-1956; $95.00
2545 Candelabra, 2-light, B Prisms,
    1937-1942 (pair); $300.00
2496 Candlesticks, 4",
    1937-1956 (pair); $85.00
2545 Candlestick, 4½",
    1937-1956 (pair); $85.00
2545 Candlestick, Lustre UDP,
    1937-1942 (pair); $165.00
2496 Candlestick, Duo,
    1937-1956 (pair); $95.00
2545 Candlestick, Duo,
    1937-1956 (pair); $200.00
2496 Candy Box and Cover, 1937-1943;
    1947-1956; $125.00
2496 Celery, 11", 1937-1956; $50.00
2496 Cheese and Cracker, 1937-1956; $115.00
2496 Comport, 5½", 1937-1956; $50.00
2496 Cream Soup and Plate, 1937-1956; $64.00
6011 Jug, 1937-1956; $350.00
2496 Mayonnaise, 6½", 2-part,
    1937-1944; $50.00
2496½ Mayonnaise, Plate, Ladle,
    1937-1956; $85.00
2496 Nappy, 3-cornered, 1937-1956; $30.00
2496 Nappy, Flared, 1937-1956; $30.00
2496 Nappy, Regular, 1937-1944; $36.00
2496 Nappy, Square, 1937-1944; $36.00
2496 Pickle, 8", 1937-1956; $40.00
2337 Plate, 6", 1937-1956; $14.00
2337 Plate, 7", 1937-1956; $18.00
2337 Plate, 8", 1937-1956; $24.00
2337 Plate, 9", 1937-1956; $45.00
2496 Plate, 10" Cake, 1937-1956; $85.00
2496 Plate, 14" Torte, 1937-1956; $115.00
2496 Platter, 12", 1937-1944; $125.00
2496 Relish, 2-part, 1937-1956; $54.00
2496 Relish, 3-part, 1937-1956; $68.00

2496 Sauce, Oblong, 1937-1944; $125.00
2496 Shaker, FGT,
    1937-1943 (pair); $175.00
2496 Sugar and Cream, 1937-1956; $65.00
2496 Sugar and Cream, Individual,
    1937-1956; $65.00
2496 Sugar and Cream Tray,
    1947-1956; $50.00
2496 Sweetmeat, 1937-1944; $50.00
2545 Vase, 10", 1937-1943; $225.00

Shirley 2545 10" Flame Vase

SHIRLEY DESIGN
PLATE ETCHING No. 331

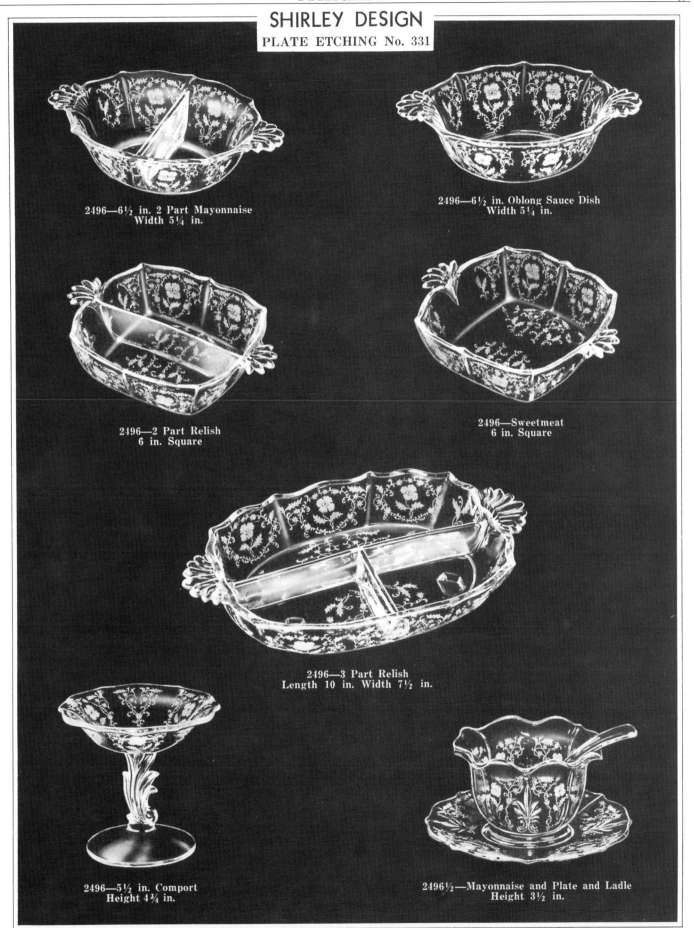

2496—6½ in. 2 Part Mayonnaise
Width 5¼ in.

2496—6½ in. Oblong Sauce Dish
Width 5¼ in.

2496—2 Part Relish
6 in. Square

2496—Sweetmeat
6 in. Square

2496—3 Part Relish
Length 10 in. Width 7½ in.

2496—5½ in. Comport
Height 4¾ in.

2496½—Mayonnaise and Plate and Ladle
Height 3½ in.

SHIRLEY DESIGN
PLATE ETCHING No. 331

2496—Footed Sugar
Height 3½ in.

2496—Footed Cream
Height 3¾ in.
Capacity 7½ oz.

2496—Shaker
Height 2¾ in.

2496—5 in. Fruit

2496—Cream Soup
2496—Cream Soup Plate

2496—12 in. Oval Platter

2496—9½ in. Vegetable Dish

2496—8 in. Pickle
2496—11 in. Celery

2496—Ice Bucket
Height 4⅜ in. Top Diameter 6½ in.
Metal Handle and Tongs
Tongs Priced Separately

2496—10 in. Cake Plate, 2 Handles

CHINTZ

Plate Etching 338

Stemware is featured in *Fostoria Stemware*, page 97.

2496 Bon Bon, 1940-1970; $48.00
869 Bowl, Finger, 1940-1943; $55.00
2496 Bowl, 5" Fruit, 1940-1944; $38.00
2496 Bowl, Flared Handled Nappy, 1940-1970; $27.00
2496 Bowl, 3-cornered Handled Nappy, 1940-1970; $27.00
2496 Bowl, 8½" Serving, 1940-1961; $68.00
6023 Bowl, 9" Footed, 1940-1943; $165.00
2496 Bowl, 9½" Vegetable, 1940-1944; $150.00
2484 Bowl, 10" Handled, 1940-1959; $110.00
2496 Bowl, 10½" Handled, 1940-1959; $125.00
2496 Bowl, 12" Flared, 1940-1970; $95.00
2496 Candlestick, 4", 1940-1970 (pair); $75.00
2496 Candlestick, 5½", 1940-1959 (pair); $87.00
2496 Candlestick, Duo, 1940-1970 (pair); $95.00
2496 Candlestick, Trindle, 1940-1959 (pair); $135.00
6023 Candlestick, Duo, 1940-1943 (pair); $150.00
2496 Candy Box and Cover, 1940-1943, 1947-1961; $125.00
2496 Celery, 1940-1959; $50.00
2496 Cheese and Cracker, 1940-1959; $115.00
2496 Comport, 5½", 1940-1959; $50.00
2496 Cream Soup and Plate, 1940-1943; $68.00
2496 Cup and Saucer, 1940-1970; $35.00
2496 Ice Bucket, Chrome Handle, 1940-1959; $125.00
2496 Jelly and Cover, 1940-1959; $87.00
5000 Jug, 1940-1943, 1947-1957; $450.00
2496½ Mayonnaise, Plate, Ladle, 1940-1961; $85.00
2496 Mayonnaise, 2-part, 1940-1943; $60.00

2496 Oil, 3½ oz., 1940-1943, 1947-1959; $135.00
2496 Pickle, 1940-1959; $42.00
2666 Pitcher, Quart, 1958-1970; $325.00
2496 Plate, 6", 1940-1970; $14.00
2496 Plate, 7", 1940-1970; $18.00
2496 Plate, 8", 1940-1970; $24.00
2496 Plate, 9", 1940-1970; $65.00
2496 Plate, Cake, 1940-1970; $80.00
2496 Plate, 14" Torte, 1940-1950, 1956-1970; $110.00
2364 Plate, 16" Torte, 1940-1944, 1947-1950, 1956-1970; $150.00
2496 Platter, 12" Oval, 1940-1944; $150.00
2496 Relish, 2-part, 1940-1969; $48.00
2496 Relish, 3-part, 1940-1970; $68.00
2419 Relish, 5-part, 1940-1944; $150.00
2083 Salad Dressing Bottle, 1940-1943; $500.00/market
2586 Sani-Cut Syrup, 1940-1943; $700.00/market
2496 Sauce, Oblong, 1940-1944; $135.00
2364 Shaker, Chrome Top "C", 1954-1970 (pair); $75.00
2496 Shaker, FGT, 1940-1943 (pair); $200.00
2496 Sugar and Cream, 1940-1970; $65.00
2496 Sugar and Cream, Individual, 1940-1970; $65.00
2496 Sugar, Cream, Tray Set, 1940-1970; $95.00
2496 Tid Bit, 3-toed, 1940-1965; $48.00
2496 Tray, 8" Oblong, 1940-1944; $85.00
2375 Tray, Handled Lunch, 1940-1970; $115.00
4121 Vase, 5", 1952-1959; $150.00
4128 Vase, 5" 1940-1943; $150.00

4143 Vase, 6" Footed, 1940-1943, 1952-1955; $165.00
4143 Vase, 7½" Footed, 1940-1943; $375.00
2660 Vase, 8" Flip, 1952-1959; $200.00
2470 Vase, 10" Footed, 1952-1959; $250.00

Sugar and Cream on Tray, 7½" Vase, Bon Bon, Oil

CHINTZ DESIGN
PLATE ETCHING No. 338

2496—Footed Cup
2496—Saucer

2496—Footed Sugar
Height 3½ in.

2496—Plate
See Price List for Sizes

2496—Footed Cream
Height 3¾ in.
Capacity 7½ oz.

5000—Footed Jug
Height 9¾ in.   Capacity 3 Pints

2496—12 in. Bowl, Flared
Height 3½ in.

2496—Trindle Candlestick
Height 6 in.   Spread 8¼ in.

2496—4 in. Candlestick

2484—10 in. Handled Bowl
Height 3½ in.

6023—9 in. Footed Bowl
Height 4⅛ in.

2496—10½ in. Handled Bowl
Height 3⅜ in.

CHINTZ DESIGN

PLATE ETCHING No. 338

2496—Individual Sugar
Height 2⅞ in.

2496—Individual Cream
Height 3⅛ in.
Capacity 4 oz.

2496—Shaker
Height 2¾ in.

2496—3 Piece Sugar & Cream Set
Consisting of:
1/12 Doz. 2496—Ind. Sugar
1/12 Doz. 2496—Ind. Cream
1/12 Doz. 2496—S. & C. Tray

2496—Cream Soup
2496—Cream Soup Plate

2496—5 in. Fruit

2496—8 in. Pickle

869—Finger Bowl
Height 2 in.
Diameter 4½ in.

2083—Salad Dressing
Bottle and Stopper
Height 6½ in.
Capacity 7 oz.

2496—3½ oz. Oil & Stopper
Height 5½ in.

2496—9½ in. Vegetable Dish

2496—11 in. Celery

2496½—Mayonnaise and Plate
and Ladle
Height 3½ in.

2496—12 in. Oval Platter

CHINTZ DESIGN
PLATE ETCHING No. 338

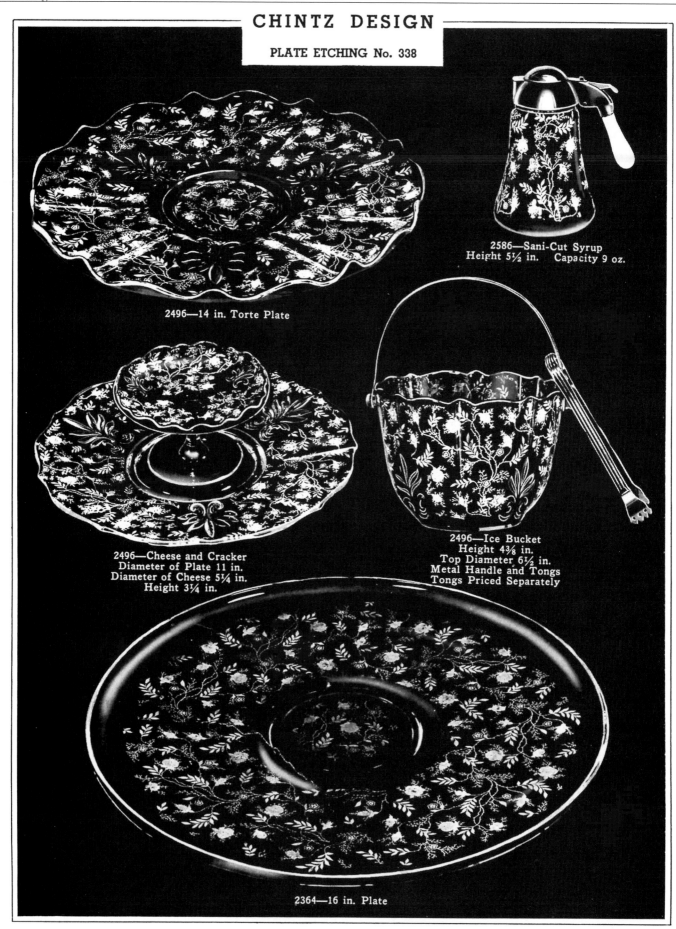

2586—Sani-Cut Syrup
Height 5½ in.   Capacity 9 oz.

2496—14 in. Torte Plate

2496—Cheese and Cracker
Diameter of Plate 11 in.
Diameter of Cheese 5¼ in.
Height 3¼ in.

2496—Ice Bucket
Height 4⅜ in.
Top Diameter 6½ in.
Metal Handle and Tongs
Tongs Priced Separately

2364—16 in. Plate

ROSEMARY

Plate Etching 339

1940 – 1943

Stemware is featured in *Fostoria Stemware,* page 40.

1769 Bowl, Finger; $38.00
6023 Bowl, 9" Footed; $145.00
2364 Bowl, 10½" Salad; $95.00
2364 Bowl, 12" Flared; $95.00
2364 Bowl, 13" Fruit; $100.00
6023 Candlestick, Duo (pair); $125.00
6011 Jug; $295.00

2337 Plate, 6"; $10.00
2337 Plate, 7"; $14.00
2337 Plate, 8"; $20.00
2364 Plate, 14" Torte; $85.00
4143 Vase, 6" Footed; $145.00
4143 Vase, 7½" Footed; $175.00

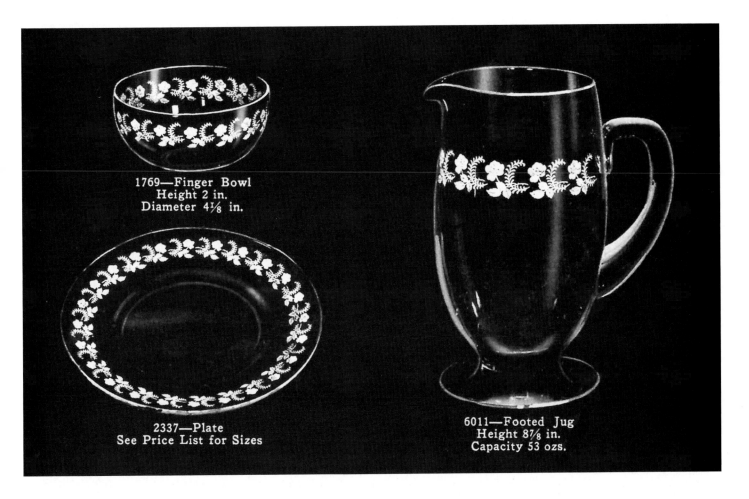

1769—Finger Bowl
Height 2 in.
Diameter 4⅛ in.

2337—Plate
See Price List for Sizes

6011—Footed Jug
Height 8⅞ in.
Capacity 53 ozs.

ROSEMARY DESIGN

PLATE ETCHING No. 339

2364—12 in. Bowl, Flared
Height 2⅞ in.

6023—9 in. Footed Bowl
Height 4⅛ in.

6023—Duo Candlestick
Height 5½ in.   Spread 6 in.

2364—13 in. Fruit Bowl
Height 2¾ in.

4143—6 in. Footed Vase
4143—7½ in. Footed Vase

2364—10½ in. Salad Bowl
2364—14 in. Torte Plate
Salad Fork & Spoon—Wood

CUTTINGS

167 Fairfax
168 Louisa
169 Trellis
170 Cynthia
175 Airdale
176 Kenmore
180 Lynn
184 Arbor
185 Arvida
186 Thelma
188 Berry
192 Kingsley
194 Orleans
195 Millefleur
196 Lattice
197 Chatteris
198 Warwick
700 Formal Garden
701 Tapestry
702 Comet
703 New Yorker
704 Royal Garden
705 Barcelona
707 Staunton
708 Nairn
709 York
710 Bristol
711 Inverness
712 Waterbury
713 Eaton
714 Oxford
715 Carlisle
716 Canterbury
717 Marlboro
718 Doncaster
719 Lancaster
720 Nottingham

721 Buckingham
722 Wellington
722½ Leicester
723 Westminster
725 Manhattan
726 Meteor
727 National
728 Embassy
729 Rocket
730 Whirlpool
731 Celestial
732 Seaweed
733 Marquette
734 Planet
735 Shooting Stars
736 Directoire
737 Quinfoil
738 Festoon
739 Rock Garden
740 Rondeau
741 Watercress
742 Orbit
743 Heraldry
744 Regency
745 Ivy
746 Gossamer
747 Fantasy
748 Allegro
749 Celebrity
751 Heirloom
752 Evangeline
754 Cavendish
755 Palmetto
756 Bouquet
757 Society
758 Bordeaux
759 Weylin

760 Wheat
761 Melba
762 Cumberland
763 Cyrene
766 Ripple
767 Beacon
768 Bridal Shower
769 Pussywillow
770 Athenian
771 Federal
772 Tulip
774 Gothic
775 Kimberley
777 Raynel
778 Lucerne
785 Cynthia
788 Chippendale
790 Hawthorne
792 Cathedral
793 Spire
794 Ingrid
795 Papyrus
796 Lyric
797 Daphne
798 Christine
799 Mulberry
800 Selma
804 Salon
805 Aloha
806 Cadence
807 Coventry
814 Christiana
816 Gadroon
817 Mount Vernon
819 Greek Key

CUTTINGS

Fostoria had not been strong on cuttings until the mid 1920s. There were cut designs on vases and candlesticks, decanters and bottles before that time, and although some of the cut designs introduced in the early part of the century continued through 1928, few cut lines became major patterns.

Several new cuttings were offered from 1922 – 1928. These usually combined stemware and some tableware and were made in crystal. With the advent of color in 1924, bowls, plates, and novelty items were made in the colors of amber, green, and canary. The Arbor pattern was the first major line cut on color. It was made in Amber, Blue, and Green from 1926 – 1927, and had no stemware. Arvida is listed in Amber, Blue, Green, and Orchid but was short lived, being listed in 1927 only. It would be well to note that the Orchid color comes alive when cut. Thelma and Berry were seen on color in 1928, and in 1929 came the intricate, complex designs of Kingsley and Orleans. Millefleur, a delicate cutting on crystal with some pieces having an Ebony base, was the first full dinner service using a cut design.

We have included all the cuttings that were introduced after 1924, but only selected patterns made before 1924 which continued to 1928. Cuttings which did not offer more than stemware and plates, and possibly a jug or decanter, are not covered in this book, having been listed in *Fostoria Stemware*. Special orders of cuttings and engravings were allowed during this period with detailed instructions about what could be ordered, the quantities that could be ordered, and a disclaimer that stated orders were subject to delay because they required individual shop attention.

The period from 1930 – 1942 saw an average of 10 new cuttings introduced each year. Few lasted longer than three years. From 1930 – 1933, some patterns were offered on crystal with a colored base, but for the most part, solid crystal was used. Many designs were polished, rock crystal, cuttings. Eighteen rock crystal cuttings were issued in 1933, all using basically the same tableware and complimentary pieces. The banner year for new cuttings was 1935 with 22.

One wonders why there was this extraordinary interest in cut designs, especially during the Great Depression. Many of the names are of British origin, such as Nottingham, Buckingham, Wellington, and the like, and many are of quite similar design, difficult to tell apart especially when offered on similar blanks. A long-time dealer in silver flatware of the same period recently remarked that one often has to place pieces side by side when trying to determine pattern identity. Wakefield was the last cut design offered (1942) during this period. Fostoria did not issue another cutting until 1950.

During the late 1920s, when Fostoria was advertising the complete dinner service in glass, not one complete service was offered with a cut design. Yet, an explosion of cuttings followed in the 1930s, only one of which was a complete dinner service, the Millefleur pattern. One possible factor could be that European influence on design had not diminished, and the beautiful European cut crystal was very much in vogue. America still was considered to be young, untried, and thus, incapable of generating its own designs. Periodicals from this time reveal that silver services, china, and cut crystal were featured most often in advertising. No doubt, Fostoria was cognizant of all design factors of the time. However, the true reason for so many cuttings during this period most likely will remain a mystery.

FAIRFAX

Cutting 167

1922 – 1928

Stemware is featured in *Fostoria Stemware*, pages 26 – 30.

880 Bon Bon; $18.00
1769 Bowl, Finger, and 1736 Plate; $18.00
2119 Candy Jar and Cover, ¼ pound; $22.00
2119 Candy Jar and Cover, ½ pound; $26.00
2119 Candy Jar and Cover, pound; $30.00
1697 Carafe; $24.00
4023 Carafe Tumbler, 6 oz.; $6.00
803 Comport, 5"; $16.00
803 Comport, 6"; $17.00
803 Comport and Cover, 5"; $23.00
803 Comport and Cover, 6"; $24.00
825 Jelly; $18.00
825 Jelly and Cover; $25.00
303 Jug 1712½; $95.00
2040/3 Jug; $65.00
2082/7 Jug; $95.00

2230/7 Jug (and Cover); $125.00
1968 Marmalade and Cover; $28.00
2138 Mayonnaise, Plate, and Ladle; $45.00
803 Nappy, 5"; $12.00
803 Nappy, 6"; $14.00
803 Nappy, 7"; $15.00
803 Nappy and Cover, 5"; $20.00
300½ Oil, Small; $27.00
840 Plate, 5" Sherbet; $5.00
2238 Plate, 8¼" Salad; $6.00
880 Salt Dip, Footed; $14.00
2263 Salt, Individual; $14.00
2263 Shaker, FGT; $15.00
1712 Sugar and Cover; $16.00
1712½ Cream; $14.00
2194 Syrup, 8 oz., Nickel Top; $37.00
2194 Syrup, 12 oz., Nickel Top; $42.00
4069 Vase, 9"; $35.00

LOUISA

Cutting 168

1922 – 1927

Stemware is featured in *Fostoria Stemware*, pages 18 and 19.

880 Bon Bon; $18.00
1769 Bowl, Finger, and 1736 Plate; $18.00
2250 Candy Jar and Cover, ¼ pound; $22.00
2250 Candy Jar and Cover, ½ pound; $26.00
2250 Candy Jar and Cover, pound; $30.00
1697 Carafe, and 6 oz. 4023 tumbler; $30.00
2241 Cologne and Stopper; $45.00
803 Comport, 5"; $16.00
803 Comport, 6"; $17.00
803 Comport and Cover, 5"; $23.00
825 Jelly; $18.00
825 Jelly and Cover; $25.00
317 Jug, Cut Neck; $95.00
317½ Jug and Cover; $125.00
1852/6 Jug; $95.00
303/7 Jug; $95.00
4087 Marmalade and Cover; $28.00

2138 Mayonnaise, Plate, Ladle; $45.00
803 Nappy, 5"; $12.00
803 Nappy, 6"; $14.00
803 Nappy, 7"; $15.00
803 Nappy and Cover, 5"; $20.00
1465 Oil, 5 oz., Cut Neck; $30.00
1465 Oil, 7 oz., Cut Neck; $30.00
840 Plate, 5", Tumbler; $5.00
2283 Plate, 8¼"; $6.00
2283 Plate, 11"; $9.00
2263 Salt, Individual; $14.00
2235 Shaker, FGT or Pearl Top; $15.00
1480 Sugar and Cream; $28.00
2194 Syrup, 8 oz., Nickel Top; $37.00
2194 Syrup, 12 oz., Nickel Top; $42.00
2209 Vase, 9"; $35.00

TRELLIS

Cutting 169

1923 – 1927

766 Bon Bon; $18.00
766 Bowl, Finger, and Plate; $18.00
810 Bowl, Finger, and Plate; $18.00
2250 Candy Jar and Cover, ¼ pound; $22.00
2250 Candy Jar and Cover, ½ pound; $26.00
2250 Candy Jar and Cover, pound; $30.00
1697 Carafe; $24.00
4023 Carafe Tumbler; $6.00
5078 Comport, 5"; $16.00
5078 Comport and Cover, 5"; $23.00
5078 Comport, 6"; $17.00
5078 Comport and Cover, 6"; $25.00
300 Decanter, Quart, Cut Neck; $28.00
825 Jelly; $18.00
825 Jelly and Cover; $25.00
303/7 Jug; $95.00
724/7 Jug; $85.00
1787/3 Jug; $45.00
2270 Jug; $95.00
2270 Jug and Cover; $125.00
1968 Marmalade and Cover; $28.00
810 Mayonnaise Set, 3-piece; $45.00
1831 Mustard and Cover; $24.00

5078 Nappy, 5"; $12.00
5078 Nappy and Cover, 5"; $20.00
5078 Nappy, 6"; $14.00
5078 Nappy and Cover, 6"; $20.00
5078 Nappy, 7"; $16.00
5078 Nappy and Cover, 7"; $24.00
5078 Nappy, 8"; $18.00
5078 Nappy and Cover, 8"; $25.00
1465 Oil, 5 oz., CN, Polished Stopper; $30.00
1465 Oil, 7 oz., CN, Polished Stopper; $30.00
2283 Plate, 5"; $4.00
840 Plate, 5"; $4.00
2283 Plate, 6"; $4.00
2283 Plate, 7"; $4.00
1897 Plate, 7"; $4.00
2283 Plate, 8"; $5.00
2238 Plate 8½"; $5.00
1848 Plate, 9", Cut Matt Star; $6.00
2235 Shaker, FGT; $15.00
2235 Shaker, Pearl Top; $18.00
1851 Sugar and Cream; $28.00
2194 Syrup, 8 oz.; $37.00
2276 Vanity Set; $38.00

Trellis Pattern, Cutting No. 169

No. 1968 Marmalade and Cover.

No. 1831 Mustard and Cover.

No. 810-3 Piece Mayonnaise Set.

No. 1697. 2 Piece Bed Room Set.

No. 300. Quart Decanter, C/N.

No. 5078 – 6 in. Nappy.

No. 766 BonBon.

No. 5078 – 6 in. Comport.

CYNTHIA

Cutting 170

1924 – 1927

Stemware is featured in *Fostoria Stemware,* pages 18 and 19.

880 Bon Bon; $18.00
1769 Bowl, Finger, and Plate; $18.00
2250 Candy Jar and Cover, ¼ pound; $20.00
2250 Candy Jar and Cover, ½ pound; $26.00
2250 Candy Jar and Cover, pound; $30.00
1697 Carafe; $24.00
4023 Carafe Tumbler, 6 oz.; $6.00
5078 Comport, 5"; $16.00
5078 Comport, 6"; $17.00
300 Decanter, 2 Quart, Cut Neck; $28.00
825 Jelly; $18.00
825 Jelly and Cover; $25.00
2270 Jug; $95.00
2270 Jug and Cover (Cover not cut); $125.00
303/3 Jug; $45.00
1852/6 Jug; $65.00
724/7 Jug, Tankard; $95.00

4087 Marmalade and Cover; $28.00
1769 Mayonnaise, Plate, Ladle; $45.00
5078 Nappy, 5"; $12.00
5078 Nappy, 6"; $14.00
5078 Nappy and Cover, 5"; $20.00
5078 Nappy and Cover, 6"; $20.00
1465 Oil, 5 oz., Cut Neck; $30.00
1465 Oil, 7 oz., Cut Neck; $30.00
2283 Plate, 6"; $4.00
1897 Plate, 7"; $4.00
2337 Plate, 7"; $4.00
2337 Plate, 8"; $8.00
2238 Plate, 8¼" Salad; $5.00
1848 Plate, 9" Sandwich; $7.00
2235 Shaker, FGT or Pearl Top; $16.00
2133 Sugar and Cream; $28.00

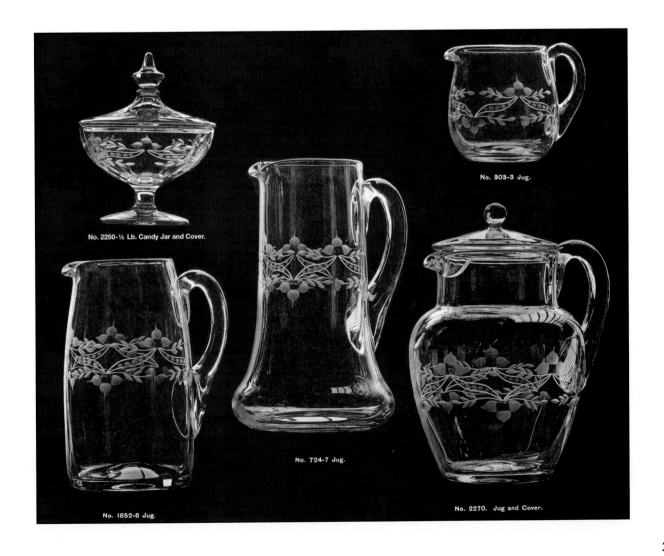

No. 2250-½ Lb. Candy Jar and Cover.

No. 303-3 Jug.

No. 724-7 Jug.

No. 1852-6 Jug.

No. 2270. Jug and Cover.

AIRDALE

Cutting 175

1924 – 1927
Stemware is featured in *Fostoria Stemware*, pages 35 and 36.

880 Almond; $14.00
880 Bon Bon; $18.00
1769 Bowl, Finger, and 2283 Plate; $18.00
1697 Carafe; $24.00
4023 Carafe Tumbler, 6 oz.; $6.00
803 Comport, 5"; $16.00
1195 Decanter, Large, Cut Neck; $28.00
2040/3 Jug; $45.00
303/7 Jug; $95.00
803 Nappy, 5" Footed; $14.00

803 Nappy, 6" Footed; $14.00
701 Plate, 5" Tumbler; $4.00
2283 Plate, 7"; $5.00
2238 Plate, 11"; $10.00
2263 Salt, Individual; $14.00
2235 Shaker, FGT; $16.00
1712 Sugar and Cream; $28.00
2287 Tray, Lunch; $18.00
4069 Vase, Cut 175½; $35.00

No. 803 – 5 in. Nappy.

No. 880 – Bon Bon.

No. 2040/3. Jug.

KENMORE

Cutting 176

Crystal unless otherwise noted.
Stemware is featured in *Fostoria Stemware*, page 64.

4095 Almond, Blue Foot, 1926; $26.00
1769 Bowl, Finger, and 1499 Plate, 1925-1926; $24.00
4095 Bowl, Footed Finger, Blue Foot, 1926-1927; $26.00
4095 Candy Jar and Cover, Blue Foot, 1926-1927; $45.00
1693½ Coaster, 3½", 1925; $7.00
303/7 Jug, 1925-1926; $95.00
2082/7 Jug, 1925-1926; $95.00
4095/7 Jug, Blue Foot, 1926-1927; $135.00
2315 Mayonnaise, Plate, 1925-1926; $18.00

2283 Plate, 6", Blue, 1926-1927; $10.00
2283 Plate, 8", Blue, 1926-1927; $12.00
2337 Plate, 7", 1925-1926; $8.00
2337 Plate, 8", 1925-1926; $8.00
2316 Plate, 8" Soup, Blue, 1926; $12.00
2283 Plate, 13", 1925-1926; $22.00
2315 Sugar and Cream, 1925-1926; $30.00
2287 Tray, Lunch, 1926-1927; $21.00

LYNN

Cutting 180

1925 – 1926

Stemware is featured in *Fostoria Stemware*, page 65.

1769 Bowl, Finger, and 2283 Plate; $18.00
2327 Compote, 7"; $15.00
2040/3 Jug; $45.00
2082/7 Jug; $85.00
2315 Mayonnaise and Plate; $20.00

2222 Plate, 7"; $4.00
2222 Plate, 8"; $4.00
2222 Plate, 10"; $7.00
2315 Sugar and Cream; $28.00

Amber Arbor 2327 Comport; Orchid Arvida 5097 Goblets, 5000 Jug

ARBOR

Cutting 184

1926 – 1927

Amber, Blue, and Green

Stemware is featured in *Fostoria Stemware*, page 31.

869 Bowl, Finger, and 2283 Plate; $25.00
2297 Bowl, 10" Shallow "A"; $30.00
2324 Bowl, 10" Footed; $35.00
2297 Bowl, 12" Deep "A"; $35.00
2324 Candlestick, 4"; $14.00
2324 Candlestick, 9"; $22.00
2331 Candy Box and Cover; $35.00
2250 Candy Jar and Cover; $30.00
2329 Centerpiece, 11"; $30.00
2329 Centerpiece, 13"; $35.00
2327 Comport, 7"; $30.00

5000 Jug; $135.00
2283 Plate, 7"; $9.00
2283 Plate, 8"; $9.00
2283 Plate, 13"; $20.00
2315 Sugar and Cream; $35.00
2287 Tray, Handled Lunch; $21.00
2276 Vanity Set; $45.00
2292 Vase, 8"; $38.00
4100 Vase, 8"; $38.00
2324 Vase, Small Urn; $40.00

"ARBOR" PATTERN, CUTTING No. 184.
MADE IN AMBER, BLUE AND GREEN.
PRICED PAGE 23 — No. 2 SUPPLEMENT PRICE LIST.

2250—¼ lb. Candy Jar and Cover

2331—3 Candy Box and Cover.

No. 2287—11 in. Hld. Lunch Tray.

No. 2327—7 in. Comport.

No. 2324—4 in. Candle.

No. 2329—11 in. Centerpiece.
No. 2309—3¾ in. Flower Block.

No. 2324—4 in. Candle.

ARVIDA
Cutting 185

1927
Amber, Green, Blue, and Orchid

In the picture on the preceding page, the 5000 Jug and two 5097 Goblets are shown in Orchid with the Arvida cutting. The Orchid color comes alive when cut, and this jug is a favorite of the authors. As far as we know, neither the jug nor the goblets were ever listed as production items; still, they do exist, one more proof that no one can ever know everything about this remarkable company.

2315 Bowl "A", 10½" Footed; $35.00
2297 Bowl "A", 12" Deep; $35.00
2372 Candle Block, 2"; $18.00
2374 Candlestick, 4"; $22.00
2331 Candy Box and Cover; $40.00
2329 Centerpiece, 11"; $32.00
2329 Centerpiece, 13"; $38.00
2371 Centerpiece, 13" Oval; $38.00
2368 Cheese and Plate; $35.00
2327 Comport, 7"; $32.00
2362 Comport, 11½"; $36.00
2378 Ice Bucket, NP Handle; $38.00
2378 Ice Bucket, NP Handle, Drainer, Tongs; $48.00

2350 Plate, 13"; $27.00
2287 Tray, Handled Lunch; $28.00
4100 Vase, 6"; $34.00
4100 Vase, 8"; $40.00
4100 Vase, 10"; $45.00
4100 Vase, 12"; $52.00
4103 Vase, 3"; $18.00
4103 Vase, 4"; $24.00
4103 Vase, 5"; $26.00
4103 Vase, 6"; $30.00
4103 Vase, 7"; $34.00
4103 Vase, 9"; $38.00
2269 Vase, 7"; $37.00
2269 Vase, 9"; $45.00

THELMA

Cutting 186

1928
Amber, Green, Rose, and Orchid

2297 Bowl "A", 12" Deep; $35.00
2342 Bowl "A", 12½" Deep; $40.00
2362 Bowl, 12½"; $45.00
2362 Candlestick, 3" (pair); $45.00
2324 Candlestick, 4" (pair); $45.00
2331 Candy Box and Cover; $40.00
2329 Centerpiece, 11"; $34.00
2329 Centerpiece, 13"; $38.00
2368 Cheese and Cracker; $37.00
2327 Comport, 7"; $35.00
2378 Ice Bucket, NP Handle; $38.00

2378 Sugar Pail, NP Handle; $85.00
2287 Tray, 11" Handled Lunch; $28.00
2342 Tray, 12" Handled Lunch; $30.00
4103 Vase, 4", Optic; $27.00
4103 Vase, 5", Optic; $28.00
4103, Vase, 6", Optic; $32.00
4100 Vase, 6", Optic; $32.00
4100 Vase, 8", Optic; $40.00
2369 Vase, 7", Optic; $38.00
2369 Vase, 9", Optic; $47.00

BERRY

Cutting 188

1928
Rose and Green

869 Bowl, Finger, and 2283 Plate; $28.00
2342 Bowl "A", 12"; $40.00
2394 Bowl, 12"; $45.00
2394 Candlestick, 2" (pair); $45.00
2324 Candlestick, 4" (pair); $45.00
2331 Candy Box and Cover; $40.00
2329 Centerpiece, 11"; $34.00
2329 Centerpiece, 13"; $38.00
2368 Cheese and Cracker; $37.00
2400 Comport; $35.00
2378 Ice Bucket, NP Handle; $38.00
5000 Jug; $150.00
2315 Mayonnaise and Plate; $35.00
2394 Mint; $16.00
2283 Plate, 7"; $9.00
2283 Plate, 8"; $9.00
2315 Plate, 13"; $27.00
2350½ Sugar and Cream; $37.00
2378 Sugar Pail, NP Handle, $85.00
2342 Tray, Handled Lunch; $30.00
4103 Vase, 6", Optic; $32.00

4105 Vase, 6", Optic; $32.00
4105 Vase, 8", Optic; $42.00
4100 Vase, 8", Optic; $42.00
2369 Vase, 7", Optic; $38.00
2369 Vase, 9", Optic; $47.00
2373 Vase, Small Window and Cover; $95.00
2373 Vase, Large Window and Cover; $125.00
2378 Whip Cream Pail, NP Handle; $85.00

Amber Berry 2297 12" Bowl "A" (Variation)

KINGSLEY

Cutting 192
1929
Crystal, Rose, and Azure unless noted.
Stemware included the 877 Goblet, High Sherbet, Low Sherbet, Parfait, Wine, and Cocktail in Crystal only. Stemware shapes are shown in *Fostoria Stemware*, page 33.

869 Bowl, Finger, 2283 Plate, 6"; $28.00
  (Crystal only)
2297 Bowl "A", 12" Deep; $35.00

2342 Bowl, "A", 12"; $35.00
2375 Candlestick, 3" (pair); $45.00
2324 Candlestick, 4" (pair); $45.00

2331 Candy Box and Cover; $40.00
2329 Centerpiece, 11"; $34.00
2329 Centerpiece, 13" ; $38.00
   (Not made in Azure)
2368 Cheese and Cracker; $37.00
2400 Comport, 6"; $30.00
2400 Comport, 8"; $38.00
2378 Ice Bucket, NP Handle; $38.00
2315 Mayonnaise, 2332 Plate; $35.00

2283 Plate, 7" (Crystal only); $7.00
2283 Plate, 8" (Crystal only); $8.00
2342 Tray, Handled Lunch; $30.00
2373 Vase, Small Window and Cover; $95.00
2373 Vase, Large Window and Cover; $125.00
2369 Vase, 7"; $38.00
2369 Vase, 9"; $47.00
2292 Vase, 8"; $45.00
4105 Vase, 8"; $45.00

ORLEANS

Cutting 194

1929
Topaz and Azure

2375 Bon Bon; $22.00
2375 Bowl, Large Dessert; $35.00
2395 Bowl, 10"; $75.00
2375 Bowl, 12"; $57.00
2394 Bowl, 12"; $60.00
2394 Candlestick, 2" (pair); $47.00
2375 Candlestick, 3" (pair); $47.00
2395½ Candlestick, 5" (pair); $55.00
2394 Candy Jar and Cover, ½ pound; $95.00
2395 Candy Jar and Cover, Oval Confection; $95.00

2368 Cheese and Cracker; $38.00
2400 Comport, 6"; $30.00
2375 Ice Bucket, NP Handle; $38.00
2375 Lemon Dish; $22.00
2375 Plate, 10" Cake; $45.00
2375 Sweetmeat; $24.00
2375 Tray, Handled Lunch; $30.00
2417 Vase, 8", Optic; $48.00
4105 Vase, 8", Optic; $45.00

MILLEFLEUR

Cutting 195

Crystal unless otherwise noted.
The only cutting during this period which was a complete dinner service.
Stemware is featured in *Fostoria Stemware*, pages 57 – 59.

2350½ Cup, 1929-1934; $12.00
2350 Cup, After Dinner, and 2419 Saucer, 1929-1934; $24.00
4020 Jug
   Crystal, 1929-1934; $195.00
   Ebony Base, 1929-1934; $225.00
2350 Plate, 6", 1929-1934; $10.00
2350 Plate, 7", 1929-1934; $12.00
2350 Plate, 9", 1929-1934; $16.00

2419 Plate, 6", 1929-1934; $10.00
2419 Plate, 7", 1929-1939; $10.00
2419 Plate, 8", 1929-1939; $12.00
2350 Saucer, 1929-1934; $10.00
2419 Saucer, 1929-1934; $10.00
4020 Sugar and Cream
   Crystal, 1929-1934; $30.00
   Ebony Base, 1929-1934; $35.00

LATTICE

Cutting 196

1929
Stemware is featured in *Fostoria Stemware*, page 33.

869 Bowl, Finger, and 2283 Plate; $22.00
2394 Bowl, 12"; $45.00
2394 Candlestick, 2" (pair); $45.00

2283 Plate, 6"; $9.00
2283 Plate, 7"; $10.00
2283 Plate, 8"; $10.00

CHATTERIS

Cutting 197

1929 – 1930

Stemware is featured in *Fostoria Stemware*, page 33.

869 Bowl, Finger, and 2283 Plate, 6"; $22.00
2394 Bowl, 12"; $45.00
2394 Candlestick, 2" (pair); $45.00
2324 Candlestick, 4" (pair); $45.00
2329 Centerpiece, 11"; $30.00
2375 Cheese and Cracker; $35.00
2400 Comport, 6"; $22.00
2378 Ice Bucket, NP Handle; $35.00
2315 Mayonnaise and Plate; $25.00

2283 Plate, 6"; $6.00
2283 Plate, 7"; $7.00
2283 Plate, 8"; $8.00
2350½ Sugar and Cream; $30.00
2375 Tray, Handled Lunch; $24.00
2369 Vase, 7"; $38.00
2417 Vase, 8"; $45.00
4105 Vase, 8"; $45.00

WARWICK

Cutting 198

1929 – 1932

Stemware is featured in *Fostoria Stemware*, page 38.

890 Bowl, Finger, and 2283 Plate, 6"; $22.00
2430 Bowl, 11"; $40.00
2394 Bowl, 12"; $45.00
2394 Candlestick, 2" (pair); $45.00
2430 Candy Jar and Cover, ½ pound; $35.00
2400 Comport, 6"; $22.00
2400 Comport, 8"; $28.00
2350½ Cream Soup and Plate; $30.00
2375 Ice Bucket, NP Handle; $35.00
2430 Jelly, 7"; $16.00
890 Jug; $135.00
2430 Mint, 5½"; $15.00

2283 Plate, 7"; $7.00
2283 Plate, 8"; $8.00
2283 Plate, 13"; $22.00
2350 Plate, 10"; $18.00
2419 Plate, 6"; $6.00
2419 Plate, 7"; $7.00
2419 Plate, 8"; $8.00
2350½ Sugar and Cream; $30.00
2375 Tray, Handled Lunch; $24.00
2417 Vase, 8"; $35.00
2430 Vase, 8"; $35.00
4105 Vase, 8"; $35.00

FORMAL GARDEN

Cutting 700

1930

Same pieces as Tapestry except 4020 Finger Bowl also made with an Ebony base.

TAPESTRY

Cutting 701

1930

Stemware for both Formal Garden and Tapestry is featured in *Fostoria Stemware*, pages 57 – 59.

4020 Bowl, Finger; $24.00
2350½ Cup, Footed; $16.00
2350 Cup, After Dinner; $18.00
2419 Plate, 6"; $6.00

2419 Plate, 7"; $7.00
2419 Plate, 8"; $8.00
2419 Saucer; $6.00
2419 Saucer, After Dinner; $6.00

COMET

Cutting 702

Stemware is featured in *Fostoria Stemware*, pages 57 – 59.

4021 Bowl, Finger
    Crystal, 1931-1942; $22.00
4020 Jug
    Crystal, 1931-1934; $175.00
    Ebony Base, 1931-1932; $200.00
    Green Base, 1934; $225.00
2419 Plate, 6"
    Crystal, 1931-1942; $6.00
2419 Plate, 7"
    Crystal, 1931-1942; $7.00
2419 Plate, 8"

    Crystal, 1931-1942; $8.00
2419 Cup and Saucer
    Crystal, 1931-1942; $18.00
2419 Cup and Saucer, After Dinner
    Crystal, 1931-1932; $26.00
4020 Sugar and Cream
    Crystal, 1931-1932; $35.00
    Ebony Base, 1931-1932; $40.00
2430 Vase, 8"
    Crystal, 1931-1932; $75.00

NEW YORKER

Cutting 703

Stemware is featured in *Fostoria Stemware*, pages 57 – 59.

4021 Bowl, Finger
    Crystal, 1930-1943; $20.00
    Green Base, 1930-1932; $24.00
    Ebony Base, 1934; $24.00
4020 Decanter
    Crystal, 1930-1932; $95.00
    Green Base, 1930-1932; $125.00
4020 Jug
    Crystal, 1930-1934; $150.00

    Green Base, 1930-1932; $225.00
    Ebony Base, 1934; $200.00
2419 Plate, 6", 1930-1943; $6.00
2419 Plate, 7", 1930-1943; $7.00
2419 Plate, 8", 1930-1943; $8.00
4020 Sugar and Cream
    Crystal, 1930-1932; $34.00
    Green Base, 1930-1932; $45.00

ROYAL GARDEN

Cutting 704

1931 – 1932
Crystal and Topaz

2430 Bowl, 11"; $45.00
2394 Bowl "A", 12"; $45.00
2433 Bowl "A", 12"; $60.00
2394 Candlestick, 2" (pair); $45.00
2433 Candlestick, 3" (pair); $55.00
2430 Candlestick, 9½" (pair); $115.00
2447 Candlestick, Duo (pair); $75.00
2430 Candy Jar and Cover, ½ pound; $55.00

2433 Comport, 6" Tall; $75.00
2443 Ice Tub, 6"; $45.00
2375 Plate, 10" Cake; $50.00
2419 Tray, Handled Lunch; $54.00
2430 Vase, 8"; $78.00
4107 Vase, 12"; $115.00
4108 Vase, 6"; $50.00

BARCELONA

Cutting 705
1931 – 1932
Rose and Azure

2375 Bon Bon; $18.00
2394 Bowl, 6"; $18.00

2375 Bowl, Large Dessert; $25.00
2297 Bowl "A", 12"; $40.00

BARCELONA DESIGN

Cutting No. 705　　　　　　　　　　　　　　Priced on page 57—1931 Price List

Made in Solid Rose—Solid Azure

1.	2297	12-in. Bowl "A"	7.	2394	6-in. Bowl	12.	2375	Bon Bon
2.	2324	4-in. Candlestick	8.	2375	7-in. Comport	13.	2375	Sweetmeat
3.	4100	8-in. Vase	9.	2331-3	Candy Box and Cover	14.	2375	Whip Cream
4.	2430	8-in. Vase	10.	2375	Large Dessert	15.	2375½	Footed Sugar
5.	2287	11-in. Handled Lunch Tray	11.	2375	10-in. Cake Plate	16.	2375½	Footed Cream
6.	2430	7-in. Jelly	11.	2375	Lemon Dish			

ROYAL GARDEN DESIGN

Cutting No. 704　　　　　　　　　　　　　　Priced on page 57—1931 Price List

Made in Solid Crystal—Solid Topaz

1.	2433	12-in. Bowl "A"	6.	2394	12-in. Bowl "A"	11.	4108	6-in. Vase
2.	2433	3-in. Candlestick	7.	2394	2-in. Candlestick	12.	2430	8-in. Vase
3.	2433	6-in. Tall Comport	8.	2443	6-in. Ice Tub	13.	2419	Handled Lunch Tray
4.	2430	11-in. Bowl	9.	2447	Duo Candlestick	14.	2375	10-in. Cake Plate
5.	2430	9½-in. Candlestick	10.	4107	12-in. Vase	15.	2430	½-lb. Candy Jar and Cover

BARCELONA

ROYAL GARDEN

2324 Candlestick, 4" (pair); $28.00
2331 Candy Box and Cover; $35.00
2375 Comport, 7"; $25.00
2430 Jelly, 7"; $18.00
2375 Lemon Dish; $18.00
2375 Plate, 10" Cake; $50.00

2375½ Sugar and Cream; $62.00
2375 Sweetmeat; $20.00
2287 Tray, 11" Handled Lunch; $55.00
2430 Vase, 8"; $95.00
4100 Vase, 8"; $90.00
2375 Whip Cream; $20.00

YORK

Cutting 709

1933 – 1943
Stemware is featured in *Fostoria Stemware*, page 77.

2470 Bowl, 12"; $38.00
2470 Candlestick, 5½" (pair); $45.00
2470 Comport, 6"; $35.00
2451 Ice Dish and Plate; $28.00

2283 Plate, 7"; $7.00
2283 Plate, 8"; $8.00
2470 Plate, 10" Cake; $34.00
2440 Plate, 13" Torte; $35.00

STAUNTON

Cutting 707

Same dates and pieces as Nairn.

NAIRN

Cutting 708

1933 – 1943
Stemware is featured in *Fostoria Stemware*, page 75.

2470½ Bowl, 10½"; $40.00
2470½ Candlestick, 5½" (pair); $45.00
2451 Ice Dish and Plate; $28.00

2283 Plate, 7"; $7.00
2283 Plate, 8"; $8.00

BRISTOL

Cutting 710

1933 – 1938
Same pieces as Inverness. Stemware is featured in *Fostoria Stemware*, page 77.

INVERNESS

Cutting 711

1933 – 1935
Stemware is featured in *Fostoria Stemware*, page 77.

2470 Bowl, 12"; $38.00
2470 Candlestick, 5½" (pair); $45.00
2470 Comport, 6"; $42.00
2451 Ice Dish and Plate; $28.00

2337 Plate, 7"; $7.00
2337 Plate, 8"; $8.00
2470 Plate, 10" Cake; $34.00
2440 Plate, 13" Torte; $35.00

WATERBURY

Cutting 712

1933 – 1943

Stemware is featured in *Fostoria Stemware*, page 72.

2424 Bowl, 8" Regular; $25.00
2451 Ice Dish and Plate; $28.00
2453 Lustre, 7½" (pair); $125.00

2283 Plate, 7"; $7.00
2283 Plate, 8"; $8.00

EATON

Cutting 713

1933 – 1938

Stemware is featured in *Fostoria Stemware*, page 77.

2470 Bon Bon; $18.00
2470½ Bowl, 10½"; $40.00
2481 Bowl, 11" Oblong; $40.00
2481 Candlestick, 5" (pair) $45.00
2470½ Candlestick, 5½" (pair); $45.00
2472 Candlestick, Duo (pair); $60.00
2451 Ice Dish, Liner, and Plate; $42.00
2470 Lemon Dish; $18.00

2337 Plate, 6"; $6.00
2337 Plate, 7"; $7.00
2337 Plate, 8"; $8.00
2470 Plate, 13" Torte; $35.00
2419 Relish, 4-part; $26.00
2440 Sugar and Cream; $34.00
2470 Sweetmeat; $20.00
2440 Vase, 7"; $65.00

OXFORD

Cutting 714

1933 – 1943

Stemware is featured in *Fostoria Stemware*, page 77.

2470½ Bowl, 10½"; $40.00
2470½ Candlestick, 5½" (pair); $45.00
2482 Candlestick, Trindle (pair); $75.00
2430 Candy Jar and Cover, ½ pound; $54.00
2400 Comport, 6"; $27.00
2451 Ice Dish, Liner, and Plate; $42.00

2337 Plate, 7"; $7.00
2337 Plate, 8"; $8.00
2440 Plate, 13" Torte; $35.00
2419 Relish, 5-part; $35.00
2440 Sugar and Cream; $34.00
2467 Vase, 7½"; $75.00

CARLISLE

Cutting 715

1933 – 1934 except where noted.

Stemware is featured in *Fostoria Stemware*, page 78.

2470 Bon Bon; $18.00
2470½ Bowl, 10½", 1933-1935; $40.00
2481 Bowl, 11" Oblong; $40.00
2481 Candlestick, 5" (pair); $45.00
2470½ Candlestick, 5½", 1933-1935 (pair); $45.00
2451 Ice Dish, Liner, and Plate; $42.00
2470 Lemon Dish; $18.00
2283 Plate, 7", $7.00

2283 Plate, 8"; $8.00
2470 Plate, Cake; $34.00
2440 Plate, 13" Torte, 1933-1935; $35.00
2419 Relish, 5-part; $35.00
2440 Sugar and Cream; $34.00
2470 Sweetmeat; $20.00
4107 Vase, 9"; $95.00

CANTERBURY

Cutting 716

1933 – 1935 except where noted.
Stemware is featured in *Fostoria Stemware*, page 78.

2470½ Bowl, 10½"; $40.00
2470½ Candlestick, 5½" (pair); $45.00
2482 Candlestick, Trindle (pair); $75.00
2430 Candy and Cover, ½ pound, 1933-1934; $54.00
2400 Comport, 6", 1933-1934; $27.00
2451 Ice Dish, Liner, and Plate, 1933-1934; $42.00
2283 Plate, 7"; $7.00

2283 Plate, 8"; $8.00
2364 Plate, 16" Torte; $48.00
2419 Relish, 4-part; $26.00
2440 Sugar and Cream, 1933-1934; $34.00
2467 Vase, 7½", 1933-1934; $75.00
4017 Vase, 9"; $95.00

MARLBORO

Cutting 717

1933 – 1938

Stemware is featured in *Fostoria Stemware*, page 78.

2470 Bon Bon; $18.00
869 Bowl, Finger, and Plate; $20.00
2470½ Bowl, 10½"; $40.00
2470½ Candlestick, 5½" (pair); $45.00
2472 Candlestick, Duo (pair); $60.00
2482 Candlestick, Trindle (pair); $75.00
2400 Comport, 6"; $27.00
2451 Ice Dish, Liner and Plate; $42.00
2470 Lemon Dish; $18.00

2470 Plate, Cake; $34.00
2337 Plate, 7"; $7.00
2337 Plate, 8"; $8.00
2364 Plate, 16" Torte; $48.00
2440 Sugar and Cream; $34.00
2470 Sweetmeat; $20.00
2440 Vase, 7"; $75.00
4102 Vase, 9"; $95.00

Doncaster through Westminster had the same pieces with exceptions noted.
Stemware for all patterns is featured in *Fostoria Stemware*, pages 79 – 80.

DONCASTER

Cutting 718

1933 – 1943
Did not have 2470 Vase or 4110 Vase.

LANCASTER

Cutting 719

1933 – 1935
Did not have a 2440 Torte, 2470 Vase or 4112 Vase.

NOTTINGHAM

Cutting 720

1933 – 1934
Did not have a 2440 Torte, 4110 Vase or 4112 Vase.

BUCKINGHAM

Cutting 721

1933 – 1934

Did not have a 2440 Torte, 2470 Vase or 4110 Vase.

WELLINGTON

Cutting 722

1933 – 1942

Did not have a 2470 Vase or 4112 Vase.

LEICESTER

Cutting 722½

1933 – 1934

Did not have a 2470 Vase or 4112 Vase.

WESTMINSTER

Cutting 723

1933 – 1938

Did not have a 2440 Torte, 4110 Vase or 4112 Vase.

869 Bowl, Finger; $12.00
2470½ Bowl, 10½"; $45.00
2470½ Candlestick, 5½" (pair); $45.00
2400 Comport, 6"; $27.00
2337 Plate, 6"; $6.00
2337 Plate, 7"; $7.00

2337 Plate, 8"; $8.00
2440 Plate, 13" Torte; $35.00
2470 Vase, 10"; $95.00
4110 Vase, 7½"; $75.00
4112 Vase, 8½"; $85.00

Manhattan through Marquette contained the same pieces except as noted.
Stemware for all patterns is featured in *Fostoria Stemware*, page 60.

MANHATTAN

Cutting 725

1933 – 1938

Did not have a 4024 Bowl, 4024 Candlestick, 6011 Decanter, or 6011 Jug.

METEOR

Cutting 726

1933 – 1939

NATIONAL

Cutting 727

1933 – 1943

EMBASSY

Cutting 728

1933 – 1937

An 11" Plate (2337) was also offered in this pattern.

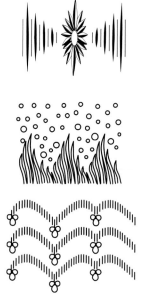

SEAWEED

Cutting 732

1934 – 1935

MARQUETTE

Cutting 733

1934 – 1935

869 Bowl, Finger; $12.00
4024 Bowl, 10" Footed; $30.00
4024 Candlestick, 6" (pair); $35.00
4024 Comport, 5"; $20.00
6011 Decanter; $135.00

6011 Jug; $155.00
2337 Plate, 6"; $6.00
2337 Plate, 7"; $7.00
2337 Plate, 8"; $8.00

The following patterns all contained the pieces listed for Shooting Stars.
Stemware is shown in *Fostoria Stemware*, pages 81 and 82.

ROCKET

Cutting 729

1934 – 1943

WHIRLPOOL

Cutting 730

1934 – 1939

CELESTIAL

Cutting 731

1934 – 1939

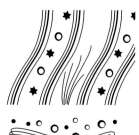

PLANET

Cutting 734

1934 – 1935

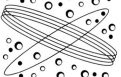

SHOOTING STARS

Cutting 735
1934 – 1935

1769 Bowl, Finger; $14.00
4024 Bowl, 10" Footed; $35.00
4024 Candlestick, 6" (pair); $45.00
6011 Decanter; $155.00

6011 Jug; $195.00
2337 Plate, 6"; $6.00
2337 Plate, 7"; $7.00
2337 Plate, 8"; $8.00

DIRECTOIRE

Cutting 736

1934 – 1939
Stemware is featured in *Fostoria Stemware*, pages 81 and 82.

1769 Bowl, Finger; $14.00
4024 Bowl, 10" Footed; $30.00
4024 Candlestick, 6" (pair); $35.00
4117 Candy Jar and Cover; $67.00
2525 Cocktail Shaker; $95.00
2525 Decanter; $80.00
6011 Decanter; $95.00

2337 Plate, 6"; $6.00
2337 Plate, 7"; $7.00
2337 Plate, 8"; $8.00
2337 Plate, 11"; $20.00
2235 Shaker, FGT (pair); $45.00
2350½ Sugar and Cream; $30.00

QUINFOIL

Cutting 737
1934 – 1937
Stemware is featured in *Fostoria Stemware*, pages 81 and 82.

319 Bar Bottle; $95.00
1769 Bowl, Finger; $14.00
4024 Bowl, 10" Footed; $30.00
4024 Candlestick, 6" (pair); $35.00
2518 Cocktail Shaker, 32 oz.; $84.00
2518½ Cocktail Shaker, 28 oz.; $75.00
2400 Comport, 6"; $27.00

2518 Decanter; $75.00
6011 Decanter; $95.00
6011 Jug; $185.00
2337 Plate, 6"; $6.00
2337 Plate, 7"; $7.00
2337 Plate, 8"; $8.00
2350½ Sugar and Cream; $30.00

FESTOON

Cutting 738
1935 – 1939

Stemware is featured in *Fostoria Stemware*, pages 83 and 84.

1769 Bowl, Finger; $14.00
2525 Cocktail Shaker; $95.00
2400 Comport, 6"; $27.00
2525 Decanter; $80.00
6011 Decanter; $95.00

6011 Jug; $185.00
2337 Plate, 6"; $6.00
2337 Plate, 7"; $7.00
2337 Plate, 8"; $8.00
2350½ Sugar and Cream; $30.00

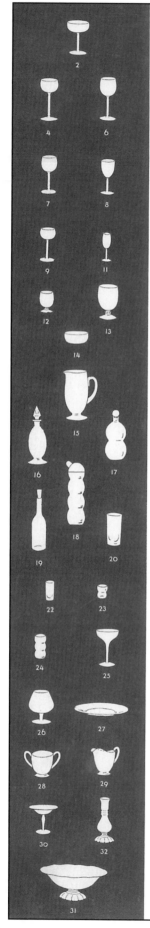

5   3   1   10   21

QUINFOIL DESIGN
CUTTING No. 737

1.	6011	10 oz. Goblet
2.	6011	5½ oz. Saucer Champagne
3.	6011	5½ oz. Low Sherbet
4.	6011	4½ oz. Rhine Wine
5.	6011	3 oz. Cocktail
6.	6011	4½ oz. Claret
7.	6011	3 oz. Wine
8.	6011	2 oz. Sherry
9.	6011	2 oz. Creme de Menthe
10.	6011	1 oz. Cordial
11.	6011	1 oz. Brandy
12.	6011	4 oz. Oyster Cocktail
13.	6011	13 oz. Footed Tumbler
13.	6011	10 oz. Footed Tumbler
13.	6011	5 oz. Footed Tumbler
13.	6011	2 oz. Footed Whiskey
14.	1769	Finger Bowl
15.	6011	Footed Jug
16.	6011	Footed Decanter
17.	2518	Decanter

18.	2518	38 oz. Cocktail Shaker
18.	2518½	28 oz. Cocktail Shaker
19.	319	Bar Bottle
20.	701	12 oz. Tumbler, Sham
20.	701	10 oz. Tumbler, Sham
21.	1185	Old Fashioned Cocktail, Sham
22.	4122	Whiskey, Sham
23.	2518	Whiskey
24.	2518	5 oz. Wine
25.	795	Hollow Stem Champagne
26.	906	Brandy Inhaler
27.	2337	6 in. Plate
27.	2337	7 in. Plate
27.	2337	8 in. Plate
28.	2350½	Footed Sugar
29.	2350½	Footed Cream
30.	2400	6 in. Comport
31.	4024	10 in. Footed Bowl
32.	4024	6 in. Candlestick

104

ROCK GARDEN

Cutting 739

1934 – 1943

Stemware is featured in *Fostoria Stemware*, pages 83 and 84.

319 Bar Bottle; $95.00
1769 Bowl, Finger; $14.00
4024 Bowl, 10" Footed; $30.00
4024 Candlestick, 6" (pair); $35.00
4117 Candy Jar and Cover; $67.00
2525 Cocktail Shaker; $95.00
2400 Comport, 6"; $27.00
2525 Decanter; $80.00
6011 Decanter; $95.00

6011 Jug; $185.00
2337 Plate, 6"; $6.00
2337 Plate, 7"; $7.00
2337 Plate, 8"; $8.00
2440 Plate, 13" Torte; $40.00
2364 Plate, 16" Torte; $48.00
2350½ Sugar and Cream; $35.00
2470 Vase, 10"; $95.00

RONDEAU

Cutting 740

July 1934 – 1935

Stemware is featured in *Fostoria Stemware*, pages 83 and 84.

1769 Bowl, Finger; $14.00
4024 Bowl, 10" Footed; $30.00
4024 Candlestick, 6" (pair); $35.00
4117 Candy Jar and Cover; $67.00
2525 Cocktail Shaker, 42 oz.; $95.00
2525½ Cocktail Shaker, 30 oz.; $85.00
2400 Comport, 6"; $27.00
2525 Decanter; $80.00

6011 Decanter; $95.00
6011 Jug; $185.00
2337 Plate, 6"; $6.00
2337 Plate, 7"; $7.00
2337 Plate, 8"; $8.00
2440 Plate, 13" Torte; $40.00
2470 Vase, 10"; $95.00

7　　　　　1　　　　　16　　　　　3

ROCK GARDEN DESIGN

CUTTING No. 739

ROCK CRYSTAL

1.	6012	10 oz. Goblet	18.	4122	1½ oz. Whiskey, Sham
2.	6012	5½ oz. Saucer Champagne	19.	6011	Footed Jug
3.	6012	5½ oz. Low Sherbet	20.	6011	Footed Decanter
4.	6012	4½ oz. Rhine Wine	21.	2525	Decanter
5.	6012	3 oz. Cocktail	22.	2525	42 oz. Cocktail Shaker
6.	6012	4½ oz. Claret	22.	2525½	30 oz. Cocktail Shaker
7.	6012	3 oz. Wine	23.	319	Bar Bottle
8.	6012	2 oz. Sherry	24.	2337	6 in. Plate
9.	6012	2 oz. Creme de Menthe	24.	2337	7 in. Plate
10.	6012	1 oz. Cordial	24.	2337	8 in. Plate
11.	6012	1 oz. Brandy	25.	2350½	Footed Sugar
12.	6012	4 oz. Footed Cocktail (Oyster)	26.	2350½	Footed Cream
13.	6012	13 oz. Footed Tumbler	27.	2400	6 in. Comport
13.	6012	10 oz. Footed Tumbler	28.	2364	16 in. Plate
13.	6012	5 oz. Footed Tumbler	29.	2440	13 in. Torte Plate
14.	1769	Finger Bowl	30.	4117	Bubble Candy Jar and Cover
15.	863	Hollow Stem Champagne	31.	4024	10 in. Footed Bowl
16.	701	12 oz. Tumbler, Sham	32.	4024	6 in. Candlestick
16.	701	10 oz. Tumbler, Sham	33.	2470	10 in. Vase
17.	1185	Old Fashioned Cocktail, Sham			

106

WATERCRESS

Cutting 741

July 1934 – 1943
Stemware is featured in *Fostoria Stemware*, pages 83 and 84.

319 Bar Bottle; $95.00
1769 Bowl, Finger; $14.00
4024 Bowl, 10" Footed; $30.00
2470½ Bowl, 10½"; $40.00
4024 Candlestick, 6" (pair); $35.00
2472 Candlestick, Duo (pair); $60.00
2496 Candlestick, Trindle (pair); $75.00
4117 Candy Jar and Cover, Bubble; $67.00
2524 Cocktail Mixer; $56.00
2525 Cocktail Shaker, 42 oz.; $95.00
2525½ Cocktail Shaker, 30 oz.; $80.00
2400 Comport, 6"; $27.00
2525 Decanter; $80.00
6011 Decanter; $95.00

6011 Jug; $185.00
2440 Lemon Dish; $18.00
2440 Mayonnaise, 2-part; $26.00
2337 Plate, 6"; $6.00
2337 Plate, 7"; $7.00
2337 Plate, 8"; $8.00
2440 Plate, 13" Torte; $40.00
2364 Plate, 16" Torte; $48.00
2440 Relish, 2-part; $24.00
2440 Relish, 3-part; $30.00
2350½ Sugar and Cream; $30.00
2440 Sweetmeat; $20.00
2440 Tray, 8½" Oval; $22.00
2470 Vase, 10"; $95.00

ORBIT

Cutting 742

July 1934 – 1936 except as noted.
Stemware is featured in *Fostoria Stemware*, pages 83 and 84.

319 Bar Bottle, July 1934 ; $125.00
1769 Bowl, Finger; $14.00
2525 Cocktail Shaker, July 1934; $125.00
2400 Comport, 6", July 1934; $30.00
2525 Decanter, 1934-1935; $80.00
6011 Decanter, 1934-1935; $95.00

6011 Jug; $185.00
2337 Plate, 6"; $6.00
2337 Plate, 7"; $7.00
2337 Plate, 8"; $8.00
2350½ Sugar and Cream, July 1934; $56.00

HERALDRY

Cutting 743

1935 – 1943
Heraldry was reintroduced in 1953.
Stemware is featured in *Fostoria Stemware*, pages 83 and 84.

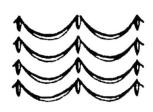

1769 Finger Bowl; $14.00
2400 Comport, 6"; $25.00
6011 Jug; $185.00

2337 Plate, 6"; $6.00
2337 Plate, 7"; $7.00
2337 Plate, 8"; $8.00

REGENCY

Cutting 744

1935 – 1943
Stemware is featured in *Fostoria Stemware*, pages 83 and 84.

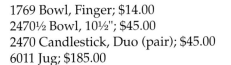

1769 Bowl, Finger; $14.00
2470½ Bowl, 10½"; $45.00
2470 Candlestick, Duo (pair); $45.00
6011 Jug; $185.00

2337 Plate, 6"; $6.00
2337 Plate, 7"; $7.00
2337 Plate, 8"; $8.00
2440 Plate, 13" Torte; $40.00

16   5   1   2

WATERCRESS DESIGN

CUTTING No. 741

ROCK CRYSTAL

1.	6012	10 oz. Goblet
2.	6012	5½ oz. Saucer Champagne
3.	6012	5½ oz. Low Sherbet
4.	6012	4½ oz. Rhine Wine
5.	6012	3 oz. Cocktail
6.	6012	4½ oz. Claret
7.	6012	3 oz. Wine
8.	6012	2 oz. Sherry
9.	6012	2 oz. Creme de Menthe
10.	6012	1 oz. Cordial
11.	6012	1 oz. Brandy
12.	6012	4 oz. Footed Cocktail (Oyster)
13.	6012	13 oz. Footed Tumbler
13.	6012	10 oz. Footed Tumbler
13.	6012	5 oz. Footed Tumbler
14.	1769	Finger Bowl
15.	863	Hollow Stem Champagne
16.	701	12 oz. Tumbler, Sham
16.	701	10 oz. Tumbler, Sham
17.	1185	Old Fashioned Cocktail, Sham
18.	4122	1½ oz. Whiskey, Sham
19.	6011	Footed Jug
20.	6011	Footed Decanter
21.	2525	Decanter
22.	2525	42 oz. Cocktail Shaker
22.	2525½	30 oz. Cocktail Shaker
23.	319	Bar Bottle
24.	2337	6 in. Plate
24.	2337	7 in. Plate
24.	2337	8 in. Plate
25.	2350½	Footed Sugar
26.	2350½	Footed Cream
27.	2364	16 in. Plate
28.	2440	13 in. Torte Plate
29.	2440	8½ in. Oval Tray
30.	2440	2 Part Mayonnaise
31.	2440	2 Part Handled Relish
32.	2440	3 Part Handled Relish
33.	2440	5 in. Handled Lemon
34.	2440	4½ in. Handled Sweetmeat
35.	2400	6 in. Comport
36.	4117	Bubble Candy Jar and Cover
37.	2524	Cocktail Mixer
38.	2496	Trindle Candlestick
39.	2472	Duo Candlestick
40.	2470½	10½ in. Bowl
41.	4024	10 in. Footed Bowl
42.	4024	6 in. Candlestick
43.	2470	10 in. Vase

108

IVY

Cutting 745

1935 – 1943

GOSSAMER

Cutting 746

1935 – 1939

Stemware for both patterns is featured in *Fostoria Stemware*, pages 83 and 84.

1769 Bowl, Finger; $14.00
2536 Bowl, 9" Handled; $45.00
2535 Candlestick, 5½" (pair); $45.00
2400 Comport, 6"; $27.00

6011 Jug; $185.00
2337 Plate, 6"; $6.00
2337 Plate, 7"; $7.00
2337 Plate, 8"; $8.00

FANTASY

Cutting 747

1935 – 1936
5000 Jug, 1935

ALLEGRO

Cutting 748

1935 – 1943

Stemware is featured in *Fostoria Stemware*, page 85.

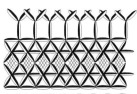

766 Bowl, Finger; $14.00
2533 Bowl, 9" Handled; $45.00
2533 Candlestick, Duo (pair); $50.00
6013 Comport, 5"; $32.00

5000 Jug; $185.00
2337 Plate, 6"; $6.00
2337 Plate, 7"; $7.00
2337 Plate, 8"; $8.00

CELEBRITY

Cutting 749

1935 – 1943 except where noted.
Stemware is featured in *Fostoria Stemware*, page 72.

869 Bowl, Finger; $12.00
2424 Bowl, 8" RO, 1935; $40.00
2481 Candlestick, 5", 1935 (pair) ; $45.00
5000 Jug, 1935 only; $200.00

2337 Plate, 6"; $6.00
2337 Plate, 7"; $7.00
2337 Plate, 8"; $8.00
2337 Plate, 11" Service, 1935 ; $30.00

HEIRLOOM

Cutting 751

1935 – 1938

2394 Bowl, 12"; $40.00
2447 Candlestick, Duo (pair); $55.00
2527 Candelabra, 2-light, UDP; (pair); $125.00
2440 Mayonnaise, 2-part; $28.00
2440 Plate, 13" Torte; $45.00
2364 Plate, 16"; $50.00

2440 Relish, 2-part; $24.00
2440 Relish, 3-part; $28.00
2514 Relish, 5-part; $67.00
2440 Sauce Dish, Oval; $28.00
2440 Tray, Oval; $24.00
2470 Vase, 10"; $95.00

2527
2 Lt. Candelabra, U. D. P.

2440—13 in. Torte Plate
2364—16 in. Plate

2470—10 in. Vase

2440—3 Part Relish

2447—Duo Candlestick

2394—12 in. Bowl

2440—2 Part Relish

2440—8½ in. Oval Tray

2440
6½-in. Oval Sauce Dish

2514—5 Part Relish

2440
2 Part Oval Mayonnaise

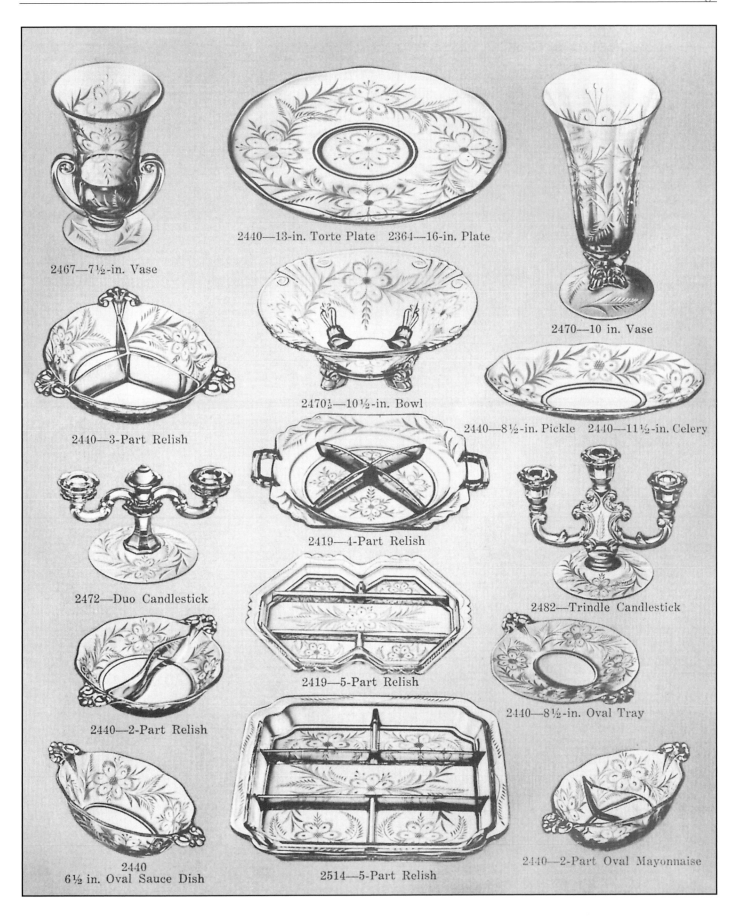

2467—7½-in. Vase

2440—13-in. Torte Plate   2364—16-in. Plate

2470½—10½-in. Bowl

2470—10 in. Vase

2440—3-Part Relish

2440—8½-in. Pickle   2440—11½-in. Celery

2472—Duo Candlestick

2419—4-Part Relish

2482—Trindle Candlestick

2440—2-Part Relish

2419—5-Part Relish

2440—8½-in. Oval Tray

2440
6½ in. Oval Sauce Dish

2514—5-Part Relish

2440—2-Part Oval Mayonnaise

EVANGELINE

Cutting 752

1935 – 1938

2470½ Bowl, 10½"; $45.00
2472 Candlestick, Duo (pair) $45.00
2482 Candlestick, Trindle (pair); $95.00
2440 Celery; $27.00
2440 Mayonnaise, 2-part; $28.00
2440 Pickle; $22.00
2440 Plate, Cake; $40.00
2440 Plate, 13" Torte; $45.00
2364 Plate, 16"; $50.00

2440 Relish, 2-part; $24.00
2440 Relish, 3-part; $28.00
2419 Relish, 4-part; $35.00
2419 Relish, 5-part; $60.00
2514 Relish, 5-part; $67.00
2440 Sauce, 6½" Oval; $28.00
2440 Tray, 8½" Oval; $24.00
2467 Vase, 7½"; $72.00
2470 Vase, 10"; $95.00

The following patterns had the same pieces as Weylin except as noted.
Stemware for these patterns is featured in *Fostoria Stemware*, pages 86 – 88.

CAVENDISH

Cutting 754

1935 – 1939
Did not have 2400 Comport.

MELBA

Cutting 761

1936 – 1943

CUMBERLAND

Cutting 762

1936 – 1939
Did not have a 6" Plate.

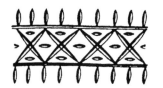

WEYLIN

Cutting 759

1936 – 1938

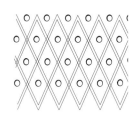

869 Bowl, Finger; $12.00
2470½ Bowl, 10½"; $40.00
2472 Candlestick, Duo (pair); $70.00
2400 Comport, 6"; $27.00

5000 Jug; $185.00
2337 Plate, 6"; $6.00
2337 Plate, 7"; $7.00
2337 Plate, 8"; $8.00

PALMETTO

Cutting 755

1935 – 1939
Stemware is featured in *Fostoria Stemware*, page 86.

869 Bowl, Finger; $12.00
2533 Bowl, 9" Handled; $95.00
2533 Candlestick, Duo (pair); $95.00

5000 Jug; $235.00
2337 Plate, 6"; $6.00
2337 Plate, 7"; $7.00
2337 Plate, 8"; $8.00

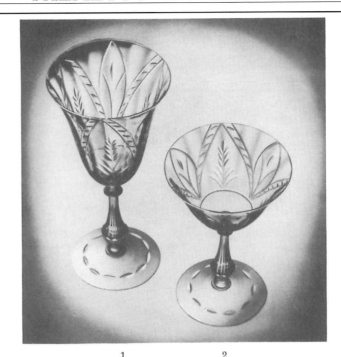

PALMETTO DESIGN
CUTTING No. 755
Rock Crystal — Optic

1.	6014	9-oz. Goblet	6.	6014	3-oz. Wine	11.	5000	Footed Jug
2.	6014	5½-oz. Saucer Champagne	7.	6014	1-oz. Cordial	12.	2337	6-in. Plate
3.	6014	5½-oz. Low Sherbet	8.	6014	4-oz. Oyster Cocktail	12.	2337	7-in. Plate
4.	6014	3½-oz. Cocktail	9.	6014	12-oz. Footed Tumbler	12.	2337	8-in. Plate
5.	6014	4-oz. Claret	9.	6014	9-oz. Footed Tumbler	13.	2533	9-in. Handled Bowl
			9.	6014	5-oz. Footed Tumbler	14.	2533	Duo Candlestick
			10.	869	Finger Bowl			

BOUQUET DESIGN
CUTTING No. 756
Rock Crystal — Optic

1.	6013	10-oz. Goblet	8.	6013	1-oz. Cordial	14.	2337	6-in. Plate
2.	6013	9-oz. Low Goblet	9.	6013	4-oz. Oyster Cocktail	14.	2337	7-in. Plate
3.	6013	6-oz. Saucer Champagne	10.	6013	13-oz. Footed Tumbler	14.	2337	8-in. Plate
4.	6013	5-oz. Low Sherbet	10.	6013	5-oz. Footed Tumbler	15.	2527	9-in. Footed Bowl
5.	6013	3½-oz. Cocktail	11.	6013	5-in. Comport	16.	2527	2 Light Candelabra, U.D.P.
6.	6013	4-oz. Claret	12.	766	Finger Bowl			
7.	6013	3-oz. Wine	13.	5000	Footed Jug			

140

BOUQUET

Cutting 756

1935 – 1938 except as noted.

SOCIETY

Cutting 757

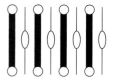

1935 – 1937 except as noted.
Stemware for both patterns is featured in *Fostoria Stemware*, page 85.

766 Bowl, Finger; $12.00
2527 Bowl, 9" Footed; $48.00
2527 Candelabra, 2-light, UDP (pair); $125.00
6013 Comport, 5"; $32.00

5000 Jug, 1935; $200.00
2337 6" Plate; $6.00
2337 7" Plate; $7.00
2337 8" Plate; $8.00

BORDEAUX

Cutting 758

1936 – 1943
Stemware is featured in *Fostoria Stemware*, page 86.

869 Bowl, Finger; $12.00
2470½ Bowl, 10½"; $40.00
2472 Candlestick, Duo (pair); $70.00
2400 Comport, 6"; $27.00
2375 Ice Bucket, NP Handle; $43.00
2451 Ice Dish, Liner, and Plate; $42.00
5000 Jug; $185.00

2337 6" Plate; $6.00
2337 7" Plate; $7.00
2337 8" Plate; $8.00
4121 Vase, 5"; $55.00
4128 Vase, 5"; $55.00
2470 Vase, 10"; $95.00

WHEAT

Cutting 760

1936 – 1939 except as noted.
This pattern did not offer stemware. Fostoria Wheat, Cutting 837, did have stemware.

2496 Bon Bon, 3-toed, 1937-1939; $32.00
2496 Bowl, 8½" Serving; $60.00
2496 Bowl, 10" Floating Garden; $55.00
2496 Bowl, 10½" Handled; $75.00
2496 Bowl, 12" Flared; $65.00
2545 Bowl 12½" Oval; $65.00
2545 Candelabra, 2-light, B Prisms (pair); $200.00
2496 Candlestick, 4" (pair); $45.00
2496 Candlestick, 5½" (pair); $55.00
2496 Candlestick, Duo (pair); $65.00
2545 Candlestick, Duo (pair); $100.00
2496 Candlestick, Trindle (pair); $75.00
2496 Candy Box and Cover, 1937-1939; $47.00
2440 Celery; $27.00
2496 Celery; $27.00
2496 Cheese and Cracker, 1937-1939; $45.00
2496 Comport, 5½"; $30.00

2496 Comport, 6½", 1937-1939; $65.00
2375 Ice Bucket, NP Handle; $45.00
2496 Ice Bucket, Gold Handle; $45.00
2496 Jelly and Cover; $75.00
2496 Mayonnaise, 2-part; $27.00
2496½ Mayonnaise and Plate,
    1937-1939; $35.00
2449 Pickle; $22.00
2496 Pickle; $22.00
2440 Plate, 10" Cake; $40.00
2496 Plate, 10" Handled Cake; $45.00
2496 Plate, 14" Torte; $48.00
2496 Nut Bowl, 3-toed, 1937-1939; $38.00
2496 Relish, 2-part; $25.00
2496 Relish, 3-part; $28.00
2496 Relish, 4-part; $45.00
2419 Relish, 5-part; $55.00

WHEAT DESIGN
CUTTING No. 760

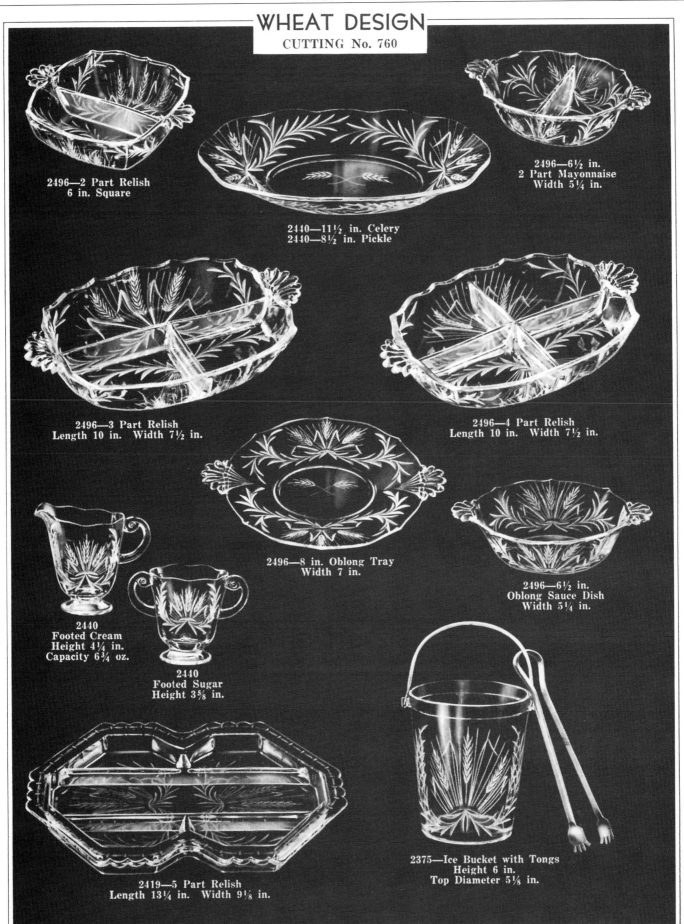

2496—2 Part Relish
6 in. Square

2440—11½ in. Celery
2440—8½ in. Pickle

2496—6½ in.
2 Part Mayonnaise
Width 5¼ in.

2496—3 Part Relish
Length 10 in. Width 7½ in.

2496—4 Part Relish
Length 10 in. Width 7½ in.

2496—8 in. Oblong Tray
Width 7 in.

2496—6½ in.
Oblong Sauce Dish
Width 5¼ in.

2440
Footed Cream
Height 4¼ in.
Capacity 6¾ oz.

2440
Footed Sugar
Height 3⅝ in.

2375—Ice Bucket with Tongs
Height 6 in.
Top Diameter 5⅛ in.

2419—5 Part Relish
Length 13¼ in. Width 9⅛ in.

WHEAT DESIGN
CUTTING No. 760

2496
Duo Candlestick
Height 4½ in.   Spread 8 in.

2496
Trindle Candlestick
Height 6 in.   Spread 8¼ in.

2496—10½ in. Handled Bowl
Height 3⅜ in.

2496—12 in. Bowl, Fld.
Height 3½ in.

2440—Oval Cake Plate
2 Handles—Length 10½ in.

2496—Sweetmeat
6 in. Square

2496
5½ in. Candlestick

2496—14 in. Torte Plate

2470
10 in. Vase

WHEAT DESIGN
CUTTING No. 760

2496—Ice Bucket
Height 4⅝ in. Top Diameter 6½ in.
Chromium Handle and Tongs
Tongs Priced Separately

2496
Individual Sugar
Height 2⅞ in.

2496
Individual Cream
Height 3⅛ in.
Capacity 4 oz.

2496—11 in. Celery

2496—8 in. Pickle

2496—5½ in. Comport
Height 4¾ in.

2496—8½ in. Serving Dish, 2 Handles

2496—10 in. Cake Plate, 2 Handles

2496—Jelly and Cover
Height 7½ in.

WHEAT DESIGN
CUTTING No. 760

2496
4 in. Candlestick

2496
10 in. Floating Garden
Width 7½ in.

2496
4 in. Candlestick

2545—12½ in. "Flame" Oval Bowl
Height 2⅞ in.

2545
"Flame" Duo Candlestick
Height 6¾ in.
Spread 10¼ in.

2545—2 Light "Flame" Candelabra
Using 12 B Prisms
Height 6¾ in.   Spread 11 in.

2496 Sauce and Tray, Oblong; $57.00
2440 Sugar and Cream; $45.00
2496 Sugar and Cream, Individual; $45.00

2496 Sweetmeat; $27.00
2496 Tid Bit, 3-toed, 1937-1939; $30.00
2470 Vase, 10"; $95.00

CYRENE

Cutting 763

1936 – 1943 except as noted.
Stemware is featured in *Fostoria Stemware*, pages 83 and 84.

1769 Bowl, Finger; $14.00
2496 Bowl, 10½" Handled; $58.00
2496 Candlestick, 5½" (pair); $45.00
6011 Jug, 1936-1942; $185.00

2337 Plate, 6"; $6.00
2337 Plate, 7"; $7.00
2337 Plate, 8"; $8.00
2350½ Sugar and Cream; $35.00

BEACON

Cutting 767

1937 – 1943
Stemware is featured in *Fostoria Stemware*, pages 89 and 90.

766 Bowl, Finger; $14.00
2496 Bowl, 8½" Serving; $60.00
2496 Bowl, 10½" Handled; $75.00
2496 Bowl, 12" Flared; $65.00
2545 Bowl, 12½" Oval; $65.00
2545 Candelabra, 2-light, B prisms (pair) $200.00
2496 Candlestick, 4" (pair); $45.00
2496 Candlestick, 5½" (pair); $55.00
2496 Candlestick, Duo (pair); $65.00
2545 Candlestick, Duo (pair); $100.00
2496 Candlestick, Trindle (pair); $75.00
2496 Celery, 11"; $27.00
2496 Cheese and Cracker; $55.00
2496 Comport, 5½"; $30.00
2496 Comport, 6½", Tall; $65.00
4132 Decanter and Stopper, 1937-1938; $95.00
4132 Ice Bowl, 1937-1938; $48.00
2496 Ice Bucket, Gold Handle; $50.00

6011 Jug; $225.00
2496 Mayonnaise, 2-part; $28.00
2496½ Mayonnaise, Plate, Ladle; $48.00
2496 Pickle, 8"; $22.00
2337 Plate, 6"; $7.00
2337 Plate, 7"; $9.00
2337 Plate, 8"; $12.00
2496 Plate, Cake; $48.00
2496 Plate, 14" Torte; $65.00
2496 Relish, 2-part; $28.00
2496 Relish, 3-part; $35.00
2496 Sauce and Tray, Oblong; $62.00
2496 Sugar and Cream; $47.00
2496 Sugar and Cream, Individual; $47.00
2496 Sugar and Cream Tray; $24.00
2496 Sweetmeat; $28.00
2496 Tid Bit, 3-toed; $32.00

RIPPLE

Cutting 766

1937 – 1943
Also included 4132 Decanter and 4132 Ice Bowl, 1937 – 1938.

BRIDAL SHOWER

Cutting 768

1937 – 1938
Stemware for both patterns is featured in *Fostoria Stemware*, pages 89 and 90.

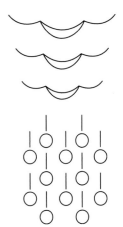

766 Bowl, Finger; $12.00
2545 Bowl, 12½"; $57.00

2545 Candelabra, 2-light (pair); $175.00
2545 Candlestick, Duo (pair); $85.00

6011 Jug; $175.00
2337 Plate, 6"; $6.00
2337 Plate, 7"; $7.00

2337 Plate, 8"; $8.00
2350½ Sugar and Cream; $30.00

Pussywillow and Athenian shared the same pieces except as noted.

PUSSYWILLOW

Cutting 769

1937 – 1943
No stemware or finger bowl.

ATHENIAN

Cutting 770

1938 – 1943
Stemware is featured in *Fostoria Stemware*, pages 81 and 82.

1769 Bowl, Finger; $14.00
4132 Decanter and Stopper; $85.00
4132 Ice Bowl; $40.00
4132 Tumbler, 14 oz. Sham; $15.00
4132 Tumbler, 12 oz. Sham; $14.00
4132 Tumbler, 9 oz. Sham; $12.00

4132 Tumbler, 5 oz. Sham; $9.00
4132 Old Fashioned Cocktail,
　7½ oz. Sham; $10.00
4132 Whiskey, 1½ oz. Sham; $10.00
2337 Plate, 7"; $7.00

Federal and Tulip shared the same pieces.

FEDERAL

Cutting 771

1937 – 1943 except where noted.

TULIP

Cutting 772

1937 – 1943 except where noted.
Stemware is featured in *Fostoria Stemware*, page 91.

766 Bowl, Finger; $12.00
4132 Bowl, Ice; $40.00
2496 Bowl, 10½" Handled; $65.00
2430 Bowl, 11" , 1938 only; $65.00
2430 Candlestick, 2", 1938 only (pair); $65.00
2496 Candlestick, 5½" (pair); $48.00
4132 Decanter and Stopper; $85.00

2430 Jelly, 7", 1938 only; $28.00
2430 Mint, 5½", 1938 only; $22.00
2337 Plate, 6"; $6.00
2337 Plate, 7"; $7.00
2337 Plate, 8"; $8.00
2430 Vase, 8", 1938 only; $60.00

GOTHIC

Cutting 774

1939 – 1942 except where noted.
Same pieces as Kimberly except for 5100 Vase.

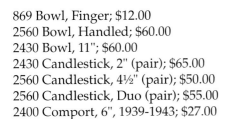

KIMBERLEY

Cutting 775

1939 – 1942 except where noted.
Stemware for Gothic and Kimberly is featured in *Fostoria Stemware,* page 92.

869 Bowl, Finger; $12.00
2560 Bowl, Handled; $60.00
2430 Bowl, 11"; $60.00
2430 Candlestick, 2" (pair); $65.00
2560 Candlestick, 4½" (pair); $50.00
2560 Candlestick, Duo (pair); $55.00
2400 Comport, 6", 1939-1943; $27.00

5000 Jug; $185.00
2337 Plate, 6"; $6.00
2337 Plate, 7"; $7.00
2337 Plate, 8"; $8.00
2560 Sugar and Cream; $40.00
5100 Vase, 10", Plain, 1939-1940; $85.00

RAYNEL

Cutting 777

1938 – 1939

LUCERNE

Cutting 778

1938 Supplement
Notice in the catalog picture how similar these two cuttings are.
Stemware for both patterns is featured in *Fostoria Stemware,* pages 89 and 90.

766 Bowl, Finger; $12.00
4132 Decanter; $85.00
4132 Ice Bowl; $45.00
6011 Jug; $175.00

2337 Plate, 6"; $6.00
2337 Plate, 7"; $7.00
2337 Plate, 8"; $8.00

CYNTHIA

Cutting 785

The second Cynthia cutting. Stemware is featured in *Fostoria Stemware,* pages 89 and 90.

2560 Bon Bon, 1938-1942; $38.00
2560 Bon Bon, 3-toed, 1938-1943; 1950-1959; $35.00
766 Bowl, Finger, 1938-1943; $16.00
2560 Bowl, 11" Handled, 1938-1943; 1950-1963; $78.00
2560 Bowl, Serving, 1938-1943; $60.00
2560 Bowl, 2-part Salad, 1938-1943; $78.00
2560 Bowl, 11½" Crimped, 1938-1943; $70.00
2560 Bowl, 13" Fruit, 1938-1943; $75.00
2560½ Candlestick, 4", 1938-1943 (pair); $65.00
2560 Candlestick, 4½", 1938-1943; 1950-1959 (pair); $65.00
2560 Candlestick, Duo, 1938-1943; 1950-1962 (pair); $65.00
2560 Celery, 11", 1938-1943; $32.00
2560 Cheese and Cracker, 1938-1943; $68.00
2560 Comport, 6", 1938-1943; $46.00
2560 Cup and Saucer, 1950-1962; $32.00
2560 Ice Bucket, Chrome Handle, 1938-1943; $75.00
2560 Ice Tongs, Chrome, 1938-1943; $35.00

6011 Jug, 1938-1943;1952-1957; $245.00
2560 Lemon, 1938-1943; $24.00
2560 Mayonnaise, Plate, Ladle, 1938-1943; 1950-1959; $75.00
2560 Mayonnaise, 2-part, 2 Ladles, 1938-1943; $87.00
2560 Oil, 3 oz. Footed, and Stopper, 1938-1943; $125.00
2560 Olive, 6¾", 1938-1943; $28.00
2560 Pickle, 8¾", 1938-1943; 1950-1959; $28.00
2666 Pitcher, Quart, 1958-1965; $250.00
2337 Plate, 6", 1938-1965; $7.00
2337 Plate, 7", 1938-1965; $9.00
2337 Plate, 8", 1938-1965; $11.00
2560 Plate, 10½" Cake, 1938-1943; 1950-1962; $56.00
2560 Plate, 14" Torte, 1938-1943; 1950-1959; $70.00
2560 Relish, 2-part, 1938-1943; $34.00
2560 Relish, 3-part, 1938-1943; 1950-1965; $60.00
2560 Relish, 4-part, 1938-1943; $85.00
2560 Relish, 5-part, 1938-1943; $95.00
2560 Sugar and Cream, Individual, 1938-1943; $60.00

299

1.   2.

RAYNEL DESIGN
CUTTING No. 777—ROCK CRYSTAL

1.	6017	9-oz. Goblet	9.	6017	12-oz. Footed Tumbler	13.	4132	7½-oz. O. F. Cocktail, Sham
2.	6017	6-oz. Saucer Champagne	9.	6017	9-oz. Footed Tumbler	14.	4132	½-oz. Whiskey, Sham
3.	6017	6-oz. Low Sherbet	9.	6017	5-oz. Footed Tumbler	15.	4132	Decanter
4.	6017	3½-oz. Cocktail	10.	766	Finger Bowl	16.	4132	Ice Bowl
5.	6017	4-oz. Claret	11.	6011	Footed Jug	17.	2337	6-in. Plate
6.	6017	3-oz. Wine	12.	4132	12-oz. Tumbler, Sham	17.	2337	7-in. Plate
7.	6017	¾-oz. Cordial	13.	4132	9-oz. Tumbler, Sham	17.	2337	8-in. Plate
8.	6017	4-oz. Oyster Cocktail	12.	4132	5-oz. Tumbler Sham			

1.   2.

LUCERNE DESIGN
CUTTING No. 778—ROCK CRYSTAL

1.	6017	9-oz. Goblet	9.	6017	12-oz. Footed Tumbler	13.	4132	7½-oz. O. F. Cocktail, Sham
2.	6017	6-oz. Saucer Champagne	9.	6017	9-oz. Footed Tumbler	14.	4132	½-oz. Whiskey, Sham
3.	6017	6-oz. Low Sherbet	9.	6017	5-oz. Footed Tumbler	15.	4132	Decanter
4.	6017	3½-oz. Cocktail	10.	766	Finger Bowl	16.	4132	Ice Bowl
5.	6017	4-oz. Claret	11.	6011	Footed Jug	17.	2337	6-in. Plate
6.	6017	3-oz. Wine	12.	4132	12-oz. Tumbler, Sham	17.	2337	7-in. Plate
7.	6017	¾-oz. Cordial	13.	4132	9-oz. Tumbler, Sham	17.	2337	8-in. Plate
8.	6017	4-oz. Oyster Cocktail	12.	4132	5-oz. Tumbler Sham			

151-D

CYNTHIA DESIGN
Cutting No. 785

6017—9 oz. Goblet
Height 7⅜ in.

6017
6 oz. Saucer Champagne
Height 5½ in.

6017
12 oz. Footed Tumbler
Height 6 in.

2560—Mayonnaise, Plate and Ladle
Height 3½ in.

2560—4 Part Relish
Length 10 in.   Width 6¾ in.

2560—11½ in. Handled Lunch Tray

2560—6¾ in. Olive
2560—8¾ in. Pickle
2560—11 in. Celery

2560—Sweetmeat, 2 Hdles.
Height 1½ in.
Diameter 5½ in.

2560—Individual Cream
Height 3¼ in.
Capacity 4 oz.

2560—Individual Sugar
Height 3 in.

2560½—4 in. Candlestick

2560—11½ Bowl, Crimped
Height 3¼ in.

2560 Sugar and Cream, 1938-1943; 1950-1961; $57.00
2560 Sweetmeat, 1938-1943; $34.00
2560 Tid Bit, 3-toed, 1938-1943; $38.00
2560 Tray, Muffin, 1938-1943; $65.00
2560 Whip Cream, 1938-1943; $34.00

2560 Tray, 11½" Handled Lunch, 1938-1943; 1950-1965; $65.00
2567 Vase, 7½" Footed, 1938-1943; $125.00
5100 Vase, 10", 1938-1943; $125.00

CHIPPENDALE

Cutting 788

1939 – 1942 except all plates made through 1943.

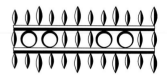

CATHEDRAL

Cutting 792

1939 – 1943

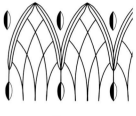

SPIRE

Cutting 793

1939 – 1943

The above three patterns shared these pieces except as noted.
Stemware is featured in *Fostoria Stemware*, pages 93 and 94.

766 Bowl, Finger; $12.00
6023 Bowl, Footed; $54.00
2324 Candlestick, 6" (pair); $45.00
6023 Comport, 5"; $28.00

6011 Jug; $175.00
2337 Plate, 6"; $6.00
2337 Plate, 7"; $7.00
2337 Plate, 8"; $8.00

DAPHNE

Cutting 797

1939 – 1943

2424 Ash Tray; $24.00
2424 Bowl, 8" Regular; $60.00
2424 Bowl, 9½" Flared; $74.00
2424 Bowl, 11½" Fruit; $85.00
2424 Candlestick, 3½" (pair); $50.00
2424 Candy Jar and Cover; $68.00
2424 Cigarette Box and Cover; $68.00

2424 Mayonnaise, Plate, Ladle; $75.00
2424 Plate, 12"; $75.00
2424 Sweetmeat, 7"; $40.00
2424 Vase, 6½" Footed Urn Flared; $95.00
2424 Vase, 7½" Footed Urn Regular; $95.00

HAWTHORN

Cutting 790

1939 – 1943
Did not have a 6023 Candlestick.

INGRID

Cutting 794

1939 – 1943

Did not have a 6023 Candlestick.

PAPYRUS

Cutting 795

1939 – 1943

Did not have a 6023 Candlestick.

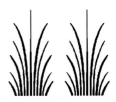

LYRIC

Cutting 796

1939 – 1942

The 7" Plate was made through 1943. No 6023 Candlestick.

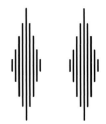

CHRISTINE

Cutting 798

1940 – 1943

No 2324 Candlestick or 6" Plate. The 6023 Bowl and Candlestick made through 1942.

CHRISTIANA

Cutting 814

1942 – 1943

No 2324 Candlestick or 6" Plate.

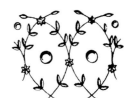

GADROON

Cutting 816

1942 – 1943

No 2324 Candlestick. All Plates made through 1956.

Stemware for listed patterns Hawthorn through Gadroon is featured in *Fostoria Stemware,* on pages 40, 96 and 100.

1769 Bowl, Finger; $15.00	6011 Jug; $175.00
6023 Bowl, Footed; $50.00	2337 Plate, 6"; $7.00
2324 Candlestick, 6" (pair); $45.00	2337 Plate, 7"; $8.00
6023 Candlestick, Duo (pair); $50.00	2337 Plate, 8"; $10.00

MULBERRY

Cutting 799

1940 – 1943 except where noted.

Stemware is featured in *Fostoria Stemware,* page 97.

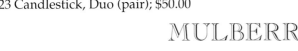

869 Bowl, Finger; $15.00	2337 Plate, 6", 1940-1958; $10.00
2563 Bowl, Handled; $77.00	2337 Plate, 7", 1940-1958; $12.00
2563 Candlestick, 4½" (pair); $75.00	2337 Plate, 8", 1940-1958; $16.00
5000 Jug; $275.00	

SELMA

Cutting 800

1940 – 1943

Stemware is featured in *Fostoria Stemware*, page 97.

869 Bowl, Finger; $15.00
6023 Bowl, Footed; $77.00
6023 Candlestick, Duo (pair); $75.00

5000 Jug; $275.00
2337 Plate, 7"; $10.00
2337 Plate, 8"; $16.00

SALON

Cutting 804

1940 – 1943

Stemware is featured in *Fostoria Stemware*, page 98.

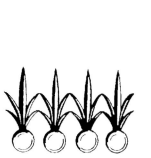

4024 Bowl, Finger; $18.00
2364 Bowl, 13" Fruit; $55.00
6023 Candlestick, Duo (pair); $65.00

6011 Jug; $175.00
2337 Plate, 7"; $7.00
2337 Plate, 8"; $8.00

ALOHA

Cutting 805

1940 – 1943

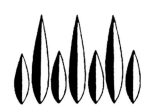

CADENCE

Cutting 806

1940 – 1943

Stemware for both patterns is featured in *Fostoria Stemware*, page 98.

4021 Bowl, Finger; $18.00
6023 Candlestick, Duo (pair); $65.00
6011 Jug; $175.00

2364 Lily Pond, 12"; $60.00
2337 Plate, 7"; $7.00
2337 Plate, 8"; $8.00

COVENTRY

Cutting 807

1940 – 1943 except as noted.

2596 Bowl, 7½" Square; $45.00
2364 Bowl, 10½" Salad; $55.00
2596 Bowl, 11" Shallow, Oblong, 1940-1942; $74.00
2364 Bowl, 12" Lily Pond; $62.00
2364 Bowl, 13" Fruit; $65.00
2596 Candlestick, 5" (pair); $65.00
2324 Candlestick, 6" (pair); $65.00
6023 Candlestick, Duo (pair); $75.00
2364 Plate, 14" Torte; $60.00

2364 Plate, 16" Torte; $64.00
2577 Vase, 6"; $67.00
4143½ Vase, 6" Footed; $67.00
2567 Vase, 7½" Footed; $78.00
4143½ Vase, 7½" Footed; $75.00
2567 Vase, 8½" Footed; $95.00
2577 Vase, 8½"; $85.00
4126½ Vase, 11" Footed; $125.00

COVENTRY DESIGN

ROCK CRYSTAL CUTTING No. 807

2364—14 in. Torte Plate
2364—16 in. Torte Plate

2364—12 in. Lily Pond
Height 2¼ in.

6023—Duo Candlestick
Height 5½ in.   Spread 6 in.

2364—10½ in. Salad Bowl
Height 4 in.
2364—14 in. Torte Plate

2364—13 in. Fruit Bowl
Height 2¾ in.

4126½—11 in. Footed Vase

2596—7½ in. Square Bowl
Height 2½ in.

2596—5 in. Candlestick

2596—11 in. Oblong Shallow Bowl
Height 2 in.

2577—8½ in. Vase   4132½—8 in. Vase   4143½—6 in. Footed Vase   2577—6 in. Vase   2567—7½ in. Footed Vase
4143½—7½ in. Footed Vase   2567—8½ in. Footed Vase

MOUNT VERNON

Cutting 817

Stemware in this pattern was made longer and is featured in *Fostoria Stemware*, on page 101.

1769 Bowl, Finger, 1942-1943; $12.00
2364 Bowl, 13" Fruit, 1942-1943; $55.00
6023 Candlestick, Duo, 1942-1943 (pair); $55.00
6011 Jug, 1942-1943; $175.00

2337 Plate, 6", 1942-1954; $6.00
2337 Plate, 7", 1942-1954; $7.00
2337 Plate, 8", 1942-1954; $8.00

GREEK KEY

Cutting 819

1942 – 1943

Stemware is featured in *Fostoria Stemware*, page 101.

766 Bowl, Finger; $12.00
2596 Bowl, 11" Oblong Shallow; $65.00
2596 Candlestick, 5" (pair); $65.00
6011 Jug; $175.00

2337 Plate, 6"; $6.00
2337 Plate, 7"; $7.00
2337 Plate, 8"; $8.00

DECORATIONS

7 Coin Gold Band
8 Cascade
9 Newport
12 Dresden
17 Daisy
19 Blue Border
20 Black Border
21 Enamel and Gold
22 Blue and Gold or Rose and Gold
23 Black and Gold
25 Vase and Scroll
29 Empress
30 Azalea
31 Laurel
32 Regent
34 Persian
35 Encrusted Gold on Oriental design
36 Poinsettia
37 Vase and Scroll
39 Royal
40 Nome
44 Rivera
46 Tinted Bands in Gold
47 Imperial, Blue and Gold
48 Dorcas
49 Coronada
52 Pasadena
53 Orange Band on Ebony
54 Alaska
55 Tinted Bands
56 Antique
57 Waveland

58 Amherst
61 Grape Stem
62 Grape Stem
63 Grape Stem
64 Grape Stem
65 Criterion
66 Hammered Silver
67 Poinsettia
68 DuBarry
69 Saturn
70 Arlington
505 Cockatoo
506 Viennese
507 Nugget
508 Butterfly
514 Italian Lace
516 Apple Blossom
517 Grape
518 White Enamel on Regal Blue
519 Colored Flowers on Crystal
603 Club Design A
604 Club Design B
605 Saturn
607 Polka Dot
608 Block
609 Lines
610 Triangle
614 Golden Swirl
616 St. Regis
Mother of Pearl
Onyx Lustre
White Edge

DECORATIONS

Amber 2324 Candlesticks, 2369 9" Vase, unknown decoration

Decorated ware was not new to the Fostoria Glass Company in the 1920s. During its earlier history, the company had become quite well known for an extensive line of decorated lamps and vases, water and table sets, novelty items, boudoir sets, trays, and so forth. Whole catalogs were devoted to presenting these skillfully hand-painted creations. Several pressed lines were offered with gold or ruby decoration. An iridescent decoration was first made in 1915. Called Iridescent Glassware when introduced, it was soon renamed Mother of Pearl Iridescent. Within this category there were more specific decorations such as Autumn Glow, Spanish Lustre, and Onyx Lustre. Mother of Pearl was not identified by decoration number but was often listed as a separate category in price lists. Knowing Fostoria shapes will be helpful in identifying Mother of Pearl pieces.

A 1916 price list describes Decoration No. 3, Crimson Rose, as roses between gold lines to form a band. Decoration 5, Rose and Blue had a large rose and leaf between two blue bands. Decoration 11, Rose and Gold had a gold rim and large roses. Also listed in 1916, Decoration 12, Dresden continued to be made through 1924 and is shown in this section. Decoration 16, Crimson Rose and Bluebird is listed in 1916 as blue bands and birds on opal glass or crystal. In that pattern, the 2104 Jug and 820 Tumbler were listed as available with an added gold band.

Decorations have been by far the most difficult category of Fostoria glass to research. Even as we go to press, there are questions about some of the designs. We have been fortunate to find examples of several decorations and to have two original booklets on decorated ware in color. Decorations 7 through 44 are reprinted from those two booklets. Note the circular Fostoria logo in use until some time in 1924 when it was changed to the brown oval. With the richness of color and design evident in Fostoria decorations and the lack of information available before now, we are convinced it is an untapped area of collecting. Our research has given us a profound appreciation for the skill needed to execute these designs.

The richest period for decorations is the mid-1920s to early 1930s. However, Fostoria continued using gold and platinum bands right up to 1982 .

This section presents all the information we currently have on decorations. Sometimes we found a decoration listed with no clue as to description. In that case, we have included the name and/or number to let you know it was listed by Fostoria, even though we cannot tell you what it looked like. A few decorations had only a name and were not numbered, i.e., White Edge and Onyx Lustre.

From time to time Fostoria pieces are found with decorations we have been unable to identify.

Amber 2324 9" Candlesticks, Gold Encrusted with Aqua Enamel; Orchid 2331 Candy Box, Gold Encrusted with Rose Enamel, unknown decoration

The 2324 amber Candlesticks might be a variation of the Vase and Scroll design, and they might be a completely different decoration. They are superbly done with gold encrustation. The 2331 three-part Candy has a delicate gold encrusted design with a light pink enamel filling in the jewel. Even the tops of the compartment dividers, and the rim and base of the bottom have gold decoration. This decoration on the Orchid color is outstanding.

Fostoria glassware may have been sold to other companies to be decorated. We have seen pieces with a Charleton decoration, for example. However, there is no doubt that Fostoria's decorating department of the 1920s and 1930s was second to none.

Should you see a Fostoria shape with a decoration, check those listed for a match, but remember that shapes other than those listed may have been made. Also, variations in color and design may have occurred. In many places elsewhere in Fostoria price lists of the 1920s, complete instructions encouraging special orders appear. It seems unusual that those same instructions do not appear on any pages listing decorations, seeming to imply that special orders were not available for decorations. We will continue to look for Fostoria decorations because, for us, the mystery creates the adventure.

We have seen so few decorations that pricing these pieces would be no more than a stab in the dark. If and when more decorations are offered for sale, we may be able to offer a guide to pricing in future editions. At present simple gold bands on the very plain designs from the 1920s are not attracting much attention. Even the gold encrusted items with enamel decoration have not been expensive when we have found them for sale.

Blue Silver Deposit 2297 7" Candlesticks

Green 2297 7" Candlesticks, Gold Encrusted, unknown decoration

COIN GOLD BAND

Decoration 7

1906 – 1928

Stemware is featured in *Fostoria Stemware*, pages 22 – 26.

5051 Almond, Large
1499 Bowl, Finger, and Plate
2219 Candy Jar and Cover, ¼ pound
2219 Candy Jar and Cover, ½ pound
2219 Candy Jar and Cover, pound
2250 Candy Jar and Cover, ¼ pound
2250 Candy Jar and Cover, ½ pound
2250 Candy Jar and Cover, pound
1697 Carafe and 4023 Tumbler
880 Comport, 5"
803 Comport, 5"
803 Comport, 6"
803 Comport and Cover, 5", Gold Knob
880 Comport and Cover, 5", Gold Knob
2252 Dish, 6" Salad
1848 Dish, 7" Salad, M.S. (Matt Star Base)
825 Jelly
825 Jelly and Cover, Gold Knob
1236/6 Jug
1968 Marmalade and Cover
803 Nappy, 5" Footed
803 Nappy and Cover, 5" Footed,
    Gold Knob
803 Nappy, 6"
1897 Plate, 7"
1848 Plate, 9" Cracker, M.S. (Matt Star Base)
2258 Plate, 11" Sandwich
2258 Relish Dish, 6"

2258 Relish Dish, 8"
2258 Relish Dish, 10"
880 Salt, Footed
858 Sweetmeat

FOSTORIA GLASS COMPANY

858-9 OZ. GOBLET OPTIC
Coin Gold Band No. 7
Cut two-thirds size.

CASCADE

Decoration 8

Coin Gold Band with Needle Etching 36½
Pre-1924 – 1928
Stemware is featured in *Fostoria Stemware*, pages 20 – 22.

766 Almond
766 Bon Bon
766 Bowl, Finger
2219 Candy Jar and Cover, ¼ pound
2219 Candy Jar and Cover, ½ pound
2219 Candy Jar and Cover, pound
766 Comport, 5" Footed
300 Decanter, Quart, Cut Neck
303/7 Jug
766 Nappy, 7", Footed
1897 Plate, 7"
701 Tumbler Plate, 5"

FOSTORIA GLASS COMPANY

766-9 OZ. GOBLET OPTIC
Coin Gold Band No. 8 with Etching No. 36½.
Cut two-thirds size

NEWPORT

Decoration 9

Coin Gold Band
Pre-1924 – 1929

Stemware in this pattern is featured in *Fostoria Stemware*, pages 20 – 22.

766 Almond
766 Bowl, Finger, and Plate
2244 Candlestick
1697 Carafe and 4023 Tumbler
803 Comport, 5"
803 Comport and Cover, 5"
825 Jelly
825 Jelly and Cover
300½ Jug
803 Nappy, 5"
803 Nappy and Cover
1897 Plate, 7"
1478 Sugar and Cream

766 – 9 OZ. GOBLET
Coin Gold Band No. 9
Cut two-thirds size.

DRESDEN

Decoration 12

Black enamel and Gold decoration.
Pre-1924 – 1926
Stemware is featured in *Fostoria Stemware*, pages 22 – 26.

1904 Bon Bon
2090 Bottle, 6 oz. Toilet
2118 Bottle, 6 oz. Toilet
858 Bowl, Finger, and Plate
1490 Candlestick, 8"
2244 Candlestick, 8¼"
2245 Candlestick, 8¼"
2219 Candy Jar and Cover, ¼ pound
2219 Candy Jar and Cover, ½ pound
2219 Candy Jar and Cover, pound
2250 Candy Jar and Cover, ¼ pound
2250 Candy Jar and Cover, ½ pound
2250 Candy Jar and Cover, pound
1697 Carafe Set, 3 pieces
2241 Cologne, 2½ oz., Drip Stopper
2242 Cologne, 3¼ oz, Drip Stopper
2243 Cologne, 2¼ oz., Drip Stopper
803 Comport, 5" Tall
1848 Dish, 7" Salad, M.S. (Matt Star Base)
724/7 Jug
1743-5 Jug and Cover
2138 Mayonnaise Set, 2 pieces
803 Nappy, 5" LD
1897 Plate, 7"
1848 Plate, 9" Sandwich, M.S. (Matt Star Base)
1719 Plate, 10½" Sandwich, M.S. (Matt Star Base)
2135 Puff and Cover
2235 Shaker

2091 Soap and Cover
1957 Vase, 7" Center
2137 Vase, Brush
2208 Vase

858 – 9 OZ. GOBLET
Enamel Decoration No. 12
Cut two-thirds size.

DAISY

Decoration 17

Enamel with Gold Band
1924
Stemware is featured in *Fostoria Stemware,* pages 22 – 26.

1904 Bon Bon and Cover
2136 Bon Bon and Cover
2090 Bottle, 6 oz. Toilet
2118 Bottle, 6 oz. Toilet
858 Bowl, Finger, and Plate
1490 Candlestick, 8"
2244 Candlestick, 8¼"
2245 Candlestick, 8¼"
2219 Candy Jar and Cover, ¼ pound
2219 Candy Jar and Cover, ½ pound
2250 Candy Jar and Cover, ¼ pound
2250 Candy Jar and Cover, ½ pound
2250 Candy Jar and Cover, pound
1697 Carafe Set, 2 pieces
2136 Cold Cream and Cover, 3"
2241 Cologne, 2¼ oz., Drip Stopper
2242 Cologne, 3¼ oz., Drip Stopper
2243 Cologne, 2¼ oz., Drip Stopper
803 Comport, 5" Tall
724/7 Jug
2104 Jug
2138 Mayonnaise Set, 2 pieces
803 Nappy, 5" LD
1848 Plate, 9" Sandwich, M.S. (Matt Star Base)

858—9 OZ. GOBLET
Enamel Decoration No. 17
Cut two-thirds size.

1719 Plate, 10½" Sandwich, M.S. (Matt Star Base)
2136 Pomade and Cover, 2"
1666 Puff and Cover
2135 Puff and Cover
2091 Soap and Cover
2137 Vase, Brush

BLUE BORDER

Decoration 19

Enamel decoration
1924
Stemware is featured in *Fostoria Stemware,* pages 22 – 26.

2136 Bon Bon and Cover, 5"
2083 Bottle, Salad, Lettered
2090 Bottle, 6 oz. Toilet
2118 Bottle, 6 oz. Toilet
858 Bowl, Finger, and Plate
1490 Candlestick, 8"
2245 Candlestick, 8¼"
2219 Candy Jar and Cover, ¼ pound
2219 Candy Jar and Cover, ½ pound
2219 Candy Jar and Cover, pound
2250 Candy Jar and Cover, ¼ pound
2250 Candy Jar and Cover, ½ pound
2250 Candy Jar and Cover, pound
1697 Carafe Set, 3 pieces
2241 Cologne, 2¼ oz., Drip Stopper
2242 Cologne, 3¼ oz., Drip Stopper
2243 Cologne, 2¼ oz., Drip Stopper

858—9 OZ. GOBLET
Enamel Decoration No. 19
Cut two-thirds size.

803 Comport, 5" Tall
1848 Dish, 7" Salad, M.S. (Matt Star Base)
2104 Jug
1743/5 Jug and Cover
1968 Marmalade and Cover
2138 Mayonnaise Set, 2 pieces
127 Mug, Handled
803 Nappy, 5" LD

1897 Plate, 7"
1848 Plate, 9" Sandwich, M.S. (Matt Star Base)
1719 Plate, 10½" Sandwich, M.S. (Matt Star Base)
2091 Soap and Cover
2208 Vase, 5"
2137 Vase, Brush
1957 Vase, 7" Center

BLACK BORDER

Decoration 20

Enamel and Gold decoration
1924
Stemware is featured in *Fostoria Stemware*, pages 22 – 26.

2136 Bon Bon and Cover, 5"
2083 Bottle, Salad, Lettered
2090 Bottle, 6 oz. Toilet
2118 Bottle, 6 oz. Toilet
858 Bowl, Finger, and Plate
1490 Candlestick, 8"
2245 Candlestick, 8¼"
2219 Candy Jar and Cover, ¼ pound
2219 Candy Jar and Cover, ½ pound
2219 Candy Jar and Cover, pound
2250 Candy Jar and Cover, ¼ pound
2250 Candy Jar and Cover, ½ pound
2250 Candy Jar and Cover, pound
1697 Carafe Set, 3 pieces
2241 Cologne, 2¼ oz., Drip Stopper
2242 Cologne, 3¼ oz., Drip Stopper
2243 Cologne, 2¼ oz., Drip Stopper
803 Comport, 5" Tall
1848 Dish, 7" Salad, M.S. (Matt Star Base)
2104 Jug
1743/5 Jug and Cover
1743/7 Jug and Cover
1968 Marmalade and Cover
2138 Mayonnaise Set, 2 pieces
127 Mug, Handled
803 Nappy, 5" LD

FOSTORIA GLASS COMPANY

858-9 OZ. GOBLET
Enamel Decoration No. 20.
Cut two-thirds size.

1848 Plate, 9" Sandwich, M.S. (Matt Star Base)
1719 Plate, 10½" Sandwich, M.S. (Matt Star Base)
2091 Soap and Cover
2199 Tray, Gold Edge only
2208 Vase, 5"
2137 Vase, Brush
1957 Vase, 7" Center

DECORATION 21

Enamel and Gold
1924
Stemware is featured in *Fostoria Stemware*, pages 22 – 26.

2136 Bon Bon and Cover
858 Bowl, Finger, and Plate
2244 Candlestick, 8¼"
2245 Candlestick, 8¼"
2250 Candy Jar and Cover, ¼ pound
2250 Candy Jar and Cover, ½ pound

2250 Candy Jar and Cover, pound
2228 Candy Jar and Cover, pound square
1697 Carafe Set, 2 pieces
2136 Cold Cream and Cover, 3"
803 Comport, 5" Footed
803 Comport and Cover, 5" Footed

880 Comport, 5" Footed
880 Comport and Cover, 5" Footed
1848 Dish, 7" Salad, M.S. (Matt Star Base)
2252 Dish, 6" Salad
825 Jelly
825 Jelly and Cover
1968 Marmalade and Cover
2138 Mayonnaise, Plate with Gold
     Edge, Ladle with Gold Edge
803 Nappy, 5" Footed
803 Nappy and Cover, 5" Footed
1848 Plate, 9" Sandwich, M.S. (Matt Star Base)
2258 Plate, 11" Sandwich
2136 Pomade and Cover, 2"
2135 Puff and Cover
2258 Relish Dish, 6"
2258 Relish Dish, 8"
2258 Relish Dish, 10"
1957 Vase, 7" Center

858-9 OZ. GOBLET
Enamel and Gold Decoration No. 21
Cut two-thirds size.

DECORATION 22

Blue and Gold or Rose and Gold
The Blue or Rose is between the Gold bands.
1924

1904 Bon Bon and Cover
2244 Candlestick, 8¼"
2245 Candlestick, 8¼"
2219 Candy Jar and Cover, ¼ pound
2219 Candy Jar and Cover, ½ pound
2250 Candy Jar and Cover, ¼ pound
2250 Candy Jar and Cover, ½ pound
1697 Carafe Set
2091 Cigarette Box and Cover
2241 Cologne, 2¼ oz.
2242 Cologne, 3¼ oz.
2090 Cologne, 6 oz and Stopper
2118 Cologne, 6 oz. and Stopper
2135 Hair Receiver and Cover
127 Mug, Handled
2238 Plate, 8¼" Salad
2238 Plate, 11" Sandwich
1616 Puff and Cover
2135 Puff and Cover, 5"
2091 Soap and Cover
725 Vase, 5"
2208 Vase, 5"
725 Vase, 8"
2137 Vase, Brush, 4⅞" x 2¼"

2219—½ L.B. CANDY JAR & COVER
Decoration No. 22—Blue and Gold
Cut one-half size.

BLACK AND GOLD

Decoration 23

1924

Stemware is featured in *Fostoria Stemware,* pages 17 and 18.

2246 Candlestick, 8¼"
2219 Candy Jar and Cover, ¼ pound
2219 Candy Jar and Cover, ½ pound
2250 Candy Jar and Cover, ¼ pound
2250 Candy Jar and Cover, ½ pound
2241 Cologne, Drip Stopper
1743/4 Jug and Cover
300/7 Tankard
896 Nappy and Cover, 6½" Footed
1897 Plate, 7"
2238 Plate, 8¼"
2238 Plate, 11"
1851 Sugar and Cream

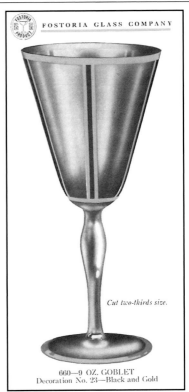

FOSTORIA GLASS COMPANY

Cut two-thirds size.

660—9 OZ. GOBLET
Decoration No. 23—Black and Gold

VASE AND SCROLL

Decoration 25

Blue tinted glass. Glass was etched on top and painted blue on the underneath side of the glass. Gold bands.

1924

2267 Bowl, 7"
2267 Bowl, 9"
2269 Candlestick, 6"
2275 Candlestick, 9"
2250 Candy Jar and Cover, ¼ pound
2250 Candy Jar and Cover, ½ pound
2283 Plate, 7"
2238 Plate 8¼"
2290 Plate , 8¼" Deep Salad
2238 Plate, 11"
2290 Plate, 13½" Deep Salad
2276 Vanity Set

Decoration 37

Rose, Light Blue, or Green Tint and Encrusted Gold, also Encrusted Gold on Amber

1924

2267 Bowl, 7" Console
2267 Bowl, 9" Console
2269 Candlestick, 6"
2275 Candlestick, 9½"
2238 Plate, 8¼" Salad
1848 Plate, 9" Sandwich
2238 Plate, 11" Sandwich, Cut M.S. (Matt Star Base)
2276 Vanity Set

2290—8¼" Deep Salad Plate
Decoration No. 25
Illustrations one-fourth size

2276 Vanity Set, Rose Tint
Encrusted Gold No. 37—Vase and Scroll
Illustration five-eights size

Vase and Scroll 2276 Vanity with Rose Tint and Gold Encrusted Bands

2298 Amber Candlesticks with Gold Encrustation

EMPRESS

Decoration 29

1924 – 1929

Stemware is featured in *Fostoria Stemware*, pages 18 and 19.

863 Almond
1769 Bowl, Finger, and Plate
2245 Candlestick, 8¼"
1697 Carafe Set
5051 Cheese, Large
1848 Cracker Plate, 9" M.S. (Matt Star Base)
803 Comport, 5" Footed
825 Jelly and Cover
1968 Marmalade and Cover
2138 Mayonnaise, Plate, Ladle
803 Nappy, 5" Deep Footed
803 Nappy, 6" Deep Footed
701 Plate, 5" Tumbler
840 Plate, 5" Sherbet
1867 Plate, 7"
2238 Plate, 8¼"
2238 Plate, 11"
2083 Salad Dressing Bottle
1759 Sugar and Cream
1852/6 Tankard

661—9 oz. Goblet—Optic
Encrusted Gold No. 29 "Empress"
Illustration half size

AZALEA

Decoration 30

Gold decoration on Green
1928

2297 Bowl "A," 12" Deep
2394 Bowl, 12"
2394 Candlestick, 2"
2324 Candlestick, 4"
2329 Centerpiece, 11"
2331 Candy Box and Cover
2391 Cigarette Box and Cover, Small
2391 Cigarette Box and Cover, Large
2350 Comport, 8"
2400 Comport, 8"
2380 Confection and Cover
2378 Ice Bucket, GF Handle
2378 Sugar Pail, GF Handle
2287 Tray, Handled Lunch
2373 Vase and Cover, Small Window
2373 Vase and Cover, Large Window
4100 Vase, 8"
2385 Vase, 8½" Footed Fan
2378 Whip Cream Pail, GF Handle

This 2324 Console Set was purchased in Rapid City, South Dakota, from a dealer who had purchased it in Arizona. We cannot be certain it is the Azalea decoration since we do not have a picture of the decoration and our information indicates that Azalea was only put on Green. We can be certain that this set is Fostoria because of the shape and color.

LAUREL

Decoration 31

Encrusted Gold
1924
Stemware is featured in *Fostoria Stemware*, pages 20 – 22.

766 Bowl, Finger, and Plate
2244 Candlestick, 8¼"
2245 Candlestick, 8¼"
2219 Candy Jar and Cover, ¼ pound
2219 Candy Jar and Cover, ½ pound
2219 Candy Jar and Cover, pound
2228 Candy Jar and Cover, pound square
2250 Candy Jar and Cover, ¼ pound
2250 Candy Jar and Cover, ½ pound
2250 Candy Jar and Cover, pound
1697 Carafe Set
2241 Cologne, 2¼ oz. Drip Stopper
2243 Cologne, 2¼ oz. Drip Stopper
2242 Cologne, 3¼ oz. Drip Stopper
803 Comport, 5" Footed
803 Comport, 6" Footed
880 Comport, 5"
880 Comport and Cover, 5"
2252 Dish, 6" Salad
1848 Dish, 7" Salad, M.S. (Matt Star Base)
825 Jelly and Cover (or no cover)
2100/7 Jug
1968 Marmalade and Cover
2138 Mayonnaise, Plate, Ladle (gold edge)

803 Nappy, 5" Deep Footed
803 Nappy, 6" Deep Footed
803 Nappy, 7" Deep Footed
803 Nappy, 5", and Cover
1465 Oil, 5 oz., Cut Neck
1896 Plate, 7"
2238 Plate, 8¼"
2238 Plate, 11"
2290 Plate, 8" Deep Salad
2290 Plate, 13" Deep Salad
1848 Plate, 9" Sandwich, M.S.
  (Matt Star Base)
1719 Plate, 10½" Sandwich,
  M.S. (Matt Star Base)
2258 Plate, 11" Sandwich
2258 Relish Dish, 6"
2258 Relish Dish, 8"
2258 Relish Dish, 10"
2083 Salad Dressing Bottle
858 Sweetmeat
2287 Tray, Handled Lunch
1957 Vase, 7" Center
2208 Vase, Sweet Pea
1465 Vinegar, 7 oz. Cut Neck

FOSTORIA GLASS COMPANY

766—9 OZ. GOBLET
Encrusted Gold No. 31 "LAUREL" Design
Cut two-thirds size

REGENT

Decoration 32

Encrusted Gold
1924
Stemware is featured in *Fostoria Stemware*, pages 20 – 22.

766 Bowl, Finger, and Plate
2244 Candlestick, 8¼"
2245 Candlestick, 8¼"
2219 Candy Jar and Cover, ¼ pound
2219 Candy Jar and Cover, ½ pound
2219 Candy Jar and Cover, pound
2228 Candy Jar and Cover, pound square
2250 Candy Jar and Cover, ¼ pound
2250 Candy Jar and Cover, ½ pound
2250 Candy Jar and Cover, pound
1697 Carafe Set
2241 Cologne, 2¼ oz. Drip Stopper
2242 Cologne, 3¼ oz. Drip Stopper
803 Comport, 5" Footed
803 Comport, 6" Footed
803 Comport and Cover, 5"
880 Comport, 5"
1848 Dish, 7" Salad, M.S. (Matt Star Base)
825 Jelly and Cover (or no cover)
2100/7 Jug
1968 Marmalade and Cover
2138 Mayonnaise and Plate, Flared
803 Nappy and Cover, 5"

803 Nappy, 5" Footed Deep
803 Nappy, 6" Footed Deep
803 Nappy, 7" Footed Deep
1897 Plate, 7"
2238 Plate 8¼"
2238 Plate, 11"
2290 Plate, 8" Deep Salad
2290 Plate, 13" Deep Salad
1848 Plate, 9" Sandwich, M.S. (Matt Star Base)
1719 Plate, 10½" Sandwich, M.S. (Matt Star Base)
2258 Plate, 11" Sandwich
858 Sweetmeat
2287 Tray, Handled Lunch

FOSTORIA GLASS COMPANY

766 – 9 OZ. GOBLET
Encrusted Gold No. 32 "REGENT" Design
Cut two-thirds size.

FOSTORIA GLASS COMPANY

ENCRUSTED GOLD NO. 34
COIN GOLD DECORATION
Etching No. 253

2219–	¼ lb. Candy Jar and Cover		$45.00
2219–	½ lb. Candy Jar and Cover		55.00
2219–	1 lb. Candy Jar and Cover		70.00
2211–	2¼ oz. Cologne, Drip Stopper		40.00
2242–	3¼ oz. Cologne, Drip Stopper		38.50
2243–	2¼ oz. Cologne, Drip Stopper		37.00

PERSIAN

Decoration 34

Coin Gold on Etching 253
1924

2419 Candy Jar and Cover, ¼ pound
2419 Candy Jar and Cover, ½ pound
2419 Candy Jar and Cover, pound
2241 Cologne, 2¼ oz. Drip Stopper
2243 Cologne, 2¼ oz. Drip Stopper
2242 Cologne, 3¼ oz. Drip Stopper

DECORATION 35

Encrusted Gold
1924

2252 Dish, 6" Salad
2258 Dish, 6" Relish
2258 Dish, 8" Relish
2258 Dish, 10" Relish
2258 Plate, 11" Sandwich

MOUNDSVILLE, W. VIRGINIA

RELISH DISH
ENCRUSTED GOLD NO. 35

2252–	6 in. Salad Dish		$26.50
2258–	6 in. Relish Dish		27.50
2258–	8 in. Relish Dish		42.00
2258–	10 in. Relish Dish		55.00
2258–	11 in. Sandwich Plate		72.00

POINSETTA

Decoration 36

Encrusted Gold and Blue
1924

2136 Bon Bon and Cover
2252 Bowl, 6" Salad
2267 Bowl, 7" Console
2267 Bowl, 9" Console
2269 Candlestick, 6"
2244 Candlestick, 8¼"
2245 Candlestick, 8¼"
2275 Candlestick, 9¼"
2250 Candy Jar and Cover, ¼ pound
2250 Candy Jar and Cover, ½ pound
2264 Cheese and Cover
2250 Cracker Plate, 9"
2136 Cold Cream and Cover
2135 Hair Receiver and Cover
2138 Mayonnaise and Plate
1897 Plate, 7" Salad
2238 Plate, 8½" Salad
1848 Plate, 9" Sandwich, Cut M.S. (Matt Star Base)
1719 Plate, 10½" Sandwich,
    Cut M.S. (Matt Star Base)
2238 Plate, 11" Sandwich
2258 Plate, 11" Sandwich
2258 Relish Dish, 6", Cut M.S. (Matt Star Base)
2258 Relish Dish, 8", Cut M.S. (Matt Star Base)

2269—6" Candle

2267—7" Console Bowl
Encrusted Gold No. 36 "Poinsetta"
Illustrations one-fourth size

2258 Relish Dish, 10", Cut M.S. (Matt Star Base)
2276 Vanity Set
2208 Vase, 5"
1957 Vase, 7"

ROYAL

Decoration 39

Encrusted Gold on Green, Amber and Canary
1924

2267 Bowl, 7"
2267 Bowl, 9"
2267 Bowl, 9" Deep, Rolled Edge
2297 Bowl "C", 9¾" Shallow, Rolled Edge
2297 Bowl "A", 10¼" Flared
2297 Bowl "C", 10½" Deep, Rolled Edge
2297 Bowl "A", 12" Deep, Flared
2245 Candlestick, 6"
2269 Candlestick, 6"
2275 Candlestick, 7"
2297 Candlestick, 7"
2245 Candlestick, 8"
2275 Candlestick, 9"
2250 Candy Jar and Cover, ¼ pound
2250 Candy Jar and Cover, ½ pound
2250 Candy Jar and Cover, pound
2249 Candy Jar and Cover, ¼ pound
2249 Candy Jar and Cover, ½ pound
2249 Candy Jar and Cover, pound
2244 Cologne

2276 Vanity Set, Amber
Encrusted Gold No. 39 "Royal"
Furnished in Green, Amber and Canary
Illustration five-eights size

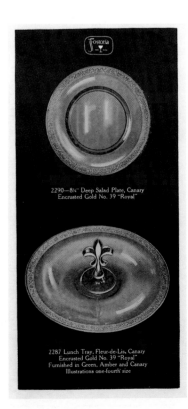

2290—8¼" Deep Salad Plate, Canary
Encrusted Gold No. 39 "Royal"

2287 Lunch Tray, Fleur-de-Lis, Canary
Encrusted Gold No. 39 "Royal"
Furnished in Green, Amber and Canary
Illustrations one-fourth size

2283 Plate, 6"
2283 Plate, 7"
2238 Plate, 8¼"
2238 Plate, 11"

2290 Plate, 8¼" Deep Salad
2290 Plate, 13½" Deep Salad
2287 Tray, Handled Lunch
2276 Vanity Set

NOME

Decoration 40

Coin Gold Band
1924 – 1929
Stemware is featured in *Fostoria Stemware*, pages 18 and 19.

1769 Bowl, Finger, and Plate
803 Comport, 5" Deep Footed
803 Nappy, 5" Deep Footed

803 Nappy, 6" Deep Footed
1897 Plate, 7" Salad
1852/6 Tankard

RIVERA

Decoration 44

Cutting with Encrusted Gold on Green, Amber, Canary, and Ebony
1924

2297 Bowl "A", 10¼" Shallow
2297 Bowl "C", 10½" Deep
2219 Candy Jar and Cover, ½ pound
2250 Candy Jar and Cover, ½ pound
2241 Cologne, 2¼ oz.

2321 Mah Jongg Set
2286 Tray, 5" Pin (Ebony)
2286 Tray, 10½" Comb and Brush (Ebony)
2276 Vanity Set

661—9 oz. Goblet—Optic
Coin Gold Band No. 40 "Nome"
Illustration half size

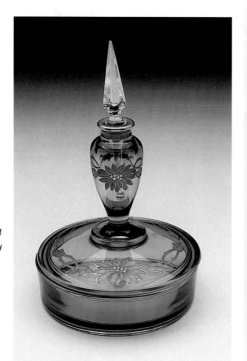

Green Rivera
2276 Vanity

2297—10¼" Shallow Bowl (A) Green
Encrusted Gold No. 44 "Rivera"

2297—10½" Deep Bowl (C) Green
Encrusted Gold No. 44 "Rivera"
Furnished in Green, Amber and Canary
Illustrations one-fourth size

2219—½ Lb. Candy Jar, Canary
Encrusted Gold No. 44 "Rivera"

2250—½ Lb. Candy Jar, Canary
Encrusted Gold No. 44 "Rivera"
Furnished in Green, Amber and Canary
Illustrations one-fourth size

2241 Cologne, Amber
Encrusted Gold No. 44 "Rivera"

2321 Mah Jongg Set, Amber
Encrusted Gold No. 44 "Rivera"
Furnished in Green, Amber and Canary
Illustrations one-fourth size

2286-5" Pin Tray, Ebony Glass
Encrusted Gold No. 44 "Rivera"

2286 10½" Comb and Brush Tray Ebony
Encrusted Gold No. No. 44 "Rivera"
Illustrations one fourth size.

DECORATION 46

Amber, Blue, and Green with Tinted Bands and Gold
Orange Tint and Gold on Crystal
1927

2267 Bowl, 7" Console
2297 Bowl "C", 9¾" Shallow
2324 Bowl, 10"
2297 Bowl "A", 10¼" Shallow
2297 Bowl "C", 10½" Deep
2315 Bowl "A", 10½"
2339 Bowl "A", 10½" with Ebony Base
2297 Bowl "A", 12" Deep
2339 Bowl "C", 19½" with Ebony Base
2324 Candlestick, 4"
2324 Candlestick, 6"
2324 Candlestick, 9"
2331 Candy Box and Cover
2219 Candy Jar and Cover, ½ pound
2250 Candy Jar and Cover, ½ pound
2329 Centerpiece, 11"
2368 Cheese and Cracker
2327 Comport, 7"
2350 Comport, 8"
2380 Confection Box and Cover
2315 Mayonnaise and 2332 Plate
2283 Plate 7"
2283 Plate 8"
2290 Plate, 13" Deep Salad
2338 Puff and Cover
2287 Tray, Lunch

Decoration 46: 2323
Crystal Cologne with
Orange Tint and Gold

2276 Vanity Set
2292 Vase, 8"

Blue 2324 Bowl and 2269 6" Candlesticks with Blue Tint and Gold Bands

IMPERIAL

Decoration 47

Gold Encrusted, 273 Royal Etching with Blue Enamel Band on underside of glass beneath etching and Gold Bands on Blue
1925 – 1927

CORONADA

Decoration 49

White and Yellow Gold Encrusted, Royal Etching on Blue
1925 – 1927

2324 Bowl, 10" Console
2297 Bowl "A", 10¼" Shallow
2315 Bowl "A", 10½" Console
2297 Bowl "A", 12" Deep
2324 Candlestick, 2"
2324 Candlestick, 4"
2324 Candlestick, 9"
2240 Candy Jar and Cover, ½ pound
2331 Candy Box and Cover
2329 Centerpiece, 11"
2322 Cologne
2323 Cologne
2327 Comport, 7"
2315 Grapefruit/Mayonnaise
2283 Plate, 7"
2283 Plate, 8"
2283 Plate, 10"
2316 Plate, 8" Soup
2290 Plate, 13"
2338 Puff Box and Cover
2315 Sugar and Cream

2287 Tray, Handled Lunch
2276 Vanity Set

Imperial Blue 2287 Handled Lunch Tray; Coronada Blue 2315 Sugar and Cream

DORCAS

Decoration 48

No information exists about this decoration.

PASADENA
Decoration 52
Gold or Silver Band on Ebony
1925 – 1926
Did not include the Smoker Set.

DECORATION 53
Orange Band on Ebony
1925 – 1926
Decoration 53 did not include the centerpiece or any plates.

2267 Bowl, 7" Console
2297 Bowl "A", 10¼" Shallow
2297 Bowl "A", 12" Deep
2324 Candlestick, 4"
2299 Candlestick, 5"
2269 Candlestick, 6"
2297 Candlestick, 7"
2331 Candy Box and Cover
2329 Centerpiece, 11"
2349 Cigarette Holder and Ash Tray
2327 Compote, 7"
2290 Plate, 7"
2290 Plate, 8"
2306 4-piece Smoker Set
2276 Vanity Set
1491 Vase, Small
1491 Vase, Large
1681 Vase, Wall Pocket
2288 Vase, Tut

Ebony 2321 Mah Jongg Set, possible variation of Decoration 53

DECORATION 55
Tinted Bands on Crystal, Amber, Blue, Green, and Canary
1926

2267 Bowl, 7"
2324 Bowl, 10"
2297 Bowl "A", 10" Shallow
2297 Bowl "A", 12" Deep
2324 Candlestick, 2"
2324 Candlestick, 4"
2324 Candlestick, 6"
2324 Candlestick, 9"
2331 Candy Box and Cover
2219 Candy Jar and Cover, ½ pound
2250 Candy Jar and Cover, ½ pound
2329 Centerpiece, 11"
2329 Centerpiece, 13"
2327 Compote, 7"
2315 Mayonnaise (Grapefruit)
2283 Plate, 7"
2283 Plate, 8"
2283 Plate, 9"
2283 Plate, 13" Cupped
2347 Puff and Cover

2287 Tray, Lunch
2276 Vanity Set

Decoration 55, Canary 2324 6" Candlesticks with Black Bands

ANTIQUE
Decoration 56
Color on Crystal: A, Yellow and Black; B, Red and Black; C, Blue and Red
1926

2267 Bowl, 7"
2324 Bowl, 10"
2297 Bowl "A", 10" Shallow
2297 Bowl "A", 12" Deep
2324 Candlestick, 2"
2324 Candlestick, 4"
2324 Candlestick, 6"
2324 Candlestick, 9"
2331 Candy Box and Cover
2219 Candy Jar and Cover, ½ pound
2250 Candy Jar and Cover, ½ pound
2329 Centerpiece, 11"
2329 Centerpiece, 13"
2327 Compote, 7"
2315 Mayonnaise (Grapefruit)
2283 Plate, 7"
2283 Plate, 8"
2283 Plate, 9"
2283 Plate, 13" Cupped
2347 Puff and Cover
2287 Tray, Lunch
2276 Vanity Set

Crystal 2250 Candy Jar with Mother of Pearl decoration and Gold finial, Blue and Red Antique 2250 Candy Jar

WAVELAND
Decoration 57

White Gold on Ebony
1926

2367 Bowl, 7" Bulb
2367 Bowl, 8" Bulb
2297 Bowl "A", 10" Shallow
2297 Bowl "A", 12" Deep
2298 Candlestick
2324 Candlestick, 4"
2299 Candlestick, 5"
2324 Candlestick, 9"
2331 Candy Box and Cover
2250 Candy Jar and Cover, ½ pound
2329 Centerpiece, 11"
2298 Clock
2298 Clock Set
2327 Compote, 7"
2317 Puff and Cover
2306 Smoker Set, 4-piece
2286 Tray, 5" Pin
2287 Tray, Lunch
2276 Vanity Set
1681 Vase, Wall Pocket
2292 Vase, 8"

Waveland 2329 Centerpiece

Waveland 2298 Clock Set

AMHERST

Decoration 58

White Gold on Etching 274, Seville, on Green
1926

2297 Bowl "A", 10" Shallow
2324 Bowl, 10"
2315 Bowl "A", 10½" Deep
2297 Bowl "A", 12" Deep
2324 Candlestick, 4"
2324 Candlestick, 9"
2250 Candy Jar and Cover, ½ pound
2331 Candy Box and Cover
2329 Centerpiece, 11"

2327 Compote, 7"
2315 Mayonnaise/Grapefruit
2283 Plate, 7"
2283 Plate, 8"
2283 Plate, 10"
2283 Plate, 13"
2315 Sugar and Cream
2287 Tray, Handled Lunch
2276 Vanity Set

GRAPE STEM

Decorations 61, 62, 63, 64

Decoration 61 – White Gold on Crystal
Decoration 62 – White and Yellow Gold on Crystal
Decoration 63 – Yellow Gold on Green
Decoration 64 – Amber, Blue or Ebony
1926
Stemware is featured in *Fostoria Stemware*, page 32.

Decoration 61, 62, and 63
4095 Nappy, 5" Footed
2384 Compote, 7"
2384 Candlestick, 9"
5084 Jug, Footed
Decoration 64
2384 Candlestick, 9"
2384 Comport, 7"

Blue Grape Stem
2384 Comport

CRITERION

Decoration 65

Coin Gold Band on Amber and Green
1926

HAMMERED SILVER

Decoration 66

Silver on Amber and Green
1926

Both Criterion and Hammered Silver shared the pieces below and used the 870 Goblet, Saucer Champagne, Fruit, Parfait, Wine, Cocktail, Cordial, and the 5084 Tumblers. Stemware in the 870 line is featured in *Fostoria Stemware*, page 32.

2350 Bouillon
869 Bowl, Finger, and 2283 Plate
2350 Bowl, Fruit
2350 Bowl, Cereal
2350 Bowl, 9" Oval Baker

2350 Bowl, 10½" Oval Baker
2324 Bowl, 10"
2297 Bowl "A", Deep
2350 Butter and Cover
2324 Candlestick, 4"

2324 Candlestick, 9"
2350 Celery
2329 Centerpiece, 11"
2327 Compote, 7"
2350 Cream Soup
2350 Cup and Saucer
2350½ Cup, Footed
5084 Jug, Footed
2315 Mayonnaise
2350 Pickle
2350 Plate, 6"
2350 Plate, 7"

2350 Plate, 8"
2350 Plate, 7" Soup
2350 Plate, 9"
2350 Plate, 10"
2350 Plate, 15" Round
2350 Platter, 10½"
2350 Platter, 12"
2350 Platter, 15"
2350 Sugar and Cover
2350 Sugar and Cream
2287 Tray, Handled Lunch

POINSETTA

Decoration 67

Decoration on Ebony
1926

2367 Bowl, 8" Bulb
2297 Bowl "A", 10" Shallow
2297 Bowl "A", 12" Deep
2324 Candlestick, 4"
2298 Candlestick
2324 Candlestick, 9"
2331 Candy Box and Cover
2250 Candy Jar and Cover, ½ pound
2329 Centerpiece, 11"
2298 Clock
2327 Compote, 7"
2347 Puff Box and Cover
2306 Smoker Set, 4-piece
2286 Tray, 5" Pin
2286 Tray, 10" Comb and Brush
2287 Tray, Lunch

Poinsetta 2297 12" Bowl "A", 2298 Candlesticks

2276 Vanity Set
1681 Vase, Wall
2292 Vase, 8"

DUBARRY

Decoration 68
No information is available about this decoration.

SATURN

Decoration 69

Amber, Blue, and Green
1927

2324 Bowl, 10"
2297 Bowl "A", 10¼" Shallow
2297 Bowl "C", 10½" Deep
2315 Bowl "A", 10½"

2297 Bowl "A", 12" Deep
2362 Bowl, 12½"
2362 Candlestick, 3"
2324 Candlestick, 4"

2324 Candlestick, 6"
2324 Candlestick, 9"
2331 Candy Box and Cover
2219 Candy Jar and Cover, ½ pound
2350 Candy Jar and Cover, ½ pound
2329 Centerpiece, 11"
371 Centerpiece, Oval
2368 Cheese and Cracker
2327 Comport, 7"
2350 Comport, 8"
2380 Confection and Cover
2315 Mayonnaise and Plate
2347½ Puff and Cover
2287 Tray, Lunch
2276 Vanity Set
2292 Vase, 8"

Saturn 2299 Candlesticks

ARLINGTON
Decoration 70

Amber, Blue, and Green
1927

2324 Bowl, 10"
2297 Bowl "A", 10¼" Shallow
2297 Bowl "C", 10½" Deep
2315 Bowl "A", 10½"
2297 Bowl "A", 12" Deep
2362 Bowl, 12½"
2362 Candlestick, 3"
2324 Candlestick, 4"
2324 Candlestick, 6"
2324 Candlestick, 9"
2331 Candy Box and Cover
2219 Candy Jar and Cover, ½ pound
2350 Candy Jar and Cover, ½ pound
2329 Centerpiece, 11"
371 Centerpiece, Oval
2368 Cheese and Cracker
2327 Comport, 7"
2350 Comport, 8"

Amber Arlington 2297 Bowl "A", Green 2327 Comport

2380 Confection and Cover
2315 Mayonnaise and Plate
2347½ Puff and Cover
2287 Tray, Lunch
2276 Vanity Set
2292 Vase, 8"

COCKATOO
Decoration 505

Gold on Ebony
1931 – 1932

2430 Bowl, 11"
2297 Bowl "A", 12" Deep
2324 Candlestick, 4"
2430 Candlestick, 9½"
2447 Candlestick, Duo
2430 Candy Jar and Cover, ½ pound
2427 Cigarette Box and Cover

2419 Jelly
2430 Jelly, 7"
2430 Mint, 5½"
2419 Plate, Cake
2430 Vase, 8"
2385 Vase, 8½"

VIENNESE

Decoration 506

Gold decoration on Ebony
1931 – 1932

2375 Bon Bon
2395 Bowl, 10"
2297 Bowl "A", 12" Deep
2324 Candlestick, 4"
2383 Candlestick, Trindle
2430 Candy Jar and Cover

2391 Cigarette and Cover, Large
2375 Lemon Dish
2375 Plate, Cake
4105 Vase, 8"
2421 Vase, 10½"

NUGGET

Decoration 507

Encrusted Gold decoration on Ebony
July 1931

2350 Ash Tray, Large
2297 Bowl, 12"
2324 Candlestick, 4"
2447 Candlestick, Duo
2456 Candy Jar and Cover, ½ pound
2391 Cigarette and Cover, Large

2400 Comport, 6"
2375 Lemon Dish
2375 Plate, Cake
5088 Vase, Bud
4105 Vase, 8"

BUTTERFLY

Decoration 508

Black Enamel decoration on Topaz
1931

2350 Ash Tray, Large
2430 Candy Jar and Cover, ½ pound
2427 Cigarette Box and Cover
2419 Jelly
2419 Lemon Dish
2419 Mayonnaise
2419 Plate, Cake
2419 Tray, Handled Lunch
4108 Vase, 6"
2430 Vase, 8"
4107 Vase, 9"

Butterfly 4108 Vase, 2419 Bon Bon

ITALIAN LACE

Decoration 514

1938 – 1942
All-over etching with Gold edge. Name changed to Gold Lace in 1943.

2496 Bowl, 12" Flared
2545 Bowl, 12½" Oval
2545 Candlestick, 4½"
2545 Candlestick, Duo
2496 Candlestick, 5½"

2496 Candlestick, Duo
2496 Candy Box and Cover
2496 Celery
2496 Cheese and Cracker
2496 Comport, 5½"
2496 Ice Bucket, Gold Handle

2496 Mayonnaise, 2-part
2496½ Mayonnaise, Plate, Ladle
2496 Nappy, Handled Flared
2496 Nappy, Handled Square
2496 Nappy, Handled 3-cornered
2496 Pickle
2496 Plate, 10" Cake
2496 Plate, 14" Torte
2496 Relish, 2-part
2496 Relish, 3-part
2496 Sauce Dish and Tray
2496 Sugar and Cream
2496 Sweetmeat
2467 Vase, 7½"
2545 Vase, 10"

Italian Lace 2394 Handled Nappy

APPLE BLOSSOM

Decoration 516
White Enamel on Regal Blue
1939 – 1942

GRAPE

Decoration 517
White Enamel on Regal Blue
1939 – 1942

4116 Bubble Ball, 4"   4116 Bubble Ball, 6"
4116 Bubble Ball, 5"   4116 Bubble Ball, 7"

DECORATION 518

White Enamel on Regal Blue
Each vase has a different design.
1940 – 1942

4123 Vase, Pansy, Decoration 518A   4137 Vase, 3¾", Decoration 518C
4130 Vase, Violet, Decoration 518B   4138 Vase, 3½", Decoration 518D

DECORATION 519

Colored flowers on Crystal
Each vase has a different flower design.
1940 – 1943

4123 Vase, Pansy, Decoration 519A   4138 Vase, 3½", Decoration 519D
4130 Vase, Violet, Decoration 519B   4144 Vase, 3", Decoration 519E
4137 Vase, 3¾", Decoration 519C   4145 Vase, 3", Decoration 519F

CLUB DESIGN A

Decoration 603

Crystal with alternating double and single Gold bands.
1929 – 1930
Design and stemware are featured in *Fostoria Stemware*, pages 57 – 59.

4121 Bowl, Finger
2350 Cream Soup
2350 Cup and Saucer, After Dinner
2419 Saucer, After Dinner
2350½ Cup and 2350 Saucer
2419 Saucer

2350 Plate, 6"
2350 Plate, 7"
2350 Plate, 9"
2419 Plate, 6"
2419 Plate, 7"
2419 Plate, 8"

CLUB DESIGN B

Decoration 604

Ebony with single Gold lines
1929 – 1932
Stemware is featured in *Fostoria Stemware*, pages 57 – 59.

2350 Ash Tray
4021 Bowl, Finger
2430 Bowl, 11"
2297 Bowl A, 12" Deep
2324 Candlestick, 4"
2430 Candy Jar and Cover
2427 Cigarette Box and Cover
2400 Comport, 6"
2350 Cream Soup
2350 Cup and Saucer, After Dinner
2419 Saucer, After Dinner
2350½ Cup and 2350 Saucer
2419 Saucer
2430 Jelly, 7"
2375 Lemon Dish
2430 Mint, 5½"
2350 Plate, 6"
2350 Plate, 7"
2350 Plate, 9"
2419 Plate, 6"
2419 Plate, 7"

2419 Plate, 8"
2375 Plate, Cake
2350½ Sugar and Cream
2404 Vase, 6"
2409 Vase, 7½"
2387 Vase, 8"
2430 Vase, 8"
4105 Vase, 8"
2421 Vase, 10½"
2373 Vase and Cover, Small Window
2373 Vase and Cover, Large Window

Design and stemware for the following patterns are featured in *Fostoria Stemware*, pages 57 – 59.

SATURN

Decoration 605

Ebony Base with Crystal bowl, Black enamel lines
1931 – 1932

4021 Bowl, Finger
2350 Cup, After Dinner, and 2419 Saucer, After Dinner
2350½ Cup, 2419 Saucer
4020 Jug, Footed

2419 Plate, 6"
2419 Plate, 7"
2419 Plate, 8"
4020 Sugar and Cream, Footed

POLKA DOT

Decoration 607

Ebony dots on Crystal bowl, Ebony base
1931 – 1932

4021 Bowl, Finger
4020 Jug
4020 Sugar and Cream

*Rose 2375 Centerpiece,
2375½ Candlesticks, possible
Triangle decoration*

BLOCK

Decoration 608
Silver on Ebony
1931 – 1932

2350 Ash Tray, Large
2430 Bowl, 11"
2430 Candlestick, 9½"
2383 Candlestick, Trindle
2430 Candy Jar and Cover, ½ pound

2427 Cigarette Box and Cover
2430 Jelly, 7"
2430 Mint, 5½"
2430 Vase, 8"

LINES

Decoration 609

Silver on Ebony
1931 – 1932

2350 Ash Tray, Small
2297 Bowl "A", 12'
2324 Candlestick, 4"
2400 Comport, 6"

2375 Lemon Dish
2375 Plate, 10" Cake
4105 Vase, 8"

TRIANGLE

Decoration 610

Silver on Ebony
1931 – 1932

2375 Bon Bon
2395 Bowl, 10"
2395½ Candlestick, 5"
2391 Cigarette and Cover, Large
2375 Lemon Dish
2375 Plate, 10" Cake
2385 Vase, 8½" Fan
2373 Vase and Cover, Large Window

*Ebony Triangle 2395½ 5" Candlesticks. Ebony with Silver fits the
Triangle description, however, with the added floral sprig, there are
questions. (Shown front and back)*

331

GOLDEN SWIRL

Decoration 614

Gold on Cutting 730, Whirlpool
1935 – 1937
Stemware is featured in *Fostoria Stemware,* pages 81 and 82.

4117 Candy Jar and Cover, Bubble
2525 Cocktail Shaker
2525 Decanter
6011 Decanter
2337 Plate, 6"
2337 Plate, 7"

2337 Plate, 11"
4116 Vase, Bubble Ball, 4"
4116 Vase, Bubble Ball, 5"
4116 Vase, Bubble Ball, 6"
4116 Vase, Bubble Ball, 7"

ST. REGIS

Decoration 616

Cut and Gold Encrusted Gold Band
1939 – 1943
Stemware is featured in *Fostoria Stemware,* pages 83 and 84.

1719 Bowl, Finger
2430 Bowl, 11" (Plain)
2430 Candlestick, 2"
6011 Jug

2337 Plate, 6" (Plain)
2337 Plate, 7" (Plain)
2337 Plate, 8" (Plain)

MOTHER OF PEARL

Decoration (Not Numbered)

Used on many complete lines as well as miscellaneous pieces.

ONYX LUSTRE

Decoration (not numbered)

Mother of Pearl Iridescence on Ebony
1926

2367 Bowl, 7" Bulb
2367 Bowl, 8" Bulb
2297 Bowl "A", 10" Shallow
2297 Bowl "A", 12" Deep
2324 Candlestick, 4"
2269 Candlestick, 6"
2331 Candy Box and Cover
2329 Centerpiece, 11"
2329 Centerpiece, 13"
2327 Compote, 7"
2283 Plate, 13" Cupped
2276 Vanity Set
1681 Vase, Wall

Onyx Lustre 2324 Candlestick

WHITE EDGE

Decoration (not numbered)

Decoration on Crystal, Green, Amber, and Canary
1924
We recently saw an Amber Cologne with White Edge Decoration. It had a simple
white enamel band on the edge of the piece.

2136 Bon Bon
2267 Bowl, 7"
2267 Bowl, 9"
2297 Bowl "A", 7" Deep, Flared
2297 Bowl "C", 7" Deep, Rolled Edge
2297 Bowl "A", 7" Shallow, Flared
2297 Bowl "C", 7" Shallow, Rolled Edge
2267 Bowl, Deep, Rolled Edge
2245 Candlestick, 6"
2245 Candlestick, 8"
2269 Candlestick, 6"
2297 Candlestick, 7"
2275 Candlestick, 7"
2275 Candlestick, 9"
2249 Candy Jar and Cover, ¼ pound
2249 Candy Jar and Cover, ½ pound

2249 Candy Jar and Cover, pound
2250 Candy Jar and Cover, ¼ pound
2250 Candy Jar and Cover, ½ pound
2250 Candy Jar and Cover, pound
2136 Cold Cream and Cover, 3"
2241 Cologne
2283 Plate, 6"
2283 Plate, 7"
2238 Plate, 8¼"
2238 Plate, 11"
2290 Plate, 8¼" Deep Salad
2290 Plate, 13½" Deep Salad
2136 Pomade and Cover, 2"
2287 Tray, Handled Lunch
2276 Vanity Set

ABOUT THE AUTHORS

Milbra Long has had a life-long passion for beauty. Emily Seate, her daughter, has had a life-long love for words and their presentation on the printed page in order to communicate an idea. For many years, the two women went their separate ways, Milbra into a 23-year career as an elementary school teacher, an antiques store owner with her husband, Frank, and finally, in her own business, Milbra's Crystal. Emily spent time in the military (she likes to say she "retired after four"), married a third-generation Texan, obtained a graduate degree from Texas Christian University, had a 10-year career as an executive secretary, and finally joined Milbra's Crystal in 1991.

The partnership they formed was unique in that it had been forged through an active and ongoing mother/daughter relationship which had long before blossomed into friendship. Emily spent the first few years following Milbra around like a puppy, soaking up information. By 1992 Milbra had shared her dream of creating a reference book for Fostoria collectors, and she and Emily talked for hours about how that could be accomplished. Very soon Milbra's passion for beautiful glass and Emily's love of words created an explosion of excitement.

Fostoria Stemware was a baptism by fire. The nitty-gritty of research, editing, proofing, and questioning demanded all their energies and experience. On July 27, 1994, they each held a copy of their first book and realized they were hooked. They had to tell the whole Fostoria story.

Reality dictated some parameters, and after some thought and discussion, they decided they could cover thoroughly the years from 1924 through the closing of the factory in Moundsville in 1986. But what about the early lamp catalog, the candlestick catalog, and the beautiful early pieces of glass Milbra had in her personal collection? It would be hard to leave those out.

When they concluded that three more books would be required to cover the period from 1924 – 1986, they decided to call the third book after the title Fostoria used on so many of its early catalogs, "Useful and Ornamental." After all, that pretty well summed up the Fostoria Glass Company and its 99 years of glass production. When the series is completed, you will have the legacy of a bygone era, with its impossible conditions, incredibly skilled workers, and extraordinarily beautiful glassware.

Milbra and Emily are delighted to be able to present this next book in the Crystal for America series to you. They welcome your questions and comments, and wish you success in the pursuit of your dreams.

INDEX